CAPTAIN
JACK CRAWFORD

Photograph of Captain Jack Crawford appearing in his first book of po-
etry, The Poet Scout: Verses and Songs, *1879. (Courtesy Rio Grande His-*
torical Collections, New Mexico State University Library.)

CAPTAIN
JACK CRAWFORD
BUCKSKIN POET, SCOUT, AND SHOWMAN

DARLIS A. MILLER

UNIVERSITY OF NEW MEXICO PRESS
ALBUQUERQUE

First paperbound printing, 2012
Paperbound ISBN: 978-0-8263-5174-6
E-ISBN: 978-0-8263-5190-6

18 17 16 15 14 13 12   1 2 3 4 5 6 7

Library of Congress Cataloging-in-Publication Data

Miller, Darlis A., 1939–
    Captain Jack Crawford—buckskin poet, scout, and showman /
Darlis A. Miller.—1st ed.
    p.   cm
    Includes bibliographical references and index.
    ISBN 0-8263-1449-X (cl)
    1. Crawford, Jack, 1847–1917—Biography.
    2. Poets, American—19th century—Biography.
    3. Scouts and Scouting—West (U.S.)—Biography.
    4. Entertainers—West (U.S.)—Biography.   1. Title.
PS1469.C3Z75   1993
811'.4—dc20

[B] 93-8611
CIP

Part of chapter 8 is drawn from "Captain Jack Crawford: A Western
Military Scout on the Chautauqua Circuit," in *South Dakota History* 21
No. 3 (Fall 1991) and used courtesy of the journal and editor.

To August Miller

Contents

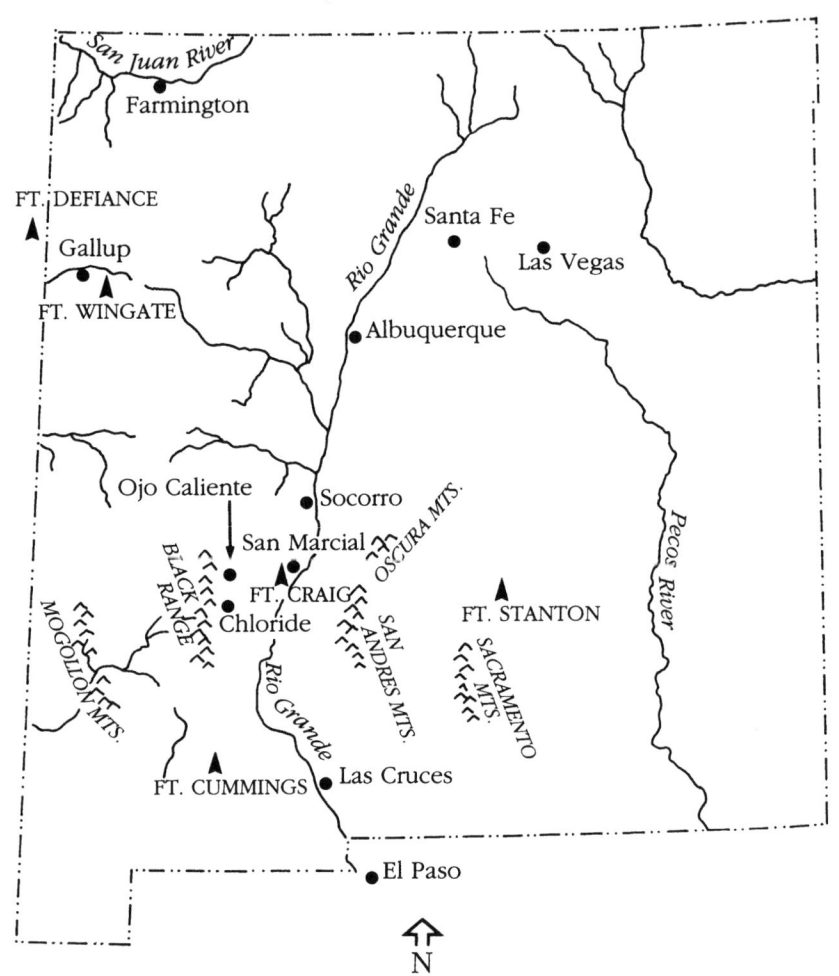

San Juan River

Farmington

FT. DEFIANCE

Gallup

FT. WINGATE

Rio Grande

Santa Fe

Las Vegas

Albuquerque

Ojo Caliente

Socorro

OSCURA MTS.

San Marcial

BLACK RANGE

FT. CRAIG

Chloride

SAN ANDRES MTS.

FT. STANTON

SACRAMENTO MTS.

MOGOLLON MTS.

Rio Grande

Pecos River

FT. CUMMINGS

Las Cruces

El Paso

N

CAPTAIN JACK'S NEW MEXICO

ILLUSTRATIONS

Illustrations

PREFACE

In 1861, fourteen-year-old John Wallace Crawford sailed from his native Ireland, with a brother and two sisters, for the United States. His parents had crossed the Atlantic a few years earlier and had established a home in Minersville, Pennsylvania, in the heart of the nation's anthracite-coal region. By the time the children reached Minersville, their father had enlisted in the Pennsylvania Ringgold Rifles and was among the first of the Union volunteers mobilized in the Civil War.

Young Johnny soon went to work in the coal mines to help support the family. Thus, the man later known as Captain Jack Crawford, poet, scout, actor, playwright, lecturer, rancher, miner, patriot, and moral crusader, began his working career in the United States as a slate picker, earning a pittance of $1.75 per week. Hundreds of Pennsylvania boys like Crawford spent their days in drudgery, stooping before the chutes amid clouds of suffocating dust, working ten or more hours a day picking slate and other refuse from coal as it moved through the breakers. Crawford was different from the other boys, however—not in his formal education, for he had none, but in his optimism and determination to make something of himself. Crawford believed in the American Dream, and he never lost faith in that dream even as he approached the end of his life. A man of action, Crawford expected to achieve fame and fortune through hard work and perseverance.

Although his success would never match that of his friend

William F. "Buffalo Bill" Cody, among the most famous of all American showmen, Crawford did become a celebrity, both in the West, where he maintained a permanent residence on an abandoned military post in New Mexico, and in the East, where he entertained a mixture of rich and common folk. What made him different from Cody and other western men of fame was his need to write and to versify, a need so compelling that his friend, the journalist James Barton Adams, described it as "an uncontrollable mania."[1] Crawford shared with Buffalo Bill a flare for showmanship, but unlike Cody, he shied away from allowing dime novelists to romanticize his achievements.

Crawford liked adventure, and although he was never foolhardy, he sometimes courted danger. As might be expected, many of his greatest adventures occurred while he was still a young man. At age seventeen, Crawford joined the Forty-eighth Pennsylvania volunteers and saw heavy fighting during the last stages of the Civil War. He was wounded twice, once at Spotsylvania and again at Petersburg, just days before Lee's surrender at Appomattox Court House. While convalescing in a Philadelphia hospital from the first wound, young Crawford learned to read and write under the tutelage of a Sister of Charity. The written word seemingly mesmerized the young soldier, and he never escaped from its spell during his lifetime.

Crawford's second great adventure occurred in the Black Hills of the Dakotas in the mid-1870s. He later claimed to have been among the first miners to enter that gold-bearing region, and in 1876 he canvassed the mining camps as a correspondent for the *Omaha Daily Bee*. Appointed chief of scouts of the Black Hills Rangers, a company organized to protect miners from angry Sioux tribesmen, he was known thereabouts as "Captain Jack," a name he forever cherished, even signing letters to his children, "Your affectionate daddy, Capt. Jack." After Custer was killed on the Little Bighorn, Crawford joined General George Crook's command as a military scout. In September 1876, Crawford endured the memorable trek known as "the starvation march," for as rations gave out the men subsisted on horsemeat. He later played a major role in the Battle of Slim Buttes, near present-day Reva, South Dakota.

At the end of Crook's summer campaign against the Sioux, Crawford joined Buffalo Bill in touring the country, performing on the stage in western melodramas. After appearing together in Virginia City, Nevada, the two showmen separated, and Crawford formed his own dramatic company. But, in 1878, the lure of adventure drew him to the Cariboo gold mines in British Columbia. Failing to find fortune, he returned to the American Southwest to engage in yet another adventure, serving as a military scout in the 1880 Victorio campaign.

Eighteen years later, the fifty-one-year-old Crawford embarked on his last major adventure when he joined the gold rush to the Klondike in the Canadian Northwest. During the intervening years Crawford had compiled a remarkable record. He made a home for his family at Fort Craig, New Mexico, 110 miles south of Albuquerque, where he served as post trader for four years. He also established ranches and worked several mining claims in the nearby mountains; and he served a four-year term as a special agent for the Justice Department, tracking down whiskey dealers selling liquor illegally to American Indians. At the same time, Crawford pursued literary and theatrical fame. During his lifetime he published seven books of poetry and more than one hundred stories, and he copyrighted four plays. He spent the last years of his life in the public spotlight, touring the country as a popular lecturer. His goal was not only to entertain but also to educate Americans about the true nature of their frontier heritage. Yet in telling his stories, Crawford romanticized the West, creating in the minds of his audience a West of mythical proportions.

Crawford lived in exciting times, witnessing several momentous events that changed the very fabric of American society.

Preface

He saw railroads span the continent, with streams of emigrants flowing west in their wake. He participated in the great Indian campaigns that hastened the removal of Native Americans to reservations. He witnessed the closing of the frontier and the emergence of an industrial society, with complex social and economic problems. Electric lights, telephones, automobiles, motion pictures, and airplanes all appeared during Crawford's lifetime. In his sixty-eighth year, Crawford even played a minor role in a movie that stressed military preparedness. He died one month before the United States entered World War I in 1917; had he lived, he would have cheered Wilson's decision to send troops to Europe.

The story of Captain Jack Crawford has never been fully told. His exploits were duly noted in some of the earliest publications about the opening of the West, but unlike Buffalo Bill Cody, Wild Bill Hickok, and other western heroes, Crawford failed to find a biographer. Until recently, primary sources for a biography have been scattered. Thanks to the generosity of Crawford's great granddaughter, Harriett Richardson of Socorro, New Mexico, the bulk of extant Crawford material has now been deposited in the Rio Grande Historical Collections at New Mexico State University. I have drawn heavily on this collection—together with government documents, correspondence, and newspapers in other repositories—to delineate the life of Captain Jack Crawford, otherwise known as the Poet Scout. But documentation is not sufficient to illuminate fully all areas of Crawford's life. Particularly disappointing is the sparsity of material relating to Maria Crawford, Jack's wife, and to his children. Thus, the people most intimately tied to the Poet Scout remain rather shadowy figures.

Because he left so few personal papers, the subject of this biography is primarily the public Jack Crawford, the frontier scout and entertainer as he appears in official reports and newspaper stories. Still, based on some family letters and Jack's own decision making, I believe that certain key events shaped his personality and help explain much of his later behavior. He was, after all, a performer during most of his life, and like all stage personalities, he craved public adulation. His need for public acclaim was probably much greater than his need for money, although achieving both fame and fortune was important to him.

Reared in poverty with an alcoholic father, Crawford came to idolize his mother. It was from her, I believe, that Jack acquired some basic assumptions about people and life in general: human beings are essentially good and well-meaning, obstacles can be overcome, conditions will improve, society can be perfected. Jack's unrelenting optimism, compassion, and sensitivity—characteristics that were at the bedrock of his personality—developed in these formative years at his mother's side. His early separation from both parents must have engendered a sense of loss and an aching need to regain the warmth of his mother's approval. Later in life, he wanted the acclaim of a much larger audience, the world. Certainly, the approval of his immediate family was never enough to satisfy his deepest longings.

When this poor, unlettered Irish lad stepped ashore with other immigrants, he dreamed of a new and better life awaiting him and his family in America. Work in the Pennsylvania coal mines, surrounded by boys his own age, merely reinforced his dream of being somebody. Never could he accept being just a face in the crowd. His desire for success, and for approval, was so strong that he was willing to take extraordinary risks—in the mines, on the battlefield, on the stage, and even within his own family circle. Although sensitive to the needs of others, he was less so, on occasion, to those nearest him. His wanderlust and longing to live on a larger stage led to long separations from Maria and his children.

Still, certain qualities in Jack's character are so outstanding that they overshadow any visible flaws. He did everything with great intensity, he genuinely liked people, and his generosity was legendary. Although relentlessly ambitious, offstage he was a decent, unassuming person. His strength of character is best seen in his resolve never to drink alcohol, upholding a promise he gave to his dying mother. Such tenacity carried over into other aspects of his life.

Crawford reached adulthood during an era that admired the self-made man and placed the millionaire entrepreneur on a pedestal. A man of his times, Crawford accepted almost as a religious principle the maxim that hard work bred success, and, like Andrew Carnegie, he came to look upon wealth as a means of helping the less fortunate. He developed a particular passion for reforming the American boy and founded a national organization for that purpose, calling it Boy Heroes of the World. That Crawford failed to achieve the wealth and stardom that he desired does not lessen the significance of his accomplishments. In fact, the well-known Boston journalist Nixon Waterman, in reflecting upon Crawford's career at the turn of the century, called him "A Genius in Buckskin," a fitting title for this talented, stout-hearted man of the West.[2]

Certainly, Captain Jack was unique among western military scouts. A poet and writer, he was also rancher, miner, reformer, and entertainer. Most important, however, his career is instructive because it illustrates one man's pursuit of the American Dream. In the unfolding of Jack's story, we see what must have been true for thousands of Americans of his generation. The American Dream suffered from defects, and reality was not the fame and fortune of their desires but more often failed companies and marriages, back-breaking labor and lost homesteads. But Jack's life-history is also a testament to the human soul's resilience in the face of disappointment and defeat.

Above all else, Crawford should be remembered as a western man of action, a man of great physical vitality, who not only participated in the closing of the frontier but also helped shape eastern views of the American West. Indeed, he captured the imagination of his audiences because he embodied qualities that they had come to expect of a western hero. Honest, brave, rugged, and self-reliant, Crawford had fought Indians, captured lawbreakers, prospected for gold, and wrangled horses during a supposedly simpler age now regarded by Americans with longing and nostalgia.

> *Soldiers, comrades, gather round me,*
> *List the story I will tell*
> *Of a noble, gallant soldier—*
> *One who loved our flag so well.*[3]

ACKNOWLEDGMENTS

This book could not have been written without the generous help of many individuals. I am deeply indebted to Harriett Richardson, who had the foresight to preserve Captain Jack memorabilia, donating much of her collection to the Rio Grande Historical Collections at New Mexico State University Library. She also gave me access to the materials she retains in her possession. Her warm friendship and constant support have been deeply appreciated. I am indebted also to other members of the Crawford family for sharing information: Evelyn M. Lewis, Marion Hageman, Harry R. Crawford, Fred Crawford, and Laurie Nauman.

A very large debt of gratitude is due several scholars who read portions of the manuscript and offered valuable suggestions for its improvement: Jo Tice Bloom, Bruce Dinges, Robin A. Fisher, Paul Hedren, Joan M. Jensen, Linda J. Lear, Shirley A. Leckie, Valerie S. Mathes, and John P. Wilson. In addition, Paul Hedren shared information and photographs from his private collection, and Linda Lear provided memorable hospitality during a research trip to the National Archives. On this same trip, I discussed aspects of the manuscript with the late Sara D. Jackson, who first introduced me to the joys of conducting research in the nation's capital. I pay tribute to her memory. Partial funding for this research trip was provided by the Arts and Sciences Research Center at New Mexico State University, award no. RC90-025.

Special thanks go to the staff of the Rio Grande Historical

Acknowledgments

Collections at New Mexico State University Library: Austin Hoover, director; Linda Blazer, assistant director; Tim Blevins, photo conservation technician; and student employees. Their cheerful assistance made working in the library a daily treat. Thanks also are due to Cheryl Wilson, head of special collections at New Mexico State University Library, for help in locating Crawford material. I am indebted also to the interlibrary loan staff at my university; their help in obtaining rare newspapers proved invaluable in the writing of this book.

I wish to thank several people who provided information, photographs, or other assistance: Peter Blodgett, Donald H. Couchman, Jim Crain, Octavia Fellin, Eleanor M. Gehres, Jerome A. Greene, Marion C. Grinstead, Joseph M. Hanney, Elizabeth Kelley, Nancy T. Koupal, Gloria Lusby, Michael T. Meier, Susan Naulty, Linda Reese, Joseph G. Rosa, Lewis O. Saum, Bob Spude, Robert M. Utley, and Robert R. White.

Thanks are also due to the staff and personnel at the following: Arizona Historical Society Library, The Bancroft Library, Buffalo Bill Historical Center, Dakota Wesleyan University Library, Deadwood Public Library, Denver Public Library, Gene Autry Western Heritage Museum, The Huntington Library, Museum of New Mexico, National Archives, New Mexico State Records Center and Archives, South Dakota State Historical Society, State Historical Society of Missouri, United States Army Military History Institute, University of British Colombia Library, and University of Washington Library.

And, finally, I would like to thank my husband, August Miller, for patiently listening to Captain Jack stories and helping to track the Poet Scout's travels in New Mexico. This book is dedicated to Gus.

CAPTAIN
JACK CRAWFORD

1
FROM DONEGAL TO FORT HELL

John W. Crawford was born March 4, 1847, in Carndonagh, County Donegal, in Northern Ireland during the Great Famine. His parents, John Austin and Susie Wallace Crawford, were of Scots descent; his father was a tailor by trade.[1] Low-thatched cottages and tiny fields dotted County Donegal, a land of unsurpassed beauty with spectacular cliff scenery along its coast. Carndonagh, a market center located on the Inishowen Peninsula, may have sheltered the impoverished Crawford family from the worst ravages of the famine.

For two years the Irish potato crop failed, and starvation, disease, and death swept the countryside. All districts were affected, but Donegal was among the counties where suffering was most severe. Bands of starving men tramped the roads—filthy, homeless, "walking skeletons" begging for food. During the spring of 1847 the mass exodus began, with hundreds of thousands fleeing Ireland to escape starvation and disease. An estimated one and one-quarter million Irish crossed the Atlantic to North America during the years of the potato blight.[2]

John W. Crawford as a young man in Pennsylvania. (Courtesy Rio Grande Historical Collections, New Mexico State University Library.)

Chapter 1

John A. Crawford joined the throng emigrating to the United States in 1854, leaving behind his wife and five small children to eke out an existence. The family was poor, living in a cottage of thatch, the children without shoes or schooling. The senior Crawford's addiction to strong drink added to their suffering. One of Jack's earliest recollections was kneeling by his mother's side "praying God to save a wayward father and husband."[3] The senior Crawford left Ireland, in part, to escape his drinking companions and to start life anew. Childhood scenes of his father's dissipation and his mother's suffering were deeply etched in Jack's memory.

Susie Crawford eventually joined her husband in the United States, leaving the children in the care of their uncle, James Wallace. By his own admission, Jack was an unruly youngster and, on at least one occasion, ran away from his uncle's home. Later, he and his older brother, William, were bound out to local farmers. Jack recalled that Charles Daugherty, the farmer for whom he worked, was "as mean an old cuss as ever drew breath." As a barefoot youth, Crawford found herding Daugherty's cows in fields of stubble to be a painful task.[4]

Jack was only seven when his father left home, and not more than ten when his mother left. Susie Crawford had been the stabilizing force in the family during Jack's formative years; her departure must have been wrenching. Still, the absence of both father and mother as Jack entered adolescence must also have fostered his self-reliance and independence. Crawford would later revere his mother's memory, and in his writings she became a saint. His father's fondness for drink, on the other hand, led to Jack's lifelong commitment to temperance. Paradoxically, after his marriage, Jack shared his father's migratory tendency that resulted in long separations from his family.

In 1861, the Crawford children sailed from Londonderry to join their parents in Minersville, one of the many coal towns that scarred the Pennsylvania countryside. By the time they reached their new home, their father had left with other Schuylkill County men to answer Lincoln's call for volunteers at the start of the Civil War. The senior Crawford served for three months with the Ringgold Rifles and then, after a brief furlough, reenlisted on August 22 as a private in Company K of the Forty-eighth Pennsylvania volunteers.[5]

Meanwhile, Jack, Austin, Elizabeth (Lizzie), and Rebecca Crawford joined their mother and new baby sister, Matilda, in Minersville, situated in the hill country of east-central Pennsylvania. It is not clear when William came to the United States, for he did not accompany the other children on the voyage.[6] Nonetheless, Jack soon found work in the mines, and his meager wages helped to feed and clothe the family while the senior Crawford was away fighting "Johnny Rebs." The family probably lived in a company-owned house and traded at a company store.

Conditions in Pennsylvania's coal mines and towns at the outbreak of the war were deplorable. Wages were low, housing wretched, and safety provisions primitive or nonexistent. The hazards of mining left hundreds of men and boys crippled and widows and families destitute. Death in the mines was an everyday event. Moreover, the labor force of English, Scots, Welsh, German, and Irish immigrants lacked cohesion and organization, and mining towns fragmented along lines of nationality. On occasion, ethnic violence rocked the coal communities.[7]

Susie Crawford may have seen too much death and destruction to allow her boys to work underground. Jack's first job in the United States was as a slate picker at Red Ash Mine, where he received less than two dollars a week in pay. Next, he drove a mule team on the dirt bank situated near the breaker. Jack claimed to have won this promotion for having stopped a runaway train. Walking to work one day, Crawford witnessed twelve loaded coal cars starting down the track after the blocking in front of the wheels gave way. He leaped on the last car, tightened the brake, and then continued over the tops of the cars until he had tightened every brake on the train, which had traveled more than a mile before coming to a stop.[8]

Soon, Crawford was promoted to firing a small engine that hoisted dirt-ladened cars up an incline from the breaker, receiving for his work $4.50 per week. Without telling his mother, he later secured a better-paying job underground as a mule driver. Because the war was draining laborers away from the mining regions, wages were on the rise, and Jack's new salary of twelve dollars a week was considered very good, indeed. To conceal his dangerous new occupation, Jack told his mother, when he presented his first month's wages, that the company had awarded him an increase for saving the lives of three mules. From a neighbor boy, however, Susie Crawford learned that Jack was working underground; the neighbor called Jack a daredevil who drove the mules too fast. Fearing for her son's safety, Mrs. Crawford stopped Jack from working inside the mine and requested his boss to return him to the dirt bank.[9]

Perhaps it was at this time that young Crawford first ran away from home to join the army. On this and a second attempt to enlist, government officials sent him home for being too small and too young. Meanwhile, John A. Crawford's company saw action at Second Manassas, in late August 1862, and at Antietam, on September 17. Later in his career, Jack often stated that his father had been badly wounded at Antietam.[10] But the senior Crawford's service records show only that he was absent from his company during the Antietam engagement and that sometime later he entered a hospital in Washington, D. C., where he remained for several months. He received a medical discharge on February 21, 1863, for "functional disease of the heart and debility . . . contracted in the service."[11]

Late in January 1864, a large portion of the senior Crawford's old regiment reenlisted and received veterans' furloughs. The men returned to Pottsville, near Crawford's hometown, where they received a hero's welcome. While the troops relaxed, recruiting agents scurried to fill vacancies in the ranks. Spurred by patriotic speeches and demonstrations, Jack and his father both enlisted as privates in Company F of the Forty-eighth Pennsylvania volunteers, the senior Crawford on February 26 and Jack on March 7, a few days following his seventeenth birthday.[12]

Crawford would later incorporate his experiences as a young soldier into his stage appearances. He often portrayed himself as a boy-soldier who had enlisted before reaching his sixteenth birthday. Interestingly, this is one of the few untruths Crawford ever told about himself. Rather than tell an outright lie, he was more likely to stretch the truth by romanticizing a situation and placing himself in the best possible light.[13]

It is possible, of course, that Jack attempted to enlist on the same date as his father, while he was still sixteen years old. Whatever the case, fudging on one's age has never been considered a major character flaw. More importantly, young Crawford managed to join the army before he was of legal age. By law, boys under eighteen were not accepted into the service, although recruiting agents often ignored this restriction. Jack's enlistment papers, in fact, erroneously state that he was nineteen when he enlisted. We may safely assume that other information in these papers is correct, that he stood five feet five inches tall and had blue eyes and brown hair.[14]

In mid-March, the Forty-eighth Pennsylvania volunteers left Pottsville to rendezvous at Annapolis, Maryland, with more than thirty other regiments comprising General Ambrose E. Burnside's Ninth Army Corps. The troops remained in camp for about four weeks, living in tents and roach-infested huts. New recruits like Jack Crawford spent long hours in performing elementary drills, learning to handle arms, and performing simple maneuvers in squads. When not involved in drills and other company routine, the senior Crawford kept busy by altering army clothing so that it would fit the new recruits. And although neither Jack nor his father could read or write, they received words of encouragement from Susie Crawford and her oldest daughter in letters that were read aloud by Jack's comrades. The training period of the young recruits was woefully short; still, they would march into combat with seasoned veterans, who would help to prepare the newcomers for the coming ordeal.[15]

On April 23, Burnside's command broke camp, and two days later the troops marched down Fourteenth Street in the nation's capital, where President Abraham Lincoln reviewed the corps from the balcony of Willard's Hotel. Thousands of spectators lined the streets to witness the military spectacle. Jack, like the other men of the Forty-eighth, would have carried on this march about forty pounds of equipment—a Springfield musket, cartridge belt with forty rounds of ammunition, bayonet and scabbard, canteen, five days' rations, frying pan, extra clothing, and a blanket. The tired troops encamped on the night of the twenty-fifth outside Alexandria, Virginia.[16]

General Ulysses S. Grant, who took command of the Union armies in March 1864, was about to unleash a series of sledgehammer blows against the Confederates that would bring final victory in 1865. Jack and his father fought together in the first and second of the bloody engagements that took place under Grant's command in Virginia. The first, the Battle of the Wilderness, occurred May 5–6, and the second, the Battle of Spotsylvania, May 8–20.

The Wilderness engagement was fought in a tangled, wooded area near Fredericksburg, Virginia. From Alexandria, Jack's regiment had marched south about twenty-six miles, where they encamped at Bristoe's Station for a half-dozen days. Grant's main forces north of the Rapidan, the Army of the Potomac under General George G. Meade and the independent Ninth Army Corps under Burnside, numbered approximately 118,000 men.[17] Meade's command crossed the Rapidan on May 4 and engaged the Confederates the next day in a battle that raged furiously until dark. The Forty-eighth Pennsylvania volunteers, as part of Burnside's command, crossed the Rapidan on May 5, and saw heavy fighting near the Wilderness Tavern on the sixth. During the conflict, Jack's regiment struggled through almost impenetrable underbrush and engaged in brisk firing at close range with the Confederates. Part of the woods ignited from the small arms and artillery fire, and many wounded soldiers were burned alive before they could be rescued.[18] At the close of the two-day battle, neither side could claim victory. Casualties approximated ten thousand for the Confederates and between fifteen thousand and seventeen thousand for the Union.[19] Undeterred by this appalling slaughter, Grant ordered his forces to advance toward Spotsylvania Court House on May 7. The following four days were spent in maneuvering and indecisive skirmishes with the enemy.

A heavy rain pelted the Spotsylvania countryside on the night of May 11, turning the roads into quagmires. On the twelfth, Grant's army made a general attack on the enemy line. Jack's regiment left the trenches at 4:00 A.M., and within the hour fighting was heavy. A dense fog obscured much of the early morning action, but the din of battle was horrendous. Rain continued to fall during the day, forcing troops on both sides to fight in the mud. The Forty-eighth Pennsylvanians made a second assault in the afternoon across an open, marshy ground under heavy fire. The fighting continued even after darkness fell. By this time, some men were so numb with fatigue that they collapsed in the mud and fell asleep under fire.[20]

On one of the final charges that fateful day, Jack Crawford was hit in the right hip with a shell fragment and severely wounded. He later recalled that he was left between the lines all night and, on the thirteenth, was evacuated to a hospital at Fredericksburg.[21] The Pottsville *Miners' Journal* reported that four men in Jack's company had been killed and nine wounded on the twelfth. Indeed, each side lost heavily in this encounter. Grant's losses for the day were approximately seven thousand, and Confederate casualties numbered between five thousand and six thousand.[22]

Despite the slaughter, Grant continued probing the enemy's line. Amid sharp skirmishing, the Forty-eighth Pennsylvanians spent the next few days in building and strengthening entrenchments. The senior Crawford, possibly not knowing how seriously his son had been wounded, slogged through mud constructing breastworks. On the night of May 14, he injured his back while carrying a log for this construction. Service records also indicate that on the eighteenth, the senior Crawford was wounded when the Forty-eighth charged the enemy's line. The *Miners' Journal* later reported that he had been shot in the head and had suffered a slight skull fracture. John A. Crawford may have spent the next three months convalescing, for muster rolls show that he was absent from his company during June, July, and August. The indecisive Battle of Spotsylvania finally came to a close on May 20, and on the following day Union troops left the area to continue their advance on Richmond.[23]

Meanwhile, Jack Crawford and thousands of other men wounded in the fighting around Spotsylvania Court House received emergency treatment at field hospitals and then were evacuated to Fredericksburg. Recent rains hampered transportation, and medical personnel were hard pressed to supply the wounded with hot soup, dry clothing, and blankets. Many were transported in army wagons on beds of straw and small evergreen boughs covered with blankets and shelter tents. In Fredericksburg, the Union army commandeered churches, warehouses, mills, and private dwellings for hospitals, and some officers and men were billeted with Southern families. From Fredericksburg, the wounded endured a rough wagon ride to Belle Plain, where they were sent to Washington by boat. Crawford was among the thousands of men received by overcrowded hospitals in the nation's capital.[24]

Young Crawford soon left Washington, en route to the Saterlee Hospital in West Philadelphia. Jack later recalled that when he and hundreds of other wounded arrived in Philadelphia, they were met by volunteer firemen with ambulances and by hundreds of ladies bearing food and drink. According to Crawford, "Philadelphia flung wide her arms to her wounded soldier-boys, returning from the front."[25] Jack, however, spent his first nine weeks at Saterlee flat on his back convalescing on a hospital cot. Although his hip eventually mended, henceforth he would walk with a slight limp.

At age seventeen, young Crawford was illiterate, impressionable, and still eager for adventure. While in Philadelphia and recovering from his wound, Jack had two experiences that helped to mold his character and shape his career as a public personality. First, he was befriended by a black-robed Sister of Charity whom Jack credits with saving his life, for when doctors thought his case was hopeless, this "angel of mercy" patiently nursed him through the crisis. Moreover, she taught him to read and write, an event that Crawford never failed to recount in his public performances and in his writing. Not surprisingly, the first letter he wrote— crude and misspelled—was to his mother in Minersville.[26]

Crawford's second significant experience in Philadelphia occurred when he attended his first dramatic performance. Having received a twenty-four-hour pass from the hospital, Jack set out to explore the city with the aid of a cane and crutch. Quite by accident, he entered the New Chestnut Street Theatre, where he witnessed *Aladdin, or The Wonderful Lamp.* The magic of the theater completely dazzled the young crippled soldier, and for many years thereafter he retained in his memory a romantic image of the play's star performer, Effie Germon.[27]

Because of his injury, young Crawford was offered a discharge from the army, which he refused. But after spending more than five months in recuperating at Saterlee Hospital, Crawford ran away to rejoin his unit. He later explained that he could no longer endure hospital life, "especially when they wanted me to act as a nurse." Hospital authorities listed him as a deserter until they were notified of his return to the front.[28]

By November 1864, Crawford had rejoined the Forty-eighth Pennsylvanians, still part of the Ninth Army Corps but now attached to the Army of the Potomac under command of General Meade. Since mid-June Meade's troops had laid siege to Petersburg, Virginia, General Robert E. Lee's stronghold. Entrenchments of the Ninth Corps were so close to Confederate lines that exposed soldiers constantly were in danger of being shot and killed by sharpshooters. A Union soldier later recalled the feeling at the front: "Life was counted of little worth—the familiarity with death almost bred contempt of the grim monster."[29]

Neither Jack nor his father was at the front on June 25, when the Forty-eighth Pennsylvanians began building their now famous mine under a Confederate strong point. Without wheelbarrows or proper mining tools, the Pennsylvanians excavated a mine shaft five hundred feet long, working night and day as the shaft neared completion. With eight thousand pounds of powder packed into the mine, the fuse was lit before sunrise on July 30. The explosion killed between three hundred and four hundred Confederate soldiers and opened a breach in their line between four hundred and five hundred feet wide. The desperate fight that ensued, known as the Battle of the Crater, involved much hand-to-hand combat. Despite the Pennsylvanians' success in digging the longest military tunnel then known to history, the Confederates repulsed the Union attack, causing General Grant to call the entire operation a "stupendous failure."[30]

By the time Jack and his father rejoined their unit near Petersburg, the Army of the Potomac had settled into regular siege life, which the men found monotonous even though picket firing was constant. On November 29, the Forty-eighth moved into Fort Sedgwick, also known as "Fort Hell" because of the constant shelling it received from nearby Confederate Fort Mahone. In fact, Confederate artillery fired on Sedgwick almost daily during the weary winter months. The bombproof shelters constructed to protect the troops failed to withstand this heavy shelling. The Forty-eighth regimental historian described the bombproofs as "excavations in the ground, seven to nine feet in depth, and then covered with heavy logs, and these [covered] with tree boughs, and the whole [covered] with from three to seven feet of earth." Confederate ten-inch shells, however, went right through the roofs "as a knife would penetrate butter."[31] Crawford later recalled having seen eight hundred-pound mortar shells in the air at one time, coming over to drop on Fort Sedgwick. He also remembered that "it was customary for the boys to stand outside of the bombproofs . . . and watch the course of the approaching messengers of death, and when one was seen coming toward any particular section of the bombproofs we would get away from it, for every one that dropped penetrated six or eight feet of earth and crushed the timbers as if they were but matches."[32]

Between Forts Sedgwick and Mahone, Union and Confederate picket lines were so close that the opposing pickets exchanged conversation and possessions. Jack later incorporated this experience in a poem entitled "Our Reunion":

> *And often when we shouted boys*
> *Across to Johnny Reb*
> *To throw us some tobacco boys*
> *And we would throw them bread*
> *How quickly they responded*
> *And the plugs came thick and fast*

Chapter 1

And we shared them with each of the other boys
And shared them to the last.[33]

Among the most memorable days of the siege was December 3, 1864, when at least thirty enemy shells exploded in Fort Hell. Some men deserted rather than face this constant and heavy shelling. A few days later, Crawford and his father undoubtedly witnessed the military execution by hanging of two New York volunteers who had been captured after deserting to the enemy. The entire division was marched past their bodies hanging from the gallows.[34]

Early in January the weather turned cold, and snow soon blanketed the countryside. A few days later, when the temperature rose the snow melted, making life miserable in the trenches. But the shelling continued, seemingly without letup, and through the winter and into early spring.[35] On April 2, 1865, however, Union troops mounted a final assault against the enemy's lines. At 4:00 A.M., Union artillery opened fire to cover the infantry's advance. Confederate guns replied with equal intensity. Jack and his comrades hastily consumed half-rations and swallowed scalding coffee before moving into assigned positions. The deafening roar of the cannons was only a prelude to the bloody battle that followed.

At 4:30 A.M., Union forces left their entrenchments for the final assault. Quickly, Jack's regiment captured the Confederate picket in front of Fort Mahone and then continued its advance in the face of destructive fire from both infantry and artillery. On the ramparts of Fort Mahone, Colonel George W. Gowen, who led the Forty-eighth, was instantly killed by a piece of shell. But the Pennsylvanians rallied and, after severe fighting, took the fort. By the end of the day, the Forty-eighth listed more than ninety men either killed, wounded, or missing, with total Union casualties numbering almost two thousand.[36]

After Gowen fell in battle, Jack Crawford assisted in carrying his body to the rear. When returning to his regiment with five canteens of coffee and extra ammunition, Jack was wounded in the left foot by a piece of shell. Two stretcher-bearers picked him up and carried him to a nearby field hospital. From there, he was evacuated to the Depot Field Hospital at City Point, on the James River, where General Grant also had his headquarters. City Point was a bustling port, with steamers, transports, and gunboats arriving night and day, delivering men and supplies, and transporting casualties to Washington. While receiving treatment for his wound at City Point, Crawford was to shake hands with Abraham Lincoln less than two weeks before the president was assassinated.[37]

Realizing that the war was coming to a close, General Grant had invited President Lincoln to visit him at City Point to be near the front when the Southern Confederacy collapsed. Bone-weary from his duties in the Executive Mansion, Lincoln left Washington on March 23, with his wife and son Tad on board the steamer River Queen, arriving at City Point the next day. The trip rejuvenated the exhausted president. In the following week, with Grant, he visited the lines behind Petersburg to review the troops, and he sailed with Admiral David D. Porter on the river. When the final assault against Petersburg was launched, Lincoln took up residence in the telegraph office at Grant's headquarters. On the morning of April 3, Lincoln wired Secretary of War Edwin M. Stanton that Lee had evacuated Petersburg during the night. Later in the day, Lincoln entered Petersburg to confer with Grant before the general followed his army, which was then moving after the retreating Confederates.[38]

Sometime before the ninth of April, when Lincoln returned to Washington, the president visited the wounded soldiers at City Point. Crawford later wrote about this momentous event in his first published book of poetry, and in an essay entitled "Lincoln in the Hospitals with His Boys, A Poem and a Story." According to

Crawford, it was announced "that all [soldiers] who could stand in line outside of the hospital tents would have the privilege of taking [Lincoln] by the hand." Crawford continues: "I never saw such a scramble in my life. Men who could scarcely move because of painful wounds sat up in their cots and begged to be carried out and held on their feet until they could feel the warm handclasp of the great president they so dearly loved." After Lincoln moved down the line, shaking the hands of the assembled soldiers, he passed the cook house where an axe lay near a pile of wood. Like many modern-day presidents, Lincoln decided to perform for his constituents. He picked up the axe and attacked a log, chips flying in every direction—much to the delight of the soldiers who scrambled for the woody souvenirs.[39]

Crawford later stated that it was while recovering from his wound at City Point that he first discovered his talent for rhyming. Lying on his bunk one day, he began singing a song to the tune of "The Old Virginia Lowlands," making up the words as he went along. A young New York soldier lying nearby wrote down the words and sent them to Jack's regiment. When Jack returned to his unit, much to his surprise the men were singing his song, one stanza of which follows:

> *'Tis of a plucky regiment*
> > *I'll try to sing a song,*
> *I hope you'll pay attention,*
> > *For I won't detain you long.*
> *They always did their duty,*
> > *And you bet they did it well,*
> *And they fought in the late engagement,*
> > *Which took place near Fort Hell.*[40]

While still on crutches, Jack rejoined his regiment in City Point when it returned from the front on April 24. By this date,

Lee had surrendered, and the nation was in mourning for its assassinated president. On April 27, the Forty-eighth embarked on transports for Alexandria, the general rendezvous for the Army of the Potomac while awaiting the close of the war. Jack may have recovered sufficiently from his wound to march with his comrades down Pennsylvania Avenue in Washington, D.C., on May 23. A grand military pageant it was—the mighty Army of the Potomac passing in review before President Andrew Johnson, his cabinet, General Grant, and other important generals. The following day, the Forty-eighth Pennsylvanians returned to camp at Alexandria and remained there until July 17, when they mustered out of the service.[41]

Although eager to return home, the veterans of the Forty-eighth were delayed in Harrisburg, Pennsylvania, while their officers completed reports. Finally, on July 22, the men boarded trains for their final destination. The homecoming celebration for the men of Pottsville, described in the *Miners' Journal,* was probably typical of celebrations held in Minersville and in other Pennsylvania coal towns on that joyous day. Homes were decorated, flags blew in the breeze, and the crowds roared as the train pulled into the depot. The veterans then paraded through town, while citizens cheered, sang patriotic songs, and fired cannons. At the town's main hotel, refreshments were served and dignitaries welcomed the returning heroes.[42]

Jack Crawford undoubtedly returned to an emotional reunion with his mother and family. Indeed, the senior Crawford may have preceded his son home, for on June 27 John A. Crawford had received a medical discharge from the army.[43] But the young man who came home from the war in July was not the same youngster who had enlisted eighteen months earlier. He had experienced heavy combat, endured intense suffering, seen the dead and mangled bodies of comrades, and listened to the moans and screaming of the wounded. He had faced the enemy's guns with courage and, although wounded twice, emerged from battle with the knowledge that he would not falter in the face of danger.

Moreover, the war had heightened the young soldier's devotion to his adopted country and left him with great respect for the fighting man. In later years, Crawford was a popular figure at Fourth of July and other patriotic celebrations, but he also devoted much time and energy to healing old wounds and cementing bonds of brotherhood between Union and Confederate veterans. And he would never forget the camaraderie of the soldier's life and the promise of adventure during a campaign. At the war's end, Jack returned home, found a job, married, and started a family. But an incessant restlessness would cause him to leave the coal towns of Pennsylvania for the distant and dangerous mining camps in the Dakota Black Hills.

> *Beyond the Mississippi,*
> *And the old Missouri, too,*
> *On the far and distant prairie,*
> *With comrades brave and true,*
> *One year ago I wandered*
> *In the hills so far away;*
> *I was happy in my cabin*
> *One year ago to-day.*[44]

2

CAPTAIN JACK IN
THE BLACK HILLS

In mid-April 1876, warm spring weather descended upon the Black Hills in Dakota Territory, melting enough snow on the hills surrounding Custer City to make water available for panning gold in nearby creeks and gulches. Gold-crazed emigrants streamed into town—as many as three hundred arriving in one week.[1] But the Black Hills swarmed with angry Sioux Indians intent upon protecting their hunting grounds from intruders. For self-defense, Custer City miners organized a 125-man militia, known as the Black Hills Rangers, and appointed Jack Crawford, described as "a quiet, unassuming young man," as chief of scouts. Crawford's job was to head a trouble-shooting unit of about twelve experienced fighting men to look for Indian signs and to escort emigrants through Red Canyon, Pleasant Valley, and Buffalo Gap, three dangerous canyons where Indians often waited in ambush.[2]

More than ten years had elapsed since Crawford mustered out of the Union army and returned to the coal mines of Pennsyl-

John W. Crawford, photograph taken in Shenandoah, Pennsylvania, probably between 1871 and 1875. (Courtesy Rio Grande Historical Collections, New Mexico State University Library.)

vania. During these years, he settled into working-class society, giving little indication that one day he would pursue a theatrical and literary career and gain distinction as a civilian scout with the army. Shortly after the war's end, the Crawford family had moved to Centralia, Pennsylvania, a small coal town in Columbia County and only a few miles northwest of Minersville. Jack went to work in the mines, but illness—later diagnosed as intermittent fever and ague—caused him to miss at least a third of his working time.[3]

Tragedy struck the family on September 7, 1867, when Susie Crawford died at age fifty after a brief illness.[4] On her deathbed she exacted a promise from her middle son Jack, fearing he would be like his father, that as long as he lived he would never drink liquor. Jack would later recount this deathbed scene countless times before audiences and in his writing, for his mother's death affected him deeply. In a letter written in 1894 to wartime friend William Wells, Crawford again described the scene:

> When mother was on her death bed and just before she died, she called me to her and asked me to give her a promise to take to heaven with her. I did not know what she was going to ask but I said I would promise anything. Then said she, my wild, reckless boy, I want you to promise me that you will never drink intoxicants and it will not be so hard to leave this world. I promised and she died with a smile on her face. I have kept that promise sacred till this day amid all the temptations of the western mining camps, the barricks [*sic*], and the officers club rooms where temptation is greater than anywhere on earth.[5]

Crawford, in fact, had pledged total abstinence even before his mother's death. Spurred by his father's addiction to drink and his mother's resultant anguish, he had joined the Cadets of Temperance (a juvenile temperance society) in Minersville before enlisting in the Pennsylvania volunteers. Crawford always said, however, that it was the pledge he gave to his dying mother and the memory of that deathbed scene that allowed him to resist temptations to drink throughout his active life.[6]

Following his mother's death, Crawford moved to Girardville, a few miles east of Centralia, finding work as a fireman at Preston Coal Company, one of the largest collieries in the Schuylkill region. He also became active in the Good Templars, a temperance organization that experienced phenomenal growth in the United States following the end of the war. Crawford frequently served as an officer in the local club and contributed original poetry to its journal. A poem entitled "My Mother's Died," which weaves together his longing for his mother's love and the cause of temperance, appeared in the journal in 1868 and may have been his first published composition.[7] The poem was attributed to "Snatcher," a nickname Jack had acquired while playing baseball on the local team and because of the way he caught or snatched the ball with his left hand.[8]

Crawford's continued sickness from intermittent fever forced him to quit his job with the Preston Coal Company probably near the close of 1868. Years later, when on the lecture circuit, he frequently eulogized the working man and, on several occasions, gave benefit performances for striking miners. Crawford, in fact, developed a keen interest in miners' welfare during the years he labored in the anthracite collieries. He and other ex-soldiers had returned from the war to face the same hazardous working conditions that had always existed in the mines. The Pottsville *Miners' Journal* grimly reported each tragedy: two miners killed and one badly crushed one week, a miner's arm mangled and another man's arm torn from his body a second week. All too often the report ended with the statement that the dead miner left a wife and several children to mourn his death.[9]

What finally caused Schuylkill miners to organize, however, was a reduction in wages at the war's end. Several local unions sprang up, and in 1868 they affiliated with the Workingmen's Benevolent Association, a new union organized by John Siney of St. Clair. Crawford became secretary of the branch established in Girardville. The miners went out on strike later that year, when coal owners again reduced wages, this time in response to a new Pennsylvania law making eight hours a legal day's work. After remaining off their jobs approximately five weeks, the men accepted a compromise; the owners would increase wages by 10 percent, and the men would work ten hours a day.[10]

Two significant events occurred in Jack's life in 1869: he was appointed postmaster of Girardville, and he married Anna Maria Stokes of Numidia, Pennsylvania. The first event involved the young veteran in controversy as well as revealing his penchant for writing letters to newspaper editors. An unidentified resident of Girardville protested Jack's appointment, complaining that the incumbent postmaster, "a crippled soldier," had been replaced by "an able bodied man." In the April 24 issue of the Pottsville *Miners' Journal,* Crawford defended himself, referring to his war record, his long bout with intermittent fever, and recommendations from his fellow soldiers. Moreover, he wrote, the former postmaster had opposed the Republican party. "He is doing a good business," Jack continued, "while I am poor and not able to do much work, and therefore I think I am fully entitled to the office, the duties of which I will perform to the best of my abilities." The *Journal* editor agreed and spoke of Crawford as a "worthy young man of temperate habits, [who] will make a good and attentive postmaster."[11]

Jack's marriage to the young and pretty Maria Stokes occurred on October 2, 1869, in Ashland, a few miles west of Girardville. Maria's father, George Washington Stokes, was a blacksmith by trade; her mother, Esther Harter Stokes, was of German descent. The young couple had known each other for about two years before their marriage, and both had been active in the Girardville branch of the Good Templars.[12]

By the time the 1870 census takers swarmed through Pennsylvania, most members of the Crawford family were living in neighboring coal communities. The senior Crawford was in Centralia, practicing his craft as a tailor; William lived in the same town, employed at the hotel as hostler; Elizabeth and Matilda stayed with Jack and Maria in Girardville; but it is not known where Austin and Rebecca resided. Changes soon appeared in the Crawford household, however, with Maria giving birth to Eva Lenore on June 28, 1870, and to Harry Wallace on August 19, 1871. A few days after Harry's birth, the senior Crawford died at Centralia at age fifty-four.[13] Although Jack had soldiered with his father, apparently they had not enjoyed a close relationship. Certainly, the senior Crawford's death did not inspire the son to memorialize his father in verse. In later years, when Jack supplied family information to the press, he said that his father had died shortly after his discharge from the army of complications arising from his war injuries.

As a young married man, Crawford remained active in the Good Templars, on occasion serving as its chief officer, and he also joined the Girardville Debating Club. He continued writing letters to the local press, typically describing temperance activities in and around Girardville. But during the summer of 1871 Crawford resigned as postmaster; and for the next four years he disappears from the public record. He may have found work in Shenandoah, Pennsylvania, where he posed for a photograph at S. Klugherz's gallery about this time. The biographical sketch that appears in his first book of poetry passes over these years, however, and merely states that after his mother's death he "struck out for the wild West."[14]

By the mid-1870s, when Crawford landed in the Black Hills, enthusiasm for developing the West had spread across the nation. The West beckoned to land-hungry settlers looking for new opportunities and independence away from the confines of older, eastern communities. Many viewed the West as a refuge for the poor, where land was cheap and opportunities plentiful. Construction of railroads after the war had hastened western settlement and led to a rapid increase in population. Indeed, railroad companies advertised their lines and the surrounding countryside to attract customers, taking advantage of the optimism that was characteristic of prospective settlers. Many veterans besides Jack Crawford must have been tantalized by newspaper reports of western settlement, such as the one published in the *Miners' Journal* in 1871 that read in part: "Westward Ho!—The claim made by the promoters of the Northern Pacific Railroad, as to the excellent character of the country traversed by that thoroughfare, seems to be verified by the fact that the settlers are moving to the line of the road in Minnesota and Eastern Dakota in unprecedented numbers." [15]

Even more young men of Crawford's age, however, learned about the West and its attractions by reading dime novels, a popular literary form that specialized in western adventure stories. The first dime novel, *Malaeska; The Indian Wife of the White Hunter,* by Ann S. Stephens, was published in June 1860 by the House of Beadle & Adams, consisting of the brothers Erastus and Irwin Beadle and Robert Adams. In this fast-paced story, the hero William Danforth shoots down a host of "savage Indians" while rescuing his Indian wife, Malaeska, from their clutches. There was nothing new about this type of adventure tale, but what distinguished the Beadle & Adams novels was their price, format, and regularity of issue. The introduction of the rotary press in the 1840s, which reduced the cost of printing, coupled with new techniques in marketing, allowed the firm to reach a mass audience. The small paperbacked booklets of about one hundred pages sold for ten cents or five cents a copy, with new issues appearing about every two weeks. [16]

The Beadle tales of adventure and romance that followed *Malaeska* proved enormously popular with the public. Writers churned out these stories with great speed, following a formula that often featured a young western hero rescuing a beautiful heroine from Indians. During the Civil War, the novels were in great demand among both Union and Confederate soldiers. Between 1860 and 1865, total sales for Beadle & Adams is said to have reached nearly five million copies.[17]

Dime novels, in fact, attracted a wide range of readers—men and women, young and old, bankers and lawyers, laborers and transients, and many others. Beadle's instructions to authors assured that the stories would be chaste, even though filled with scenes of combat and violence: "We prohibit all things offensive to good taste in expression and incident; we prohibit subjects or characters that carry an immoral taint." But as imitators entered the field, sensationalism increased, and the dime novel became synonymous with blood-and-thunder literature.[18] In response to this new competition, the Beadle's editor explained: "we had to kill a few more Indians than we used to."[19] For the rest of the century, however, dime novels provided mental relaxation to readers whose humdrum lives lacked the spontaneity and excitement of dime-novel heroes.

Later, Crawford would campaign against the reading of dime novels, blaming them for leading many young men into a life of crime, poverty, and dissipation. But during his young adulthood, he became an avid reader of western adventure stories. And even before he learned to read, he listened as others read them aloud. He later told one audience: "As I sat listening, spellbound, with every nerve tuned up to the highest pitch, I wanted to go out into the world and become a hero as much as any boy." Writing to his friend Wells in 1894, Jack stated that before going West, his soul "was aflame with the stories of adventure in the land of the setting sun . . . . Hence like thousands of boys, full of vim and adventure, reckless and fool hardy, I plunged into the heart of the untamed West."[20]

Crawford never recorded the titles he read, but the novels were readily available, even in small Pennsylvania coal towns. In 1869, the *Miners' Journal* published two chapters of Leon Lewis's thriller, *Red Knife; or Kit Carson's Last Trail,* and then advised readers that the story would be continued in the *New York Ledger,* for sale in bookstores and news depots.[21]

Crawford may even have read the first Buffalo Bill dime novels that Ned Buntline wrote in 1869 and 1872. William F. "Buffalo Bill" Cody, in fact, was just beginning his career as an entertainer after gaining prominence as a military scout. No one can accurately judge the impact that dime novels had on Cody's subsequent rise to fame. But most scholars probably would agree with Albert Johannsen that Cody was "made famous in part by the fiction written about him." And, indeed, dime novelists capitalized on their readers' fascination with stories that recounted the adventures of western characters such as Buffalo Bill Cody, Wild Bill Hickok, Kit Carson, and Daniel Boone, even if these thrillers bore little resemblance to the real men or to their actions.[22]

For many readers, including young Jack Crawford, these fictional accounts not only aroused their curiosity about the West but also helped to establish Cody and a host of other frontiersmen as public heroes. Authors projected into their literary characters the qualities that Americans most admired in other people. Dime-novel heroes were rugged individualists, self-made men who epitomized the rags-to-riches success story. In glorifying western expansion, novelists also glorified the men who carried out the nation's grand design of conquering a wilderness. As they helped to tame the West, dime-novel heroes had to surmount unbelievable obstacles, providing readers with a great adventure story and also corroborating their system of values.[23]

It is possible that Crawford met Buffalo Bill sometime during Cody's first or second theatrical tour through the East. In December 1872, Cody made his debut on stage in Chicago, where he starred in Buntline's melodrama, *The Scouts of the Prairie.* In his second season, Cody appeared in *The Scouts of the Plains,* costarring Wild Bill Hickok and Texas Jack Omohundro, in which action focused on these heroic frontiersmen fighting and killing Indians. The play opened at Pittsburgh, Pennsylvania, on November 17,

1873, and moved to Pottsville in December. Crowds flocked to the playhouses; young men and boys particularly delighted in the noise and tumult of the sham Indian battles.[24] We cannot be certain that Crawford witnessed Buffalo Bill's performance at this time, but in less than three years he had become Cody's friend and would later name a child after the great showman. Apparently, however, Jack never recorded how or when he first made Cody's acquaintance.

Undoubtedly, western adventure stories—and perhaps a budding friendship with Cody—influenced Crawford's decision to leave his family and head west. But the importance of newspapers in stimulating interest in overland travel among young men like Crawford cannot be overestimated. Even small presses like the one in Pottsville gave ample coverage to westward expansion and to military maneuvers west of the Mississippi. In July 1873, for example, the *Miners' Journal* published a long article on the Yellowstone expedition of Lieutenant Colonel George A. Custer and provided a map of Montana and the Dakotas to accompany it. Custer and the Seventh Cavalry were in the field as part of a larger expedition commanded by Colonel David S. Stanley, sent north to explore the Yellowstone region and to protect surveyors of the Northern Pacific Railroad.[25]

Crawford very likely read this or some other account of Custer's expedition, and he undoubtedly read stories about Custer the following year, when the flamboyant colonel verified the presence of gold in the Black Hills. Prior to this, the army had prevented prospectors from entering the Hills, since the Hills were part of the Sioux reservation. But rumors abounded that they contained millions in gold. As pressure mounted to open the area to prospectors, the army sent Custer and more than one thousand troops into the Black Hills, in the summer of 1874, to report on their mineral wealth and to locate a suitable site for a new fort. In early August, while still in the field, Custer sent a messenger to Fort Laramie, Wyoming, to telegraph east a long official report, which contained news that gold had been found along French

Creek in paying quantities. This story made newspaper headlines from coast to coast, and almost overnight the nation became infected with gold fever.[26]

Across the country—in Boston, New Orleans, San Francisco, and numerous other cities—men organized in groups to head for the gold fields. The army subsequently patrolled the Black Hills to evict intruders, but it fought a losing battle. During the summer of 1875, an estimated eight hundred miners were illegally panning for gold. And even more would attempt to reach the gold region after geologist Walter P. Jenney verified Custer's discovery later that year. Hired by the U.S. government to conduct a careful survey of the Hills, Jenney left Fort Laramie on May 25 and spent the entire summer in the field. In mid-October, the *Cheyenne Daily Leader* quietly announced his return to Cheyenne, where he was preparing a final report that would confirm the presence of gold.[27] Not even the approach of winter or reports of Indian hostility would keep gold-crazed Americans from striking out for the Dakotas.

Exactly when Crawford first entered the Black Hills remains a mystery. Years later, after becoming a public personality, Crawford received an amazing amount of publicity, but most published accounts of his life are riddled with errors. Not surprisingly, stories describing his arrival in the Black Hills are often contradictory.

The authors of the biographical sketches that appear in the first and second editions of Crawford's book of poetry, *The Poet Scout,* simply call him one of the pioneers of the Black Hills. They both assert, however, that Crawford headed west armed with a letter of recommendation from Pennsylvania Governor John F. Hartranft. This document, reproduced in the first edition, is dated May 8, 1875, which seems the most reliable starting date for tracing Crawford's journey into the Black Hills.[28]

The Hartranft letter also makes credible a story appearing in an 1885 issue of the *Black Range,* a newspaper published in

Chloride, New Mexico, where Jack was engaged in mining. According to this account, after starting west, Crawford "attached himself to Prof. Jenny's [*sic*] exploring expedition then just starting on its tour through the northern territories." In fact, several firsthand accounts of Jenney's expedition mention that it encountered stray civilians along the way. Crawford probably left the Jenney party, however, while it leisurely explored the Hills; for by mid-September he was in Omaha, Nebraska, a distant outfitting town for Black Hillers.[29]

But how was Crawford supporting himself? A partial answer is found in a notice appearing in the *Omaha Daily Bee* for October 7, 1875: "Captain Jack Crawford, who was, for a time, traveling correspondent of the *Bee,* has gone to Indianapolis to go into business." [30] This announcement is noteworthy for several reasons. First, it indicates that Crawford had adopted the sobriquet "Captain Jack" even before he became a semipermanent resident of the Black Hills. Second, it suggests that Crawford was funneling news about the Hills to the *Bee* in 1875, although none of his signed correspondence appears in the paper until the following year. And, finally, the announcement may conceal Jack's plans to return illegally to the gold region, for it is highly unlikely that he established a business in Indianapolis. Jack states in his unpublished Black Hills reminiscences that sometime before the spring of 1876 he was "captured by the troops and twice removed" from the Hills. The 1885 *Black Range* article offers a similar story, claiming that Crawford was a member of a company that Captain Edwin Pollack's troops captured in December 1875 and escorted to the Fort Laramie guardhouse. This story is entirely plausible, although the episode probably occurred a month or two earlier since Pollack left the Hills in the latter part of November. Moreover, both the Cheyenne and Laramie newspapers published reports that month about the army arresting miners for trespassing on Sioux territory.[31]

Unable to keep whites out of Indian territory, U.S. officials tried unsuccessfully to purchase the Black Hills from the Sioux during the fall of 1875. When negotiations failed, the government changed its policy, much to the delight of gold seekers. In November, the army withdrew its troops and stopped arresting trespassers. At the same time, the government tried to restrict Sioux hunting bands to their reservation, ordering all Sioux to return to their agencies by January 31, 1876.[32] Despite the risks involved, thousands of whites now rushed to the Black Hills to claim their share of the gold.

Several frontier towns on the edge of Indian territory advertised their locations as jumping-off points for the gold fields. Among the most important outfitting towns to emerge in the competition for customers were Cheyenne, Wyoming, and Sidney, Nebraska—both located on the Union Pacific Railway. After reaching Cheyenne, the adventurer found a well-marked wagonroad to Fort Laramie, ninety-three miles to the north, and, after December 1875, an iron bridge for crossing the North Platte. Custer City was about 150 miles beyond Fort Laramie. The route to the Hills via Sidney was slightly shorter, but it suffered a major drawback. Thirty-five miles north of Sidney, travelers had to cross the Platte River, "dangerous when flooded and treacherous with quicksand when shallow." But the problem was solved in May 1876, when an industrious entrepreneur completed a bridge at this spot.[33]

As gold fever swept the country early in 1876, the *Omaha Daily Bee* dispatched two paid correspondents early in 1876 to report on conditions in the Black Hills. J. H. Pierce ("Ranger") traveled to Cheyenne to keep readers informed of movements through that portal, and John W. Crawford ("Capt. Jack") journeyed to the heart of the gold fields.[34] During the first six months of this centennial year, the *Bee* published more than thirty of Jack's letters, filled with details about camp life, practical advice to emigrants, and descriptions of Dakota scenery and skirmishes with Indians. Crawford's letters, in fact, contributed to his fame as a local celebrity, as well as revealing his wit and resourcefulness as frontier scout and journalist.

Crawford was in Sidney the first week in January purchasing supplies for his trip into the gold region. He told readers of the *Daily Bee* that flour, bacon, and other staples could be purchased here as cheaply as in Omaha and that ponies cost between thirty dollars and eighty dollars and good ox teams between sixty-five dollars and one hundred dollars. He would travel north in a party of ten men, guided by Zeb Swaringen, a Black Hills pioneer. The men driving ox teams left Sidney on the morning of January 5. Jack departed the following morning on horseback, joining the party late that same evening near the crossing of the Platte. They slept comfortably that night, despite intense cold. When the temperature fell below zero, the river froze; yet the ice was not thick enough to bear oxen. After venturing about halfway across the river the next morning, the animals broke through the ice, forcing Crawford and the other men into knee-deep water to cut a path to the shoreline. With oxen and supplies safely on the north bank, they built a huge fire to dry clothes and then fixed a meal of venison, pork, and coffee. A keg of brandy was also tapped, and everyone but Jack imbibed. But even this stimulant did not prevent four men from suffering frostbite.[35]

The road north was in excellent condition. Despite one evening of snow and gale-strength winds, Crawford's party reached Red Cloud Agency on the night of January 12 without much difficulty. Jack dined that evening with agency personnel, with the conversation turning to Indians and the Black Hills. He gained the impression that nearby Sioux were friendly since large parties had passed through Red Cloud without harassment. There would be no trouble, he claimed, if travelers would refuse to give Indians liquor. "Besides," Jack wrote, the Indians "fear their supplies being stopped should they interfere."[36]

Crawford continued northeast toward Spotted Tail

Agency, encountering both Sioux and Cheyenne. He informed his readers that "we have not had a night watch on since we came among [the Indians], and we have been assured that no stealing or interference will be indulged in by the Indians." Beyond Spotted Tail, and after crossing the Cheyenne River, his party ran into a severe snowstorm, which delayed them a day. Another outfit joined them at this point, and together they struggled through drifting snow to Buffalo Gap, where they camped in a sheltered spot and "made our camp merry with story-telling [and] singing." On January 22, Crawford's party approached Custer City at sunset, seventeen days after leaving Sidney.[37]

From atop a hill, Jack surveyed the mining camp, surprised by its size. "Beautifully situated in a native park, surrounded by fine forests of white pine," Custer City had a population of about three hundred miners and boasted four stores, four saloons, and forty houses, with more than sixty other buildings under construction. A large well in the center of the one-mile-square town supplied water for miners and stock.[38]

In his first letter to the *Daily Bee* from Custer City, dated January 25, Crawford provided useful information for the would-be emigrant: flour cost twelve dollars per one hundred pounds; bacon, thirty cents per pound. A newly established sawmill would soon furnish lumber for thirty-five dollars per thousand feet. Having learned of rich discoveries in the northern Hills, he predicted a stampede there in the spring. Jack also described activities of Custer residents, most of whom were feverishly constructing cabins. He and several other miners were helping to build a house for the only woman in town, a "grass widow" with two children, "her husband having been scared off by some misdemeanor."[39]

Captain Jack devoted part of this lengthy missive to claim jumping, a common problem because of the town's transient population. He described the plight of Zeb Swaringen, who found upon his return to Custer that others had taken possession of his house and lot. Still, Crawford claimed, only law-abiding citizens lived in camp. No gamblers were yet in residence, and miners were determined to keep "roughs and sharpers" from disturbing the peace. "Woe be to the wretches who may be deserving of [the miners'] vengeance," he concluded.

Crawford spent the next several days prospecting, working on his cabin, and writing letters, thereby documenting for posterity the great 1876 gold rush. Despite the cold and sometimes stormy weather, gold seekers were arriving in Custer City almost daily. They staked claims on nearby creeks and in dry gulches, and they acquired town lots, on which they erected log cabins or frame houses. By the end of February, more than six hundred lots had been claimed (some selling for five hundred dollars) and three hundred houses constructed. Still, Jack reported, hundreds of people were waiting for places to put in their goods. "The streets are covered with teams, and almost every other lot is occupied by a tent, wherein people are living, waiting till their houses are built." The sound of the axe could be heard throughout Custer City. When Crawford tried to locate a ranch outside of town, he found that every desirable spot within a radius of five miles had been located.[40]

By April 5, three sawmills were operating night and day, but demand for lumber still exceeded supply. The busiest men in town, Captain Jack avowed, were carpenters and liquor dealers. A teetotaler himself, Crawford did not shy away from the company of men who imbibed, and he added spice to his letters by describing the town's popular drinking spots. Custer's first fire, in fact, eliminated one favorite establishment, John Dion's saloon (as well as the coffee and bake stand next door). Through the early morning hours, Crawford labored with other residents to keep the fire from spreading. A popular watering hole that escaped the blaze was Al Swearingen's Hall, a hurdy-gurdy house. For fifty cents a miner could purchase a dance with a young lady, a drink or a cigar for himself, and a treat for his partner. In April, Crawford reported that because business was so good Swearingen had expanded his building to extend an entire city block. When remodeling was completed, the hall would contain a bar and gambling room, dance hall, a complete kitchen, and sleeping and dining rooms for dance girls and boarders.⁴¹

Jack kept readers apprised of the misfortunes of another saloonkeeper named Fritz Drougmond. In March, a U.S. marshal arrested Drougmond and took him to Yankton, the capital of Dakota Territory, to stand trial for selling liquor on an Indian reservation. Drougmond left behind a nineteen-year-old wife and a small infant as well as an unfinished two-story hotel. Under Mrs. Drougmond's supervision, work on the hotel continued. But saloonkeeper D. B. Moody soon proffered the young woman his services as friend and business manager. All seemed serene, Jack noted, "until it began to be whispered around that Moody was not only managing the business affairs of old Fritz, but was also attending to family matters." When Drougmond returned to Custer some weeks later, he drove Moody from the premises. But Fritz's troubles were not over. His hotel burned down shortly after his return, and then, after opening a new saloon in Deadwood in the northern Hills, he learned that his wife (having remained in Custer) had run off with Moody. Fritz dropped everything, headed south, and the last Jack saw of him "he was galloping over the hills towards Red Cloud" to reclaim his wife. Fortunately for other saloonkeepers, U.S. officials decided in June that liquor could be brought into the Black Hills as long as it was not sold to Indians.⁴²

As a newspaper correspondent and practical miner, Crawford became a well-known figure in Custer City. Many new arrivals greeted him on the street, saying "Jack, how are you? We have read your letters; is the country as good as you say?" Readers of the *Daily Bee* even had some knowledge of Jack's personal appearance, for a drawing of "Captain Jack" appeared in a four-page special supplement on the Black Hills. Dressed in buckskin shirt and pants, with a revolver and bowie knife at his waist, and a rifle resting on his shoulder, he is sporting shoulder-length hair and a trim mustache and goatee—the same appearance he would affect before audiences in later years. Richard B. Hughes, who arrived in Custer during the spring of 1876, later recalled that many frontiersmen had worn their hair long, desiring to be considered Indian fighters—thus earning for themselves the name "Bad Haired Long Men," a term of derision. But Hughes held Jack in high esteem, noting "there was nothing of brag or bluster about Crawford either in speech or manner." [43]

With spring advancing, hundreds of people streamed into Custer City. Doctors, lawyers, businessmen, gamblers, and entertainers rubbed shoulders with rough-clad miners. One of the first men Crawford met in Custer, in fact, was Dick Brown, a professional banjo player who temporarily abandoned the stage to hunt for gold. Almost every evening "Banjo Dick" played for his friends, and Jack added to the merriment with his own songs and poetry. [44] The arrival of "good" women in town provided new opportunities for socializing. In April, for example, a Mr. Felix staged Custer's first ball at Roberts's new store, "tastefully decorated with evergreens." One hundred people, including twenty-two women, enjoyed an evening of dining and dancing. The supper Felix served, Jack maintained, was one of the finest ever eaten in Custer—pies, cakes, cold meats, coffee, wine, cider, bottled ale, and fresh milk were some of the delicacies on the bill of fare. [45]

Among the gold seekers were men of such bravery that Crawford felt compelled to record their stories. Early in February, Jack wrote about John A. Byers, the first man known to have reached the Black Hills alone and without previous knowledge of the country. Byers had walked the entire distance of 495 miles from Jefferson (near Sioux City), Iowa, accompanied part of the way by eighteen-year-old Charley Holt. Twenty miles from Spotted Tail Agency, the two men were nearing exhaustion, having lived several days on parched coffee. At this point, four Sioux rode up, cooked some antelope, and left them with enough so they could reach the agency. Holt decided to stay at Spotted Tail, but Byers continued to Custer, making the one-hundred-mile trip in five days through snow. "Old trappers and hunters who met Mr. Byers at the agency," Crawford wrote, "said they would not undertake such a trip for all the wealth in the Hills." After recuperating in Crawford's cabin, Byers headed to Deadwood. Holt eventually reached Custer and, with another boy, constructed a primitive dugout for shelter. A few nights later the roof collapsed, killing Charley instantly and almost killing his partner. "The saddest point about this affecting incident," Crawford later recorded, "was that no letters, papers, or even the slightest clew to his home or friends could be found; all that we knew was that he had walked all the way from Sioux City to the Black Hills to die and start a graveyard." [46]

Crawford soon became close friends with Charles Whitehead, special correspondent of the Kansas City *Times,* who arrived in Custer City in late February or early March. The two men took an instant liking to each other and shared personal histories over many campfires. During their travels together, Whitehead encouraged the young correspondent to persevere with his poetry. Later Jack expressed his gratitude in a poem entitled "To Charley," which begins:

> *Lonely tonight in my little log cabin,*
> > *I am thinking of you and the days long ago,*
> *When together we sat on the peak of old Harney,*
> > *Drinking the grandeur of nature below.* [47]

The two men shared some memorable experiences, among them a trip to Harney's Peak, which is mentioned in the poem. Early one morning in March, they started for its summit, about twelve miles north of Custer, with four days of rations and blankets strapped to their ponies. They rode through magnificent country: "Parks almost as green as in summer, natural amphitheaters surrounded by walls of granite, and stately trees, from one to three feet through, and a natural arch of [willows] growing on each side of the creek for miles." In one superb park, they camped for a dinner of slap-jacks, bacon, and boiled coffee. A few hours later, they climbed a peak adjacent to Harney, christening it "Bee Mount," and then descended the large ravine that divided the two pinnacles. At the base of Harney, they made an evening camp just as snow began falling. They found splendid shelter. "Eight trees, from one to two feet through, stood in a circle and formed one of the prettiest natural bowers we ever saw, and all came together at the top, making it look like an Indian tepee on the ground." They stretched a lariat from tree to tree, then covered this frame with boughs to form a roof.[48]

After a meal of pancakes and an evening of storytelling, the two men retired for the night. Snow was still falling. At 1:00 A.M., they awakened to the sound of their ponies leaving camp. Jack dashed after the animals on foot—without rifle, revolver, or gloves. He followed their trail most of the way into Custer, arriving there at 5:00 A.M., cold and exhausted. After a short nap, he started out again to look for his horse and was surprised to see Charley riding down the creek two miles above Custer. Whitehead had remained at the campsite nearly all night, feeding a big fire to guide Crawford to shelter. But in his haste to discover what had become of his friend—he feared Indians had captured him— Charley left most of their gear behind.

A couple of days elapsed before they started for the foot of Harney's Peak to gather their belongings. When they reached their old campsite, they discovered that almost everything was missing. Thieves had made away with two buffalo robes, two blankets, two saddles, and four days of rations, and then set fire to the camp. Jack's biggest loss was an old scrapbook lodged in his saddle bag that contained more than five hundred poems composed since Civil War days. He also lost cherished letters from soldiers and statesmen. Readers gained a sense of his woe from a poem that subsequently appeared in the *Daily Bee,* a portion of which follows:

> *Farewell, companion of my soul,*
> *No other book your tale can tell,*
> *No other lines my heart console;*
> *Old book of yore, farewell, farewell.*[49]

Crawford wasted little time in bemoaning his bad luck, however. The *Omaha Daily Bee* had sponsored his trip into the Black Hills to assess their mineral wealth, and he faithfully carried out his mission, not only by talking to experienced miners but also by digging into the Hills himself. As much as any man, he hoped to strike it rich.

Jack prospected north and south of Custer City, locating both placer and quartz claims. In mid-February he was prospecting near Hill City, about fourteen miles north of Custer and at the junction of Newton's Fork and Spring Creek. He staked a placer claim on Spring Creek on the sixteenth and spent the next two days sinking a prospect hole eight feet long, three feet wide, and twelve feet deep. Three days later, on Newton's Fork he sank a similar hole that reached bedrock, but "only got small prospects."[50]

In an April 5 letter, Crawford described Hill City, second in importance to Custer in the southern Hills. Situated "in a very pretty little park," it was a company-owned town, where lots sold for five dollars, although company officials held the best locations, offering them for "big prices." Most of its 150 houses were still under construction. Jack reported working a half-day on his claim three miles above Hill City, then marking on a stake "represented, April 1, 1876, J.W.C." Mining districts, he later explained, established "representation days," typically one day in each week when every miner had to do a small amount of work on his claim to show good faith. If he did not appear on that day, other parties could "jump" or relocate the claim.[51]

In this same letter, Captain Jack lectured prospective gold seekers: "No man should come to this country expecting to pick up gold as soon as he gets here. He has to work hard and long to get to the bed rock. There are ditches to dig, sluices to make, and, first of all, the pay streak to be found." He went on to say that a man frequently had to dig twenty prospect holes across his claim before finding any pay, and sometimes he found nothing at all. He advised men to enter the Hills with at least three months of rations and one or two hundred dollars. Many who arrive with few resources, he warned, will have to desert their claims just as they are about to strike pay dirt. He wrote of one successful Hill City miner who was making five dollars per day washing out dirt, "which he had to carry over two hundred yards to water." He also reported that the eight sluices about to start operating near Hill City had cost five hundred dollars. In short, it required hard work and adequate finances to locate gold.

Scarcity of water prevented Custer City miners from working their claims on French Creek until mid-April. Crawford recorded the good fortune of some: three men had panned forty dollars in one day; Dave Olston, sluicing with three other men, had taken out forty-five dollars in half a day. Jack began working his claim just above Custer City on May 1, "representation day." "Merchants, mechanics, lawyers, doctors, and everybody might be seen in the afternoon with rifle, pick and shovel, hastening to be on their ground." The problem with Jack's claim, however, was its location on a high bar, which would necessitate cutting a ditch a mile long to get water.[52]

Crawford never "struck it rich" in the Black Hills, but he

did help to create a viable mining community. Although he entered the gold region as a paid correspondent, he was not content simply to observe and record the actions of others. He immersed himself in the affairs of the community and helped to write the laws that governed Custer City during the heady days of its early growth.

On the evening of February 9, residents of Custer City gathered in a public meeting to voice fears that the expected influx of miners would bring into their midst a lawless element that would prey on the community. City recorder P. J. Keefer was elected president of the meeting, and Crawford was chosen secretary. After some discussion, Keefer appointed Jack and five others to devise a government that would preserve law and order and protect life and property in Custer City. The following evening, this committee recommended to assembled citizens that a provisional government be established immediately, and one which would enlarge the powers of the town's trustees so they could enact new laws or amend existing ones for the good of the community. The committee also advised that two police justices and one city marshal be elected to enforce the laws. After approving these recommendations, the crowd nominated men for the newly created offices and scheduled an election for the following week.[53]

Apparently, the provisional government operated smoothly until a lawyer by the name of Haskell arrived in March and convinced the trustees that they lacked the power to settle claim disputes. Thereafter, a justice and a jury of miners ruled on questions of property. But according to Crawford, "Haskell the rascal" laid the foundation for lawsuits for twenty years to come, for claim jumping became the order of the day, with lawyers reaping all the benefits. Although Haskell soon departed for Deadwood, the people of Custer revamped their provisional government in late March by enacting new laws and electing new officers, including a new board of trustees. The election generated a great deal of interest. Following the balloting, Crawford reported, saloon-keepers conducted a booming business while miners anxiously awaited the outcome. But Jack had reason to be pleased, for he was elected to be one of the town's twelve trustees.[54]

It was about this time that Crawford became involved in one of the first lawsuits ever tried in the Black Hills. The story is best told by Annie D. Tallent, a Black Hills pioneer, whose book *The Black Hills; or, The Last Hunting Ground of the Dakotahs* has become a minor classic. Tallent states that when Captain Jack arrived in Custer City he took possession of a substantial log build-ing that Dr. D. M. Flick had constructed in 1875 and that Captain Pollack subsequently used as military headquarters. When Flick returned to the Hills in April 1876, he installed his family and be-longings in the building while Jack was absent—and refused to budge when he returned. Crawford brought action against Flick, with attorney Tom Harvey arguing his case before Justice Keefer and a five-man jury. The verdict favored the defendant, forcing Crawford to find new lodgings. Not surprisingly, "Capt. Jack" failed to report these events to his Omaha readers, and in his reminis-cences he simply remarks that he moved out of a larger and into a smaller dwelling to accommodate a family.[55]

The men and women who entered the Black Hills in 1876 tried to build law-abiding communities, in which everyone had equal opportunity to exploit the gold-bearing gulches and creek beds. Their lives were filled with hardships typical of any mining frontier opened during winter months. But the Black Hillers faced another danger—Indians who increasingly resented their intru-sion. With the coming of spring, Sioux warriors stepped up their harassment of white trespassers. The U.S. Army and local miners retaliated. And in the ensuing conflict that swept the reservation and beyond, Jack Crawford would gain distinction as chief of scouts for the Black Hills Rangers and then as a civilian scout with the army. It would be a bloody contest to control the land, one that pitted hero against hero, soldier against warrior. And with Custer's defeat on the Little Bighorn, the nation awoke to the tragic consequences of total war.

> *Did I hear the news from Custer?*
> *Well, I reckon I did, old pard;*
> *It came like a streak of lightin',*
> *And, you bet, it hit me hard.*
> *I ain't no hand to blubber,*
> *And the briny ain't run for years;*
> *But chalk me down for a lubber,*
> *If I didn't shed regular tears.*[56]

3
CHIEF OF SCOUTS

The "Sitting Bull Campaign" of 1876 coincided with the nation's celebration of one hundred years of independence. As tourists flocked to the Philadelphia Centennial Exposition to view the country's industrial achievements, columns of U.S. troops invaded the western hunting grounds of Sioux and other northern tribes. The Fort Laramie Treaty of 1868 had granted Sioux hunters the right to range beyond the boundaries of their reservation, which included nearly all of present-day South Dakota west of the Missouri River. But plenty of evidence existed to show that hunting bands frequently turned into raiding parties that swooped down on white settlements on the periphery of Indian territory. When the hunting bands failed to return to the reservation by January 31, 1876, General Phil Sheridan, commanding the Division of the Missouri, plotted a winter campaign to break the power of the off-reservation Indians, whose dynamic leader, the Hunkpapa Sioux Sitting Bull, looked with scorn upon his brethren who submitted to the white man's rule. [1]

Custer City, on French Creek, where Captain Jack served as Chief of Scouts of the Black Hills Rangers during the 1876 gold rush. (Photo by D. S. Mitchell, courtesy Jim Crain.)

Chapter 3

While military officials in Chicago and Washington perfected plans for war, angry Sioux warriors increased their attacks on the Black Hills intruders. Although the Indians had appeared docile when "Capt. Jack" visited their agencies in mid-January, three weeks later he informed readers of the *Omaha Daily Bee* that Indians had attacked a party of whites on the Cheyenne road and had run off six horses. He warned people coming into the Hills to travel in parties of not less than fifty and to keep a vigilant night watch after passing the agencies.[2]

About two weeks after Crawford issued this warning, Charles Whitehead, in a letter dated March 5, described for readers of the Kansas City *Times* a daring Indian raid on Custer City, calling attention to Crawford's bold performance as a frontier scout. On the previous morning, a party of Germans had encountered a large band of Sioux camped about seven miles from Custer. They wasted little time in returning to town to sound the alarm. Meanwhile, the Sioux broke into small bands and attacked several emigrant trains coming into Custer, running off their stock. Crawford, Whitehead, and some other men were camped at Calamity Bar, a claim about three miles from town, when Indians swooped down and captured most of their horses.[3]

At noon, five or six Indians galloped through the upper end of Custer and "drove off all the stock grazing on the commons west of the city." Indians concealed in pines on the edge of town fired at the herders to cover the raiders' escape. "Talk about a panic in a town!" Everyone rushed for their firearms and then scattered into nearby parks and hills to bring in horses and mules still at large. Within thirty minutes of the attack, twenty armed and mounted men assembled at the west end of town, elected Jack their leader, and struck out on the Indians' trail, going in the direction of the Cheyenne River. By nightfall, the pursuit party had dwindled to seven men—and soon only Crawford and George Hoyt remained on the trail. The rest returned to Custer the next morning about daylight, "tired, hungry and half frozen." White-head reported having seen Indian signal fires burning on the mountaintops during the night.

While Crawford and the Black Hillers prepared for new attacks, General George Crook was leading an expedition of about nine hundred officers, soldiers, and civilians against off-reservation Indians in Montana. The command had left Fort Fetterman, Wyoming, on March 1 and headed north on the Bozeman Trail. Drifting snow and below-zero temperatures, however, slowed their progress. On March 17, the troops attacked a large encampment of Sioux and Cheyennes on Powder River, but withdrew in the face of strong resistance after destroying only part of their village. While the Indians suffered few casualties, Crook's command lost four killed and six wounded. In a letter dated March 28, however, Crawford told his readers about a report circulating in Custer City that "Gen. Crook has made a big fight with the northern Sioux, and whipped them."[4]

Early in April, Crawford received word that young warriors had left the Red Cloud Agency. "There is little doubt," he concluded, "that they are prowling about the Hills in search of plunder." Indians recently had attacked three miners camped outside Rapid City, fifteen miles north of Hill City, wounding one, killing and scalping another. The next day they returned and drove off twenty-eight head of stock. In fact, Jack reported, stock were being run off every week from some part of the Hills.[5]

A second raid on Custer City occurred on April 10, when Indians came within one hundred yards of the city limits and ran off about thirty animals. Crawford organized a pursuit party, but failed to overtake the culprits. About this same time, new reports were circulating that Indians had captured both Crook and Lieutenant Colonel (by brevet, Major General) George A. Custer. Although Crawford doubted that Sitting Bull could outflank either man, he feared that army activity in the north would drive the

Sioux toward the Black Hills. In case of new raids, Crawford warned, "we have not a horse fit for duty." Custer City's greatest need was grain to feed the horses, and he appealed to residents in Omaha and Cheyenne to send in a carload of corn. Thousands of emigrants are coming into the Hills, Crawford wrote; with cornfed horses, Custer City men could fly to the aid of any party coming under attack.[6]

Because of increased Indian hostility, Custer citizens in mid-April organized a company of militiamen, known as the Black Hills Rangers, to protect the town. Major Edward W. Wynkoop, a native of Philadelphia, commanded the unit, and Crawford was appointed chief of a smaller party of scouts. Within days, Indians came within a half-mile of town and drove off ten head of stock. Crawford went in pursuit, employing a young Cheyenne, Jule Seminole, as trailer. After pressing the Indians for nearly fifty miles, they recovered seven animals that the raiders had abandoned.[7]

On his return to Custer, Crawford learned of the massacre of the Metz party in Red Canyon, "the most famous of all Indian atrocities" in the Black Hills, according to historian Watson Parker. Charles Metz, his wife, and their black servant were killed on their way to Cheyenne, and their bodies were horribly mutilated. Three men in their party escaped to a nearby stage station, but two died later from their wounds. The black woman's husband, Crawford reported, was in Custer swearing vengeance. In writing of this tragedy, Jack expressed amazement that emigrants continued arriving in Custer in small, poorly armed parties. But he also noted that property prices were dropping—frightened residents were "selling out for little or nothing" and leaving town.[8]

Attacks on Custer residents continued without any perceivable letup. About April 21, five Indians fired on German-born John Hanson as he rode toward Custer. Using his fallen horse for a breastwork, Hanson wounded at least two before the attackers departed. He then walked into town and gave the alarm signal—

three shots fired in quick succession. More than fifty rangers responded, but only Crawford, Wynkoop, and a few others located mounts for following the Indians' trail. Crawford later wrote that pursuit had been useless since the Indians were riding good horses and had at least an hour's head start. Nonetheless, Custer residents were building a stockade near the center of town, where "several good horses will be fed for the use of our scouts." Crawford predicted that with grain-fed mounts, the rangers would soon report success against the Indians.[9]

A few days after the attack on Hanson, Crawford, Jule Seminole, "Antelope" Frank Smith, and four others left on a scout that lasted about four days. They saw hundreds of Indian signs and fired on four tribesmen driving stock, but they encountered no large parties of Indians. Seminole, however, came down with pneumonia, and, upon returning to Custer, took up residence in Crawford's cabin. In fact, Crawford spent several nights attending two very sick men. In addition to Seminole, Jack had befriended a man by the name of Hughes, suffering from a gunshot wound that had shattered his arm. Jack's ten-by-twelve-foot cabin contained two single bunks, one on each side, with a dry-goods box between them and against one wall serving as a table and writing desk. Hughes slept on one bunk, Seminole on the other, and Hughes's nine-year-old boy curled up at his father's feet. Jack bedded on the floor.[10]

During the first week in May, snow fell steadily for two days, but emigration to the Hills continued unabated. In a letter dated May 5, Crawford again told readers of dangers facing the Black Hillers. "The Indians are continually skulking about the outskirts of the city and on the roadway," he wrote, "stealing at every opportunity, and when it requires little risk they go so far as to take scalps." The previous night Indians had entered Custer and had run off seven horses; and the night before that, they had made away with eight horses and two yoke of oxen. Jack also told the tragic story of sixty-eight-year-old J. Leggette, whose body had just been brought into Custer. Leggette had been traveling with a party of fifty men on the Cheyenne road, when, about twenty miles from Custer, Indians fired into the wagon train. Men and horses panicked, dashing ahead to look for safety. When Leggette fell behind the stampeding riders, he was shot and killed. A money belt containing nearly four thousand dollars was later recovered from his body.[11]

On May 10, Crawford left Custer City to report on conditions in the northern Hills, where rich strikes reportedly had been made in Deadwood Gulch and along Whitewood Creek. Since his arrival in the Black Hills, Jack had witnessed a steady migration north. He also had become acquainted with William Gay, one of the early locators in Deadwood Gulch, who spent an evening in Crawford's cabin in early March testifying to the great wealth buried in the northern Hills. The great stampede to Deadwood got under way later that spring as soon as roads became passable for miners and teamsters bringing in supplies.[12]

With a party of about sixty men, Crawford started for the northern gold fields with spirits and expectations high. He had closed his letter to the *Omaha Daily Bee* the night before with a jaunty verse:

> *And now I reckon I'll jest let up,*
> *And prepare for a jolly old time;*
> *I'll pack my grub, and wipe my gun,*
> *As soon as I close this rhyme;*
> *And tomorrow, when day begins to dawn,*
> *With hearts as light as the air,*
> *We'll start for the far-off northern land,*
> *For they tell us the gold is there.*[13]

Jack made the trip to Deadwood City, located just below the confluence of Deadwood and Whitewood creeks, in six days, although the party with whom he had started soon splintered into several small groups. Crawford, in fact, covered most of the sixty-five miles with five stalwart companions: M. B. Goodell, a merchant; Dick Brown, the banjo player; John Powers of New York; Charles Stone of Boston; and James T. Irion of Alabama. On the fourth day out, after crossing Elk Creek, they encountered terrible roads—"mud holes, stumps, dead mules and oxen, broken wagons, rocks and side hills, corderoy crossings made of willow branches, and mud to the hub." About 4:00 P.M. their wagon struck a stump, breaking the front axle. Three of the men quickly retraced their route to find a replacement among the broken wagons that littered the trail.[14]

On Sunday, May 14, mule teams and oxen passed Jack's party all day long as the men worked to repair the wagon. "And ye Gods! what swearing, it was terrible to bear on the Sabbath morning," Crawford reported. "Sometimes ten and fifteen men [were] around each wagon, pushing and lifting, while the crack of the teamster's whip, as he flung it around his team" was accompanied by a blasphemous oath. By mid-afternoon, Crawford's party was under way again, but broke down after traveling only two miles. Brown and Goodell unhitched the team and started for Deadwood to borrow a wagon—and found an abandoned one only a short distance away. That evening, they encountered a large camp of about one hundred miners at Two-Bit Gulch and spent the rest of the evening, until nearly midnight, singing songs and having a good time. They arrived in Deadwood the next day after traversing the worst part of the road, which required easing the wagons down a steep hill with ropes.

For the next two weeks, Crawford canvassed the mining camps that sprawled through Deadwood Gulch and neighboring valleys. Nobody knew for certain how many prospectors were digging in the northern Hills. Edwin A. Curley, who toured the Black Hills in the summer of 1876 and later wrote an account of his journey, consulted with Crawford to arrive at an estimated population for the Deadwood area of twenty-five hundred. In May, Jack reported that Deadwood sported at least one hundred houses, and possibly as many more were under construction. Hundreds of recent arrivals like Jack, however, lived in tents, or in dugouts, shanties, and brush shelters.[15]

Crawford described for Omaha readers a typical Sunday in Deadwood. Forty teams had arrived that day from Custer or Cheyenne, and some came in from Sidney. No mining was going on, but men were busy putting up buildings. Five or six hundred miners from neighboring gulches were in town to purchase supplies and frequent the saloons. The place, he said, was "a perfect mass of humanity." Richard Hughes, reaching Deadwood a day before Jack, later recalled that "on any Sunday [in Deadwood] nearly the entire population of the northern Hills was concentrated on Main Street."[16]

Soon after reaching Deadwood, Crawford, Dick Brown, and some other friends walked two miles up the gulch to Gayville to enjoy an evening of banjo playing with brothers Alfred and William Gay. The Gays reported rich diggings nearby and exhibited 150 dollars in gold dust, which two men had panned that same day. Although Gayville consisted of only thirty-seven houses, every town lot had been taken. Sometime later, Jack returned to Gayville and built a house on a lot that William Gay had reserved for him.[17]

On his first trip north, Crawford also visited Crook City, a bustling mining camp nine miles from Deadwood at the mouth of Whitewood Creek. And on May 29, he joined about thirty other locators in laying out the original townsite of Spearfish, fourteen miles northwest of Deadwood on the banks of a dashing stream from which it derives its name. Like many modern-day travelers, Crawford was captivated by the beauty of Spearfish, soon to be called the "Queen City" of the Black Hills. He later served as secretary of a meeting called to organize a government for the camp.[18]

When Crawford returned to Custer City, he was convinced that reports about the richness of Deadwood had not been exaggerated. But too many miners were in the northern Hills for the number of placer locations available. Every claim of any value, he told his readers, had already been staked out. But still the "pilgrims" came, willing to work for others and making a few dollars a day, hoping for a chance to acquire a claim. To illustrate the magnitude of the northern influx, Crawford reported that on June 1, the day before his party pulled into Custer, he encountered thirty-five different teams loaded with supplies and passengers headed for Deadwood.[19]

Upon his return south, Jack discovered that the entire populace of Hill City had joined the stampede to Deadwood—"not one solitary soul remains." Custer City also presented a gloomy appearance, for the stampede north had reduced its population to about two hundred people. Crawford found only "nine stores, four saloons and one billiard hall still remaining, and many property holders have left their buildings without a representative." Still, he believed that Custer City had a promising future as a winter resort for miners wishing to stay year-round in the Hills. With a touch of wit, Crawford noted that all the lawyers had gone north, which was "one reason why we have still greater faith in Custer, for as soon as the people discover the lawyers coming into Deadwood many who left here to avoid them will return to live in peace."[20]

Crawford remained in Custer City for about a week before starting out on an expedition with Cheyenne photographer D. S. Mitchell to photograph points of interest between Custer and Deadwood. Several of Mitchell's photographs have survived, but Jack left no written account of this journey, except for a brief report of his visit to the Deadwood region in the latter part of June. Some three hundred people now resided in Gayville and about fifty in Spearfish. Deadwood, with a population of two thousand, continued to be the mecca for wandering prospectors. Jack made note that a Mrs. McKelvy, a boarding-house operator, "sets the best table in Deadwood, and is making money." Jim VanDaniker also was raking in gold dust from his saloon, boarding house, and restaurant, where he charged one dollar per meal.[21]

While Jack was in the northern Hills, miners in Deadwood and Gayville persuaded him to carry specimens of gold-bearing ore to Chicago in hopes of gaining financial backing for development. By this time, he probably had acquired part-interest in at least one quartz lead in the Deadwood region. He shipped more than sixty pounds of ore by stagecoach to Cheyenne, and then rode there on horseback. Crawford was in reduced straits, however, and could not afford train fare to Omaha. When the Cheyenne station manager learned of Captain Jack's identity, however, Union Pacific Railway officials quickly provided free transportation in gratitude for his letters publicizing the Black Hills.[22]

On the Fourth of July, the nation celebrated its one hundredth birthday with an outpouring of patriotism and self-congratulations. At the Philadelphia Centennial Exposition, ceremonies included a grand parade, music, speeches, and fireworks. In Sidney, Nebraska, businessmen decorated their stores with flags, citizens fired guns and cannons, politicians gave speeches, and fireworks lit up the evening sky. And the *Cheyenne Daily Leader* informed its readers that "Mr. J. Crawford, well known in the Black Hills as the *Omaha Bee* correspondent, passed through Cheyenne yesterday en route for Omaha."[23]

Two days later, on July 6, newspapers across the land stunned readers with news of the Little Bighorn disaster. With columns edged in black, the *Daily Leader* headlined its feature story with these words: "Gen. Custer's Command Slaughtered Like Sheep." The *Omaha Daily Bee* shouted: "Custer and Reno's Commands, Consisting of Twelve Companies, Annihilated by the Indians."[24] Months earlier, from his rustic cabin in the Black Hills, Crawford had predicted a major clash between Sitting Bull and the U.S. Army; but on June 25, the day that Custer made his bold and final stand, Crawford's most consuming interest—like that of almost every other Black Hills resident—had been gold and the acquisition of capital to mine the gold. Black Hillers, in fact, had only limited knowledge of the army's plans to subdue the off-reservation Indians.[25]

Although General Sheridan had hoped to defeat the non-reservation Sioux before spring, the severity of winter delayed the campaign until summer. Military strategy was simple: three columns would converge on Sioux hunting grounds, crush resistance, and force the hunting bands back to the reservation. Colonel John Gibbon, first in the field, left Fort Ellis, Montana, on March 30, moving east along the banks of the Yellowstone River with about 450 men in his command. General Alfred H. Terry, on May 17, marched out of Fort Abraham Lincoln, in present-day North Dakota, with 925 men, including the Seventh Cavalry under Lieutenant Colonel George A. Custer, and headed west, across Dakota and into Montana. On May 29, General George Crook left Fort Fetterman and headed north with more than 1,000 men in his command.[26]

No one had any idea of the number of Indians grouping on the Little Bighorn. Army officials believed that commands could expect to meet no more than between 500 and 800 hostile warriors. With the coming of spring, however, increasing numbers of Indians had left the reservation to join the off-reservation bands in an unusually large village in the area of the Little Bighorn. When Custer ordered his final advance, he unwittingly sent his men against a fighting force that may have numbered 2,000 warriors. All of Custer's command of 216 men died on that hot Sunday afternoon, and Major Marcus A. Reno lost 47 killed and 53 wounded in the Little Bighorn engagement.[27]

The nation was grief-stricken over Custer's death, and newspapers everywhere screamed for vengeance. Embittered by the military disaster, Sheridan's soldiers intensified their efforts to crush the hostiles. Joining in the push to avenge Custer's death was Buffalo Bill Cody, who had cut short a theatrical tour in June to rejoin his old regiment, the Fifth Cavalry, as chief of scouts. Cody learned of Custer's death on July 7, while in the field north of Fort Laramie with Colonel Wesley Merritt's command. Shortly thereafter, he dispatched a telegram to his friend Jack Crawford in Omaha, which read: "Have you heard of the death of our brave Custer?" Jack immediately wrote a nine-stanza poem, "The Death of Custer," which he sent to Cody and which appeared in the July 11 issue of the *Omaha Daily Bee.* Among the best known of Crawford's poems, the first stanza is reproduced at the end of Chapter 2.[28]

Crawford soon journeyed to Chicago to exhibit quartz specimens to skeptical bankers and businessmen. In previous months, Chicago newspapers had condemned the Black Hills gold rush as a great humbug, apparently perpetrated by greedy capitalists who preyed on hapless gold seekers. Charles Swartout, a pioneer in the Black Hills with ten years of mining experience, reached Chicago a few weeks before Jack, and in an interview with the press, he asserted that the Deadwood region was "the richest quartz bearing country ever thrown open in the Union." Crawford probably was among the first of the Black Hillers to appear in Chicago with evidence to back this claim.[29]

In Chicago, Crawford also met with General Sheridan, who quizzed him about the Black Hills and the accuracy of government maps. Jack later claimed that upon examining Crawford's specimens of quartz, Sheridan remarked: "Captain, this is the first substantial evidence I have seen of gold-bearing quartz in the Black Hills." While at army headquarters, Jack received another telegram from Cody, asking Jack to join him immediately to help in avenging Custer's death. According to Crawford, Sheridan thereupon appointed him as a scout with Merritt's Fifth Cavalry. Indeed, quartermaster records show that Crawford's employment with the army began on July 22, while he was still in Chicago.[30]

Crawford returned to Omaha on July 24, en route to Fort Laramie to join the Fifth Cavalry. Before he boarded a train the following morning for Cheyenne, his friends presented him with appropriate gifts: a new Winchester repeating rifle, cartridge belt, holster, hunting knife and sheath, and a buckskin suit. The management of the *Omaha Daily Bee* contributed "liberally to his outfit" and paid tribute to its intrepid correspondent with these words:

> Captain Jack is a right good fellow, and we hope to see him distinguish himself alongside of his old friend Buffalo Bill. Jack has done some good in advancing the interests of the Black Hills, and it was on this account that his Omaha friends took occasion to give him a handsome testimonial of their appreciation of his labors.[31]

When Crawford reached Cheyenne, he discovered that the Fifth Cavalry had already left Fort Laramie and was en route north to Fort Fetterman. On July 27, railroad officials provided him free transportation to Medicine Bow, a station on the Union Pacific about 110 miles beyond Cheyenne and less than 90 miles south of Fetterman, where Jack hoped to join Merritt's command. He left Medicine Bow alone on horseback on the twenty-eighth, at the beginning of what proved to be a 400-mile chase to catch up with Merritt. Crawford camped that evening with Charley Hecht's wagon train carrying supplies for the military. Early the next morning, the train moved on about five miles to good grass, where Crawford shared the teamsters' breakfast of tomatoes, fried bacon, deer, chicken, bread, and coffee. Jack continued on alone to Fetterman, covering the remaining fifty-five miles in ten hours and thirty minutes.[32]

But Merritt and his command had already left to join Crook, bivouacked on Goose Creek in northern Wyoming near the Montana border and awaiting reinforcements before resuming the campaign. On August 3, Merritt's force finally joined with Crook's, and on the following day Crook announced the organization of the Big Horn and Yellowstone Expedition. He placed Merritt in charge of all cavalry regiments, leaving Lieutenant Colonel Eugene A. Carr in command of the Fifth Cavalry. Crook's entire force consisted of about 2,200 men: 1,500 cavalry, 450 infantry, 240 Indian scouts, and a contingent of civilian employees, including 44 white scouts and guides.[33]

Anxious to make contact with the Sioux, Crook departed Goose Creek on August 5, leaving his 160-wagon supply train behind, in charge of Quartermaster John Furey. Because Crook wanted his men to be as mobile as the Indians, each soldier carried on the march only a few essentials—a blanket, tin cup, frying pan, eating utensils, and four days of rations. Pack mules carried extra ammunition and rations sufficient to last fifteen days, but tents remained with the supply train. When Crawford caught up with Crook's command on August 8, it was camped on Rosebud Creek in Montana.[34]

Crawford later wrote an exciting account of his ride to join Crook, which appears in the first edition of *The Poet Scout,* published only three years after these events took place. Jack had left Fort Fetterman on August 2, accompanied by a military courier named Graves. Because the days were uncomfortably warm, the men soon jettisoned overcoats and blankets, each retaining only a rubber blanket and the clothes they wore. Before reaching the Powder River, where canteens were replenished, they suffered severely from thirst. They kept constantly alert for Indian signs. A day or two into their journey, after crossing a trail of an estimated fifty Sioux warriors, they pulled off their horses' shoes "in order to throw the reds off our trail by making believe we were Indians, should any of them chance to cross us in the rear."[35]

Upon reaching the wagon train bivouacked on Goose Creek, Crawford and Graves learned that Crook and his entire command had departed for Bighorn country. With fresh mounts, the two men continued on Crook's trail, even though Captain Furey warned that the entire country "was swarming with Indians." Furey, in fact, would not allow them to carry dispatches to Crook, fearing that Indians would overpower the lone riders. They rode nights and kept out of sight during the day, although daytime heat made sleeping difficult. A day or two after leaving Goose Creek, they spied an Indian scouting party, which, Jack said, showed that Crook's command was close at hand. "There are always a band of Indians on the trail for the purpose of picking up played-out horses, or anything thrown away by the soldiers, such as old clothes, pots, pans and kettles."

They soon reached the Rosebud mountains, climbed the summit, and in descending chose a route they thought would connect with Crook's trail. Graves realized they were off the track, however, and riding into the same valley where Custer had fought his last battle. The night was murky, a storm threatening. But the men rode on to investigate the battleground, finding it strewn with bones and skulls, the work of wolves and coyotes that had disturbed the hastily dug graves. The two riders quickly moved out of the valley and reached the headwaters of the Rosebud at daylight. They slept during the day and continued their ride that evening, reaching Crook's command on the morning of the eighth.

After a brief nap, Crawford located his friend Buffalo Bill, handed him some letters, and distributed other communications to officers and newspaper correspondents accompanying the expedition. He then turned over to Cody a present from a Mr. Jones, proprietor of the Jones House in Cheyenne. The gift was a bottle of sour-mash whiskey, which Jack had carried unharmed on his perilous journey to the Rosebud. In writing of this incident in his autobiography, published in 1879, Cody whimsically remarked: "Jack Crawford is the only man I have ever known that could have brought that bottle of whiskey through without *accident* befalling it, for he is one of the very few teetotal scouts I ever met."[36] Indeed, Crawford made a good impression upon both officers and enlisted men, who considered his ride from Fetterman "a plucky undertaking."[37]

Crook's army continued its march down the Rosebud, and

on August 10 it met General Terry's column of about seventeen hundred men in the Rosebud Valley, where the trail of the Sioux turned eastward. After Crook's men drew rations from Terry's wagon train (which then returned to the Yellowstone), the combined commands followed the trail to the Powder River amid cold rain and heavy mud. At the mouth of the Powder, the expedition bivouacked for a week, waiting for supplies to arrive by boat. Although Captain Jack's "yarns and rhymes" would help to relieve the monotony of camp life, Buffalo Bill grew bored by the inactivity and left the expedition to continue his theatrical career in the East. According to one newspaper account, it was on Cody's recommendation that Merritt subsequently appointed Crawford to succeed Cody as chief of scouts of the Fifth Cavalry.[38]

With his men rationed for fifteen days, Crook departed from the Yellowstone on August 24, traveled up the Powder to relocate the Indian trail he had abandoned a week earlier, and then, on the twenty-sixth, followed the trail eastward toward the Little Missouri. According to historian Jerome Greene, Crook's departure from the Powder River "marked the beginning of one of the most grueling marches in American military history." The weather turned cold, and unseasonable rains lashed the men almost daily. Men and horses alike became mired in the resulting mud. John F. Finerty, the *Chicago Times* correspondent with the expedition, later recalled: "The horses sank in the mud to their kneejoints, and the soldiers' shoes were pulled off in trying to drag their feet through the sticky slime." Most vexatious for Crook, the Indian trail disappeared on the Little Missouri in present-day North Dakota, indicating that the tribes had scattered.[39]

On September 5, camped at the head of Heart River, several miles east of the Little Missouri, Crook decided to head for the Black Hills, 180 miles to the south, to offer the miners protection from hostiles returning to the agencies. That evening he sent a dispatch to General Sheridan, requesting that rations for his command be sent to Custer City, where he planned to establish a base camp; and he ordered his soldiers on half-rations. But even with this effort to conserve food, the men were facing starvation, for their supplies were nearly exhausted and the Black Hills lay at least seven days away.[40]

On the following day, Crook's command began the long journey south in a steady rain. Without grain and adequate forage, horses and mules had weakened and many now collapsed in the mud. Crook already had given orders to shoot abandoned animals for food, and for several days his soddened, ragtag army would exist on a diet of mule and horse meat. But the soldiers were nearing total exhaustion—wet, hungry, disheartened by constant hardships. One officer wrote that he saw "men who were very plucky sit down and cry like children because they could not hold out." Years later, Colonel Andrew S. Burt would reminisce with Crawford about the hardships they had shared on this grueling march: hunger; marching in rain; sleeping on wet, muddy ground; eating horse meat. He vividly recalled Jack squatting on the ground before a campfire, "gnawing at a horse's rib fresh from the coals and glad to get the rib!"[41]

On September 7, Crook detailed Captain Anson Mills to take 150 men on the strongest horses and ride to the northernmost mining camps in the Black Hills to obtain food for his starving troops. Lieutenant John W. Bubb, the expedition commissary, would have charge of the pack train and oversee the purchasing of supplies. Accompanying Mills's command were civilian scouts Crawford and Frank Grouard and newspaper correspondents Robert Strahorn of Denver's *Rocky Mountain News* and Reuben Davenport of the *New York Herald.*[42]

Mills's command left camp that same evening in "a thick mist," guided by Grouard, Crook's favorite scout. About 1:00 A.M. the column stopped to rest, and then moved on at daylight. On the afternoon of September 8, Crawford and Grouard were ranging a mile or more in advance of the troops when Grouard spied some Indian ponies. Further investigation revealed the presence of a Sioux village in the ravines of Slim Buttes, rocky formations near present-day Reva, South Dakota.[43]

After consulting with his officers, Mills moved the column back to the shelter of a deep ravine to spend the night, planning to attack the village at daylight. Since it was not known how many Indians were in the village, Crawford volunteered to ride back to inform Crook "so that reinforcements could be hurried forward." Mills rejected the offer, saying that "no man could find his way back at night." The captain's statement amused Jack and other men, knowing that even on a pitch-black night a horse would have no difficulty in keeping a trail made by 150 animals on ground softened by rain.[44]

Hardly anyone slept that night because of the cold, mud, rain, and hunger. Crawford and Davenport had messed together earlier that evening on weak tea, one hardtack each, and some bacon rind. When Tom Moore, the chief packer, shared some coffee with them, their spirits soared. About 2:00 A.M., on September 9, the command moved forward in total darkness, with Crawford and Grouard in the lead. About a mile from the village, Mills left the pack train and horses in the care of Lieutenant Bubb, the packers, and twenty-five soldiers. Davenport, quite ill at this time, remained with the pack train.[45]

Mills's plan called for three columns of soldiers to attack simultaneously the sleeping camp at dawn. Lieutenants Emmet Crawford and Adolphus H. Von Luettwitz, each accompanied by fifty men on foot, would diverge to the right and left of the village. Once they were in position, Lieutenant Frederick Schwatka, with twenty-five mounted men, would sweep through its center and stampede the herd of Indian ponies. Then, Crawford and Von Luettwitz's forces would catch the village in a withering crossfire.[46]

Long before daylight, however, and before Von Luettwitz's men were in position, Mills ordered the general attack, fearing that a small herd of ponies that stampeded through the village had eliminated the chance for total surprise. Jack Crawford joined Schwatka's men as they charged through the village, yelling and firing into tepees. Quickly, the dismounted soldiers began firing on the Indians as they burst from their lodges. By a circuitous route, Captain Jack and Schwatka's men rejoined the main command, but in the darkness little could be seen except the flashes of gunfire. Mills now ordered Jack to ride to the pack train to hurry it to the front, and he also sent a courier to General Crook, asking for reinforcement. Although the Indians had been taken by surprise, most escaped the deadly entrapment that Mills planned for them since the troopers had failed to encircle the village. And even though Schwatka captured the main portion of the pony herd, several mounted warriors were seen at daybreak riding westward to obtain assistance from neighboring bands.[47]

Mills took immediate steps to defend his position overlooking the village while awaiting Crook's arrival. Lieutenant Schwatka, Jack Crawford, and three enlisted men dug rifle pits for protecting the pack train and wounded soldiers, while other troopers took up positions atop nearby ridges. Sometime later, Captain Jack, Robert Strahorn, and about fourteen volunteers entered the deserted village to survey its contents, drawing fire from Indians concealed in the bluffs and hiding in a nearby deep ravine. In a dispatch written for the *Omaha Daily Bee*, Crawford described the cornucopia they encountered: "tepees full of dried meats, skins, bead work, and all that an Indian's head could wish for." The lodges also contained a guidon from Custer's cavalry, an officer's coat, and several saddles from Custer's command. The forage party returned to the command post with a mule ladened with dried meat, which "was quickly pounced upon by the hungry troops." Other detachments entered the village to salvage whatever the command could use, and then set fire to the lodges later that afternoon.[48]

About noon Crook's force reached the Slim Buttes battleground, thus relieving anxieties among Mills's soldiers, who had feared a disaster like the one that had struck down Custer. By this time firing had almost ceased, except for an occasional shot from the densely wooded ravine that sheltered an unknown number of warriors. All efforts to dislodge them had failed, but after Crook arrived the scouts were ordered to advance to the ravine for a final effort to end the stalemate. While engaged in this maneuver, "Buffalo Chips" White, a scouting partner of Buffalo Bill, was shot through the heart and killed. Crawford later told Colonel Andrew S. Burt that White had seen a dog near the ravine, which he had mistaken for an Indian. When he rose from his prone position to fire, "Jack reached to pull him back from exposure but too late, for he was instantly killed by a shot from the ravine." At this point, soldiers and officers alike rushed to the edge of the stronghold and poured in a withering fire. The battle was soon over. From the blood-drenched ravine, more than twenty survivors emerged, among them the warrior American Horse, who died later that night from a wound in the abdomen. They left behind the bodies of three women, one man, and an infant.[49]

Late in the afternoon, mounted Indians swarmed on nearby ridges and made a strong effort to regain their horses and free the captives. During the fighting that followed (according to reporter Davenport), "Captain Jack killed and scalped an Indian a mile from the column." By nightfall, however, the Indians had been repulsed, and the tired troopers enjoyed an evening meal of roasted Indian pony, dried fruit, and other provisions confiscated from the village. Captain Jack told readers of the *Omaha Daily Bee* that "a good night's rest, on ground high and dry, with plenty of buffalo robes, blankets and big fire, was the result of our day's labor." Crawford also became the proud owner of a mare and colt, his share of the captured pony herd, distributed among men who had charged the village. In this same dispatch, Jack admitted that he had taken "one top-knot" during a fight in which he "came near losing" his own hair. He later regretted this bloody deed and never spoke of it in his public performances.[50]

About 9:00 A.M., on September 10, Crook's force left Slim Buttes and moved south toward the Black Hills seventy miles away. In the early afternoon, the column halted to care for the wounded being carried on mule-drawn litters. Because the dried meat and fruit captured in the Indian village were not sufficient to sustain the command, soldiers resumed the practice of butchering horses for rations. In the evening, Crook directed Frank Grouard to carry dispatches to Fort Laramie, but the scout refused to leave before morning.[51]

Grouard finally left camp about 10:00 A.M. on the eleventh, in company with Captain Mills, Lieutenant Bubb, and about seventy-five mounted troopers who were riding ahead to the mining camps to purchase provisions for Crook's starving command. At Crook's request, Captain Jack joined Mills's party, accompanied also by reporters Strahorn and Davenport. They departed in a bitter storm, rode until midnight, and then started out again at 6:00 A.M. on the twelfth. Upon reaching the mouth of Whitewood Canyon that evening, a small detail galloped on to Crook City, with Crawford leading the way. Bubb quickly purchased supplies from citizens anxious to cooperate with the army and, on September 13, returned to the main command with fifty head of beef cattle and ten ox-drawn wagons filled with provisions.[52]

Meanwhile, Crawford had embarked upon a daring ride to carry dispatches for Reuben Davenport to Fort Laramie, a feat that Jack proudly described to countless audiences in later years, even though it had led to his release as a military scout. When Mills's party left camp on September 11, Grouard was carrying Crook's dispatches as well as those of the correspondents—with instructions to telegraph official messages first. Davenport, however, offered to pay Crawford five hundred dollars if he would beat Grouard to the telegraph and place his dispatches on the wire ahead of all others. Jack later stated that he accepted Davenport's offer only after receiving permission from Colonel Merritt to leave the command.[53]

Upon reaching Crook City on the evening of September 12, Grouard slept while Crawford rode to Deadwood in the pitch dark. It was a dangerous undertaking, for Indians were still harassing the mining communities. Only two days earlier a Sioux party had come within two hundred yards of the main street in Crook City, and Indian outrages were being reported almost daily. Jack arrived in Deadwood at 6:00 A.M. on the thirteenth, secured a new horse, and then started for Custer City. Grouard, on Crook's authority, purchased fresh mounts along the route and passed Crawford ten miles north of Custer.[54]

Totally exhausted, the two men agreed to spend the night in Custer City and resume the race the next day. Unknown to Crawford, Grouard hired Frank Smith to carry the dispatches to the army camp at Red Canyon, forty miles beyond Custer, where military couriers would carry them forward. Smith departed about midnight. Crawford left at 9:00 A.M. and reached Red Canyon in mid-afternoon, where the commanding officer persuaded him to spend the night since he had no chance of overtaking the couriers. Jack continued his ride on the fifteenth and reached the telegraph line at Sage Creek, about sixty miles from Fort Laramie, at 8:00 P.M.[55]

Although the line was down, Captain Jack capitalized on a hasty action Grouard had taken in Custer City, when, in anger, he had handed Davenport's dispatches to Crawford. Having duplicate copies enabled Jack to leave one copy with the operator at Sage

Creek, requesting that it be placed on the wire as soon as it was repaired, and to continue with the other copy to Fort Laramie. At the next camp, forty-eight miles beyond Sage Creek, Crawford learned that the line had been repaired and that Davenport's dispatches were on the wire "ahead of all others." Captain Jack reached Fort Laramie at 7:00 P.M. on September 16, nine hours behind the government courier. Two days later, the *New York Herald* published Crawford's own story under the headline: "Captain Jack's Ride as a Bearer of Herald Despatches."[56]

Crawford's feat was truly remarkable, for he had been living on starvation rations before leaving Crook's command on the eleventh and then riding three hundred miles or more in the next six days. In what was clearly an understatement, he concluded his report to the *Herald* by saying he was "pretty well exhausted." Some months later, James Gordon Bennett of the *Herald* paid Crawford the 500 dollars that Davenport had promised and an additional 222 dollars to cover expenses.[57]

The story of Jack's ride has a final twist, which in no way detracts from his accomplishment. When the government courier reached Fort Laramie, Davenport's story was being transmitted from Sage Creek. During a pause in the transmission, the operator at Laramie broke in with Crook's dispatches and continued sending without interruption, so that only a portion of Davenport's report was sent over the lines before Crook's. Still, Crawford had Davenport's dispatches on the wire five hours ahead of all other correspondents.[58]

On the same evening that Crawford reached Fort Laramie, he met with General Sheridan, who had journeyed west to consult with Crook. But Jack remained at the post only a day or two before returning to Custer, where he learned from Colonel Merritt of his discharge as an army scout, apparently for having left the command at Crook City. Crawford lost little time in writing to Crook to explain the circumstances of his departure, since he believed that the general was "laboring under a misunderstanding." But Jack was not reinstated. Quartermaster records show that his employment with the military terminated on September 15.[59]

Crawford may have spent the month of October in the mining camps. But by November 10 he was once again in Omaha. From there, he traveled to Philadelphia to join Buffalo Bill's theatrical troupe for its winter tour, planning to return to the Black Hills in May. While starring as "Captain Jack" opposite "Buffalo Bill" in western melodramas, however, Crawford discovered that his talents for entertaining extended beyond the glow of an evening campfire. Rather than returning to the gold region, Crawford stayed with Cody through the spring season, and then continued his quest of fame and fortune with his own theatrical company.[60]

Crawford's experiences in the Black Hills, covering no more than eighteen months, dramatically affected his later career and taught him some valuable lessons. He learned the fundamentals of gold mining, for example, and discovered that investment funds were essential for development. For the rest of his life, he retained a consuming interest in mining, working hard to interest capitalists in his mining schemes. Crawford also experienced the excitement of Indian campaigning and learned the techniques of trailing. Within four years of leaving the Dakotas, he was again on the government payroll as a civilian scout, tracking the elusive Victorio in Mexico. Moreover, he acquired first-hand knowledge of Native Americans. Later, as his ideas about Indians and their place in American society matured, he would side with humanitarians in trying to ease their transition to a new way of life. And finally, Crawford's friendship with Bill Cody deepened with the shared experiences of scouting on the Powder and exchanging stories around the campfire. Their relationship was often stormy, however, and Crawford's stage career with Cody ended on a sour note. Still, despite setbacks in his theatrical career, Captain Jack moved through life with an optimism that would not be vanquished.

> *I never like to see a man a 'rastlin' with the dumps*
> *'Cause in the game o'life he doesn't always catch the trumps;*
> *But I can always cotton to a free and easy cuss*
> *As takes his dose, and thanks the Lord it isn't any wuss.*[61]

4

CODY, CARIBOO, AND THE
VICTORIO CAMPAIGN

Capt. Jack Crawford.
HOUSEWORTH & CO.   PHOTOGRAPHERS.
No. 12 Montgomery Street, near Market Street, San Francisco.

On January 8, 1877, the Buffalo Bill Combination thrilled a large audience at Boston's Beethoven Hall. The occasion was its performance of the sensational melodrama, *The Red Right Hand; or, Buffalo Bill's First Scalp for Custer,* loosely based on William F. Cody's exploits as a military scout. The Boston press commented favorably on Captain Jack Crawford's appearance in a leading role, as did newspapers in other towns where the combination performed. Nearly all the stories also described Crawford's "perilous journey" following the Slim Buttes engagement. And nearly all misrepresented the facts by exaggerating the distance of his ride or the amount of money he had received from the *New York Herald.* [1]

When Crawford left the Big Horn and Yellowstone Expedition, he was facing a major crossroad in his life. He had received an impressive salary of 150 dollars a month as a scout, and he still had hopes of striking it rich in the Black Hills. But he also had a family to support in Pennsylvania. Consequently, when Cody of-

Captain Jack Crawford, as he appeared on stage in San Francisco, 1877. (Courtesy, The Bancroft Library.)

fered him a position with the Buffalo Bill Combination, Jack accepted, planning to return to the Dakotas when the theatrical season ended in the spring. Once launched on a dramatic career, however, Crawford's course was set. Henceforth he would find his greatest happiness on the stage, entertaining audiences with stories about the American West.[2]

Jack was twenty-nine years old when he teamed up with Cody, and his essential personality had already developed. Described as brave, generous, witty, and unpretentious, he was also a sensitive, kindhearted man, who wrote forthrightly of his love and affection for both male and female friends. Above all else he was honest and temperate, retaining in adulthood the values his mother had instilled in him as a child. His talent for versifying was so well known that publicists for the Buffalo Bill Combination touted him as "The Poet Scout of the Black Hills." A pen portrait of Jack, written by a military friend in 1884, indicates how he probably appeared to audiences on his first theatrical tour through the East. Crawford, according to his friend,

> is a tall, wiry built man, with a nervous, sensitive face, which his open frank, demeanor dignifies when you have once entered into conversation with him. His manner is simple and easy, entirely free from [affectation]. His long, light-brown hair falls below his shoulders, and a moustache and goatee of the same color ornament his youthful face. A large light felt sombrero crowns his head and his body is covered with a blue shirt with wide, flowing collar. Buckskin trousers, with fringed sides, cover his long, muscular legs, and a belt, with a "persuader" attached, usually circles his waist.[3]

Crawford was also a family man, and in later years he took great pride in the accomplishments of his children. Unfortunately, there is a dearth of material about Maria Crawford and the children prior to 1881, when they joined Jack in New Mexico. Since Crawford was an inveterate letter writer, we can safely assume that he corresponded regularly with Maria and shared with her his dreams of financial success. Jack's long absences from home, however, would tarnish the luster of their youthful romance.

Cody, Cariboo, and the Victorio Campaign

Whether Crawford saw Maria and the children after leaving the Black Hills can only be speculated. The *Omaha Daily Bee* announced that Jack had left Omaha on November 25, 1876, to join the Buffalo Bill Combination in Philadelphia. Almost immediately thereafter, Captain Jack's name and image appeared in the publicity for the troupe's winter tour through the East.[4]

In many respects, Buffalo Bill and Captain Jack, the two leading performers in the combination, were much alike. Both were noted for their good fellowship, sunny dispositions, generosity, optimism, and willingness to undergo hardships to achieve their goals. Each had gone to work at a young age to help support his family, thereby neglecting a formal education, although Cody occasionally had attended county schools in Iowa and Kansas. Cody, a year older than Crawford, had married in 1866 and, within seven years, had fathered three children. Like Crawford, Cody frequently left his family for extended periods. In fact, when Cody's five-year-old son Kit Carson ("Kitty") Cody was fatally stricken with scarlet fever in April 1876, Cody was on tour in the East, starring in *The Scouts of the Plains*. Kitty's death gives us the first documented evidence of the Cody–Crawford friendship, for Cody notified Crawford (then in Custer City) of the tragedy. Jack responded with a poem, which began: "My friend, I feel your sorrow / Just as though it were my own."[5]

By the time Crawford joined the Buffalo Bill Combination, Cody had gained distinction on the Northern Plains, serving continuously as chief-of-scouts for the Fifth Cavalry from September 1868 through November 1872. Cody embarked upon his stage career during the winter of 1872–73, and thereafter he alternated winter theatrical tours with summer enlistments with the army or as a hunting guide for parties of European and eastern dignitaries. Shortly after Custer's defeat on the Little Bighorn, Cody added to his fame by killing and scalping the Cheyenne warrior Yellow Hair (also called Yellow Hand)—hence, "the first scalp for Custer."[6]

Despite Cody's acclaim as a frontiersman and stage personality, the name of Buffalo Bill had not yet become a household word in 1876. His greatest financial success and recognition as a showman would come after he initiated his magnificent outdoor Wild West exhibitions in 1883. Thus, when Crawford joined his friend on the stage and shared with Cody the applause of boisterous audiences, the Poet Scout had reason to compare his talents favorably with Cody's. The key to understanding Cody's remarkable success in later years is the publicity he received—in the form of dime novels that depicted Buffalo Bill as bigger than life and through the efforts of Cody's press agent, John M. Burke, a master in selling his associate to the public. Crawford pointedly rejected dime novels as an avenue to fame and never stumbled upon a talented press agent like Burke.[7]

In October 1876, Cody opened the new season in Rochester, New York, by staging an old favorite, *Life on the Border.* From there he traveled to New York City and then to Philadelphia, where Crawford joined his tour of the eastern states. A traveling theatrical combination like Cody's offered audiences one or two select plays before moving to another city; in contrast, a stock company remained indefinitely in the same theater, performing a variety of plays.[8]

For the 1876–77 season, in which Crawford costarred with Cody, the Buffalo Bill Combination usually alternated *Life on the Border,* a play advertised as "depicting True Frontier Life," with the more sanguinary *The Red Right Hand,* a new performance arranged for the stage by actor J. V. Arlington. One critic described *The Red Right Hand* as "a bloodthirsty drama." "The rifle and the scalping knife," he went on to say, " with unlimited gunpowder and slaughter of Indians pervade the play from first to last." Another writer claimed that the drama was "equal to ten or fifteen dime novels"; so much blood flowed that "miners of the Black Hills might have used the vital liquid for the purposes of sluicing." Cody took a more whimsical view of the drama, describing it as "a five-act play, without head or tail, and it made no difference at which act we commenced the performance. . . . It afforded us, however, ample opportunity to give a noisy, rattling, gunpowder entertainment, and to present a succession of scenes in the late Indian war, all of which seemed to give general satisfaction." [9]

Audiences, in fact, loved the performance. A boisterous crowd in Pittsburgh filled the playhouse "clear away to the ceiling." During a two-day engagement in Wheeling, West Virginia, in March 1877, large audiences loudly applauded Buffalo Bill and Captain Jack, who, according to the local press, rendered "their respective parts in handsome style." [10]

The Wheeling engagement would remain indelibly imprinted on Captain Jack's memory, for it coincided with a local temperance crusade that brought to town the great evangelist Francis Murphy. An Irish immigrant and reformed drunkard, Murphy had achieved phenomenal success as a temperance crusader after initiating a series of thirty-two lectures in Chicago late in 1874. Subsequently, the zealous reformer had persuaded thousands of people to sign the "Murphy pledge" and to encourage others likewise to abstain from all intoxicating liquors. [11]

In Wheeling, the Murphy Movement got under way at the Fourth Street Methodist Church about four weeks prior to Jack's arrival, and soon several local churches were holding regular temperance meetings. Hymns were sung, testimonials rendered, and pledges signed by hundreds of new converts. Enthusiasm peaked early in March, when it was announced that Murphy himself would soon appear in the city. Advertisements in the *Wheeling Daily Register* offered residents two unique forms of entertainment for the evening of March 9: Buffalo Bill and Captain Jack performing in *The Red Right Hand* at the Hamilton Opera House, and Francis Murphy speaking at the Fourth Street church temperance meeting. [12]

As it turned out, Murphy rescheduled his lecture for the

afternoon, thereby enabling Cody and Crawford to be among the throng that listened to the evangelist tell of his early addiction to intoxicants. When Murphy cut short his address to catch a train, Captain Jack was called from the audience to recount his experiences in fighting demon rum. Crawford later claimed that because of his long talk and continual begging, he persuaded Buffalo Bill to sign the Murphy pledge. Apparently Cody, whose drinking sprees were notorious, honored the pledge for about four months. Had his former acquaintances read the announcement in the *Wheeling Daily Register* that Buffalo Bill and Captain Jack would address a temperance meeting on the Sabbath, their laughter might have awakened the dead.[13]

In April, the Buffalo Bill Combination traveled to Kansas City, where Jack met his old friend Charley Whitehead, and then moved on to Omaha for a two-night stand. The press in both cities tendered Captain Jack favorable notices. Whitehead summarized, for readers of the Kansas City *Times,* Jack's remarkable history, comparing his childhood to "that of Oliver Twist." A writer for the *Omaha Daily Bee* recalled Jack's valuable services as a newspaper correspondent advertising the Black Hills and, upon witnessing a performance of *The Red Right Hand,* avowed that he also "gave evidence of being a good actor."[14]

After closing in Omaha, the combination temporarily disbanded. But before parting company, Cody and Crawford squabbled over money. Neither of the two performers were good businessmen, a shortcoming reflected in the casual way in which they handled the matter of Jack's pay. When Crawford joined the Buffalo Bill Combination, Cody had promised him ample remuneration if business were good. Cody apparently paid all the troupe's expenses while on the road and never gave Crawford an accounting until the season ended. Much to his chagrin, Jack learned that he was to receive the same salary as the chief property man, twenty dollars per week.[15]

At this juncture, Crawford planned to leave Cody's employ and guide a party of prospectors into the Black Hills. Cody, however, received a good offer to perform at the Bush Street Theatre in San Francisco and persuaded Jack to go along, promising that he would make the salary "all right."[16]

The Buffalo Bill Combination opened in San Francisco on May 14. During its five-week engagement, the troupe regularly filled the theater with enthusiastic playgoers who loudly applauded Buffalo Bill and Captain Jack in performances of *Life on the Border, The Red Right Hand,* or *The Scouts of the Plains.* Because of their success (the opening night's receipts amounted to fourteen hundred dollars), Crawford asked for a salary of one hundred dollars per week; Cody offered forty dollars, but settled on fifty dollars after Crawford threatened to leave.[17]

During the second half of the nineteenth century, audiences throughout the country delighted in frontier melodramas such as those performed by Cody and Crawford. The plays followed a basic formula that featured resourceful frontier heroes enduring a seemingly endless number of brawls and narrow escapes to triumph over villainous foes. Conditioned by textbooks, newspapers, and other published accounts to view westward expansion as a national goal, audiences eagerly applauded these genuine western army scouts who only recently had returned from the Sioux wars. Moreover, by the mid-1870s, the nation already had developed a western mythology, viewing the West as a place of freedom and limitless opportunity. Consequently, when Cody and Crawford stepped on stage, the "myth-visions" in the minds of the audience so colored their perceptions that the ex-scouts appeared as "crusading heroes [helping to spread] civilization over savagery."[18]

While in San Francisco, Jack left the theater long enough to take part in Memorial Day ceremonies sponsored by the local post of the Grand Army of the Republic (G.A.R.), the nation's largest veterans' organization. More than three hundred ex-soldiers gathered at the Odd Fellows' Cemetery on May 30, where they listened to Captain Jack deliver an original nine-stanza poem honoring comrades who had fallen in the late war. The full text appeared a few days later on the front page of the San Francisco *Daily Alta California.* [19]

After their successful run in San Francisco, Buffalo Bill and Captain Jack appeared in Oakland and Sacramento and then traveled to Virginia City, Nevada, in late June for a six-day engagement. The Virginia City *Territorial Enterprise* gave ample coverage to the two famous scouts and praised their ability to please the crowds that nightly "packed the hall to suffocation." The audience on June 29 witnessed an accident on stage that widened the rift between the two stars and led to Crawford's decision to form his own dramatic company.[20]

For their final evening performance in Virginia City, Cody and Crawford staged *The Red Right Hand,* with Captain Jack impersonating Yellow Hand. Crawford and Cody (both on horseback) were exchanging shots at short range in the final act, when suddenly Jack fell from his horse. He quickly recovered and was engaging Cody in hand-to-hand combat when the audience noticed blood streaming down his tights. Gertie Granville, an actress with the combination, fainted in her box seat, as stage hands quickly lowered the curtain.[21]

Rushing to the wounded actor's side, Crawford's friends discovered an ugly and painful wound below his left groin. Although the *Territorial Enterprise* reported the next day that Crawford had accidently shot himself, privately Captain Jack blamed the accident on Cody. He later stated that Cody had been so drunk on the night of the performance that the actor scheduled to play Yellow Hand had refused to appear on stage. Cody had twice slashed Jack during the knife scene.[22]

Both the *Daily Alta California* and the *New York Herald*

printed accounts of Jack's accident. As for Cody, he made a final stage appearance in Virginia City the next day, in a matinee production of *Life on the Border,* playing both his own part and that of Captain Jack. After settling his financial account with Crawford, Cody left the city and subsequently disbanded the combination for the second time in Omaha. Later, he traveled to Ogallala to meet Major Frank North, who—in partnership with Cody—had established a ranch a few months earlier on the South Fork of the Dismal River, sixty-five miles north of North Platte, Nebraska. Cody and North spent the rest of the summer stocking their range with cattle. Years later, in a letter to Cody dated September 19, 1894, Crawford took credit for helping Cody save the twenty-two thousand dollars needed for the ranching venture. Had he not persuaded Cody to sign the Murphy pledge and then watched over him "as a she bear would watch her first cub," Crawford implied, Cody would have squandered the money during his marathon drinking bouts.[23]

Even though Crawford's wound was not life-threatening, it kept him confined to a bed for more than two weeks. He hobbled about a little on crutches as he slowly regained his strength, but not until August 2 was his familiar form seen again on the streets of Virginia City, walking with the aid of a crutch and cane. On the fifth, Cody wired Crawford from North Platte, asking if he would open with him on September 1—"salary fifty per week for season." But Crawford had already decided to strike out on his own, and he made his intentions known in a letter that Cody labeled as "unkind." Cody denied that Jack's accident had been his fault, saying that he had "never wanted to put the horses on the stage," implying that the animals had been the culprits. Still, Cody wished Jack success in his venture but advised his friend: "dont build your castles to [*sic*] high."[24]

Aware of Crawford's reduced circumstances, the leading citizens of Virginia City invited Jack to stage a benefit performance on the evening of September 6. In its announcement, the *Territorial Enterprise* erroneously reported that Buffalo Bill had been paying Crawford only twenty dollars per week. A copy of the article was forwarded to Cody, who immediately wired Crawford "to correct the slander." Crawford willingly complied, and on the day before the benefit, the local press published Jack's letter explaining his financial arrangement with Cody. Nevertheless, Crawford deeply resented Cody's lack of gratitude and his insensitivity. Jack's sense of betrayal by a friend whom he loved and admired like a brother would deepen in the coming years.[25]

For the Virginia City benefit performance, Crawford staged an old favorite, the *Ticket of Leave Man,* with the help of local actors and Gertie Granville, who traveled from San Francisco to take a leading role. Crawford played before a packed house and drew receipts of eight hundred dollars. James G. Fair, the mining magnate who later became a U.S. senator, was among those who attended the play, having bought up one hundred tickets at one dollar apiece. Four days later, Crawford left Virginia City for San Francisco to appear in a G.A.R. benefit for widows and orphans. He also collaborated with San Francisco playwright Sam Smith in writing a new drama, entitled *The Plains; or, The Trials in Death Valley.*[26]

At the request of San Francisco friends, Crawford staged another benefit performance on November 18 at Baldwin's Theatre, where he starred in *Nick of the Woods.* An olio of songs, dances, and acrobatic acts completed the night's entertainment. To advertise his appearance, Crawford issued a complimentary program, entitled "The Lariat," which contained several of his poems and a letter thanking the people of San Francisco for their kindness. San Franciscans responded by packing the playhouse "from pit to dome." The local press labeled the evening "an immense success."[27]

Within a week, Crawford embarked upon a tour through

California with his own Captain Jack Combination, consisting of fifteen professional actors. As it turned out, the company was too large and travel expenses too costly in such a sparsely settled state. But Crawford must have been ecstatic when he opened in Oakland on November 24, performing in one of three new dramas that comprised the troupe's stock of plays: *The Plains; or, The Trials in Death Valley,* by Sam Smith; *Captain Jack,* by Fred G. Maeder, author of at least two of the melodramas that had helped catapult Buffalo Bill to fame; and *The Poet Scout,* by William L. Visscher, a poet and journalist who joined Crawford's combination as a comedian.[28]

The Captain Jack Combination played San Bernardino in early January 1878, but a heavy rain on opening night kept the turnout small. The foul weather dogged Jack to Los Angeles, where he opened on January 14 at Turnverein Hall with another of Fred Maeder's melodramas, *On the Trail.* The *Los Angeles Herald* described the play as abounding in "exciting and romantic adventures"—a suitable vehicle to display the talents of Captain Jack, "the very beau ideal of a frontier hero." On subsequent nights, the combination staged Sam Smith's *The Plains* and Maeder's *Captain Jack.* But continued inclement weather forced cancellation of one performance and otherwise limited the size of audiences. Even a January 22 benefit performance could not save the financially struggling troupe. Less than two weeks later, the *Daily Alta California* marked its demise with the announcement that Crawford had canceled a performance in Oakland because of a "split in the company."[29]

The Captain Jack Combination disbanded in San Francisco just as the nation was emerging from a major depression that had begun in 1873. Labor unrest had led to a massive railroad strike in 1877, the first great industrial disruption in U.S. history. Reformers were beginning to attack the country's social and economic system and suggesting new ways for improving society. By the end of the decade, Henry George, the most important of the reformers, would publish his best-selling *Progress and Poverty,* a forthright attack on the maldistribution of wealth in the United States.

Because he had a family to support, Crawford must have been aware of some of these changes in the national economy. But while the eastern states were rapidly industrializing, the West of Cody and Crawford remained the domain of the rancher and miner. Indeed, the discovery of gold and silver in western mountains had helped to populate the region with risk-taking Americans eager to exploit its hidden treasures. Rumors of a gold discovery anywhere on the continent prompted masses of citizens to abandon home and hearth for the new El Dorado.

With characteristic enthusiasm, Crawford embarked on his next great adventure during the spring of 1878, when he journeyed to the gold fields of the Cariboo Region in British Columbia. The initial mining push into the Cariboo had taken place more than a decade earlier. California miners had stampeded to the lower Fraser River in 1858, after the news of recent gold discoveries there circulated in San Francisco. Eventually prospectors ventured further up the Fraser, about four hundred miles north of Yale, where spectacular strikes were made along Antler and Williams creeks. William Barker, who struck pay dirt on Williams Creek in 1862, gave his name to the new settlement of Barkerville, which became the chief supply center for the gold region. During the stampede that followed Barker's strike, more than fifteen thousand miners entered the Cariboo. But the shallow diggings along the creeks were soon exhausted, and the population decreased rapidly after 1865.[30]

Still, Barkerville and surrounding camps survived into the next decade, when attention focused on quartz rather than placer mining. In fact, while Jack was recovering from his accident in Virginia City, the *Daily Alta California* carried a story of new discoveries. Increasingly optimistic reports of Cariboo wealth appeared in later issues, and on New Year's Day 1878, the paper avowed that "rich veins are constantly being discovered." Soon a small-scale rush was under way; a news release from Victoria, British Columbia, dated February 28, announced: "A steamer with her decks black with passengers sailed yesterday [for the gold fields], and another, in which all the berths are engaged, will sail tomorrow."[31]

Whether Jack returned to Maria and the children in Pennsylvania before heading north is not known. In late March 1878, however, he was in Seattle with a new theatrical troupe for a two-night engagement at Yesler's Hall, where he starred in *The Plains.* On April 8, he performed the same play before a packed house in Victoria, British Columbia. By the end of the month the Crawford combination had performed in New Westminster, Nanaimo, and again in Victoria, where the local press told its readers that "besides being a famous scout Capt. Jack is beyond all doubt, a first class actor."[32]

Crawford's first trip to the gold fields was in the company of his fellow actors. On May 7, he and his troupe boarded the steamer *Wilson G. Hunt* for the start of a trip of more than five hundred miles to Barkerville. They traveled by steamer to Yale, the head of navigation on the Fraser, and then boarded a stagecoach for the ride north on the Cariboo Road, a mighty highway that wound along rock cliffs and canyons and twice crossed the river on two enormous bridges. Along the way, Jack and his companions viewed some of the continent's most spectacular and rugged scenery, with their journey punctuated by stops at roadhouses that offered shelter and meals to travelers.[33]

Upon reaching his destination, Crawford performed at the Barkerville Theatre Royal, but he also found time to evaluate the gold fields. To a friend in New Westminster, he wrote that he was satisfied "there is no richer country than Cariboo." He also declared, "As soon as I take my company below I will return to Cariboo, take off my coat, and help to prove that Cariboo is rich." True to his word, Crawford left with his troupe in early August, reaching Victoria on the twenty-fourth. During a performance of *The Plains*, which was staged that very same evening in the Victoria Theatre Royal, Jack announced that he would reembark on the journey north during the following week.[34]

Crawford spent the next seven months in the Cariboo, where, according to one biographical sketch, he "entered into mining operations which were not particularly successful." Either on this trip or shortly after reaching the gold fields, Crawford was joined by his brother-in-law, William K. Nattress, (married to Jack's sister, Lizzie). They had entered a demanding environment where temperatures of thirty below zero were not unusual in the winter and five to ten feet of snow often remained on the ground into late March. During these months, Jack continued writing poetry and worked at revising *The Plains*. The poems he composed that winter suggest that even he could succumb to melancholy during the long nights in the north country. "I'm Sad To-Night" speaks of Jack's success in masking his melancholy during a Cariboo Christmas party. Alone on his thirty-second birthday, Jack penned these lines:

> *Lonely in my cabin musing,*
> > *How the time does pass away—*
> *Not a soul to wish me gladness,*
> > *Not a friend to pull my ears;*
> *While my heart is filled with sadness,*
> > *Thinking of the passing years.*[35]

Crawford left the Cariboo on April 10, 1879, and arrived in Victoria three weeks later. From there, he proceeded by steamship to San Francisco to negotiate the publication of his first book of poetry. Although the Victoria *British Colonist* announced that Crawford planned to return to the Cariboo in six or seven weeks, Jack was to spend the remainder of the year in San Francisco, concentrating on his theatrical and literary career.[36] Indeed, for the rest of his life, Crawford would try to balance his public ambitions with his equally burning desire to strike it rich in the gold fields.

Crawford experienced several triumphs during his stay in San Francisco. On June 28, the *Golden Era* published "Sour Mash," in which Jack recounted his ride from Medicine Bow to the Rosebud, carrying a bottle of whiskey to Cody. Two weeks later, Jack was the recipient of a testimonial benefit staged at the Grand Opera House.[37] Meanwhile, H. Keller and Company of San Francisco had agreed to publish his poetry book for five hundred dollars. Jack apparently raised the money through subscriptions—a common method of financing publication in that era. *The Poet Scout: Verses and Songs* appeared in the fall of 1879. A handsome volume containing seventy of Jack's best poems and several fine engravings, it is a book collector's item today.[38]

About the same time that his book appeared, Crawford also copyrighted *The Plains,* the play he had written with Sam Smith and which he had continued to edit and rework in later months. This time he gave it a new title, *California through Death Valley.* He would again copyright the play in 1888, calling it *Fonda; or The Trapper's Dream.* [39]

On August 19, 1879, Crawford opened a six-day engagement of *California through Death Valley* at the Bush Street Theatre. He took the leading role of Jack Croff, a scout and hunter, who teams up with old Bill Williams, a mountain trapper, to rescue a girl named Fonda from the Mormons. Loosely based on the Mountain Meadows Massacre, the play appealed to the strong anti-Mormon bias then prevalent in American society. Although San Franciscans applauded Jack's performance, a local drama critic judged that the story was not "very coherent nor artistically developed." Still, he conceded, "the characters were no better nor worse played than we usually expect."[40]

A month later, Crawford joined the city of San Francisco in welcoming former President Ulysses S. Grant on his return to the United States after a two-year tour around the world. Thousands of residents turned out on September 20 to cheer Grant's arrival aboard the steamship *City of Tokio.* Cannons roared, whistles blew, and bells rang as the vessel steamed into port. As darkness descended, a gigantic procession escorted the general's party to the Palace Hotel, the route lit by torches, rockets, and Roman candles, and in some places by electric lights. Clad in his buckskin suit, Crawford rode on a black stallion, near the head of the parade, with the Oakland Light Cavalry.[41]

The following morning, Jack met the illustrious war hero. According to a story that Crawford never tired of telling in later years, a crowd had descended upon the Palace Hotel intent upon greeting the former president. Among the hopefuls was the G.A.R. post from San Jose. Learning that the veterans had less than thirty minutes before they must catch a train, Crawford intervened on their behalf by sending his calling card to Colonel Fred Grant, the general's son and a former acquaintance of the ex-scout. Informed of the problem, General Grant invited the men to come right up. With Crawford in the lead, the former Union soldiers marched in formation up the stairs and down the hallway to Grant's room. The general shook each man warmly by the hand, after which they dashed off to meet their train.[42]

On his third evening in San Francisco, Grant attended the opening performance of *The Color Guard,* a military drama sponsored by the local G.A.R. post. Crawford played the leading role of Bob Mason, a Union scout, assisted by the well-known California actor Tom Keene. San Franciscans eager to catch another glimpse of the general crowded the theater decorated with red, white, and blue bunting, flags, shields, and other military paraphernalia. The play was already in progress when Grant arrived with his two sons and other military guests. Immediately, the curtain dropped, as the crowd cheered and the orchestra played "Hail to the Chief." When the play resumed, Jack stepped to the front of the stage and recited a new composition, "A Mountain Boy's Letter to General Grant," expressing the admiration and loyalty of the boys who had followed the hero of the Union. The former president so greatly admired the poem that he reproduced it in the published account of his world tour.[43]

Since his return from the Cariboo, and possibly even before, Crawford had been making plans to tour Australia with *California through Death Valley*. Alfred Dampier, director of the Theatre Royal in Melbourne, had watched Crawford perform in Sacramento in 1877, and subsequently he encouraged Jack to make the trip, asserting that his play was "the best frontier picture play he had even seen, not excepting Davey Crockett." Jack also learned that the Williamsons, another theatrical company, had cleared more than ten thousand dollars on their first engagement in Australia, performing Sam Smith's *Struck Oil*. Crawford obviously hoped to do as well.[44]

In need of funds to underwrite the venture, Jack turned to Bill Cody for assistance. The two men had kept up a regular correspondence since parting in Virginia City, and in a letter to Jack dated April 22, 1879, Cody expounded on his recent success. He had cleared six thousand dollars on an engagement in San Francisco and was making "big money in the cattle business." His family had moved to North Platte, where he had opened a farm and was breeding fine stock with a fifteen-hundred-dollar stallion, a seven-hundred-dollar jack, and thoroughbred mares, bulls, and cows. Cody, however, backed away from loaning Jack anything. In a letter dated June 24, he told Crawford: "I am hard pushed for money just at present. . . . as soon as I can get hold of some money, am not afraid to trust you."[45]

Still, Crawford remained optimistic and intended to sail for Australia in late September. Probably for lack of finances, these plans fell through, and Crawford remained in California for several more months, occasionally making public appearances. On December 6, for example, he joined other performers in staging a benefit performance that raised eight hundred dollars for the ten orphan children of former Confederate General John Hood and his wife, who recently had died of yellow fever in New Orleans. Jack recited a poem he had written for the occasion, "Hood's Children," in which he celebrated the brave fighting men of the Blue and the Gray.[46]

With the coming of the new year, Crawford's departure for Australia seemed assured. In a letter dated January 24, 1880, Dampier gave Jack final instructions: bring Indians, a trained horse and dog, and novelties—skins of animals and buffalo heads—to decorate the theater. No scouts or American Indians had ever been in Melbourne, Dampier stated, and a ride around the city with the Indians "would be the greatest advertisement ever known in this country."[47]

Although the management of the Melbourne Theatre promised to pay for his passage, Jack needed five hundred dollars to outfit his crew. He again appealed to Cody. Crawford later claimed that Cody agreed to loan him the money and even wired Jack to meet him in Denver in ten days. Crawford traveled east for the reunion with his old friend, but neither Cody nor the money appeared. Cody soon told Jack that he could not advance the loan until after the spring roundup. Crestfallen, Crawford canceled the Australian venture. Apparently, he stayed on in Denver to perform with yet another Captain Jack Combination.[48]

From Denver, Jack's troupe traveled to Las Vegas, New Mexico, for a brief engagement and then on to Santa Fe, where it opened on May 23, 1880, with a performance of *California through Death Valley.* The Santa Fe *Weekly New Mexican* praised the production and called the knife fight between Captain Jack and Piute Sam "one of the most terribly real and thrilling enactments ever put upon the stage." [49] But the show was in financial difficulty. On June 1, the Santa Fe press announced that "the Captain Jack Combination has busted—dissolved—their baggage being held at the Grand Central Hotel for a board bill of one hundred and thirty dollars." Nonetheless, Captain Jack had made many friends in Santa Fe, both among military officers and businessmen, and they proposed to sponsor a special benefit performance to help Crawford pay his creditors. [50]

On the evening of June 3, playgoers "jammed and packed" Mottley's Theatre "from orchestra to entrance door." Jack and his troupe delighted Santa Feans with another production of *California through Death Valley.* The press pronounced the entire affair a success "from beginning to end," and judged as excellent Crawford's portrayal of "Captain Jack." One hundred seventy-five dollars in ticket sales enabled Crawford to pay the hotel bill and retrieve the company's baggage. [51]

In the midst of his financial crisis, Crawford offered his services as a scout to Colonel Edward Hatch, commanding the Military District of New Mexico. Hatch and his soldiers were then engaged in a frustrating campaign against the dynamic Indian leader Victorio and his Warm Spring Apache followers. For years, Victorio's people had camped at Ojo Caliente (Warm Springs) near the northern edge of the Black Range in southwestern New Mexico. In 1877, however, the government forced their removal to the San Carlos Indian Reservation in Arizona. Unhappy on this barren reserve, the Warm Spring Apaches slipped away in September of that year and returned to their former haunts in New Mexico. Two years later, in September 1879, Victorio and his warriors clashed with U.S. soldiers near Ojo Caliente, killing five troopers and three civilians in the opening skirmishes of what became known as Victorio's War. [52]

Chapter 4

For more than a year, Victorio led his people in a bloody campaign against inhabitants in Texas, New Mexico, and Chihuahua, Mexico, eluding both Mexican and U.S. soldiers sent out to subdue them. By the time Hatch accepted Jack's offer, the people of New Mexico were clamoring for an end to the bloodshed.[53]

By mid-June 1880 Crawford's name appeared on the roster of civilians employed at Fort Craig, located on the tableland west of the Rio Grande and about 110 miles south of Albuquerque. The post had been abandoned in 1878, but it was reactivated during the Victorio War, serving as a base for Indian operations. Sometime in late June, Jack left Fort Craig on a reconnaissance of the San Francisco River region near the Arizona–New Mexico border. The trip provided Crawford with ample opportunity to survey mining prospects in the Black Range and in the Mogollon Mountains.[54]

Upon his return to Fort Craig, Crawford received orders to scout the country east of the post as far as the Mescalero Agency north of the Sacramento Mountains. He was instructed to examine all water holes in the area and determine the number of Mescalero Apaches off the reservation who might be expected to join Victorio's band.[55]

Crawford left the post on the afternoon of August 12 and the next day rode into the San Andres Mountains, where he came upon a "beautiful pool of cold, sparkling water," known as Dripping Spring. Jack would later file on the spring as a mill site, and then spend a small fortune trying to develop this and other sites in the San Andres.

Late in the afternoon of the thirteenth, after descending the east side of the San Andres and moving onto the plains, Jack encountered a lone horseman, who was as wary of Jack as the scout was of the young man. Crawford soon guessed the rider's identity—William Antrim, alias Billy the Kid—wanted by the authorities for murder. They shared conversation and rations and then went their separate ways. Jack later expanded on their meeting in his diary and in an essay entitled "How I Met Billy the Kid," which he intended to publish in a book for boys. Jack used his encounter with Billy to underscore the baneful influence of dime novels. According to Jack, the Kid expressed regret for his wild ways and admitted that "Dime Novels, and a reckless love of adventure, drove him from a good home and a loving mother, and frontier whiskey and bad associates did the rest." Although Jack could have conjured up this episode for didactic reasons, more than likely the Antrim tale contains a strong element of truth, as did most of the stories that Crawford told of himself. Billy, it might be added, was shot and killed by Sheriff Pat Garrett less than twelve months after his chance meeting with Crawford.[56]

On August 14, Jack reached the Mescalero Agency, where he dined with Lieutenant Patrick Cusack and other military officers. He spent the rest of the evening swapping stories and reciting poetry before a blazing campfire. Two days later, Crawford rode into the Sacramentos with two companions looking for signs of hostile Indians. For more than a week they scoured the countryside, finding plenty of evidence that hostiles had swept through the area. Fred Asbeck's ranch on the lower Sacramento River had been burned to the ground, but the old rancher had left an ugly bait for his tormentors—a box of arsenic-laced raisins, which Crawford claimed had caused the death of four Apaches.[57]

Jack continued scouting down the base of the Organ Mountains southwest of the Sacramentos, and he reached the Rio Grande on August 25. Two days later he rode into Fort Cummings, fifty-three miles west of the river near Cooke's Spring. There, he reported to Colonel George P. Buell of the Fifteenth Infantry. Buell was mounting a massive expedition into Mexico to find Victorio.[58]

Crawford remained at Cummings for about a week, washing clothes, writing letters, and dining with officers. On September 3, Buell ordered him into Chihuahua to locate Victorio's camp. Casimero Grigalba accompanied Jack as Spanish interpreter, together with Navajo Charlie (said to be Victorio's son-in-law), who would enter the chief's camp and try to persuade him to surrender.[59]

On September 8, Crawford's party reached the town of Ascension, where they remained several days, allowing their horses to rest while two Mexican scouts tried to find Victorio's trail. Jack spent part of this time in writing letters to newspapers and conferring with Mexican officials. Upon receiving news of Victorio's movements, he left for Lake Guzman on September 14, and the following day he camped beside Lake Santa Maria, where he pored over a recent letter from Maria, which closed with these words: "Remember, my dear boy, that while you are struggling for us amid dangers and hardships, you have little ones at home praying for you." The beauty of the evening inspired Jack to compose a tender poem, entitled "Little Ones Praying at Home." He wrote the words down on a piece of brown paper that had been wrapped around a chunk of jerked meat.[60]

From Lake Santa Maria, Jack traveled toward the Candelaria Mountains, about sixty miles south of El Paso, Texas, pausing to make smoke signals from hilltops along the way to attract Victorio's attention. Finally, on the seventeenth, he located the Apache camp. The story of its discovery and the disappointment that followed is best told in Crawford's own words:

> On the second day after leaving Lake Santa Maria we reached the Candelaria range, and much to my gratification while sweeping the country with my field glass I discovered Victorio's camp. I at once pushed forward to within a mile of his camping place, and gave Navajo Charlie explicit instructions to enter the camp, explain to the old Chief our mission and bring himself and not more than two of his warriors out to meet me and have a talk. To my astonishment and dismay he absolutely refused to go. He would give no explanation of his conduct. Coaxing and threats alike failed to move him. . . . In my anger I would have taken desperate chances and have gone myself to the hostile camp, but I knew not enough of the Apache tongue to intelligently converse with Victorio, and he nor none of his warriors could speak English.[61]

Reluctantly, Crawford returned to El Paso, where he wired Buell at Fort Cummings of his discovery. On September 23, he met the colonel at the Mexican town of Palomas, a few miles south of the border. Buell designated Crawford as his chief of scouts and ordered him to proceed east toward the Rio Grande to cut across Victorio's trail should he attempt to make a dash northward. Meanwhile, the colonel, with a large contingent of infantry and cavalry, pushed into the Candelarias only to discover that Victorio had moved further south. On October 1, Crawford rejoined Buell at El Lucero, about fifty miles southeast of Lake Santa Maria, where Buell received word from the Mexican commander, Colonel Joaquin Terrazas, that Victorio had gone toward the Pinos Mountains to the southeast. A few days later, Buell ordered Crawford and two other scouts to proceed "not less than 100 miles down the Rio Grande . . . below Fort Quitman" to look for Indian signs.[62]

While scouting south of Quitman, Jack learned that Terrazas had ordered American troops to leave Mexican soil; thus, on October 13, Crawford turned north to rejoin his command, reaching El Paso on the eighteenth. Here, Crawford heard that three days earlier Mexican troops had killed Victorio at Tres Castillos, in a bloody encounter that left sixty Apache warriors and eighteen women and children dead. The long, brutal Victorio campaign had ended. After conferring with Buell in Mesilla, New Mexico, Crawford resigned as chief of scouts on October 23. Sometime later, Buell wrote Crawford a letter of commendation, which reads in part: "There is no doubt but what your scout after Victorio into old Mexico, and the rapidity with which you located him in the Candelaria Mountains, and your fast ride to the nearest post, from whence you wired me at Fort Cummings, was the cause which led directly to his death by the Mexican troops."[63]

During the year following his resignation as Chief of Scouts, Crawford decided to make New Mexico his permanent home. Prospecting trips into the mountains of southern New Mexico had convinced him that a fortune awaited the industrious miner. To gain a steady income, he accepted an appointment as post trader at Fort Craig and then sent for Maria and the children to join him at the post. For the first time in more than six years, the Crawfords would be united in a stable household.

Among Jack's greatest strengths was his ability to rebound quickly from setbacks. He had tasted celebrity status with the Buffalo Bill Combination and yet had been unsuccessful financially with his own theatrical troupe. The desire for fame and fortune that still burned inside would now propel him in other directions. Jack's friendship with Cody survived the Virginia City and Australia mishaps, and the two men continued exchanging letters. The seeds of mistrust had been planted, however, and Captain Jack and Buffalo Bill would never again experience the harmony and goodwill they once had shared on the trail and on the stage. Still, Crawford found contentment in his growing family and looked forward to his reunion with little Eva and Harry as a moment of pure joy.

There are little ones praying for me far away,
There are little ones praying for me;
With tiny hands pressed before each little breast,
Their sweet faces in dreamland I see.[64]

5
POST TRADER AT FORT CRAIG

When Crawford parted company with Colonel Buell in Mesilla, his life entered a new phase. For the next five years, he devoted his energies to exploiting the economic resources of southern New Mexico, a region poised on the brink of a dynamic mining boom. His decision to relocate his family in New Mexico signaled his boundless faith in the territory's future. Like other frontier entrepreneurs, Captain Jack would engage in multiple enterprises. While serving as post trader at Fort Craig, he also filled government contracts, developed mines, established a dairy ranch, and expanded his landholdings. He would later build a horse ranch in the foothills of the San Andres Mountains. During these same years, Jack continued to write poetry, but he appeared on the stage infrequently. The fires of his dramatic ambition were not dampened for very long, however. About the time that Fort Craig closed as a military instal-

Crawford family, 1882, while Captain Jack was post trader at Fort Craig, New Mexico. Posed in the photo are Jack, Maria, baby May Cody, Harry, and Eva. (Courtesy Rio Grande Historical Collections, New Mexico State University Library.)

lation, Crawford was planning another theatrical tour through the East.

Crawford's first great mining venture in New Mexico was a harbinger of later financial disasters. Soon after resigning as Buell's chief of scouts, Jack became "Chief Scout and Prospector" for the Lode and Placer Prospecting and Mining Association head-quartered in Denver, Colorado. James Cherry, a Chicago mining engineer, was the company's president, and several well-known Ohio and Colorado capitalists served as trustees. According to its prospectus, the company planned to raise sufficient funds to employ fifty men to prospect in New Mexico, Arizona, and Colorado, and "to erect mills and smelters for the treatment of ores" to be taken from the newly discovered mines. [1]

In mid-November 1880, Jack was in Denver outfitting a party of about twenty-five prospectors, each contributing one hundred dollars and receiving, in return, one thousand shares in the company. They also were to receive two dollars per day and board while in the field. Upon his return to New Mexico, Crawford established a base camp near the military outpost at Ojo Caliente, about thirty-five miles directly west of Fort Craig. From there, the miners dispersed west into the Black Range and Mogollon Mountains. [2]

Hostile Apache bands posed a constant threat to the gold seekers. On January 31, 1881, Captain Jack narrowly escaped death when five Indians surprised him and two companions while prospecting in a canyon between Ojo Caliente and the village of Cañada Alamosa. In the fierce gunfight that followed, a bullet struck the breech of Jack's rifle "and glancing down cut a gash along the palm of his hand." When Jack reached Cañada Alamosa, the Catholic priest dressed his wound and then discovered that bullets had pierced his coat in two places. [3]

Despite the Indian scare, Crawford's party continued prospecting and locating claims. But Jack soon learned that the white man's perfidy could be as deadly to his plans as an Apache ambush.

After spending two months in the field, the men had exhausted their supplies, and company officials failed to send additional funds. Jack concluded that the Denver capitalists were trying to sell stock in the company solely on the basis of his reputation, without investing a penny of their own money. He did everything within his power to alleviate the suffering of his stranded miners, even selling his gold watch and other possessions to buy food. On February 28, Captain Jack wrote a long letter to the editor of the *Las Vegas Daily Optic,* exposing the company. "It is all up," he began. "The cloud that has so long darkened my sky has burst at last. Lode and Placer is gone under." [4]

Despite this setback, Crawford found means to continue prospecting. On April 25, he penned a humorous letter to the Santa Fe *Military Review* from his cabin in Chloride City, the center of the recently established Apache Mining District, located about twenty miles south of Ojo Caliente. "Houses are going up one after another in rapid succession," he reported, and "doctors, lawyers, and other 'tender-feet' are coming in by the dozens." A few weeks later, the Santa Fe *Daily New Mexican* reported that Jack had "pulled through" his rough times and "now owns a fine mine in the Black Range." This may have been a reference to the Little Maud, a claim Crawford located earlier in February with F. A. Richards and Captain John W. Bean, Fort Craig's commanding officer. In June, Crawford acquired half-interest in an even more valuable property, the Monte Christo Mine, located one mile south of the Chloride post office. [5]

Even while prospecting, Crawford was seeking other sources of income. In mid-May 1881, the army awarded him contracts to supply Ojo Caliente with forage and fuel. On June 1, a board of officers recommended his appointment as post trader at Fort Craig, a potentially lucrative position highly sought after by other frontier entrepreneurs. [6] Although confirmation of his appointment was delayed several weeks, Crawford must have been corresponding regularly with Maria about moving the family to New Mexico. Sometime later that summer, Captain Jack was re-united with Maria, Eva, and Harry at San Marcial, a station on the Atchison, Topeka and Santa Fe Railway about five miles north of Fort Craig.

Years later, Eva recalled the happy reunion. Dashing down the steps of the train, the ten-year-old threw herself into her father's arms. "Eva! It's my little Eva," Jack cried. "How is my little bronco girl, anyway?" Simply fine, she responded, now that she was with her Papa.[7] The family traveled by wagon to Fort Craig with a military escort, for Apache activity in the surrounding countryside was reason for caution. The contrast between New Mexico's dry, barren mesas and Pennsylvania's lush, green hills must have jolted all of Maria's senses. But Maria would soon adapt to the desert environment and create an attractive home for Jack and the children.

For nearly two decades the Crawfords resided at this isolated military outpost, remaining as caretakers even after troops were withdrawn. Established in 1854 to guard the northern end of the Jornada del Muerto, Fort Craig had a long and distinguished history. During the Civil War, Union troops assembled there to block Texas Confederate soldiers en route to the north to capture Santa Fe and the military supply depot at Fort Union. On February 21, 1862, the two armies met in combat at Valverde ford six miles above Fort Craig. After a fierce all-day battle, Union troops retreated to the safety of the post, and the Texans continued north to face ultimate defeat in the Battle of Glorieta Pass near Santa Fe.[8]

After the war, troops routinely left Craig to scout the surrounding countryside for marauding Indians. With an eye to economy, however, the army closed the post in July 1878, leaving a small detail behind to guard government buildings. But the outbreak of Victorio's War forced the military to regarrison Fort Craig two years later. By this date it was in miserable condition, for upon deactivation the army had "stripped [it] of everything that was regarded of value." San Marcial villagers then pillaged what remained "until only the bare walls were left." When the Crawfords drove through its gates in the summer of 1881, the post was still "a dilapidated, tumbledown, miserable place." [9]

An adobe wall, possibly ten feet high in places, enclosed the military compound. Officers' quarters lay along the north wall; directly opposite were enlisted men's quarters and the commanding officer's residence. Commissary and quartermaster offices, blacksmith shop, wagon yards, stables, and other miscellaneous buildings abutted the east wall. [10] Crawford established the trader's store temporarily in an unoccupied building within the walled garrison. In December, however, the commanding officer ordered him to vacate this space, since the quartermaster wanted it for storage. [11]

Shortly thereafter, Captain Jack moved his store to a building outside the east wall. Nearby stood the former "Valverde House," which he had purchased prior to Maria's arrival for the family residence. Renamed "The Scouts' Hotel," the Crawfords soon boarded a handful of officers and civilians, with Maria taking charge of domestic arrangements. Eva helped to wait upon guests at mealtime, and vegetables from Jack's garden added variety to Maria's menu. [12]

From all accounts, Maria Crawford was a remarkable woman, providing stability for the family when Jack was away on business and entertainment trips. Not only would she worry about the health and education of her children, but she also took care of practical matters—washing and sewing clothes, caring for the house, and working in Jack's store when needed. She became pregnant soon after reaching Fort Craig, however, and some of these activities necessarily were curtailed as her pregnancy advanced. Dr. John Kane, the highly regarded post surgeon, may have been on hand when Maria gave birth on May 22, 1882, to May Cody, named after Jack's longtime friend, Buffalo Bill Cody. Captain Jack worshiped the child; to his newspaper friend, Jim Carlin, he avowed, "Old pard, the Lord must have taken a big liking to us when he sent that little angel to flood our western home with heaven's purest sunshine." The Crawfords affectionately called their youngest daughter "Little Nugget." [13]

Army children found much to enjoy at frontier posts, and the Crawford offspring were no exception. They spent considerable time outdoors in play, and Harry undoubtedly joined other boys in playing at soldiering. Both Eva and Harry, under their father's guidance, became expert riders and marksmen. Like other army youngsters, they would enjoy the excitement of military reviews and the constant influx of new people. But they also quickly discovered a more serious side to military life. [14]

When the Crawfords arrived at Fort Craig, it was garrisoned by two companies, one white and one black from the Ninth Cavalry. These soldiers spent much time in performing routine garrison duty and repairing buildings, but they also stood guard at Ojo Caliente and scouted for hostile Indians. Although the Ninth Cavalry established an excellent record for discipline and bravery, on November 17, 1881, a black recruit disrupted normal routine. During the morning stable call, he stole 550 dollars from his sergeant's locker and then deserted. Other black soldiers tracked him three miles beyond San Marcial, where he shot and killed one of his pursuers. Soon captured, the recruit himself was killed trying to escape his guard. [15]

In December, Eva and Harry probably witnessed the departure of the "buffalo soldiers" for Fort Riley, Kansas. Thereafter, Fort Craig was garrisoned by white soldiers, typically two companies of cavalry and one of infantry. Early in January 1882, two patrols left the post to scout for Indians reportedly committing depredations along the river. Although they failed to discover any Indian signs, Eva later recalled that during similar scares, women and children were rushed into the fortresslike commissary buildings for protection.[16]

Despite living on this isolated military post, Jack and Maria arranged for their children's education. Shortly after the family's arrival, Jack hired Professor Frederick W. Spencer of Wisconsin to tutor Eva and Harry in exchange for room and board. An excellent violinist in addition to being a schoolteacher, Spencer so charmed Jack with his virtuosity that the Poet Scout exclaimed: "You can stay here all your life and all you will have to do will be to play one piece a day." In April 1882, the local press reported that the professor was organizing a "select school for the children of the post" and would also offer guitar and violin lessons to interested students.[17]

How long Spencer remained at Fort Craig is unknown. In late February 1883, however, Jack accompanied Eva to Santa Fe, where she enrolled in Rev. Horatio O. Ladd's University of New Mexico, advertised as "a Protestant Christian College," offering both primary and secondary instruction for three dollars per month. Out-of-town young ladies like Eva boarded with the Ladd family. But Eva probably studied in Santa Fe no more than a year or two, for at age fourteen (in 1885), she traveled with her father to Denver, where she entered another private school.[18]

Before its final deactivation, Fort Craig developed into a lively military community in which the Crawfords assumed a prominent position. In late 1882, at least 3 officers' families resided on the post, then garrisoned by 8 officers and 139 enlisted men. A Fort Craig baseball club was flourishing, and the post's amateur dramatic company announced plans to give monthly entertainments. Professor Spencer, his friend A. J. Way of Cleveland, and Captain Jack also planned to perform. Described as "one of the greatest guitar players and soloists in the United States," Professor Way had traveled to New Mexico for his health.[19]

Crawford's store provided a congenial meeting place for

area residents. Men and women alike, civilians as well as military personnel, entered his establishment to purchase a wide variety of commodities: shirts, shoes, calico, thread, tobacco, matches, paper, envelopes, candles, lamp shades, flour, bacon, coffee, medicine, canned peaches, canned sardines, and so forth. Prospectors from the San Mateo and San Andres mountains also traded with Jack, packing supplies on mules for their return to the mountains. Moreover, because Crawford served as the Fort Craig postmaster, residents daily streamed into his store to collect their mail.[20]

At every western military post, a council of army officers fixed the price of the trader's commodities and also made sure that he kept on hand a wide assortment of merchandise desired by the soldiers, including alcoholic beverages. Simply stated, to keep the post tradership, Crawford had to sell liquor to soldiers, which contradicted his lifelong commitment to temperance. Although Jack never recorded how he resolved this dilemma in his mind, it is evident that he set aside his scruples with regard to alcohol to take advantage of a business opportunity, which, in turn, allowed his family to join him in New Mexico.

The post trader's store, in fact, did a brisk business in beer, brandy, and other spirits. A surviving daybook from 1882 indicates that most of Jack's sales were for alcoholic beverages, dispensed in separate saloon rooms for officers and enlisted men. Civilians also frequented these areas to drink and play billiards. Professor Spencer and rancher Henry Toussaint, for instance, were two of Jack's most faithful patrons. By military edict, the enlisted men's clubroom closed at 9:00 P.M. (taps), though officers were allowed to keep later hours.[21]

Crawford hired local men to help run his various enterprises, including a small dairy he built about two miles from the post to supply the garrison with milk and butter. In filling government hay contracts at Fort Craig and Ojo Caliente, he employed between six and twelve men to cut grama grass with mowing machines. One laborer recalled that in putting in hay at Ojo Caliente, the men slept with their carbines, for the hay field was only five miles from an Apache trail.[22]

Captain Jack should have received a nice income from the post tradership, dairy, and government contracts, and undoubtedly profits from these activities helped to finance his mining and ranching schemes. But he did not amass great wealth. In 1885, a reporter declared that although Jack was "by no means a pauper . . . his generosity will always keep him short of ready cash." The journalist went on to explain, "No ragged miner or worn tramp ever called upon Jack in vain and legions of unprincipled scalawags have taken advantage of this softness of heart to dupe him of his money."[23]

A handful of travelers that Jack befriended left written descriptions of the Poet Scout's household. All agreed that the Crawfords lived "very comfortably" at Fort Craig. Jim Carlin's observations, published in 1885 in the *Albuquerque Evening Democrat,* provide a written commentary for the much-published photograph of the Crawford living room, which appears elsewhere in this book.

> Nowhere on the face of the earth is refinement and frontierism brought into more striking contrast than in Jack Crawford's home. In one room the finest pictures, richest carpets, modern furniture and exquisite draperies; in the next rifles, pistols, saddles, and all the paraphernalia of the western horseman. In one room can be heard the sweet notes of the piano and the cultivated voices of happy children practicing the latest songs; in the next the voices of the scout and the writer wrangling over who played low in a spirited game of seven-up. The hum of the sewing machine drifts out through the open window and blends with the lowing of the herd in the corral.[24]

Carlin also left pen-portraits of Jack's family. He described Maria as "one of those genial, pleasant, home-like ladies who possess the happy facility of making one feel perfectly at home in her neat and comfortable house." Fifteen-year-old Eva, he said, was "a perfect specimen of the typical frontier girl. In the parlor she is a finished and refined little lady, and accomplished pianist, but when she springs upon the back of a restless broncho and dashes away over the plain at a breakneck speed . . . she presents a striking picture of the wild frontier girl, daring, reckless, and full of adventure." Strong, muscular fourteen-year-old Harry was already an accomplished horseman, "skilled in every feature which goes to make up the perfect cowboy." And Carlin described three-year-old May as sweet, enchanting, "idolized by all who know her." [25]

At the time Carlin penned these remarks, New Mexico was undergoing a dynamic transformation, brought about by the arrival of the railroad. A land of great cultural and physical diversity, New Mexico had suffered chronic poverty both before and after becoming a territory of the United States. Anglo and Hispanic settlers lived in uneasy accommodation with a large Indian population, with each group struggling to control resources of the territory's rugged mountains, grassy plains, and inhospitable deserts. Small settlements, predominantly Hispanic, clung to the banks of life-giving streams and rivers, the villagers living in one-story adobe houses and cultivating fields of corn, beans, and wheat.

The Atchison, Topeka and Santa Fe Railway entered New Mexico late in 1878 and built south from Raton Pass the following year. The first locomotive steamed into Albuquerque in April 1880 and reached San Marcial in September.[26] With the arrival of the Iron Horse, mining and ranching industries boomed, and Anglo emigrants streamed into the territory to share in the wealth.

The impact of the railroad could be seen in all the larger communities. Albuquerque and Las Vegas, for example, sprouted new commercial districts adjacent to railroad depots that were built a mile or more from the original town plazas. Socorro, thirty-five miles north of Fort Craig, was transformed from a quiet little farming village of about five hundred people in the early 1860s into a bustling mining and smelting town of more than four thousand in 1885.[27]

The coming of steel rails also created new railroad towns, such as Raton, near the New Mexico–Colorado border, and "New" San Marcial, a predominantly Anglo town built near the largely Hispanic village of "Old" San Marcial. Since the Crawford family history is intimately connected with New San Marcial, a brief look at its origins and subsequent growth will be helpful.

Hispanic farmers settled Old San Marcial in 1866, after floodwaters destroyed their village on the opposite (east) side of the Rio Grande. By 1880 it was a typical Hispanic settlement of about seventy-five families, most of whom lived in small adobe houses, attended Mass in the Catholic church, and cultivated small plots of farmland that they irrigated with water from the river.[28] In 1882, the Santa Fe built its division headquarters a mile from Old San Marcial, thus sparking a construction boom and the emergence of New San Marcial as a railroad town. By the end of the year, the railway had erected a two-story station house, a roundhouse capable of servicing eight engines, repair shops, a commodious section boarding house, and tenement houses for its employees.[29]

About the time this construction began, Martin Zimmerman, owner of the Armendaris land grant on which San Marcial was located, organized the San Marcial Land and Improvement Company and laid out the new town in regular squares. He advertised the sale of town lots and farmland in leading territorial newspapers. In December 1882, a writer for the *Las Vegas Daily Optic* marveled at San Marcial's remarkable growth. "Building material," he asserted, "cannot be procured fast enough for the people to build houses." In the same issue, the *Optic* reported that "Capt. Jack" had bought four town lots, on which he planned to build a livery stable.[30]

By mid-1885 San Marcial resembled an eastern, urban community, having a population of about 350 permanent residents. Streets were "wide, clean, and bordered with luxuriant shade trees." The town boasted two churches (one Catholic, the other

Methodist) and a schoolhouse. The business district stretched along Railroad Avenue, facing the depot and other railroad facilities. A Harvey House (officially named the Depot Hotel) was on the north side of the depot, and the San Marcial House, a combination concert hall, lecture room, and dance hall, stood nearby.[31] As if to celebrate the town's coming of age, residents staged a magnificent ball at the San Marcial House in late November 1885. A special train brought in sixty Socorro residents for the occasion, and a Silver Cornet Band greeted them at the station. Captain Jack, Maria, and Eva attended the festivities, which included a midnight supper at the Depot Hotel, "where the tables were groaning under their burden of good things."[32]

Although its chief industry was railroading, San Marcial also functioned as a supply center for nearby mountain mining camps. People commonly believed that great wealth could be found in these areas. Optimism, in fact, reached fever pitch during the years when Crawford managed the Fort Craig store.

Jack's own passion for mining was unsurpassed. He was firmly convinced that with his practical knowledge and willingness to work, coupled with outside development funds, a fortune was there for the taking. Typical of most western miners, Crawford located several promising claims and then attempted to raise capital for further expansion. But unlike many others, he retained faith in his properties even after initial efforts proved to be disappointing. For more than thirty years, he poured money into his claims, always hoping that eastern financiers would underwrite the cost of large-scale mining.

Crawford located most of his claims in two areas—the Black Range west of Fort Craig, and the South Oscura and San Andres mountains to the east. Chloride, the most promising camp in the Black Range, became a gathering place for the Crawford clan. Jack's younger brother Austin and sisters Lizzie Nattress and Rebecca James, with their families, were among the three hundred to five hundred people living there during the peak years of the 1880s.[33] Jack himself was a familiar figure in camp. Besides staging entertainments, he owned a half-interest in its livery stable, and he acquired several nearby promising claims. In 1884, for example, he paid 350 dollars for a one-third interest in two mines about eight miles from Chloride and 1,500 dollars for a one-third interest in the Monte Christo, making him its principal owner.[34]

Crawford expended most of his energy, however, in developing copper and lead claims in the South Oscura and San Andres mountains, about forty miles east of San Marcial. Only a few hardy miners ever found their way into these isolated ranges. A wagon road cut through the area, connecting Fort Craig with Fort Stanton in Lincoln County, but it never supported a mining community the size of Chloride. Today, these ranges are within White Sands Missile Range, off-limits to private citizens.

Captain Jack explored these mountains during the Victorio campaign, but whether he located the first mining claim there, as one newspaper alleged, cannot be verified. By the close of 1882, however, he had filed on at least seventeen locations, naming three after his children.[35] These claims were located only a few miles southeast of Trinity Site, where scientists detonated the first atomic bomb in 1945.

Crawford enjoyed exhibiting his mines to reporters, hoping that their stories would attract investors. An account of one visit appeared in a December 1882 issue of the *Las Vegas Daily Optic.* Although amusing, the story underscored the uncertainties of travel in this isolated region—even for an experienced scout. Jack's party of three, including *Optic* correspondent Ed W. Freeman, left Fort Craig on December 18, expecting to reach Crawford's camp in the South Oscuras by nightfall. They were still groping their way through the foothills when darkness fell. Without blankets, provisions, or even water, the men hobbled their horses, lit a fire, and attempted to sleep. About midnight, the horses struggled free and "started on a bee line for the Rio Grande." At daylight, the men struck out on foot, finally locating Jack's camp at about 8:00 A.M. "The boys [two men working Jack's claim] soon had a nice breakfast of coffee, sowbelly and warm bread prepared for us and with ravenous appetites we devoured the meal," Freeman later reported.[36]

Despite the night's discomfort, the *Optic* newsman made a thorough exploration of the mountains. He told his readers that the mineral belt started in the San Andres and extended in a northeasterly direction into the Oscuras. Within a distance of thirteen miles, 160 claims had been staked, but only 25 were being worked. This region, Freeman avowed, was "the best copper district that has as yet been discovered in New Mexico." He revealed also that an experienced mineralogist, Edward Brown, was to oversee work on Crawford's claims.[37]

These ranges attracted even more attention in later months. On August 1, 1883, the *Socorro Bullion* predicted that the San Andres would soon become the territory's major copper district.[38] And Crawford took the lead in scouring the area for promising sites. During a two-year period, 1883–84, he or his agents located at least forty-one mining claims in the South Oscuras and San Andres. He also filed on or acquired title to a half-dozen or more mill sites. Thus, by controlling major sources of water in the area (natural springs), he also controlled several miles of fine stock range. Dripping Spring and Grapevine Spring, two of Jack's mill sites, would figure prominently in his plans to establish a horse ranch.[39]

Maintaining legal title to so many mining properties, however, was expensive. Federal law required owners to expend one hundred dollars annually on each claim; otherwise, the property was subject to relocation by other parties. Since the ordinary price of labor in mining camps was three dollars a day, one man would have to perform thirty-three and a third days of labor to complete this "assessment work."[40]

In a letter to the *Socorro Bullion,* dated April 10, 1883, Crawford stated that in the previous two years he had spent more than three thousand dollars on his claims.[41] He hired local men to perform much of the required labor, but often he worked in the mines himself. A newspaper correspondent, writing of a visit to the South Oscuras the following year, focused on Crawford's industry and generosity. He had found Jack's camp deserted, but a note penned to a tent advised passersby:

> Miners, prospectors and others passing this way will find water in keg. If not good, one and a half miles north on trail is plenty. There is bacon and flour and potatoes in the chest—help yourselves. . . . I have finished assessment work upon 6 claims and have moved to my camp in the San Andres where two men will be at work during the year. . . .
>
> Yours,
> Capt. Jack Crawford

The amount of work Jack had accomplished surprised the journalist. On one location, he discovered a tunnel forty feet long and from six to eight feet wide, from which "at least five hundred tons of good ore have been taken . . . piled up on three large dumps or piles outside." Other nearby sites showed similar development. Predicting that the region was destined to make men wealthy, he concluded, "I know of no one more deserving of success than the 'Poet Scout.' "[42]

Since it took more money to work these mines than he possessed, Crawford spent a good deal of time in seeking additional funds from friends and eastern capitalists. He made several attempts to enlist the support of Bill Cody, sending him ore specimens and lengthy letters outlining his plans. Initially, Cody expressed interest. Writing from Massachusetts on April 8, 1882, nearing the end of his winter tour, he informed Jack: "You may look for me[,] the Major [North] and one or two friends this summer after we get through with the round up." Business had been "something wonderful," he reported; even during Holy Week, he expected to clear three hundred dollars a day on the stage. Writing from North Platte on May 25, Cody announced that he was about to sell the Dismal Ranch, after which he and North would travel to New Mexico to discuss Jack's schemes. He ended the letter on a cautious note, however, saying that he was "afraid of mines." [43]

Throughout the month of June, Cody held forth the possibility of visiting Jack's mines. In a letter dated June 10, he chided Jack for being "so impatient." As soon as the ranch was sold, he promised to travel to New Mexico with the best mineral expert in Colorado. "If he pronounces your prospects & claims good," Cody wrote, "I can in side of twenty day[s] organize the wealthyest [*sic*] stock co. in America." [44]

But Cody did not visit Crawford's mines that summer. Rather, he helped stage North Platte's Fourth of July celebration, called the "Old Glory Blow Out," an event that "would reshape the rest of his life." [45] The celebration began at 10:30 A.M. with Buffalo Bill, dressed in white corduroy pants and a black velvet coat, leading a street parade. Thereafter, local cowboys competed for cash prizes in horse racing, steer riding, and buffalo roping. The success of this pioneer rodeo inspired Cody, in 1883, to organize "Buffalo Bill's Wild West," an outdoor exhibition of cowboy skills, Indian fights, and frontier adventure. By the end of the decade, Cody had gained international fame with his great outdoor traveling extravaganza and was well on his way to becoming one of the world's greatest showmen. [46]

Crawford also sought financial backing from Ned Buntline, author and dime novelist who had launched Cody on his theatrical career. Buntline, whose real name was Edward Z. C. Judson, had been supporting himself since 1846 by writing lurid fiction. [47] Exactly when Crawford became his friend remains a mystery. But, in 1879, Buntline featured Captain Jack in a dime novel entitled *The Terrible Dread; or, The Seven Scouts*. Three years later, Jack again appeared as the hero in Buntline's *Merciless Ben, The Hair Lifter*, published in the *New York Weekly*. [48]

According to his biographer, Ned experienced "one of the great sorrows of his life" in 1881, when his four-year-old daughter died after a brief illness.[49] Deep in sorrow, he cried out to his friend: "Three words speak the agony which volumes could not describe, the loss which all the gold in your mines could not replace, the shadow which hangs darkest in all my long, eventful life—*Irene is dead!*" Jack immediately responded with a touching poem, entitled "Irene is Dead," in which he admonished Ned:

> *Bow not thy aged head in grief,*
> *For Irene knows no pain,*
> *And all is love, and joy, and peace,*
> *Where you shall meet again.*[50]

In following years, Ned wrote several times of wanting to visit Crawford in New Mexico and invest in his mines. In a letter dated October 26, 1882, written from his estate at "Eagles Nest" in Stamford, New York, Buntline avowed, "I believe there are a hundred fortunes in your mines out there needing only capital to develop them." Two months later, he informed Jack, "I want to be with you in those mining enterprises and will surely come as soon as my home affairs will let me." Buntline died, however, without ever having set foot on Jack's property.[51]

Although he clearly valued Buntline's friendship, Crawford wrote a stinging rebuke of dime novelists in the second edition of *The Poet Scout,* published in 1886 and only a few months before Ned's death. Because a modern-day writer has questioned Jack's sincerity in denouncing dime novels, it is appropriate to examine the issue more closely before continuing the story of his mines.[52]

Crawford's bias against dime novels was of long standing, and only three are known to exist that featured Captain Jack as the central character. In addition to Buntline's two, the prolific author

Prentiss Ingraham wrote a third, entitled *The Adventurous Life of Captain Jack, The Border Boy,* published in 1883.[53]

Crawford was not dissembling when he stated in *The Poet Scout* that his name had "never yet figured in one of these trashy concerns with my consent." His forthright stand against this literature kept the figure of "Captain Jack" from appearing as the central hero in any of the dime novels that flooded the newsstands in later years. Consequently, Captain Jack received far less public exposure than Buffalo Bill, the hero of more than five hundred original dime novels.[54]

Jack set forth his objections in a short essay entitled "A Chapter for Boys," which appears in his book of poetry. He pulled no punches in his opening paragraph, which began:

> I wish I could sit down and take every dime-novel-reading little boy in America by the hand and point out to him the destination he will reach if he persists in reading the vile trash which depicts such Indian scenes as never occurred, and points out "blood-and-thunder" heroes who never lived, and of such a type as were never heard of in the West. If I had the power I would catch every dime-novel publisher in America and confine him in prison for life, where he could not pursue his criminal work—for it is criminal—and lead so many bright boys to ruin and disgrace.[55]

Crawford went on to say that many boys who traveled West for adventure found themselves washing dishes in hotels or serving as "lackeys in some subordinate position until their parents could send for them." Moreover, he blamed dime novels for some of the tragedies he had witnessed in the Black Hills—youngsters lured west by adventure stories, only to die from exposure or in brushes with the Sioux. He also claimed that many inmates in western prisons had been "brought to their present shame and disgrace through reading dime novels." "They longed to be heroes or highwaymen or noted robbers," Jack continued, "and their first attempt at crime invariably led to their imprisonment for a long term."[56]

Although sincere in his beliefs, Crawford's crusade against dime novels was fueled in part by his desire to be recognized as an honest spokesman for the West, an ex-scout who portrayed the region more accurately and sympathetically than other westerners. The fact that he had appeared on stage with Bill Cody in highly sensational melodramas may even have propelled him in this direction, for Jack increasingly found it necessary to establish a public identity that differed from Cody's. Jack's harshest condemnation of dime novels, in fact (and, by implication, sensational melodramas), came several years after his stint with the Buffalo Bill Combination. And true to his convictions, Crawford's own plays were remarkably free of violence, although in other respects they were conventional nineteenth-century melodramas.

Crawford was not alone in railing against dime novels. Attacks on the genre emerged early and gathered steam in the 1880s, when sensationalism increased. Clergymen, teachers, and moralists condemned the violence and bloodshed featured in nearly every story. Frank Tousey, who began publishing dime novels in 1878, added to the controversy with his sensational stories about Jesse James and other outlaws. In 1883, the postmaster general banned sixty-six issues of Tousey's Wide Awake Library, fearing that they would incite murder. The following year, the *New York Tribune* claimed that blood-and-thunder thrillers had led scores of boys to rob their parents before heading into the wild and woolly West. Some parents forbade the reading of dime novels, though writer Booth Tarkington later recalled having read the forbidden stories concealed inside the covers of an approved book, such as *Pilgrim's Progress.* [57]

Despite his anti–dime novel preachments, Crawford mourned Buntline's death. And although he persuaded neither Buntline nor Cody to advance funds, he found others willing to invest in his mines. Starting in August 1883 (and continuing for nearly two years), Wall Street businessman Samuel K. Schwenk handled Jack's mining properties, financing assessment work and seeking additional development funds. Schwenk became so confident of their worth that he subsequently resigned as president of Iron King Mining Company to devote all of his energies to Jack's claims.[58]

During the years Crawford was locating mines, he also established at least two ranches in New Mexico. On September 20, 1882, he preempted 160 acres in Nogal Canyon, about sixteen miles southwest of Fort Craig, where he ran a small herd of cattle. Although information about the "No-Gal Ranch" is sparse, we do know that he received a patent for the land in 1890.[59] Crawford also kept a mixture of cows, horses, and beef cattle on property adjacent to the family residence at Fort Craig. After the army abandoned the post, he filed on this land as a Soldier's Homestead in 1885, maintaining ownership until after the turn of the century.[60]

These enterprises—mines, ranches, government con tracts, the trader's store—left little time for Crawford to perform on stage. On occasion, however, he recited poetry at public gatherings, and he also remained active in the Grand Army of the Republic.[61] The theater was in Crawford's blood, however, and by mid-1884 he was contemplating a return to the stage. Exactly what Jack had in mind is unclear, but eventually he teamed up with his old friend, Will L. Visscher, a member of the first Captain Jack Combination.

After parting company with Jack in California, Visscher had pursued a career as actor, comic lecturer, poet, and newspaperman. He was in Denver working as a journalist when Crawford arrived in January 1885 to place Eva in school. The two comrades held a joyous reunion and appeared twice together before large audiences. Their reception was so encouraging, they decided "to join destinies and take the road professionally," traveling first to New Mexico and then touring the continent. They opened in Albuquerque on February 26 and subsequently played before enthusiastic audiences in Socorro, Las Cruces, El Paso, Fort Wingate, Santa Fe, and Las Vegas.[62]

The crowd that packed Van Patten's Hall in Las Cruces included a judge and several prominent lawyers, who were in town for district court. In praising the duo's performance, the local press accorded those residents who had not attended a glimpse of what they had missed. "Captain Jack gave recitations and songs from his own compositions," the press recorded, "and won unlimited and well deserved applause." But Visscher completely captivated the audience with his flashing wit and droll humor in a brilliant monologue of war reminiscences. "With the attendant music, the two gave one of the most delightful entertainments of a literary character, which it has ever been our good fortune to attend."[63]

After touring New Mexico, the Visscher–Crawford combination moved on to Kansas and then appeared in St. Louis about the time that Dr. William F. Carver arrived with his Wild West show.[64] A dentist by trade, Carver began his career as an "exhibition marksman" in 1877. He later toured Europe as a champion rifle shot and helped Buffalo Bill organize the first Wild West show in 1883. After one season together, however, the partners separated, and thereafter each toured with his own Wild West company.[65]

Wild West shows, as developed by Cody and Carver, were something entirely new in popular entertainment. Staged in outdoor arenas, they combined demonstrations of skills required of a working cowboy—bronco-busting, bulldogging, roping, shooting—with reenactments of exciting incidents from western life: an Indian attack on the Deadwood stagecoach, a sham buffalo hunt, Indian war dances. The shows were enormously successful in their day, with as many as six million people witnessing Cody's performances in 1893, the year of the Columbian Exposition in Chicago. Audiences everywhere were thrilled by scenes of danger and hardship thought to be characteristic of the western movement. That genuine westerners starred in the exhibitions added to their appeal. Similar to the Beadle Dime Novels, the Wild West shows dramatized the American West "as a place of romance and glamour."[66]

For unknown reasons, Visscher and Crawford ended their partnership in St. Louis, and Jack teamed up with Doc Carver. Carver's show, "Life on the Plains and the Great Wild West Combination," opened for a four-day stand at the St. Louis fairgrounds on May 3, 1885.[67] On the morning prior to the show's opening, however, Carver staged a giant parade, complete with cowboys, Mexicans, Indians, and a ten-thousand-dollar gold cornet band mounted on an English tallyho coach. The next day, the St. Louis *Missouri Republican* featured Captain Jack in a long article, based on an interview with Will Visscher. Visscher's depiction of Jack as one of the nation's most heroic Indian hunters would only increase the public's curiosity about the exhibition and its performers.[68]

In fact, more than thirty thousand people thronged the fairgrounds on opening day. Those arriving early had an unexpected encounter with the famous Poet Scout. In their haste to enter the grounds, the crowd surged against a locked gate, breaking it open. As the horde moved forward, Crawford "jumped out of [the ticket] box, drew his revolver, and planting himself at the gates forced the crowd back." He was subsequently arrested for this hasty action and taken to a police station, but quickly released when police discovered that his revolver contained only blank cartridges. Carver's biographer rather lamely defends Crawford's conduct, avowing that not only had Captain Jack feared for his life but he also feared how Indian and cowboy performers would react to the advancing mob.[69]

At 3:00 P.M., Carver galloped into the arena to open the show dressed in a purple velvet hunting shirt, black boots and riding pants, and white sombrero. A buckskin-clad Captain Jack rode in the procession of cowboys and Indians that followed. The afternoon's entertainment included pony races, bronco riding, a reenactment of the pony express, a buffalo hunt, an Indian war dance, and Indians attacking a stagecoach. A newspaperman described the closing segment, in which Indians creep up on a sleeping traveler (a role played by Crawford) and then engage him in fight: "After a brave defense, Captain Jack is killed and just as the Indians are about to scalp him, a band of scouts led by Dr. Carver rush to the rescue and after the Indians are put to flight Captain Jack's body is placed on a horse and borne away." [70]

Buffalo Bill's Wild West exhibition followed on Carver's heels, opening at the St. Louis fairgrounds on May 10. Since dissolving their partnership, the two showmen regarded each other with disdain while competing for the public's patronage. During the week of May 3, each company placed advertisements in the *Missouri Republican,* claiming to be the original Wild West exhibition.[71] The two companies tangled later that summer in New England, following Carver's successful appearance in New Haven before a crowd of ten thousand. Cody's biographer sums up the Wild West imbroglio in this manner: "Each sued the other for libel; there were attachments and court hearings. What it was all about is unclear and perhaps not worth untangling." Eventually the two parties settled out of court, but not before Carver's company had folded.[72]

Crawford rebounded from the company's demise with characteristic drive and determination. After parting with Carver in New England, Jack arranged with a New York firm to republish *The Poet Scout,* and he interested a millionaire grocer in his copper mines. He also spoke of returning to the stage. Although his theatrical plans were not fully developed, within twelve months he would perfect a lecture style that would entertain audiences for nearly thirty years. In September, Crawford returned to New

Chapter 5

Mexico in high spirits, even though financial worries constantly threatened his equanimity.

> *I'm an optimistic warbler*
> *And I whistle, laugh and sing,*
> *Bringing gladness out of sadness*
> *With the sunshine that I fling.*[73]

6

"THE CAMPFIRE AND THE TRAIL"

Carl Sandburg once wrote, "Nothing happens unless first a dream." He was referring to the birth of the American republic, but the idea he expressed helps to explain the character of Captain Jack. Crawford's dream was the American Dream— the belief that anyone could rise above his or her origins, and through hard work and perseverance, achieve success. This dream was almost as old as the country itself. Early European settlers found such an abundance of resources in the New World that anything seemed possible.[1]

The American Dream, in fact, continued to serve as a magnet drawing tens of millions of immigrants across the seas in search of a better life. The tremendous nineteenth-century expansion in the United States helped to fuel the idea that anyone, no matter how poor, could achieve fame and fortune. During the second half of the century, the dream came to mean (more than anything else) material success, the accumulation of money. And for

Captain Jack Crawford, The Poet Scout. (Photo by Ben Wittick, courtesy School of American Research Collections in the Museum of New Mexico, Neg. No. 15747.)

Crawford's generation, Andrew Carnegie's rise from poverty to wealth was the most striking evidence that the dream could become a reality.

Crawford's brief stint with Carver's Wild West show would strengthen Jack's dream rather than diminish it. The thunderous applause that greeted him in the arena rang in his memory long after the company folded. The dream constantly ignited his energy and imagination, propelling him in several different directions at the same time.

After the collapse of Carver's show, Jack traveled to New York City to arrange for a new edition of *The Poet Scout* and to raise money for his mining ventures. On Wall Street, he consulted with Samuel K. Schwenk and then met with the millionaire grocer H. K. Thurber, reportedly one of the owners of the Copper Queen Mine in Bisbee, Arizona. Thurber apparently agreed to help finance both projects. According to one account, he advanced five hundred dollars to Funk and Wagnalls to publish the poetry book, the author to reimburse his benefactor by taking subscriptions at two dollars a copy on delivery.[2] Then, in August, the New York capitalist traveled to New Mexico to check on cattle interests in Lincoln County and to survey the San Andres copper mines. Although the local press announced that Thurber planned to erect a smelter in New Mexico if Jack's property "be as represented," records fail to disclose whether he invested more than a token amount in Crawford's mines.[3]

Before Jack returned to New Mexico, he attended the funeral of General U. S. Grant, serving as an aide on the staff of General Daniel E. Sickles, former commander of the Third Army Corps at the Battle of Gettysburg. Grant's body was brought to New York on a special train shrouded in black curtains. For two days the body lay in state at City Hall, while an endless stream of city residents filed past to pay their last respects. The day before the funeral, the *New York Evening Telegram* published Crawford's touching poem "Mustered Out," in which Jack eulogized his dead commander. On August 8, 1885, Crawford joined hundreds of other veterans and celebrities in accompanying Grant's body to the tomb on Riverside Drive.[4]

During this time of national mourning, Crawford published a fourteen-page pamphlet, entitled "In Memoriam, The Hero's Departed," featuring a photograph of Grant on the cover. Dedicated to comrades in the Grand Army of the Republic, the pamphlet contained a program of the Grant memorial services, several of Crawford's poems, and two articles about Crawford's career.[5] Someone sent a copy to Bill Cody, then on tour in Canada, and Cody wasted little time in registering his complaints about its contents. The prickly nature of the Cody–Crawford friendship is evident in Cody's letter to the Poet Scout dated August 11.

Two statements in the booklet had raised Buffalo Bill's hackles: that Crawford was "the only scout who can claim any merit as an actor," and that during the Sioux campaign Jack had "superseded Mr. Cody as chief of scouts." The second statement, Bill claimed, read as though Crawford had been placed in command over Cody while the latter was still in the field. In response to the first statement, Cody suggested a unique method for comparing their dramatic abilities—something like a theatrical shoot-out!

> Now Jack, you say you are the only scout with any dramatic ability. Now if you wish to prove that you start your company. I will start me one and we will play the same towns this winter at the same time. And let the public decide that question. And this I will do if you don't stop your slurring me.[6]

Crawford's written response to Cody's outburst has not survived, but whatever he wrote caused Buffalo Bill to dispatch a second missive of nearly twelve pages, examining their separate careers as scouts and their subsequent association. He began his letter with these words: "Now you dont understand me at all—or my friendship toward you." After scolding Jack for laboring under several misconceptions, Cody concluded that "if at any time I can do anything for you, if it lays in my power, command me."[7]

In September, Jack returned to New Mexico. By this date the army had abandoned Fort Craig and turned the property over to the Department of Interior.[8] The Crawfords, however, continued residing on their Fort Craig ranch, although much of its daily management must have fallen into Maria's hands. After Jack's death, Maria remarked on her husband's roving disposition in her application for a widow's pension: "he would absent himself for long periods, and then would come home for a while and then go off again."[9]

Jack's absences undoubtedly placed a strain on the Crawford marriage, and, in fact, late in life Jack and Maria separated. Because of his frequent and lengthy stays away from home, Crawford does not fare well as husband and father in the eyes of modern readers grown accustomed to the warm family unity portrayed on old television programs such as *Little House on the Prairie* and *The Waltons*. But Jack deserves to be judged against the standards of his own time, when it was not unusual for men to be gone from home, leaving women alone to head the households. Tamara Hareven has said of the nineteenth-century family that it was "often more complex, more diverse, and less orderly than [it is] today" and that the major burdens of family relationships "were heavily weighted toward economic needs and tasks" rather than emotional needs.[10] From most nineteenth-century vantage points, Jack would be viewed as a worthy husband and father since he was industrious, temperate, honest, kind, and willing to share decision making with his wife. Certainly his career mandated the vast majority of his travels.[11]

Family tradition has it that when Jack followed the lecture circuit in later years, Maria declined his invitation to accompany him. We do Maria a disservice, I think, to suggest that she needed a doting and protective husband to give life its meaning. Very likely she experienced the same inner satisfaction in her ability to manage the household when left on her own as did many of her contemporaries when faced with a similar situation, including Susan McSween Barber, the most famous of New Mexico's women ranchers.[12]

Because of her strength of character, Maria gained a reputation as "a typical pioneer woman, equal to any emergency."[13] Family members also remember her as a jovial woman with a good sense of humor. Like Jack, she had little formal education, although unlike her husband, she showed little inclination to record her observations on paper. Jack later paid tribute to Maria's courage and resourcefulness, telling a New York reporter that during one of his absences from home a tramp stopped at the Fort Craig ranch and told Maria that he was an old scouting partner of Jack's. "He said his name was 'Dashaway Gus' and that he was a regular terror. Mrs. Crawford had taken his measure, and quietly producing the Winchester which she always keeps by her bedside loaded, she asked him to take a walk, which he very obligingly did."[14]

Living in a country still trying to shed the last vestiges of the frontier, Maria had many opportunities to show her mettle. Take, for example, the time when she and two other women were pursued by six gray wolves while returning from the Hardy Ranch in the San Mateo Mountains. They had left home with a loaded shotgun in their buggy, but at the ranch the gun had been used and not reloaded. The local press reported that "after several ineffectual attempts on the part of Mrs. Crawford to fire the empty piece, she discovered the trouble and loaded it." But the team had become skittish, and Maria decided not to fire unless absolutely necessary. The wolves kept up their pursuit for several miles before giving up the chase.[15]

Jack spent just three months in New Mexico during the fall of 1885 before again embarking on a trip to the East Coast. But even during this short stay, he often was away from home taking care of business affairs. In early September he met Thurber at Fort Stanton, and together they went to examine Crawford's San Andres mines. Later that month, he began soliciting subscriptions for *The Poet Scout* in towns and villages north of San Marcial. While in Albuquerque, he also attended the Territorial Fair and a Grand Army campfire. Continuing north, he spent three days in Santa Fe drumming up subscriptions. Finally, on October 10, the Albuquerque press recorded his departure for home on the early morning train.[16]

Although tragedy lurked around the corner, Crawford was experiencing some of the most joyous days of his life. During his three-month stay in New Mexico, he was reunited with James Carlin, a true soul mate who would remain Crawford's loyal friend during good times and bad. Carlin was not his real name. Crawford knew him as Arty Brace back in 1877, when Jack was touring in Nevada with Buffalo Bill and Arty was working on small-town western newspapers.[17] A classic friendship developed; but exactly when the two men first crossed paths is not clear.

The world would later know Jim Carlin as the talented and witty Denver journalist James B. Adams, the name bestowed upon him at birth. Born in 1843 in Richmond, Ohio, Adams served in the Union army and was captured by Confederates at the Battle of Chattanooga. Like Jack, he later served as a government scout. For a time he was attached to Frank North's company of Pawnee scouts and later took part in the 1879 Ute campaign in northern Colorado.[18] The major flaw in Adams's character (and the reason he assumed bogus names) was a weakness for drink.

In 1885, Carlin—still unwilling to assume his real name—landed a job on the *Albuquerque Evening Democrat* and then learned of his friend living at Fort Craig. On September 18, he penned a long letter to the Poet Scout, apparently the first communication between the two men since their association in Nevada. "I cannot tell you how many thousand times I have thought of you," Carlin wrote, and he expressed a desire to renew their old friendship. In explaining his change of names, Carlin confessed, "I gave my name as Brace in Nevada because I was on a protracted spree, and had sense enough to not disgrace my own name."[19] But he had not yet conquered his addiction to alcohol.

In short order, Carlin received a letter from his old "pard," which, in Carlin's words, "gave [my] heart a pretty severe attack of the mumps." Opening with a long poem, one of Jack's best, Crawford expressed joy upon rediscovering his friend. The first stanza follows:

Let my heart speak out in a simple song,
To the echo of days long ago—
Let my soul burst forth in a friendship strong,
That grows stronger as older I grow.
For many a night when I laid me down,
With the star-spangled heavens above me,
I thought of a friend in a far away town
Whom I loved, and I knew that he loved me.

Carlin later published the entire poem in the *Evening Democrat.* "The same old Jack!" he exclaimed. "The same old noble chum, with a heart as true as the steel of his hunting knife." But the text of Jack's long letter, he insisted, was "too sacred to put into print."[20] In mid-November, Carlin spent almost a week as Jack's house guest, and it was following this visit to Fort Craig that he wrote the charming description of the Crawford household that appears in Chapter 5.[21]

During the first week in December, the two friends boarded a train for New York, where Jack completed arrangements for publishing *The Poet Scout: A Book of Song and Story.*

Released in February 1886, the volume of nearly one hundred poems received favorable notices in several leading newspapers. The New York *Graphic's* review began: "There is a bubble and a sparkle from nature's spring that makes this volume refreshing. The author is not a Byron or a Tennyson or anything of the sort. He is simply a man who sings, well or ill as may be, out of his heart." A San Francisco reviewer echoed the same sentiment: "Captain Jack is not, and never will be, a Burns, but nevertheless he is a born poet. Not a mere stringer of re-echoing words, but he writes because he feels the sentiments he expresses, and speaks because of the fullness of the heart." Among the poems singled out for praise was "Our Nugget," dedicated to little May Cody Crawford.[22]

Sometime in 1886, Crawford also published *From Darkness into Light and Other Poems,* a slender volume probably intended to advertise the larger collection of poetry. On the page immediately following the fifth and final poem were instructions for ordering *The Poet Scout.*[23]

Jack never made any money from *The Poet Scout,* primarily because he gave so many copies to friends and celebrities, each inscribed with an appropriate greeting. Written on the flyleaf of the volume he sent to Maria are these words: "To My Wife—The sun is peeping out again, The clouds are fading fast; While hope is lighting up my sky, And fortune smiles at last. Yours Affectionately, J. W. Crawford, Capt. Jack."[24]

The sunshine that warmed Jack's soul stemmed, in part, from his recent success as an entertainer. His career as a public lecturer, in fact, began on this trip to New York, where he spent Christmas with Mr. and Mrs. James Tanner at their home in Brooklyn.[25] Jim Tanner, a well-known figure among Union war veterans, would become Jack's confidant and business partner. During the Second Battle of Bull Run, an exploding shell had so severely injured the young corporal's legs that both had to be amputated below the knee. Tanner later learned to walk on artificial limbs. After the war, he was admitted to the bar, became deputy collector in the New York customhouse, and then served many years as collector of taxes for Brooklyn. Billed as "Corporal Tanner," he also became a much-sought-after orator at Grand Army functions.[26] Crawford remained good friends with Tanner until about 1906, when Mrs. Tanner was killed in an auto accident. After that, as Jack and Maria's marriage continued to unravel, the two men drifted apart.

Jack always claimed, however, that it was Mrs. Tanner's encouragement that propelled him onto the rostrum. Shortly after the start of 1886, he gave his first two-hour entertainment as a benefit for Mrs. Tanner's Methodist church. He had written a lecture for the occasion, but once in front of the audience and struggling with the text, he set aside his prepared remarks. He then spoke directly to the audience, telling them stories of his western adventures and reciting his poetry. A born storyteller, Crawford so delighted the congregation that he was invited to repeat the performance.[27]

Before his return to New Mexico, Captain Jack spoke to twenty-nine different audiences. He entitled his entertainment "The Campfire and the Trail" and insisted that it was not a lecture, but "a frontier monologue and medley." When he spoke to veterans' organizations, flags and a miniature campfire adorned the stage. Dressed in buckskin, with a wide-brimmed sombrero covering his "flowing locks," a six-shooter at his waist, and a rifle in hand, Crawford was a living example of the western hero. After witnessing Jack's performance, Nym Crinkle of the New York *World* wrote: "The world longs for a fresh individuality, and fresh, strong character. I never was so struck by this as when I sat the other night in a crowded house, and listened to a talk by the celebrated Captain Jack Crawford, while he held his audience spellbound for two hours by a simple narration of his life."[28]

Chapter 6

While in the East, Crawford attended a Grand Army encampment in Scranton, Pennsylvania, where he was reunited with some boyhood friends. Several subscribed for a copy of his book, and all were eager to have him perform in their hometowns. Prospects were looking so good that Crawford jubilantly wrote Maria from Brooklyn on February 14: "I shall be well fixed and out of debt this time one year hence. Then we will have a neat little house somewhere where the children can go to school and where we can have some comfort." [29]

But Jack's newfound literary and platform success did little to soften the impact of the shocking news that arrived on April 4, 1886—little May had died of scarlet fever. Jack's grief was profound; yet in his great sorrow his chief concern was for Maria, again pregnant. We will never know what words of comfort Crawford sent to his wife. Jim Carlin's letter to Maria, written on April 5, said that Jack told everyone who offered him sympathy that "it breaks his heart to think how you must be suffering under the blow." Carlin went on to say that Jack had been "toiling and laboring day and night to push back financial clouds and was almost worn out when this last affliction overtook him." [30]

Still, what are we to make of the fact that Crawford did not rush home to be at the side of his grieving wife? Did she resent his continued absence and harbor this resentment for years to come? Or did she try to console and reassure him, in the manner of Maggie Brown, a contemporary of Maria's who later resided in Rincon, New Mexico, about ninety miles south of Fort Craig. When Brown's two-year-old daughter became ill and it looked as if she might die, Maggie wrote to her husband, then absent in the Colorado gold fields: "Others have to lose, we must too. Darling, bare up, I have good kind friends to support me. I will pray for you." [31] Although unsure of Maria's reaction, we do know that Jack submerged his own grief in practical matters some two thousand miles from home, honoring his platform engagements and working for his family's financial security.

Jack's poignant poem, written on this sad occasion and entitled "Our Lost Nugget," was published in a New York newspaper. A stanza follows:

> *God help me, and God help her mother,*
> > *Her grief must be crushing indeed,*
> *And God help her sister and brother,*
> > *Since hearts that so loved her must bleed.*
> *And mine reaches out o'er the prairie*
> > *In a sad and a solemn refrain,*
> *When I think I shall never behold her,*
> > *And ne'er kiss her sweet lips again.*[32]

Before Crawford returned to New Mexico in June, he visited Secretary of Interior Lucius Q. C. Lamar in Washington and received an appointment as custodian of the Fort Craig reservation. In announcing this selection, the New Mexico press reported inaccurately that Captain Jack also had been named chief of scouts and would join the campaign being waged in Arizona against Geronimo and his handful of Apache followers.[33]

Throughout the summer, in fact, General Nelson A. Miles and more than four thousand U.S. troops were in the field trying to capture the elusive Apache leader. Although Jack raised the possibility of joining the campaign as a correspondent for the *New York Herald,* family and business matters kept him closer to home.[34] In July, Maria gave birth to their fourth child, May, later christened Elizabeth Esther May Crawford.[35] And during that summer and fall, the Poet Scout worked with renewed vigor on his Oscura and San Andres mines, for he had struck a promising business deal with a Philadelphia capitalist.

For one hundred dollars, Crawford turned over to W. S. Thomas forty-eight claims and three mill sites, with Thomas agreeing to finance assessment work and to organize a company to develop the property if he was pleased with the results. But once the mines began to realize a profit, Crawford was to be reimbursed for his original expenditures—now amounting to about thirteen thousand dollars—and then share profits equally with his new partner.[36] Jack employed a four-man crew that summer to work the Copper Bottom Mine, the most promising of his claims. Although he was optimistic that a rich vein of copper would be uncovered, the men found only low-grade ore, which, coupled with the distance from a railroad, hindered extensive operations.[37]

The isolation of his mines, in fact, almost cost Crawford his life. One Sunday afternoon in late July, he left camp in the South Oscuras en route to Fort Craig, intending to drive his team all night to avoid crossing the desert in the daytime. At one point, a rattlesnake spooked the horses. Having left his Winchester in camp so that his men could hunt game, Crawford leaped from the buckboard and attacked the rattler with his whip. Meanwhile, the team took off without him, and in catching up to it he stepped on a second rattler, "which sprang up and fastened its fangs in the back of his right hand." Jack managed to fling the snake to the ground and then stamped it to death. Even though he tried to suck out the venom, he arrived home deathly sick, with his arm and hand greatly swollen.[38]

In August, Jim Tanner, his wife, and two daughters visited the Crawfords at Fort Craig following Tanner's appearance at the national G.A.R. encampment in San Francisco. The *Albuquerque Morning Democrat* warmly welcomed the ex-soldier, calling him "the greatest orator in America . . . next to Bob Ingersoll." Before leaving New Mexico, Corporal Tanner "spoke most eloquently" to a small audience at the Albuquerque Opera House.[39] Most importantly, however, he left the territory with a better understanding of Crawford's business opportunities, and he would soon help to promote Jack's mining and ranching schemes.

Early in 1887, Captain Jack made plans to tour the territory with "The Campfire and the Trail." Although a complete itinerary has not been found, local press announcements help in documenting his busy schedule. In February he was booked for appearances in Chloride and Lordsburg, and in March he traveled to Arizona, performing before sell-out crowds in Tucson and Phoenix. Later in the spring, he entertained at the Garcia Opera House in Socorro and at Union Hall in Albuquerque. A writer for the *Socorro Bullion* who witnessed Crawford's performance avowed, "Captain Jack not only possesses talent, but what is far greater, genius, the rare gift of God to artists and poets." [40]

The Socorro press also published a lengthy article in March, captioned "A Coming Star—Our Poet Scout," announcing Jack's forthcoming departure for New York to appear in a frontier drama, for the impressive salary of 125 dollars per week and expenses. Crawford's star, indeed, was on the rise. The same article reported that publishers were beginning to pay for his compositions. For a poem published in *Texas Siftings,* a popular humor magazine, Crawford had received a twenty-five-dollar check.[41]

While Captain Jack was enjoying public acclaim, Jim Carlin had fallen on hard times. Undoubtedly, the underlying cause of Jim's problems was alcohol. That Jack came to his rescue on this and later occasions attests to facets of Crawford's character already touched upon—his generosity and warmheartedness.

In November 1886, Carlin and a former associate, Joe Dixon, started working on the *Inter-Republics,* an El Paso, Texas, newspaper. Within three months, however, they resigned their jobs and joined local businessman Captain W. H. Kingsbery on a trip to San Lucas Springs, Mexico, apparently in an effort to spy out investment opportunities. In a letter to Jack describing his plight, Carlin said that in Mexico he got into a "row and had to skip." Most likely his row had been a drunken brawl, for when rumors of his extradition surfaced, he became "scared to death," fearing he had killed a man.[42]

Possibly not knowing the reason for his hasty departure, Dixon publicly accused Carlin of having decamped with Kingsbery's horse, money, and other valuables. Meanwhile, Crawford sent his friend sufficient funds to tide him over until the controversy died down. Fearing arrest, Carlin had planned to leave New Mexico under yet another assumed name, promising to keep Crawford informed of his whereabouts. But Carlin was not arrested, nor did he leave the territory under another name. In May 1887, the *Las Vegas Daily Optic* announced that the two friends had passed through the city, Jack to star on the New York stage and Jim apparently going with him.[43]

En route east, Crawford staged "The Campfire and the Trail" in a number of towns stretching from Trinidad, Colorado, to Kansas City, Missouri.[44] While in St. Louis, in mid-August, he wrote to Maria of financial matters. He had received word that someone had jumped Grapevine Spring, intending to sell it; consequently, he urged his son Harry to ride out to investigate. Jack also suggested that Maria sell the piano and other household goods if she needed cash. He would leave for New York City in a few days, he assured Maria, and hoped to secure funds there from business associates W. S. Thomas and H. K. Thurber.[45]

Crawford arrived in New York about the time that newspapers reported on new disturbances among Ute Indians in Colorado. At least four different New York City journals carried long interviews with the Poet Scout, presenting his views on "the Indian question." His experience as a military scout had shaped his thinking about Indian policy, and like most army officers, he believed that the War Department should control Indian affairs. The army, Jack maintained, would see that Indians received their supplies instead of having them stolen by "thieving Indian agents." Then, if Indians left their reservation, the army would quickly go in pursuit and punish them severely. Crawford believed that Indians should be treated fairly, but he depicted the leader of the disgruntled Utes as a treacherous, cunning savage who should be separated from other members of his tribe.[46] Crawford would have even more to say about Indian policy after serving four years with the Justice Department investigating illegal liquor sales to Indians.

Upon reaching New York City, Crawford immersed himself in preparations for opening *On the Trail; or, Daniel Boone, the Avenger,* in which he played the leading role. On September 4, he wrote Maria a long letter, only a portion of which survives. He again referred to financial difficulties, but confidently predicted that he would "soon be fixed and all of us will share in the glory." "Remember now," he admonished Maria, "we are pulling together." He concluded his letter: "Love to all. I must go for my costume. . . . Your affectionate husband, Jack."[47]

Crawford opened with the play in Brooklyn and then toured throughout the East. His company of thirty-four people, including cowboys and Indians, traveled in its own special railway cars. A parade, featuring a brass band and two dens of wild animals, was staged each day of the performance. Although one publicist denied the show was a "blood-and-thunder" drama, plenty of thrilling scenes and desperate encounters enlivened this portrayal of pioneer life in Kentucky. Crawford played to packed houses in Pennsylvania and New York, invariably receiving praise in the reviews. One critic wrote, "Capt. Jack was very much at home in the title role and proved that a scout, this one at least, can portray thrilling scenes on the stage as well as pass through them in real life."[48]

Jack spent Christmas with the Tanners in Brooklyn and then started through the East again with *On the Trail.*[49] But he had become disenchanted with the play, disliking some of its "vulgar gags and suggestive witticisms." He also claimed that the role of Daniel Boone was "an utter exaggeration." Consequently, he left the company in late January or early February 1888.[50]

Meanwhile, Maria continued supervising family affairs in

New Mexico. Tradition credits her with writing the reports that Jack submitted as custodian of the Fort Craig reservation. She also oversaw the activities of her growing children. As popular teenagers, Eva and Harry frequently attended social events in San Marcial and nearby communities. In September 1887, seventeen-year-old Eva boarded a train for Topeka, Kansas, to enroll in Bethany College, a woman's institution that the Episcopal church operated.[51]

On the ranch, Maria was assisted by an Hispanic couple living on the premises. Jack employed other workers as well to help manage his substantial ranching activities. Tax assessment records for 1887 show that he kept on his Fort Craig ranch four horses, eight ponies, four colts, two mules, two burros, thirty cows, five bulls, thirty-five stock cattle, and ten oxen. He also paid taxes on five wagons, two carriages, and a blacksmith shop in San Marcial, which he probably rented to another party.[52]

After leaving the Daniel Boone Company, Captain Jack remained on the East Coast to further his stage career. He spent about three months in Boston, entertaining in homes of the elite, reciting poetry at Grand Army functions, and performing "The Campfire and the Trail." In the spring he signed a contract with Sheridan Corbyn, a theatrical manager, to tour in *Fonda; or, the Trapper's Dream*, previously staged in San Francisco with the title *California through Death Valley*. Corbyn agreed to finance the venture, while Crawford agreed to write several new songs to strengthen the performance. *Fonda* opened in Keyport, New Jersey, on August 24—and closed two days later, when Corbyn failed to come up with funds to keep the company afloat.[53]

The irrepressible Captain Jack immediately traveled to New York City, promising to secure a new manager and to continue touring with *Fonda*. To gain pocket money, he performed "The Campfire and the Trail," receiving fifty dollars for an evening's entertainment.[54] By mid-September, however, he was stumping the city on behalf of the Republican party and in support of Benjamin Harrison's bid for the presidency. Crawford delivered more than fifty speeches and contributed several campaign songs and verses before the electioneering ended.[55] Although this was his first plunge into national politics, Jack had labored unsuccessfully with other territorial Republicans in 1884 to elect L. Bradford Prince as New Mexico's delegate to Congress.[56] Neither Prince nor the Republican party would forget Crawford's loyalty.

Following the campaign, Jack organized a new theatrical company and toured with *Fonda* throughout the East. He struggled financially to keep the show afloat, driving himself nearly into exhaustion. Mrs. Tanner admonished Jack in a Christmas letter: "Do begin to take some rest, in some way. Do let some one else do what they can do to relieve you. You were worn out and run down when you started and have been in hell ever since."[57]

Crawford's play was well received, judging from extant reviews. A writer for the Charlottesville, Virginia, press avowed: "Those who failed to see 'Fonda' at the Opera House last week missed a great treat, perhaps the best play that has been presented this season, certainly the most unique." After praising Jack's talent as actor and writer, the reviewer asserted, "Captain Jack Crawford is today the most picturesque figure of American *genre.*"[58]

The same writer announced that Crawford was at work on a new play, which he hoped to perform the following season. This announcement, in conjunction with a reference in Mrs. Tanner's Christmas letter, suggests that Carlin was traveling with the Crawford theatrical company. Later, in 1889, the Poet Scout copyrighted a drama that he had written with his friend's aid, entitled *Tat; or, Edna, the Veteran's Daughter.* He again copyrighted the play in 1896 with the title, *The Mighty Truth; or, In Clouds or Sunshine.*[59] When Carlin later achieved distinction as the western journalist James Barton Adams, he refused to allow his name to be associated with the play. He preferred giving Crawford all the credit, he said, in gratitude for his steadfast support and encouragement.[60]

While critics were lauding Jack's performance in *Fonda,* the Senate confirmed the appointment of James Tanner as commissioner of pensions on March 26, 1889. A true friend of veterans, Tanner quickly informed the nation of his philosophy: "A pension for every surviving soldier who needs one; and no soldier's widow, father or mother should be in want."[61] By reversing the previous administration's conservative approach, the new commissioner became entangled in bitter controversy and was forced to resign in mid-September. Nonetheless, like thousands of other veterans, the Poet Scout benefited financially from his friend's generous policy, with his pension increasing from seventeen dollars to twenty-four dollars per month.[62]

During Tanner's short tenure as commissioner, Crawford sought employment with the government as special agent in the Justice Department. He solicited letters of recommendation from influential friends, including L. Bradford Prince, recently appointed governor of New Mexico, and H. K. Thurber, the New York capitalist. Both Tanners supported Jack's quest. In a letter to Attorney General William H. H. Miller, dated May 28, Commissioner Tanner wrote: "I will come and see you daytime or nighttime, sunshine or storm, to advance [Crawford's] interest." Mrs. Tanner and twenty other members of the Women's Christian Temperance Union also petitioned Miller.[63]

With a family friend as commissioner, Eva Crawford journeyed to Washington in late May to "accept a position in the pension bureau."[64] Apparently, she had remained at Bethany College no more than a year or so; and how long she stayed in Washington cannot be determined. Nonetheless, during the month of June, Eva and Captain Jack took in the "magnificent sights" of the nation's capital. On one occasion, she helped her father stage a temperance lecture at Fort Myers, proudly noting in a letter published in the

San Marcial Reporter that she had persuaded six soldiers to sign the pledge.[65]

Meanwhile, eighteen-year-old Harry Crawford also was receiving public notice. In June 1889, he succeeded Captain Jack as custodian of the Fort Craig reservation, a fitting replacement since young Crawford already was managing the family ranch. An excellent horseman, Harry took first place in San Marcial's Fourth of July horse-racing and steer-roping contests. By this date, however, his father had left Washington for St. Joseph, Missouri, where he proudly informed the local press of his son's achievements.[66]

Crawford was in St. Joseph to assume duties as a director of the New Era Exposition, billed as the greatest fair held in the U.S. since the Philadelphia Centennial Exposition. The month-long affair, opening September 3, called attention to the West's agricultural and mineral resources. Captain Jack's celebrity status, the press predicted, would help draw crowds to the exposition grounds. The *St. Joseph Herald,* in fact, referred to Crawford as "the famous poet-scout . . . who divides with Buffalo Bill the honor of being the most noted frontiersman of the country."[67]

Placed in charge of outdoor amusements and mineral displays, Crawford quickly dispatched letters to New Mexico soliciting ore specimens and planning to exhibit them in a building shaped like an Indian lodge, to be called the "Poet Scout's Wigwam." The New Mexico press enthusiastically supported his efforts. The *San Marcial Reporter,* for example, looked upon the exposition as the territory's golden opportunity to attract outside capital and urged every mining camp to send displays.[68]

Advertisements for the St. Joseph extravaganza, however, focused on Jack's primary role as amusement director, for Crawford planned to establish an Indian village at the fair and reenact scenes of Indian warfare by using Apaches from the San Carlos reservation. One scholar believes that to secure government permission for the Apaches to leave Arizona, Crawford had to strike a deal with Secretary of Interior John W. Noble. To appease Noble and other policymakers opposed to romanticizing tribal life, Jack agreed to place Apaches "in juxtaposition" with a group of Indian students from Haskell Institute at Lawrence, Kansas, so that visitors would clearly see the contrast between old Indian ways and progress achieved through education.[69] Although Noble eventually approved this plan, he required the Poet Scout to give bonds for the Apaches' safe return to Arizona.[70]

Crawford left St. Joseph in mid-August to visit his family, gather material for New Mexico's exhibit, and recruit Apaches. En route home, however, he encountered Major Trevanion T. Teel of El Paso, a former officer with Sibley's Confederate army. While exchanging war stories, Teel spoke of having buried several cannons in Albuquerque during the Confederate retreat from New Mexico in 1862. Before Crawford continued to San Marcial, Teel showed him the exact spot where the weapons had rested undisturbed for twenty-seven years. This revelation created a minor sensation among local residents, and workers soon excavated eight twelve-pound brass howitzers, "as bright as on the day when they were buried."[71]

Jack spent two days with his family before departing for San Carlos. There, he signed contracts with about fifty Apache men "to give public exhibitions of Indian life and character," in return for a fifteen-dollar monthly salary, traveling expenses, and "proper food and raiment."[72] When the northbound train carrying this contingent pulled into San Marcial a few days later, an eager throng crowded the depot, hoping to catch a glimpse of the Indians.[73]

Captain Jack and his charges reached St. Joseph on the evening of September 3. The Apaches immediately erected tepees on the southeast corner of the exposition grounds, amid tall trees and near a running stream. The forty-five-acre fairgrounds, in fact, contrasted sharply with the barren San Carlos reservation. Trees, lakes, waterfalls, and beautiful buildings dotted the landscape, while hundreds of electric lights were scattered through the trees. The five thousand prismatic lights encircling the central lake and festooning the bridges turned the grounds into a nighttime fairyland.[74]

Captain Jack pitched his tent at the Indian camp, making this his headquarters. Advertised as presenting a true picture of Indian life, the Apache village quickly became a main attraction. Its fifty-one men and ten women soon settled into a routine, preparing daily meals and bathing in the stream, seemingly unbothered by the stares of fairgoers. What struck white observers most forcibly was the natural beauty of the Indians—their slim bodies and muscular physiques. Initial disdain, which was apparent in newspaper stories announcing the Apaches' arrival, gave way to admiration. One reporter admitted that the "muscular development [of Apache men] is the envy of three-thirds of the dudish young gentlemen around town."[75]

Under Crawford's direction, the men gave daily exhibitions of Indian fighting in the amphitheater. On September 10, Jack added a new event to the program. In midafternoon, Apaches and "soldiers" staged a running battle along the creek banks, and in the fight culminating in Custer's last battle, Captain Jack portrayed the gallant Custer. The *St. Joseph Daily News* proclaimed in its evening edition: "This was decidedly the most realistic and exciting piece of work yet done by Captain Jack and his Indians." Thereafter, the "Custer Massacre" was staged each afternoon.[76]

The local press also called attention to the Haskell Indian students' encampment southeast of the "Temple of the Muses." Here, nineteen boys and nine girls demonstrated crafts taught at the institute, and the Haskell boys' band performed patriotic airs for the crowds.[77] By exhibiting the students in this manner, Secretary Noble wished to demonstrate the success of the government's assimilation program, but fairgoers exhibited a decided preference for Captain Jack's Apaches and their portrayal of Indian fighting and traditional culture. In interviews with the press, however, Crawford extolled the government's progress in "civilizing" Indians. The contrast between the San Carlos Apaches and the Haskell students, he stated, "shows that the government is doing a good work." But he also praised army efforts to change Indian behavior. Thanks to the work of men like Captain John L. Bullis, acting agent at the San Carlos Agency, Apaches only recently off the warpath, Crawford avowed, were becoming self-sufficient farmers.[78]

On September 12, Harry Crawford arrived in St. Joseph with a carload of broncos and burros that Captain Jack employed in his amphitheater entertainments.[79] Three days later, on a Sunday evening, young Crawford witnessed a devastating fire that broke out in Main Hall, which housed some of the most valuable machinery exhibitions. Within minutes, the building "was a roaring, seething mass of flame." Hundreds of men rushed to the scene to save the displays, but intense heat and suffocating black smoke drove them back. The shouts of men could be heard above the noise of falling timbers, crashing glass, and roaring flames. Into this inferno rushed Captain Jack and a man called Bronco John, leading a group of Apaches and cowboys who succeeded in rescuing the valuable coach of Revolutionary War hero LaFayette. Hardly anything else from the building was saved, with the total property loss amounting to more than a quarter of a million dollars. According to one report, the Studebaker Company (owners of the historic coach) sent Crawford's daughter a pony cart and harness in appreciation for Jack's courageous deed.[80]

Before the exposition closed in October, Captain Jack received expressions of gratitude from two very different delegations. Local stockmen adopted resolutions thanking him for the camp scenes staged each evening in the amphitheater. "Such startling realism," they claimed, "was never before placed before the public."[81] The Apaches also expressed appreciation by presenting him with small presents they had made themselves. An Apache spokesman told Crawford "that his followers thought well of the captain; that he had ever proven true to them, and they wanted him to remember them individually as they remembered him."[82]

Although twentieth-century reformers would decry placing Indians on display in Wild West and other exhibitions, this form of employment gave them a chance to see new places, earn money, and escape the boredom of reservation life. For the most part, the San Carlos Apaches must have enjoyed their stay in St. Joseph. Before leaving the city, they descended on Emery's Department Store to purchase blankets, undershirts, mirrors, beads, and other goods, and packing them in newly purchased trunks for their return trip to Arizona.[83]

On October 9, family and friends gathered at the San Marcial depot to await the arrival of Jack and the Apaches en route to the San Carlos reservation. Within two weeks of his reunion with Maria, however, Crawford received a telegram from Attorney General Miller informing him of his appointment as a special agent in the Department of Justice. By the end of the month, Jack was in Washington to receive instructions for his new assignment.[84]

Crawford had spent the last four years struggling for financial success on the stage. He would spend the next four on the government payroll, thereby achieving a measure of financial security for his family. Although his new work kept him constantly on the road, traveling to most western states and territories, Captain Jack continued writing poetry and staging "The Campfire and the Trail." He also collaborated with Jim Tanner and his son Harry in establishing a horse ranch in New Mexico. In his travels, however, Crawford missed the company of his children. And he never quite recovered from the loss of little May Cody Crawford, the child he called "Little Nugget."

> *Some call her blue eyes,*
> *And some call her pet,*
> *Violet and sunshine,*
> *And sweet mignonette;*
> *Golden hair, blue bird,*
> *And sweet little love,*
> *But I call her May flower,*
> *My little white dove.*[85]

John W. Crawford, photograph taken in Pottsville, Pennsylvania after the Civil War. (Courtesy Rio Grande Historical Collections, New Mexico State University Library.)

Captain Jack Crawford (center) at Cold Springs, six miles north of Custer City, 1876. (Photo by D. S. Mitchell, courtesy Jim Crain.)

*Deadwood City, in Whitewood Gulch, during the
Black Hills gold rush. (Photo by D. S. Mitchell, courtesy
Jim Crain.)*

*Captain Jack Crawford with actress Gertie Granville, as
they appeared on stage in San Francisco, 1877. (Courtesy,
The Bancroft Library.)*

Military quarters at Fort Craig, New Mexico, where Captain Jack served as post trader in the 1880s. (Courtesy Rio Grande Historical Collections, New Mexico State University Library.)

Captain Jack with Eva and Harry Crawford, ca. 1881, Fort Craig, New Mexico. (Courtesy Rio Grande Historical Collections, New Mexico State University Library.)

Captain Jack's general store at Fort Craig, New Mexico. (Courtesy Museum of New Mexico, Neg. No. 50893.)

Interior of Crawford residence at Fort Craig, New Mexico. (Courtesy Rio Grande Historical Collections, New Mexico State University Library.)

A second view of the interior of the Crawford residence at Fort Craig, New Mexico. (Courtesy Rio Grande Historical Collections, New Mexico State University Library.)

RESIDENCE AND STORE OF "CAPTAIN JACK,"
THE POET SCOUT,
CRAIG N.M.

Drawing of the Crawford residence and store at Fort Craig, New Mexico, 1885. (Courtesy Clarence Chrisman Album, Arizona Historical Society Library, Tucson.)

"Little Nugget," May Cody Crawford and dog Hero (beside carriage). (Courtesy Rio Grande Historical Collections, New Mexico State University Library.)

Publicity photograph of Captain Jack Crawford, probably taken in the 1880s. (Courtesy Rio Grande Historical Collections, New Mexico State University.)

Captain Jack Crawford and Will Visscher with a group of 6th U.S. Cavalry troopers at Tunnel Springs, near Fort Wingate, New Mexico, 1885. (Photo by Ben Wittick, courtesy School of American Research Collections in the Museum of New Mexico, Neg. No. 67682.)

The Crawfords and friends, Fort Craig, New Mexico. Numbered individuals are Captain Jack, Eva, Maria, and the second May Crawford. (Courtesy Rio Grande Historical Collections, New Mexico State University Library.)

Publicity poster showing Captain Jack as he appeared on stage in "The Campfire and the Trail." (Courtesy Rio Grande Historical Collections, New Mexico State University Library.)

Captain Jack and San Carlos Apaches at the New Era Exposition, St. Joseph, Missouri, 1889. (Courtesy Rio Grande Historical Collections, New Mexico State University Library.)

Family photograph taken in El Paso, Texas, 1895, showing left to right, Maria, Harry, Captain Jack, Dan Reckhart, Eva Reckhart, and May. (Courtesy Rio Grande Historical Collections, New Mexico State University Library.)

Eva, May, and Maria Crawford. (Courtesy Rio Grande Historical Collections, New Mexico State University Library.)

Captain Jack and crew sluicing on the banks of the Hootalinqua, 1898. (Courtesy Rio Grande Historical Collections, New Mexico State University Library.)

Captain Jack Crawford entertaining at Northwest Mounted Police Square, Dawson, Yukon Territory, 4th of July, 1899. (Photo by E.A. Hegg, courtesy Special Collections Division, University of Washington Libraries, Neg. No. 2353.

Captain Jack Crawford, social gathering, Dawson, Yukon Territory. (Photo by E.A. Hegg, courtesy Special Collections Division, University of Washington Libraries, Neg. No. 3146.)

Captain Jack entertaining at Onekama, Michigan with Isabel Crawford, 1909. (Courtesy Rio Grande Historical Collections, New Mexico State University Library.)

James Barton Adams, alias James Carlin, friend and confidant of Captain Jack. (Courtesy Rio Grande Historical Collections, New Mexico State University Library.)

Popular philosopher Elbert Hubbard and Captain Jack Crawford. Hubbard and his wife Alice drowned in 1915 in the sinking of the Lusitania. (Courtesy Rio Grande Historical Collections, New Mexico State University Library.)

Captain Jack Crawford and bust by sculptor August Zeller. (Courtesy Rio Grande Historical Collections, New Mexico State University Library.)

John W. Crawford in his later years. (Courtesy Rio Grande Historical Collections, New Mexico State University Library.)

Captain Jack Crawford, publicity photographs. (Courtesy Rio Grande Historical Collections, New Mexico State University Library.)

Captain Jack in "The Battle Cry of Peace," 1916. (Courtesy Rio Grande Historical Collections, New Mexico State University Library.)

7

SPECIAL AGENT

On November 10, 1889, Special Agent John W. Crawford wrote in a small notebook: "Arrived at Roman A. Baca's Ranch 3 miles from San Mateo at 7:30 . . . had supper and sent Juan my Indian guide to town. Two big campfires in the foot hills. Evidently Indians having a big dance and lots of drunks." Crawford was in the field on his first assignment for the Justice Department. He had orders from Attorney General Miller to investigate reports that Thomas Hye, accused of operating "a disreputable den" at the Chaco ruins, about twenty miles east of the Navajo reservation, was selling whiskey to the Navajos.[1]

Captain Jack and San Carlos Apaches at the New Era Exposition, St. Joseph, Missouri, 1889. (Courtesy Rio Grande Historical Collections, New Mexico State University Library.)

Chapter 7

Since the colonial era, government officials had tried to prevent the sale of whiskey to American Indians. Under the influence of alcohol, Indians behaved like other inebriates. They were unpredictable, prone to violence, and willing to exchange their finest possessions for the troublesome substance. Although congressional trade and intercourse acts made it illegal to sell liquor to Indians, whiskey dealers reaped such enormous profits from the illegal trade that complete prohibition was impossible.[2]

Crawford was ideally suited for the job of investigating violations of the intercourse acts. A longtime foe of intoxicants, Crawford took special delight in ferreting out unscrupulous whiskey dealers who preyed on Native Americans, and he was not afraid to take chances while pursuing his quarry. Moreover, he respected Indians and felt comfortable in their company. He also was sympathetic to the government's assimilation program, and like other reformers he viewed whiskey as a great evil threatening to undermine this undertaking.

Although his job with the Justice Department was a mere interlude in his entertainment career, Crawford's experiences as special agent added to his credentials as a western personality. In the course of his travels he met all sorts of people—tough characters, dedicated public servants, and disgruntled Indians and white citizens. From all sections of the country, he gathered material that he would later use on stage and in printed compositions. And he continued to entertain before select audiences, perfecting his lecture style and keeping his name before the public.

At the time Crawford assumed duties as special agent, the Navajo tribe lived on a vast reservation stretching across northeastern Arizona and northwestern New Mexico. With a population of about eighteen thousand, the Navajos were enjoying greater prosperity "than at any previous time in their history." Conflicts between Navajos and settlers were on the increase, however, as each group vied to control public grazing on lands adjacent to reservation boundaries.[3] The seemingly endless flow of whiskey into this contested area further exacerbated relations.

In late October, Crawford traveled to the Navajo reservation to begin a five-month investigation into violations of the intercourse acts. He would receive a salary of six dollars a day plus expenses. A diary he kept during part of this time, in conjunction with his expense account and the report he submitted to Attorney General Miller, document his extensive travels—by train, buckboard, and on horseback—in gathering evidence to combat the illegal whiskey trade.

At the start of his investigation, Crawford consulted with Indian Agent C. E. Vandever at the Navajo Agency at Fort Defiance, a few miles west of the New Mexico–Arizona border. Later at Fort Wingate, near modern Gallup, he acquired the services of a guide and interpreter who was fluent in English, Spanish, and Navajo.[4] Shortly thereafter, Jack met with a handful of local ranchers who bitterly complained of off-reservation Navajos stealing cattle, attributing much of the trouble to the ease with which the Indians acquired liquor. W. H. Hulvey claimed that whiskey dealers paid only $1.25 per gallon for whiskey in Albuquerque and then traded a bottle of this "poison" to Indians for a sheep or other valuables—horses, silver belts, bridles, saddles, and rawhide lariats (made from the hides of stolen cattle).

On his way to the Chaco ruins, Crawford spent a night at the Baca Ranch, northeast of modern Grants, where he learned that Indians had stolen a mare and colt from Baca a few days earlier. At George Howard's Hidden Spring Ranch, on the continental divide, he met with ten Navajo headmen who were eager to speak "with the long-haired chief from Washington." Their spokesman, identified by Crawford as Nah-Bone, remarked that the majority of his people were opposed to whiskey and wanted to help Crawford "kill the whole business." On November 14, Jack continued on to Hye's place, but the suspected culprit was already in Albuquerque

Chapter 7

standing trial on two indictments, "one brought by Agent Vandever for selling liquor to Indians and one for polygamy." Finding
no further evidence of wrongdoing at Chaco, Crawford returned
to Fort Wingate.

With less than two days of rest, Crawford was on the move
again. This time his destination was Chavez Station, about twenty-
five miles east of Wingate on the Atlantic and Pacific Railroad,
where Navajos reportedly obtained whiskey at José E. Montoya's
store. Disguised as a cowboy, Jack sauntered into the establishment, purchased a cigar, and then returned outside, observing several Indians going around to the rear of the building. He later
learned that liquor had been handed to the Indians "through a
dark hole from the cellar" to conceal the identity of the whiskey
dispenser. Crawford spent the night sleeping on the depot floor,
before boarding a morning train for Wingate. Shortly thereafter, he
presented his findings to a grand jury in Albuquerque.

Jack seemed to thrive on this constant movement. Moreover, he derived pleasure from the rough camaraderie of the men
he encountered, and he relished the dangerous nature of his work.
In fact, his boundless energy and a work ethic that sanctified long
hours and tired limbs made him an exemplary public servant. But
he saw his family infrequently. He did spend Thanksgiving at
home, however, and then worked a day or two on his mining
claims in the San Andres. On December 1, he awoke to a beautiful
Sunday morning and wrote in a small notebook: "All quiet and still
as a summer's dream. The sun shines as brightly and as warm as if
it were the first of June instead of December." That afternoon, he
and Maria entertained a few friends with an elaborate dinner and
poetry recitations.[5]

The next day Crawford boarded a train for Albuquerque,
where he received appointments as deputy U.S. marshal for Arizona and New Mexico. He soon took a night train to Gallup, and
then spent a day or two in the area gathering evidence of illegal

liquor sales. On December 10, he started for Fort Defiance with Agent Vandever.[6]

But the Navajo agent was too ill to accompany Jack on the next leg of his investigation, a forty-mile horseback ride to Ganado, a trading post operated by the now-famed Indian trader Clinton N. Cotton. Cotton had worked as a telegraph operator for the Atlantic and Pacific Railroad before joining Lorenzo Hubbell, in 1884, as a partner in Hubbell's expanding Indian trading business. Crawford described Cotton as a genial fellow, who treated "the white man and the Indian as brothers."[7] While spending the night at Ganado, Crawford learned that two men in a spring wagon had camped between Ganado and Keam's Canyon and were selling liquor to Indians. Before they had disposed of all their wares, however, Indians not only stole their horses but fired at them— sufficient warning to cause the whiskey dealers to flee the reservation. Crawford thoroughly enjoyed his visit to Cotton's emporium and, in fact, purchased thirty dollars worth of Navajo blankets before leaving.[8]

A snowstorm and train wreck delayed Crawford's return to Albuquerque. But two days after his arrival, he left that city to investigate illegal liquor sales at La Posta, a way station on the main road between Santa Fe and Fort Wingate. Jack reached his destination late on the afternoon of December 20. Immediately, he spied some Indians camped on the edge of the village drinking whiskey from beer bottles. He asked an Indian who spoke some English where he got the whiskey; the man pointed to the village. Accompanied by W. J. Johnson, a local rancher who had joined him earlier that day, Jack rode into the settlement. From an Anglo resident, he learned that two Hispanic traders had been "selling liquor to the Indians almost openly and . . . sending it to them by Mexican sheep herders." Jack concluded that the only way to catch the lawbreakers was to send a Hispanic deputy to investigate, since Anglos were "looked upon with suspicion and watched." Crawford's investigations were not without personal risk. He later told Attorney General Miller that he had concealed his identity as a special agent in La Posta, fearing "an assassin's bullet."[9]

From La Posta Crawford rode to the Chaco ruins to investigate new reports that Thomas Hye and his partner were again selling liquor. He found "no truth" in these rumors, but two miles from the ruins Crawford encountered Nah-Bone and four other Navajos, who directed him to a clump of trees about two miles away. There, Jack came upon Thomas Hurley sound asleep beside a smoldering fire, with two five-gallon kegs and several beer bottles littering the ground. While the Indians observed from the sidelines, Crawford awoke and questioned Hurley. Captain Jack then handcuffed the man, informing him that there was sufficient evidence "to send him [away] for a long term." Crawford then implemented a rusc that convinced him that Hurley had been selling liquor to Indians. Jack asked the handcuffed man if he had ever seen him before; the answer was no. "Yes, you have," said Jack, "but you did not recognize me when I was disguised as an Indian." Crawford later reported to Miller that this announcement had caused Hurley to "blanch and tremble."[10]

Still, Crawford had no intention of escorting Hurley to the nearest jail, for the evidence—all hearsay—would not hold up in court. Consequently, Crawford intentionally relaxed his guard that night, allowing his captive to sneak away under cover of darkness, eventually making his way into Mexico. Hurley's escape, Crawford contended, "was better than half a dozen arrests," for news of his encounter with Crawford had caused at least half of the illegal whiskey dealers to leave the country.

Jack returned to his family on Christmas Day. But, on December 28, he boarded a train for Albuquerque and spent the next week in conferring with Agent Vandever, who was in town with nine prominent Navajos visiting the Albuquerque Indian school.

School officials staged a special program for the visitors, during which Captain Jack "delivered one of his characteristic and [inimitable] lectures" and a young Indian student recited the address of Spartacus to the gladiators.[11]

Shortly thereafter, Crawford traveled to the Navajo Agency with Vandever to prepare for a trip north to the San Juan River country, near the New Mexico–Colorado border. A report of deep snow in the mountains, however, forced Jack to cancel his journey. Meanwhile, he had received information from a friend in Tularosa, a small village near the Mescalero Apache reservation in southeastern New Mexico, that several Hispanos "were selling liquor to Indians openly." Consequently, Crawford returned to Fort Craig in mid-January 1890 and then spent four days driving a team and buckboard east across the desert to the Mescalero Agency. By the time he reached the agency, however, the whiskey dealers had already been arrested and were in jail awaiting trial.[12]

Crawford enjoyed a few days of rest at home before continuing his investigations. During this respite, he staged a two-hour entertainment in San Marcial to benefit the school-building fund.[13] On February 2, however, he boarded a train for Albuquerque and then traveled to Fort Defiance to join Agent Vandever and Indian investigator Arthur M. Tinker for a trip north to investigate the recent murder of an Indian. The passions of the northern Navajos had become so inflamed that newspaper stories raised the specter of another Indian war, claiming that Navajos threatened to massacre white settlers in the area.[14]

After battling snowdrifts, the three government agents reached the San Juan on February 23, and two days later they held a council with the Indians. According to the Navajos, their kinsman had been killed while hunting on grazing lands claimed by whites. Cowboys discovered him skinning a deer and opened fire, thinking the animal was one of their steers. The agents could do nothing more than listen; newspapers later announced, however, that the courts would intervene in this tragedy. Crawford went on to investigate rumors of illegal whiskey sales in nearby Farmington, before rejoining Vandever and Tinker for the return trip to Defiance. From there he proceeded to Fort Craig for a two-day visit with his family, and then on March 10 he departed for the nation's capital.[15]

Jack spent more than five weeks in Washington, conferring with Justice Department officials and socializing with his old friend Jim Tanner. Following his resignation as commissioner of pensions, Tanner had remained in Washington to become a pension agent, filing claims for hundreds of veterans seeking government pensions. In late March, the Tanners staged a reception for Crawford at their home in Georgetown. A Washington correspondent reporting on the event referred to Captain Jack as "one of the best known characters of the wild and wooly west." While in the capital, Crawford also addressed a large gathering at the Foundry Methodist Church on behalf of the Women's Christian Temperance Union.[16]

Crawford's next assignment was to investigate illegal whiskey sales on the Cheyenne River Indian Reservation in South Dakota. He reached Forest City, on the east side of the Missouri River and across from the reservation, on May 2 and devoted the next two weeks to gathering evidence. One informant, Agnes Lockhart, ran the government school at what was known as Charger's Camp. She assured Jack that Indians had been getting liquor off the reservation. Other informants who had encountered drunken Indians in Jacob Kluth's store, on the east side of the river, were in full agreement. Although it was difficult to persuade Indians to testify against Kluth, Jack compiled evidence of illegal whiskey sales, turning it over to a U.S. attorney before starting on another assignment.[17] From South Dakota, Crawford traveled to the Flathead Agency in Montana and then south to Indian Territory, a land seemingly awash in illegal whiskey. On both assignments, Crawford interviewed local residents, conferred with government agents, and then submitted detailed reports to Washington.[18]

Jack returned to New Mexico in mid-July 1890. By this time he was making plans to establish a horse ranch in the San Andres Mountains east of Fort Craig. During his recent stay in Washington, he and Jim Tanner had sat "very late for several nights," discussing the future. Tanner, who was making good money from the pension business, predicted that within fifteen months he could invest twenty-five thousand dollars in Jack's mining and ranching ventures. Tanner envisioned a first-class horse ranch, with young Harry Crawford managing the enterprise.[19]

Jack already had begun making improvements on Grapevine Spring, preparatory to stocking the site with horses. While in the East, he purchased and shipped to his son three blooded stallions with the intention of offering stud services to other ranchers for a fee. With characteristic optimism, Jack wrote to Maria in late April, while en route to South Dakota, "Jim [Tanner] is going to put all the money into the business that I will want, and in 24 months from today I will owe no man a dollar." By the close of the following year (1891), about forty mares grazed on the Grapevine ranch.[20]

Crawford spent the last two weeks of July at Fort Craig, before departing on his next assignment. During this time, he traveled to his mines in the San Andres, where he undoubtedly visited with Jim Carlin, who had returned to New Mexico several weeks earlier. In announcing Carlin's arrival, the *Las Vegas Daily Optic* had stated that he planned "to rusticate for several months" on the ranch of his old friend Captain Jack. In fact, Carlin soon took up residence in a tent at Dripping Spring, where, during the next two years, he performed editorial work for Crawford—typing reports to Washington and revising Jack's manuscripts. Years later, long after Carlin had shed his bogus name, Crawford would intimate that his friend had sequestered himself in the San Andres to "dry out"—time well spent since he apparently conquered his addiction to alcohol.[21]

On July 30, Crawford departed for the Ponca Agency, in northeastern Nebraska, to investigate violations of the intercourse acts. He solicited testimony from Indian Agent James E. Helms and Rev. John E. Smith, missionary and teacher at the Ponca day school. This was about the time that the Poncas were allotted land in severalty, allowing the rest of their reservation to be opened to settlement by non-Indians—a change that may have contributed to a rise in illegal liquor sales. A year after allotment was implemented, Reverend Smith reported a "great deal of drinking" among the Poncas: "Many dollars which should be spent for useful and necessary articles are spent in the saloons of Niobrara." Jack kept detailed notes of his conversations with Billy Bingham, a local resident who admitted to having furnished Indians with liquor but claimed only to be a middleman for local saloon keepers. After spending three weeks in collecting testimony, Crawford left Nebraska for the Pacific Northwest.[22]

Crawford's ten-week stay on the coast would conclude with yet another brush with death—a terrifying train crash that left at least five people dead and scores injured. Jack plunged into his new assignment, however, with characteristic energy, investigating violations of the intercourse acts in Oregon, Washington, and Idaho. During these weeks he also gave entertainments, including one in Fairhaven, Washington, for the benefit of his friend Will Visscher, then working on the Fairhaven *Herald.*[23]

A case involving the Yakima Indians of Washington consumed most of Crawford's time. Jack had traveled west with specific orders to protect the rights of the Yakimas to traditional salmon-fishing grounds on the Columbia River, south of their reservation. Establishing his headquarters at The Dalles, Oregon, near the site of the fisheries, Crawford quickly went into action. He and other government agents believed the Yakimas were being victimized by O. D. Taylor, a minister of the gospel who wanted to monopolize the fisheries. Although Taylor was under a court order restraining him from interfering with the Indians' fishing privileges, Taylor had cut off their access by fencing the trails leading to the fisheries. Shortly after his arrival, Crawford removed these obstructions, justifying his actions by saying that the Yakimas, "poor inoffensive wards of our big government, were being abused and cruelly ill treated." In fact, on three different occasions, Jack removed Taylor's fences, only to have Taylor's agents rebuild them.[24]

Finally, during the first week of November, Taylor was tried in federal court in Walla Walla for ignoring the court's restraining order. Although Crawford escorted five Indian witnesses to testify against the preacher, the case went against the government. Special Indian Agent Thomas Lang, in reporting the verdict to Indian Commissioner Thomas J. Morgan, claimed that Taylor had bribed witnesses and employed money in other ways to destroy the government's case. But he praised Captain Jack, stating that Crawford had "been unwearying in preparing the cause for the court and [had] done what but few men could do so efficiently and understandingly."[25] Despite the government's efforts to protect Indian fishing rights, a year after Taylor's trial the Yakimas still were not catching many fish because of "trails being fenced and fish wheels being placed in the Columbia River."[26]

On November 12, 1890, Crawford boarded an evening train in Portland, bound for California and then home. At about 8:15 P.M., near Salem, Jack was tossed from his berth when the trestle crossing Lake Labish collapsed under the front engine's weight. Several people in Jack's car were badly hurt in this terrible disaster, which left five dead and more than one hundred injured, including the Poet Scout. The most severely injured were carried to nearby farmhouses on litters and in wagons filled with straw. Although Jack's injuries were less serious, for weeks after returning home he would walk with the aid of a cane.[27]

Crawford returned to Fort Craig on November 20 and

spent the next week or two with Jim Carlin at Dripping Spring, recuperating from his injuries. From this "mountain resort," Jack wrote to a friend in Spokane Falls that he was enjoying the "rough life, wearing old clothes and eating unrefined grub." He found the mountain air invigorating and relished strolls up the canyon, where a tiny stream issued from an overhanging cliff.[28] This break from official duties also allowed Jack time to write, to exchange ideas with Carlin, and to reflect on his recent experiences among Indians. It may have been at this time that Crawford wrote "Philip Faithful," a short story that revealed Jack's optimism about the future of American Indians. Because of his growing celebrity status and his importance as an interpreter of the American West, Crawford's thoughts on Indians are of more than passing interest.

Crawford's short story focused on Tahashta, a young Indian lad averse to waging war on white settlers. On his first war party, Tahashta saved the life of a white baby girl, whom he would later marry. Taking the name of Philip Faithful upon marriage, Tahashta thereafter chose to follow the path of the white man. In this story, Crawford not only exhibited faith in the government's assimilation program, but he also confirmed the Indians' humanity. He believed that Indians shared universal emotions with whites—love, grief, loyalty, and the desire for justice.[29] For his time, Crawford held liberal views of Indians, including the sanctioning of interracial marriages, which he depicted in poetry and short stories.

As a special agent for the Justice Department, Jack had the opportunity to know and to be associated with Indians of every kind. This experience, he believed, in addition to his work as a military scout, rendered him a reliable commentator on Indian policy. Crawford set forth his ideas in official reports, in published interviews, and in his public performances. His position on "the Indian question," however, was not too different from that of many army officers.

Jack had long supported the War Department in its efforts

to control Indian affairs. Nearly every Indian war in the West, he maintained, had been caused directly or indirectly by the Indian Bureau and by "dishonest, unscrupulous Indian agents." He believed that Indian agents rarely had control over reservation Indians, who frequently laughed at the ineffectual and often cowardly agents. Army officers, on the other hand, commanded respect with their six-shooters. Crawford claimed that Indians universally hated a coward and revered a brave man. He often told audiences that he and other scouts wore long hair because Indians believed it to be a badge of courage: a man going into battle with long hair showed that he was not afraid his scalp would be lifted.[30]

Like most army officers, Crawford looked upon reservations as temporary reserves where Indians would begin to learn about the American way of life. He fully supported the Dawes Severalty Act of 1887, which allotted reservation land to individual Indians. Like the optimistic reformers who sponsored the bill, Crawford believed Indians were capable of great change and that private ownership would lead to their ultimate assimilation into American society. Inspired by their white neighbors cultivating the land, Indians would begin to think that "if the white man can raise grain and make himself comfortable, they can do likewise."[31]

Crawford also promoted Indian education, a key ingredient of the government's assimilation program. By the end of the 1880s federal schools were to be found on every reservation. Moreover, the success of the Carlisle Industrial Training School, founded in Carlisle, Pennsylvania in 1879, led to the establishment of additional off-reservation Indian boarding schools. During the Harrison administration (1889–93), however, Indian Commissioner Morgan unveiled a plan to establish a hierarchy of Indian schools: primary schools for each Indian village, then reservation boarding schools, culminating in off-reservation industrial schools.[32]

With firsthand knowledge of conditions on reservations,

Crawford advocated a system of schools that differed slightly from Morgan's. Crawford believed that education should be provided close to home and "under the eyes of the parents, who must thereby learn to respect education." During his travels, he had listened to Navajos complain about graduates of eastern schools who were of no benefit to their people when they returned to the reservation. Moreover, Jack abhorred the manner in which some children were secured for the off-reservation schools. He had witnessed "a child torn from his screaming mother's arms and hurried away." "Don't you suppose that mother has the same feeling in her breast for her young as your mother had for you?" he asked a reporter. Crawford advocated teaching reading and writing in reservation day schools. Students would then advance to reservation industrial schools, where boys would learn to farm and to breed horses, and girls would acquire homemaking skills. Graduates of reservation schools who wanted more education would be sent east for training in law, medicine, and other professions.[33] More sensitive to parental feelings than most reformers, Crawford continued to advocate this commonsense approach to Indian education in later years.

Still, Crawford was only one of many reformers advocating a comprehensive Indian education program. Neither his vision nor that of Commissioner Morgan, however, had much impact on the educational policies that government officials implemented in the early twentieth century. Superintendent of Indian Education Estelle Reel and Commissioner Francis Leupp, for example, now advocated manual training for Indian children to the exclusion of all other educational programs. In effect, they simply gave up the assimilation effort, believing as they did that Indians "occupied a station inferior to that of white Americans."[34]

Crawford remained in New Mexico about two months before resuming his official duties. While recuperating at Dripping Spring, he inscribed a copy of *The Poet Scout* for seven-year-old

Irma Cody, the daughter of Buffalo Bill. This was about the time that Cody returned to the U.S. following a successful tour of Europe with his sensational Wild West show. Earlier in the year, Jack had visited with Mrs. Cody in North Platte and was well posted on Cody's activities. Jack even composed a poem entitled "A Welcome to Papa," which Irma recited when Cody returned to his family.[35]

Crawford's days at home were filled with activity—trips to Chloride with Harry and other family members, excursions to the San Andres, and recitations at social gatherings.[36] On January 22, 1891, however, he left Fort Craig for Salt Lake City, where he received an appointment as deputy U.S. marshal for the district of Utah. He spent about three weeks investigating illegal liquor traffic on the Uintah and Ouray Ute Reservation and then departed for Green Bay, Wisconsin, to continue his investigations.[37]

The Green Bay press lionized Jack, with the *State Gazette* calling him "one of the best known Indian fighters and scouts the world has ever known—his fame as a poet is national."[38] During his stay in the city, Crawford entertained a large audience at the local G.A.R. hall and also took part in memorial services for the recently deceased General William T. Sherman. Most of his time, however, was spent in investigating affairs at the Green Bay Agency.[39]

Before leaving on his next assignment, Jack wrote a long letter to military author Captain Charles King, then embroiled in a literary dispute with Reuben B. Davenport, the *New York Herald* correspondent during the 1876 Sioux campaign. In his book *Campaigning with Crook*, published in 1880, King accused Davenport of cowardice and unmanly conduct during the Slim Buttes engagement. Davenport came across the book a decade later and threatened suit for libel. The "unjustly accused reporter" also solicited Captain Jack's aid. On February 2, 1891, Crawford's account of the Battle of Slim Buttes, which exonerated Davenport, appeared in the Milwaukee *Evening Wisconsin,* published in King's hometown. King soon admitted his error, but not before he and Captain Jack had exchanged barbs through the mail.[40]

During March and part of April, Jack was constantly on the road, investigating illegal sales of liquor in North Dakota and Montana. Whenever possible, he staged entertainments to benefit a worthy cause. At Fort Keogh, Montana, for example, proceeds from his platform appearances went to the Sunday schools, and at Miles City, to the G.A.R. relief fund.[41]

Crawford returned to New Mexico in mid-April and spent the next two and a half months at home, taking care of financial matters. He exchanged a series of letters with potential investors, discussing schemes for developing his properties. To Albert Scheffer of Saint Paul, Minnesota, Jack offered a half-interest in his San Andres mines, ranches, and horses, in exchange for five thousand dollars. Among other improvements, the money would be spent to build a three-mile pipeline "to bring water down Grape-vine canon, so my mares will not have so much climbing." Crawford went on to say: "There is also a house to build, a large canal, water troughs, etc., and I cannot do this, employ two men as I now do, pay taxes, and support my family on $6 per day." He made a similar offer to his friend Jim Tanner, who promised financial help as soon as he paid his own debts.[42]

Crawford also made improvements on his Fort Craig ranch. He recently had purchased a "New Pulsometer Steam Pump" to help in irrigating his fields. Having seen the pump at work in the Snake River country, Jack was convinced it would revolutionize farming in New Mexico. In late June, he demonstrated this pump to a group of invited guests. In less than eight minutes, he filled a tank with twenty-four hundred gallons of water pumped from his well. The local press matched Jack's enthusiasm, predicting the pump would "prove of untold benefit to the people of the arid regions of the southwest." Later, Jack composed "The

Song of the Pulsometer," a ten-stanza poem that the Pulsometer Steam Pump Company of New York used in its advertisements.[43]

On July 5, Crawford again left Fort Craig on official business. He would spend the next five and a half months in investigating violations of the intercourse acts in Minnesota and New York. In late November, he conferred with officials in Washington, D.C., where the *Post* ran a one-column article on the famous scout, noting that he had recently cut his hair. Jack explained, "I saw so many cranks here in the East wearing long hair that I thought I'd take mine off." A New Mexico wag, learning of this development, begged Jack in a five-stanza poem, published in the *San Marcial Reporter:* "Flee the barber's murderous scissors, / Seek no more his fatal chair; / Let it never more be spoken[,] / 'Captain Jack has cut his hair.' "[44]

At the end of November, Attorney General Miller ordered Crawford to return to New Mexico to investigate liquor traffic on or near the Navajo reservation. For several months local residents had been inundating government offices with new complaints about drunken Indians. C. N. Cotton claimed that "lots of whiskey" was being sold to Navajos at a saloon north of Wingate Station. In a letter to Indian Agent David L. Shipley, Cotton suggested that a special agent "be sent to stop this cursed traffic," adding that "special agent Crawford did good work in stopping it [a] couple years ago."[45]

A blizzard delayed Crawford's return to New Mexico, and then illness further curtailed his movements. Jack did not resume his official duties until late January 1892.[46] He spent the next seven months in New Mexico, but reports documenting his investigations during this time have not been found. It is evident, however, that Jack juggled his official responsibilities with an incredibly diverse range of other activities.

On January 26, for example, Crawford was in Santa Fe to help Governor L. Bradford Prince and other city luminaries in welcoming more than eighty members of the International League of Press Clubs en route east from San Francisco. The local press called this "by far the most important body that has ever visited New Mexico." By hosting a gala reception and then showing the eastern journalists as much of historic Santa Fe as possible on their overnight stay, Prince hoped to gain favorable coverage for New Mexico in the eastern press. The visitors included two of the nation's most celebrated women journalists, Kate Field, editor of *Kate Field's Washington,* and Mrs. Frank Leslie, a successful businesswoman who had taken over her late husband's bankrupt publishing house a decade earlier and turned it into a prosperous enterprise. It was Mrs. Leslie who invited Captain Jack, described in the press as "an old acquaintance," to join the party the next day for the short train ride to Las Vegas. From there the party was whisked away in carriages to the elegant Montezuma Hotel, where the visitors were treated like royalty. During this two-day interlude, Kate Field interviewed Captain Jack for her journal, and he entertained the journalists with his recitations.[47]

In February, Crawford twice traveled to the Navajo reservation to investigate liquor sales. A report from Chavez Station indicated that a large number of "armed and drunken Navajoes threatened to wipe out the population of that vicinity." The trouble arose over the shooting of a Navajo in a dispute with local cattlemen. One observer avowed that if whiskey were kept away from the reservation "these troubles would not occur."[48] Jack continued looking into these matters in March. But it is no longer possible to construct a complete itinerary of his travels or even to speculate on what he discovered.

During Jack's stay in New Mexico, however, the press kept readers informed of his many stage appearances. On March 2, for example, Crawford and his two daughters performed in a play in San Marcial to benefit the Methodist church. About two weeks later he was in Santa Fe, where Eva assisted him in entertaining a large audience at the courthouse. Described in the press as "the pride and glory of Jack Crawford's life . . . a charming and gifted girl," Eva delighted Santa Feans with several renditions of her father's poems. A few days later, she accompanied her father to Las Vegas for the opening of an irrigation convention. And still later that month, Jack and Eva were in El Paso, Texas, where they entertained a "large and cultured audience" that filled Myar Opera House during a Grand Army reunion.[49]

Jack spent much of April in traveling on official business. But he also found time to attend two important territorial events: the G.A.R. encampment that opened in Las Vegas on the seventh, and the Republican Convention held in Silver City a week later.[50] At the Las Vegas encampment, Jack was one of several speakers who entertained veterans and invited guests. The *Daily Optic* later reported that Captain Jack had been "the hit of the evening." The *Optic*'s review of Crawford's performance testifies to his amazing ability to capture an audience:

> From the time he opened his mouth till he shut it and sat down, amidst thunders of applause, he kept the audience in one continuous uproar. The *Optic*'s stenographer threw down his pen in despair and joined the general merriment. Humor flows from Capt. Jack like water from a sprinkling cart. Sometimes it falls upon you in a gentle and enjoyable shower, and then it pours upon you like a thousand torrents. . . . After he had occupied what he considered his proper portion of the time, he attempted to sit down, but the people would not have it. The encore was so deafening and showed so plainly that he must respond or it would continue all night, that the captain again took the stand and was funnier than before.

Jack closed the evening's campfire with a thirteen-stanza poem he had prepared especially for the occasion, entitled "The War's Humorous Side."[51]

On May 10, Crawford left Albuquerque on the evening train en route to the San Juan on official business. At Fort Wingate he joined up with members of the Navajo Commission, recently appointed by Secretary of Interior John W. Noble to investigate and report upon the mineral resources of the Carrizo Mountains on the Navajo reservation. For several years rumors had circulated that the Carrizos, in the extreme northeastern corner of Arizona, contained rich deposits of gold and silver. In 1890, a band of prospectors secretly began mining the area—only to be driven out by the army. Thereafter, pressure mounted to open this part of the Navajo reservation to mining.[52]

Crawford planned to ride north with the commission and then proceed to the San Juan with a guide. Not far into the journey, however, he became disenchanted with the government appointees, later voicing his complaints in correspondence published in the *Daily Optic.* Jack pointed out that the delegation included only one experienced prospector, hardly sufficient to survey such a large mineral district. According to Crawford, General Alexander M. McCook, who headed the commission, made only a cursory examination before concluding that the mountains lacked precious ores. Despite Jack's belief that the Carrizos contained immense wealth, the government dropped plans to negotiate their sale.[53]

Upon reaching the San Juan, Crawford wrote a twenty-five-page letter to Jim Carlin, describing his experiences since leaving Fort Wingate. Carlin subsequently edited and rewrote the letter, reducing it to twelve pages. He apparently then sent the letter to a San Francisco newspaper for publication under Crawford's signature.[54] Mention already has been made of Carlin's editorial work for Crawford. But, in fact, Carlin's importance to Captain Jack went beyond mere editorial assistance. During his stay at Dripping Spring, Carlin served as Jack's confidant, literary collaborator, and financial advisor. Their mutual dependence is revealed in a series of letters that Carlin wrote to Jack while the latter was traveling on official business.

While in residence at Dripping Spring, Carlin wrote to Jack as often as two and three times a week. In whimsical passages designed for his friend's amusement, Jim described the vicissitudes of New Mexico's weather and the eccentricities of an odd assortment of riding animals. Carlin's whimsy, however, failed to conceal a deep despondency occasioned by his reduced circumstances.[55] Still, the affection that flowed between the two men shines through Carlin's prose. In closing a lengthy missive, Carlin wrote: "Hope you will get here soon, and that you can stay long enough to get acquainted next trip. These flying visits are durned uncomfortin'. Like eating soup with your fingers." [56]

Carlin was not totally isolated at Dripping Spring. Freighters and military personnel from Fort Stanton occasionally stopped on their way to the railroad station at Lava. Carlin also traveled there to pick up mail and supplies. And during the summer of 1891, he left Dripping Spring for the Midwest, returning to New Mexico several weeks later with his son, Frank.[57] But during long stretches of solitude, Carlin turned his facile pen to Crawford's literary projects. He probably even helped to write some of Jack's poems, including "The McGinty Club," which Crawford dedicated to the famous El Paso club that enlivened the town's social life in the 1890s. Eva Crawford later married Daniel W. Reckhart, president of the organization, and its roster listed Jack as its official "Poet Liar-ate." The McGintys had given Jack a royal welcome in March 1892, during the Texas encampment of the G.A.R. Carlin's references, in two letters written shortly thereafter, to "[making] another try at McGinty tomorrow" and "I have a fair start on McGinty" leave little doubt that Jim had a hand in composing the poem.[58]

Carlin left New Mexico in August 1892, to visit his mother in Salina, Kansas. He soon reentered the world of journalism, writing under the name of James Barton Adams. In one of his final letters from Dripping Spring, however, Carlin outlined what Jack must do to achieve fame and fortune. First, he advised Jack to quit his government job and return to the lecture circuit. With only two lectures a week, he said, Crawford would double his present salary. Jack must also keep up his literary work. "When you are before the public every bookseller would want your books in stock—and your newspaper work would, like [Bill] Nye's, command a fancy price." To reduce expenses, Carlin advised Jack to move his family east, lease his Fort Craig and Dripping Spring ranches, and dispose of his cattle and low-grade mines, all of which never "made you a dollar." Carlin's parting advice became the road that Jack soon traveled: "Make the platform and literary field your leading calling." [59]

About the time that Carlin left New Mexico, James Tanner and son arrived to visit the Crawfords at their Fort Craig ranch. There is no way of knowing how much money Tanner eventually invested in Jack's enterprises. On this trip, however, Tanner purchased Austin Crawford's interest in the Monte Christo Mine in Chloride, making Tanner and Captain Jack its principal owners. About a month later, Crawford was in Washington, D.C., to attend the national encampment of the Grand Army. Undoubtedly, the two friends again discussed Jack's financial prospects. But Jack's stay in Washington was brief. After obtaining a leave of absence from the Justice Department, Crawford left the capital for New York City, to campaign for the Republican party. [60]

The 1892 presidential campaign focused on personalities more than on issues. Still, incumbent Benjamin Harrison and other Republican leaders vigorously upheld the protective tariff. Crawford parroted the party line, writing a campaign song, entitled "God and Protection," to woo Irish voters. Captain Jack stumped tirelessly for the Republicans. According to one account, he addressed one or more political meetings every night. A Republican official called him "a vote maker," since he both entertained and instructed his audience. People looked forward to his campaign ditties. A favorite, entitled "When Grover Cleveland Gets a Second Term," began:

Some funny things will happen, just as sure as you are born,
When Grover Cleveland gets a second term.
The sun will in the evening rise, and set in early morn,
When Grover Cleveland gets a second term.[61]

Unable to extend his leave, Crawford resumed his official duties about the time that Cleveland achieved his resounding victory at the polls. In late November, Crawford was in Tama, Iowa, investigating violations of the intercourse acts at the Sac and Fox Agency. After spending Christmas at home, he traveled to Wisconsin to continue his investigations.[62] In late January 1893, Jack was in the Dakota Black Hills, where, in addition to his official duties, he gave two entertainments in Deadwood to raise funds to protect Wild Bill Hickok's grave. While in South Dakota, Crawford received his first letter from seven-year-old "Darling Little May." In honor of the occasion, he composed a poem for his daughter, enclosing it in a letter, which he ended with these words: "Give my love to Mama, Eva, and don't forget to corall [*sic*] a big lot for yourself."[63]

Crawford returned to New Mexico, in late March, to undertake yet another investigation on the Navajo reservation. But his work for the government was coming to an end. Faced with a Democratic administration in Washington and buoyed by Carlin's advice, Crawford resigned his post as of June 1.[64]

For almost four years, John W. Crawford had served his government as special agent for the Justice Department. With energy and determination, he compiled evidence that helped to rid Indian reservations of "vile" whiskey dealers. His association with Indians allowed him to speak with authority on Indian policy. His celebrity status gave his views more importance nationally than would otherwise have been the case. But the dream of fame and fortune—to match that of Bill Cody—remained as strong as ever.

Chapter 7

Still optimistic that the dream was within reach, Captain Jack spent
the next five years on the lecture circuit, entertaining thousands
of Americans with his unique mixture of humorous and heartrending western stories. On the stage, Crawford was able to capitalize
on the nation's growing nostalgia for bygone days. The same nostalgia often seared Jack's spirit, but unlike most people in his audience, Captain Jack had experienced the dangers and wild scenes
that he so vividly described.

> *Ah! yes, it is the same old trail I rode in other days;*
> *It winds along the Mesa to the top of yonder raise,*
> *And echoes that are borne to me sing peace on every side,*
> *And yet there's something missing from the trail I used*
> *to ride.*[65]

8

IN SEARCH OF
FAME AND FORTUNE

The year 1893 was not soon forgotten by the American people. Ushered in with a smug optimism that was reflected in the Chicago World's Columbian Exposition, it ended twelve months later with the nation reeling from a full-scale depression. The winter of 1893–94 saw 20 percent of the work force unemployed and ill-clad men wandering the countryside looking for work. It was an inauspicious time for the forty-six-year-old Poet Scout to embark on a platform and writing career. Indeed, while the nation struggled to overcome this economic crisis, Crawford labored relentlessly to propel himself into the front ranks of public speakers. At the same time, he schemed to develop his mining claims and inundated popular magazines with his manuscripts. He was to experience both joy and disappointment in his quest of the American Dream.

Yet despite the Panic of 1893, middle-class Americans continued their pursuit of self-education with almost as much intensity as they had done so in earlier years. They flocked to chautauqua grounds in the summer and filled lecture halls throughout the

Crawford and dog Hero in tent, probably on the banks of the Hootalinqua, 1898, during the Klondike gold rush. (Courtesy Rio Grande Historical Collections, New Mexico State University Library.)

year. Captain Jack was one of many professional speakers to benefit from this long-entrenched American habit of listening to lectures for amusement and enrichment. By the time the economy regained stability in 1898, he would be recognized as among the country's most popular platform entertainers. More significantly, he had also become an important molder of public opinion; through his poetry and stories, he taught Americans about the western experience.[1]

Before the depression hit bottom in 1894, Crawford had reason to feel confident of success. The previous year, a Detroit news story described both Jack and California poet Joaquin [Cincinnatus Hiner] Miller, a literary sensation in England and the United States during the 1870s, as established poets and men of action. Entitled "Western Warblers," the article featured a drawing of Captain Jack dressed in the buckskin outfit he wore on stage. Although Miller was only a few years older than Crawford, the story referred to him as "quite an old man, in complete retirement, almost a hermit," while "Crawford is considered quite a young man [whose] latest effusions breathe the very spirit of ardent and aspiring youth."[2]

Crawford also received wide recognition that year, during the Chicago Exposition commemorating the four-hundredth anniversary of Columbus's discovery of the New World. White City, the name bestowed on this "neo-classical wonderland" on the Lake Michigan shore, celebrated America's progress and inspired an outpouring of praise from many of its twenty-seven-and-a-half million visitors. The Chicago *Herald,* for July 30, carried a one-column story headlined "Scout and Reformer, Jack Crawford Visits the Fair," in which the Poet Scout recorded his delight with the spectacle. Calling Jack "the modern Leather-Stocking and pathfinder of the Black Hills," the *Herald* summarized his eventful career for its readers.[3]

Crawford had traveled to Chicago to oversee publication

of a new book of poetry and to take part in a New Mexico Day celebration at the exposition. For more than a year, territorial politicians labored to make sure that New Mexico was well represented at Chicago. Foremost in their minds was the issue of statehood. By advertising New Mexico's agricultural and mineral resources, they hoped to remind easterners that New Mexico was part of the U.S. and deserving of statehood.[4]

On New Mexico Day, September 16, Jack and other New Mexicans mingled in the territorial building, with each sporting a blue badge bearing the inscription "New Mexico, World's Fair, September 16, 1893" and, underneath this, "The Sunshine State." At noon, the crowd moved to the New Liberty Bell near the administration building, where "thousands of spectators gathered about to witness the ringing of the great national bell in honor of our Territory." An even-dozen New Mexicans made up the ringing party, including Captain Jack, his daughter Eva, ex-Governor L. Bradford Prince, and Republican stalwart Bernard S. Rodey of Albuquerque. Lusty cheers for New Mexico and statehood followed the pealing of the bell.[5]

Later that afternoon, visitors packed the lawn in front of the New Mexico building, awaiting the formal exercises. First on the program was New Mexico Governor William C. Thornton, followed by Prince, and then Captain Jack. One visitor later claimed that "Captain Jack made the most ringing speech ever heard within the borders of the White City." His eloquent statements on New Mexico's behalf were greeted with cheers and "the waving of men's hats and women's 'kerchiefs in the air." Jack concluded his presentation by reading "The Sunshine State," a lengthy poem he had written especially for the occasion. The poem so impressed ex-Governor Prince that he had at least a thousand copies printed for distribution through the audience. Following the fifth and last speaker, Captain Jack took the stage again, this time dressed in his buckskins. He devoted his talk to correcting eastern beliefs about cowboys, depicting them as "honest, generous, hard-working" men rather than as wild desperadoes. His recitation of "Pony Bill's Sermon" drew round after round "of the most uproarious laughter and applause."[6]

New Mexico's day was a grand success for Captain Jack and its organizers. Fairgoers carried away as souvenirs the territorial blue badges and copies of "The Sunshine State," and the Chicago Sunday *Tribune* featured a drawing of Captain Jack and the other New Mexicans ringing the Liberty Bell. Folks at home learned of these events in both the *Las Vegas Daily Optic* and the *Santa Fe New Mexican Review,* which printed part of Jack's poem, calling it "a good immigration document besides being good poetry." The *Review* summed up Jack's contribution by saying he had been "a very popular feature at the celebration."[7]

It is ironic, though understandable, that Crawford received more publicity in the Chicago press than did a young Wisconsin history professor who participated in the "World's Congress of Historians" held at Chicago's new Art Institute in conjunction with the exposition. The paper that Frederick Jackson Turner delivered at this meeting, "The Significance of the Frontier in American History," would generate an entirely new approach in interpreting the nation's history. Turner probably never encountered either Captain Jack or Buffalo Bill, who was in town with his Wild West show. Yet the scholar who wrote about the frontier and the two showmen who had helped bring about its end held similar ideas about the westering experience—that it had set men free and honed their self-reliance. What distinguished the three men was the manner in which they conveyed this message to the American people.[8]

Before the exposition closed in October, the Chicago firm of Charles H. Kerr and Company released Crawford's *Camp Fire Sparks,* a small volume containing sixteen of the Poet Scout's best soldier-poems. Jim Carlin had encouraged Jack to publish this collection, predicting that it would be in great demand among veterans at Grand Army encampments. Reviews of the book must have elated Jack. The New Mexico *Optic* called him a genius. A Boston critic proclaimed him "the people's poet." "His is not true poetry," the critic wrote, "but ringing, manly, straight forward verse, speaking straight to the heart of battle and of home and home love, never above the comprehension of the simplest man who can fight, the simplest woman who loves her country, but never, as far as it goes, unworthy of a genuine poet." The same writer avowed: "no reader who has lived through a war can be unmoved by" Crawford's poems.[9]

Other literary successes followed. In November, Jack's essay "The Government Scout" appeared in *Outing,* a magazine for the amateur sportsman. Theodore Roosevelt had published a series on ranch life in previous issues, and several of Frederic Remington's western illustrations had appeared in the magazine. Later contributors included such notables as Jack London and Owen Wister. Crawford depicted the life of a scout as "one of constant danger, privation and exposure to all kinds of weather." Little romance entered this story, for his purpose was to introduce dime novel–reading boys to the realities of western campaigning.[10]

In all of his prose compositions, Crawford tried to present accurately the West he had experienced. By writing about distinctive western characters and picturesque landscapes and by using dialect speech, he clearly belongs to the local-color movement in literature, which gained prominence in the U.S. during the last half of the nineteenth century. Local-color authors such as Bret Harte, Joaquin Miller, and Mark Twain presented for readers a more realistic portrayal of American society than was found in the writings of antebellum romanticists. Yet almost all local colorists laced their stories with strong doses of sentimentality, mixing romance with realism. The Poet Scout was no exception. In "Justice on the Frontier," for example, in which Jack describes the first legal execution in Wyoming, the condemned man, "Big Foot Ed," assists the sheriff in making his hanging a pleasant occasion for the entire community. Just moments before his death, Ed asserts, in fractured English, that justice has been served. Despite his devotion to realism, Crawford helped to promote, however unconsciously, a mythic American West, a West in which a condemned man faced his executioner with a smile, although in reality he probably trembled so badly that he required assistance to reach the floor of the scaffold.[11]

Although a new literature of realism appeared in the Gilded Age, poetry remained highly romantic and sentimental. Crawford's verses were no different, as can be clearly seen in his poems on mothers' love, women's uplifting influence, nature, and tragic death. Like other nineteenth-century poets, Crawford also sounded a moralistic note. In "A Message from the Dead," for example, he preached against cigarettes, dime novels, wine, and wicked women; and in "Does It Pay?" he counseled young men to be true to mothers and sweethearts and not to aggrieve them by drinking whiskey. Many of his poems celebrated the abundant optimism that sustained middle-class society in its mad rush to achieve material success.[12]

Several other Crawford stories appeared in print following the Chicago Exposition. In April 1894, the Chicago journal *Banner of Gold* published "The Professor," a poignant story unfolding in Tres Pinos, a rough mining camp on the San Juan River. Crawford's account of "How I Stepped onto the Platform" appeared in the May issue of *Home and Country,* a New York publication. And in June, the Chicago *Evening Lamp* published his sprightly "The Fourth at Jimtown." During these same months, Jack produced and copyrighted (in collaboration with Edward Maro) a comic song entitled "The Oriental Bum Bum," inspired by the Chicago Fair's Midway Plaisance. He also completed his first serial story, "Private Brown: A Romance of a Frontier Military Post," which one military author compared favorably with the stories of Captain Charles King.[13]

Buoyed by his literary success, the energetic and hard-working Crawford rejoined the lecture circuit with heightened enthusiasm. He felt most alive when performing before an audience. And he continued calling his performance "The Camp Fire and the Trail," although he developed five different programs to accommodate groups that engaged him for repeat appearances. His entertainments remained much the same, however; he told stories about the Indian wars, recited his own songs and poetry, and gave "highly humorous talks on the peculiarities of western characters and their customs."[14]

In mid-November 1893, Crawford staged his professional debut in Chicago before the prestigious Illinois Club. Following the performance, club members unanimously agreed that "a more fascinating entertainer never stood before" them, and a writer for the Chicago *Herald* declared that Jack's "power over an audience borders on the wonderful. . . . by his remarkable versatility he sways his hearers from laughter to tears, and from tears to laughter."[15] Later that winter in Chicago, Crawford talked to fifteen hundred schoolchildren one afternoon at the Marlow Opera House and to thirteen hundred adults that same evening. He spent the rest of the winter and spring speaking before audiences in the Midwest—primarily in Illinois, Michigan, and Wisconsin.[16]

Among the most memorable of Jack's entertainments was one staged in Janesville, Wisconsin, in January 1894. Crawford appeared on stage with a talented violinist, Professor Frederick W. Spencer—the former Fort Craig schoolteacher. Jack began his performance by telling his listeners that years ago Spencer had tutored the Crawford children along the banks of the Rio Grande. Reunited with his old friend after nearly a decade, Spencer functioned as Crawford's business agent for the next two or three years.[17]

During the summer of 1894, Crawford made plans to travel to England to secure evidence in Scotland linking Jack and his relatives to a wealthy estate on Staten Island. Now worth an estimated twenty million dollars, the estate had originated with William Wallace, said to be a relative of Jack's mother, who had settled on Staten Island early in the nineteenth century. Wallace died without leaving a will, and a fire subsequently destroyed papers that would connect Captain Jack with this wealthy Staten Islander.[18] Newspaper stories about his trip suggest that Crawford held little hope for securing the estate; rather, he looked upon his visit to England as a chance to achieve recognition as a western writer—in the manner of Bret Harte and Joaquin Miller, who had visited there several years earlier.

In late July, Crawford sailed on the steamship *Teutonic,* at the start of his seven-week adventure. He first visited his childhood home in Carndonagh, Ireland, where he staged an entertainment. "It did my heart good to receive such a reception as that granted me by my townspeople," he later declared. Scenes of his boyhood brought forth intense emotions. Standing in the house where he was born, he recalled the "sunny smile—the sad sweet smile" of his mother's face, an image he included in a poem about his birthplace. He also performed before an audience of one thousand in Londonderry. In attendance was the Lord Bishop of Derry, who found some of Crawford's ballads and poetry "not unworthy of Brete [*sic*] Harte." [19]

Crossing to England, Jack worked at advancing his writing career. He called on George R. Sims, playwright and author, whose column "Mustard and Cress" appeared in the London *Referee.* Sims later wrote an amusing account of this meeting, which was published in the *Referee* along with a large portrait of the Poet Scout. Sims concluded his article by stating: "If [Captain Jack] entertains the public as well as he entertained me his success is assured." [20]

London society lionized the Poet Scout. Crawford later

recalled that he was invited out more frequently than he could accept and that his picture stared at him in so many English newspapers that "I got quite familiar with myself." The *Westminster Budget* devoted a full page to Captain Jack, and the *Westminster News* gave him two columns. He staged at least one entertainment in London, at St. John's Mission Hall, for the benefit of the Young People's Temperance Club.[21]

Crawford was especially pleased by the reception his poems and stories received from London editors. After reading poetry at a luncheon hosted by the editor of the *Strand* magazine, he received two guineas from Robert Frazier, editor of *Tid-Bits,* who agreed to publish "Dot Leetle Cripple Boy Vot Died" in a forthcoming issue. The *Strand* editor accepted two of Crawford's stories, and J. B. Boyle, editor of the *Westminster Budget,* later published "The Cowboy Preacher." By the end of his trip, the Poet Scout had placed seventeen stories and five poems with the London journals.[22]

About the time that Crawford visited England, he wrote to an old boyhood friend in Wichita, Kansas, saying that "it seemed strange . . . that while the original and real Buffalo Bill was living in quiet modest retirement in Wichita, another claiming to be the original was setting the world on fire with stories of his wonderful deeds and hair breadth escapes." By the "original Buffalo Bill," Jack was referring to William Mathewson, an old buffalo hunter active on the plains prior to Bill Cody's rise to fame. A Wichita newspaper subsequently published Crawford's letter, causing John Burke, Bill Cody's press agent, to denounce Captain Jack in the press "as a fraud and fake frontiersman."[23] What followed was an exchange of sharply worded letters between Cody and Crawford, each extolling his own accomplishments and accusing the other of misdeeds.

Crawford's side of the exchange, the only side that has survived, makes clear that the Cody–Crawford friendship had fallen on hard times. In his many interviews with the press, however, Crawford rarely mentioned Buffalo Bill; and the Wichita communication is the closest he ever came to attacking the famous showman publicly, in print. But in this exchange of letters, Crawford allowed his resentment to boil over. Writing from the Hotel Metropole in London, Crawford cataloged Cody's past wrongs: paying a miserly salary when Jack traveled with the Buffalo Bill Combination, deserting a wounded Crawford in Virginia City, and failing to advance a promised loan so that the Australia tour had to be canceled. He also reminded his old friend that it had been through Crawford's influence that Cody had stayed on the wagon long enough to accumulate funds to buy his ranch.[24]

In this and a second letter written upon his return to New York City, Crawford attacked Cody's integrity. He denied that Cody had killed Yellow Hand, for example, and he claimed that others had written the dime novels attributed to Cody's authorship. He also alluded to Cody's excesses (and he was neither the first nor the last of Cody's associates to do so)—heavy drinking, consorting with fast women, neglecting his wife.[25]

Crawford's troubled friendship with Cody, in fact, was an important factor behind the Poet Scout's devotion to realism on the platform and in his writing. Above all else, Crawford thought of himself as an honest man, and he wanted to project this image before the public. In essays and on stage, he assured the public that he was depicting the authentic West—not the sensational West of dime novelists. By the 1890s, when Cody was at the height of his popularity both in Europe and the United States, Crawford had come to view his Wild West show in the same light as dime novels—lacking in authenticity and portraying an unreal West. It is too simple to dismiss Crawford's stand as mere envy. Beyond question, Crawford desired fame and fortune equal to that of his friend. Crawford was making a name for himself, however, as a public speaker, whose entertainment was popular among middle-class families. He could not duplicate Cody's success in the arena, but he could achieve his own unique distinction for portraying the true West—portraying it more honestly than Buffalo Bill and his sidekick, John Burke. Despite Crawford's angry accusations, however, his affection for Cody continued to find expression in later years; in 1899, for example, Crawford presented a Winchester carbine to Cody, with the inscription "Col. W.F. Cody, from Captain Jack." [26]

Crawford returned from England in October and spent the next twelve months in staging entertainments in New York, Pennsylvania, New Hampshire, Ohio, and Illinois. Publicity brochures soon listed his permanent address as 162 West 103d Street in New York City, although he still maintained his New Mexico residence. In December 1894, the *New York Mercury* devoted two columns to the popular entertainer, calling him "the most picturesque and interesting character in New York at present." The article went on to say that Captain Jack had "captivated everybody . . . when he appeared last Thursday evening at Mrs. Frank Leslie's reception in the Gerlach." Thursday evenings in Mrs. Leslie's parlors at the Gerlach Hotel had become "one of the social institutions of New York." "In her gown of white brocade, glittering with diamond comb, brooch, and bracelets," Mrs. Leslie—head of the Frank Leslie Publishing House—graciously received her guests in a drawing room crowded with authors, artists, musicians, titled foreigners, and other "elaborately dressed ladies and well-groomed men." On this particular Thursday evening, Captain Jack recited at least two poems, eliciting "a full volume of the heartiest applause" from Mrs. Leslie's other guests. [27]

One of the most memorable events in Crawford's career occurred at the national Grand Army encampment held in Louisville, Kentucky, in September 1895, where Jack appeared among the principal speakers. Thousands of Union and Confederate veterans poured into town for an unprecedented joint meeting on

Southern soil. During the encampment, Crawford served as aide-de-camp to Grand Army Commander in Chief Thomas G. Lawler; and in the gigantic Grand Army parade, the buckskin-clad Crawford made a picturesque figure riding among other aides dressed in regular uniform.[28]

Whether Jack returned to New Mexico in the year following his European adventure is not known. He did send money to Maria during these months, however, and corresponded regularly with family members. In a letter to little May, dated February 21, 1895, Papa Jack admonished his daughter to practice her handwriting; and in another letter, dated March 16, he praised her efforts on the typewriter. But he probably was not present for the weddings of his two eldest children. In May, Eva married Daniel W. Reckhart, a graduate of Columbia University, in a quiet ceremony in El Paso, Texas; and in June, Harry married Maude Richards, formerly of Chloride, in the Methodist church at San Marcial.[29]

Crawford's literary career continued to flourish following his return from England. The April 1895 issue of *Central Magazine* contained two of Jack's poems, in addition to a long essay by John G. Scorer, entitled "A Unique Character in American Literature, Capt. Jack Crawford, 'The Poet Scout.' " After summarizing the Poet Scout's early history, Scorer expanded on Crawford's commitment to portraying the real West as opposed to the sensational West of dime novels and wild west shows. Scorer's essay would later appear as the introduction to a new volume of Crawford's poems, published in 1904.[30]

Captain Jack's short story, "The Death of Wild Bill," published in the *New York City Life* in May, is a good example of Crawford's realistic essays. It is a factual account of the murder and burial of Wild Bill Hickok in Deadwood, followed by an assessment of Hickok's character—"he would get drunk, gamble and indulge in the general licentiousness characteristic of the border in the earlier days, yet . . . he was gentle as a child . . . loyal in his friendship, generous to a fault." Crawford concludes the story with a poem he wrote following Hickok's death, dedicated to Hickok's good friend Charlie Utter.[31]

In subsequent months, Crawford became a regular contributor to *Home and Country,* a family magazine that soon began offering a free copy of Jack's *Camp Fire Sparks* to new subscribers. The June issue carried his "Life among the Cowboys," which, according to one reviewer, "tells the story of the cowboy as he really is." Crawford's short story entitled "Joe," appearing in the July issue, was called "mediocre" by another reviewer.[32] One of Jack's most delightful poems, "Broncho vs. Bicycle," appeared in August in *The Bicycling World,* the country's leading bicyclist's journal. Accompanying the poem was a photograph of Crawford and the story of how he came to compose the verse. Bicycle manufacturer Colonel Albert A. Pope of Boston, having befriended Jack years earlier, asked the Poet Scout to attend a dinner given by the Bicycle Club, at which Tom Stevens, the famous cyclist, would appear. Pope suggested that Crawford write something on the bicycle and read it at the dinner. The result was a thirteen-stanza poem depicting a fanciful race between Stevens on the bicycle and a cowboy on his fast bronco. The poem made such a hit with audiences that Jack recited it in nearly all of his platform appearances. The first stanza began:

> *The first we saw of the high-toned tramp*
> *War over thar' at our Pecos camp;*
> *He war comin' down the Sante Fe trail*
> *Astride of a wheel with a crooked tail,*
> *A skinnin' along, with a merry song,*
> *An' ringin' a little warnin' gong.*
> *He looked so outlandish, strange an' queer,*

That all of us grinned from ear to ear,
An' every boy on the round-up swore
He had never seed sich a horse afore.[33]

Crawford's compositions continued to appear in print. To a boyhood friend, Jack acknowledged that all of his manuscripts were edited "by a newspaper man before I send [them] to the printers"—otherwise, he implied, his lack of training in spelling and punctuation would consign his efforts to the wastebasket.[34] Starting about 1895, however, Crawford's "newspaper man" was a woman—Marie Madison, a playwright and essayist about whom very little is known. During her lifetime, she copyrighted at least sixteen plays, including *Colonel Bob,* in 1908, which she co-authored with Captain Jack. Madison's *The Witch* was performed in Los Angeles in June 1892, but she was living in New York when she first began editorial duties with Crawford. Sometime in 1896, Madison published a lengthy essay, entitled "A True American, Capt. Jack Crawford, the Poet Scout," in *The Western Veteran,* a patriotic magazine. Accompanied by a photo of the Poet Scout and four of his poems, the article recounted Crawford's early history and described his debut as a platform lecturer. Madison also discussed Crawford's writing, calling some of his comic verses "equal to Brete [*sic*] Harte's." [35]

Crawford's publications in the popular press, in addition to articles like Scorer's and Madison's, contributed to Jack's fame as a public personality. When he opened a new lecture season in mid-October 1895, he had reason to expect a rousing reception from audiences. The entertainment managers Bragg & Muller handled most of Captain Jack's bookings, while Frederick Spencer continued to serve as Jack's business agent in New York City, answering mail and securing additional engagements. Crawford also traveled with a paid secretary, A. C. Wendell, who served in this capacity until 1898, when Crawford left for the Klondike. Wendell remained a lifelong friend. In fact, when Wendell was nearing the age of seventy, his associates at the Minneapolis post office, where he was employed, affectionately called him "Captain Jack" after his old friend.[36]

Crawford was booked solid from October 19, when he opened the season in St. Paul, Minnesota, through mid-January 1896, when he closed in Dallas, Texas. Between these dates, he performed "The Campfire and the Trail" in a multitude of western towns and cities, stretching from Minnesota through North Dakota, Montana, Washington, Oregon, and California to New Mexico, Colorado, Kansas, and Oklahoma. On his return trip to the East Coast in late January, he staged entertainments in Nebraska and then spent the following four months lecturing in Canada, Pennsylvania, and the Midwest.[37]

During this 1895–96 tour, Crawford spoke before audiences that often numbered in the hundreds. On occasion, he gave three performances in a single day before boarding a train for the next day's assignment. He reportedly received between 50 dollars and 125 dollars for an evening's performance.[38] And he was as popular in the West as he had been in the East. The editor of the Billings (Montana) *Daily Gazette* headlined his review of Jack's performance: "A Rare Entertainment, Everyone Delighted with Capt. Jack Crawford, The Poet Scout." He went on to report:

> The large audience which greeted Capt. Jack Crawford at the court house last night was delighted with the entertainment. . . . the rich vein of humor which pervaded some of the scout's anecdotes and experiences provoked the most genuine mirth, the audience at times being fairly convulsed. For two hours, without intermission, Capt. Crawford held the closest attention of his hearers and all were sorry when he closed that he did not talk longer.[39]

A writer for the *Spokesman-Review* of Spokane, Washington, reported that "laughter, tears and applause demonstrated the pleasure of an audience of 400 last night at the First Methodist church, while John W. Crawford, better known as Captain Jack, the Poet Scout, spun yarns, recited poetry and depicted the evils resulting from the use of strong drink and the circulation of pernicious literature." The writer called Jack "one of the best single handed entertainers now before the public."[40] And still another writer, in reviewing Jack's performance in Woodland, California, recorded that Crawford "captured his audience like a whirlwind. The entertainment might be termed a 'panorama of surprises,' for nobody, probably not even the speaker himself, can tell what is coming next."[41]

Although these reviews may reflect the journalistic license that was typical of Gilded Age writing, clearly Crawford found support and affection among newswriters. He was, after all, a colorful and attractive public figure; newseditors found him to be readily promotable. Their positive accounts probably are a genuine measure of Crawford's personality.

On his tour through Montana, Captain Jack conferred with an old friend who had fallen on hard times. William Gay, founder of Gayville, South Dakota, and a pioneer in the Black Hills gold rush, was in the Helena jail, under sentence of death by hanging for the murder of a deputy sheriff. Gay previously had served a jail term for the murder of young Charles Forbes, who may have been romantically involved with Gay's attractive young wife. Although the presiding judge in the Forbes case considered Gay a scoundrel, Captain Jack and other friends believed he did not deserve to die for the killing of the deputy. Gay appealed to Captain Jack for funds to pay lawyers seeking a new trial for the condemned man. Whether Jack supplied money is not known, but he did advise Gay to write an article for publication in *Home and Country.* Unfortunately for Gay, the Supreme Court denied a second trial. In Gay's last letter to Jack, dated April 7, 1896, he asked for more funds to mount a campaign to have the governor commute his sentence. Two months later Gay was executed.[42]

A high point for Captain Jack on the 1895–96 tour was a reunion with his family in El Paso, where he staged a three-hour entertainment in Chopin Hall on the evening of December 16. The *El Paso Daily Herald* reported that the Crawfords celebrated being together "for the first time in years" by having a group photograph taken. Appearing in the picture are Jack and Maria Crawford; Eva and her husband, D. W. Reckhart; Harry Crawford; and little May Crawford. It was a brief reunion, however, for on December 18 Crawford was in Las Vegas, New Mexico, for a performance, and the following night he entertained in Raton. Thereafter, he lectured in several Colorado towns, spending Christmas Day at the Brown Palace Hotel in Denver.[43]

Crawford's public image as a rugged western hero was reinforced by an incident that took place in late January 1896, while he was en route to Scranton, Pennsylvania, to fill an engagement. A two-hundred-pound bully, known as "Tombstone Bill," boarded Crawford's train and then began to taunt Jack about his appearance, remarking that he had never seen such a freak before. Jack's patience finally evaporated after Bill insulted and then cursed Jack's G.A.R. badge. Crawford struck the fellow in the nose, and in the fistfight that followed Crawford clearly bested his opponent, much to the delight of fellow passengers. In reporting the event, a sympathetic Scranton newspaper carried a drawing of Captain Jack dressed in buckskin and a headline reading: "He Thrashed the Fellow, Capt. Jack Crawford's Experience on a Train Today."[44]

With the advent of spring and a new political season, Crawford used his talents to back William McKinley's bid for the presidency. Speaking to a crowded hall in Lincoln, Nebraska, on the night of March 30, Jack recited verses favoring McKinley and the protective tariff. Two days later, in a long letter to the editor of the *Las Vegas Daily Optic,* Crawford avowed: "McKinleyism everywhere and at all times!" In June, he attended the Republican National Convention at St. Louis and then accompanied the notification committee to Canton, Ohio, to convey to McKinley the official notice of his nomination. From McKinley's front porch, Jack spoke to guests assembled on the lawn and also recited a poem written especially for the occasion.[45]

Crawford soon rejoined the lecture circuit, entertaining across the northeastern quarter of the United States. In early September he was in St. Paul to attend the national G.A.R. encampment, where he again served as special aide to the commander in chief. On the evening of September 7, fifteen hundred people gathered in an open-air campfire to listen to patriotic speeches delivered by Captain Jack, his old friend Corporal Tanner, and a Major Wilkinson of Fort Snelling. During the G.A.R. festivities, Jack also gave a two-hour entertainment at the state prison in Stillwater. In mid-September, he appeared in Burlington, Vermont, as the official poet for the reunion of the Army of the Potomac.[46]

Soon after the Vermont engagement, Crawford entered directly into the presidential campaign, accepting employment in Mark Hanna's army of publicists for McKinley, Ohio's favorite son. While the Democratic nominee, William Jennings Bryan, crisscrossed the country making speeches, Hanna—McKinley's campaign manager—invited hundreds of thousands of Americans to McKinley's residence, where the candidate delivered appropriate little speeches on prosperity and moderation. To counteract the emotionalism of Bryan's stumping for "free silver," Hanna hired speakers like Crawford to educate the people about the gold standard.[47]

Many of Crawford's New Mexico friends denounced his stand in the election. The silver question became an emotional issue, touching the lives of many thinking citizens. Republicans from western silver-producing regions like New Mexico crossed lines to support the dynamic Bryan. Earlier in the decade, silver mines in Chloride had closed on account of the low price of silver. The Chloride *Black Range* announced, in its issue of August 28,

1896, that Captain Jack had agreed to take the stump for McKinley at a salary of two hundred dollars a week. "For the love of notoriety and a fat salary," the article concluded, "Capt. Jack has turned traitor to his old mining associates by aiding to overthrow and destroy silver, the back-bone of this great republic."[48]

It is doubtful that Crawford received such a munificent sum for his political speeches. Writing from Mannington, West Virginia, on October 7, Crawford informed Maria that the Republican Committee had reduced his promised compensation by one-half. Still, Crawford remained loyal to the Republican cause. "The last three weeks," he informed Maria, "I have driven nearly two hundred miles through the mountains of West Virginia . . . where I have been doing good work for McKinley and the Republican party." He also told his wife that the "free silver craze" was dying out "among all thinking and reading people."[49]

Later that month, Crawford teamed up with New York Congressman John Murray Mitchell to speak to a large gathering of workingmen in New York City. The local press reported that Mitchell explained the financial question in a simple, straightforward manner, but that "it remained for the Poet Scout with his flowing locks and picturesque figure to fairly electrify the immense crowd." In this and in another speech given at Pleasant Valley, New York, Crawford talked as a workingman to fellow workers.[50]

The Pleasant Valley speech, the complete text of which appeared in print, reflected Crawford's version of the American Dream. Jack identified himself as a workingman and friend of labor who, thirty years earlier, had served as a secretary of the first miner's union organized in the coalfields of Pennsylvania. He was not opposed to capitalists and rich men, Crawford insisted, even though he recognized that some had been guilty of crushing the working classes. Many rich men, he declared, had started out as "poor boys like myself. They won their fortunes by hard work and earnest toil. . . . They are the mainstays of our country." This was the same great country offering the same opportunities. "Get a move on you. Any of you may become capitalists, aye, millionaires. That's what I am struggling for, and I am going to get there or die trying." Jack gave the workers a vision of how he would use such wealth. He would scatter it among the people, doing good; he would employ thousands of needy men in some business that would need protection from foreign competition so that he could provide decent wages. The vision Crawford invoked was one upon which his listeners had been reared—an American Dream of prosperity for those who worked hard. Protective tariffs and the gold standard were almost extraneous to his central message, but he linked them through his own self-interest as the owner of several mines. The "free silver craze" had shaken the confidence of eastern capitalists, the very men who might invest in his enterprises, and, he told his listeners, he would be a fool "to work and vote against the interests of the man that I am begging to help me save my property." [51]

Like many Americans, Crawford believed in a mythical economic world, where free competition allowed the most competent and hard working to rise to the top of the social order. When he made his speech at Pleasant Valley, he largely ignored the world of large corporations and monopolies that limited opportunity for small businessmen and common laborers. He also ignored the fact that most virtuous and hardworking people of his generation died as they had lived, virtuous and relatively poor, lacking the material success that would help to ease their working-class existence. But unlike many others who developed a cynical view of millionaires, believing that "behind every great fortune there was a crime," Crawford continued to praise their drive and perseverance. [52]

In November, Crawford spent election night at the national Republican headquarters in New York City and rejoiced with other Republican stalwarts in McKinley's victory. The next day, he wrote a lengthy letter to the editor of the *Las Vegas Daily Optic* to explain, to his New Mexico friends, his position in the campaign. He also announced his imminent departure for New Mexico.[53]

Sometime later that year, or possibly early in January 1897, Crawford traveled west, accompanied by a New York investor named Reynolds, who planned to thoroughly investigate Crawford's mines. While lecturing across the country, Jack had continued searching for development funds. For a time, he relied upon Samuel K. Schwenk to finance assessment work so that the claims could be protected until a wealthy investor like Reynolds was located. Crawford also employed A. J. Harrison, an experienced miner, to work full time on the claims. Harrison was as confident as Crawford about their potential value. Writing to Crawford on April 19, 1896, Harrison avowed: "You have a copper proposition, second in importance only to those found in Michigan and Montana. . . . they only await the magic wand of capital (and not a great deal of that) to develop hidden wealth." [54]

Reynolds, however, was not to be the source of that capital. In a letter published in the *San Marcial Bee* on February 6, 1897, Crawford summarized the result of Reynolds's investigation, prefacing his remarks by saying, "As I have never yet written a false report, I will not do so now." The expert employed by Reynolds to assess Jack's claims had found plenty of ore, but of low grade. "Scarcity of water and timber and the long distance from the railroad are also obstacles in the way of small capital undertaking the development." But for a rich company, the expert concluded, Jack's mines were a fine prospect. Although disappointed that Reynolds lacked resources to develop the claims, Crawford vowed to continue searching for the necessary capital to prove the correctness of his dreams. He would "strike it rich or die trying," he wrote, "and no power on earth can make me believe otherwise than that I will strike it." [55]

The American Dream of Jack's fantasy, in fact, was flawed.

No matter how hard he worked, he would not become wealthy from his mines. And this held true for almost all men lured west by hopes of striking it rich in the mining districts. For most miners, reality was fatigue, danger, despair, and lost dreams.

Still, Crawford persevered. In February 1897, he tried to interest Colonel Albert A. Pope, the bicycle manufacturer, in developing his mines. He asked Pope to advance five thousand dollars over the next two years to develop the best of the San Andres claims. For collateral, Jack offered his ranches and Dripping and Grapevine springs. Although Crawford promised to split profits equally should they strike it rich, the colonel apparently passed up his offer.[56]

While waiting to find a backer, Crawford continued to work for a living. By mid-January 1897 he was on the East Coast again, pursuing his platform career. On the fifteenth, he entertained in Burlington, Massachusetts, where General O. O. Howard introduced him to a large audience in the opera house. On the twenty-first, Jack spoke at a banquet in New York City honoring the Republican Editorial Association. He shared the stage with Chauncey M. Depew, president of the New York Central Railroad; Lieutenant Robert Peary of Arctic fame; and other luminaries. The crowd of two hundred must have appreciated Captain Jack's brief two-minute speech, in which he recited a satirical poem contrasting the styles of eastern and western editors.[57]

During the next four months, Crawford staged entertainments before a multitude of audiences throughout the Northeast. He spent several weeks in Boston, where he made a hit with the well-known literary personality Nixon Waterman, who later wrote a column on Jack entitled "A Genius in Buckskin." Waterman, the associate editor of the *League of American Wheelmen Bulletin,* probably was responsible for Jack joining the League later that spring. In announcing Jack's membership, the *L.A.W. Bulletin* noted: "Capt. Jack Crawford, the 'Poet Scout,' who has trailed more bad Indians and written more good poetry than any other man, living, dead or yet to be born . . . is an enthusiastic wheelman, and an earnest advocate of good roads."[58]

Crawford may have returned to New Mexico to supervise work on his mines during June or July of 1897. In mid-July, he most certainly read the electrifying news, relayed from Seattle and San Francisco, that miners heavily ladened with gold had just returned from the Canadian Klondike. This news sparked the greatest gold rush in history. Seemingly no industrious American male, least of all Captain Jack, was immune from the gold fever that swept across the nation. Crawford was no tenderfoot, however. He refused to join the stampede that headed for the gold fields later that summer. Instead, he announced plans to form a mining company that would systematically explore for gold in the Klondike the following spring.[59]

While organizing his new company, Crawford continued staging entertainments with characteristic energy. By this time, he had broken with lecture management bureaus and was securing his own speaking dates with the help of his paid secretary. Crawford's November bookings brought in about 660 dollars, and in December his engagements would total 733 dollars. *Talent,* a New York quarterly for lecture bureaus, labeled Jack's season "a great one, artistically as well as financially."[60] During the eight months preceding his departure for the Klondike, Crawford crisscrossed the northeastern states, speaking to chautauquas, veterans organizations, schoolboys, prison inmates, private clubs, YMCA boys, and middle-class Americans in general. In November, his audience in Albany, New York, numbered one thousand people, while in January 1898, fourteen hundred witnessed his performance in Leominster, Massachusetts.[61]

As in past years, Jack stepped on stage dressed in buckskin pants, blue homespun shirt, and fur-trimmed buckskin coat. Small American flags made of silk adorned the legs of his trousers. With his handheld rifle and belted six-shooter, Crawford appeared before his audience as a true western scout and hero.[62]

A western hero, in fact, was what the audience had paid to hear. Local newspapers frequently carried long articles on Jack prior to his appearance, reviewing his career as a military scout and publishing bits of his poetry. The men who introduced Crawford's performances continued to build this image. A Massachusetts audience was told that "living for years amid the wild and exciting incidents of savage border warfare accustomed to scenes of bloodshed and violence, dealing as an officer of the government with the most vicious and depraved criminals, [Captain Jack] has preserved through it all an honest manhood and a character of which he is justly proud." For two hours and more, Crawford would regale his audiences with stories of his western adventures, songs and poems of his own composition, and humorous anecdotes about western personalities.[63]

The Crawford stories that raised listeners' emotions to fever pitch were those about campaigning against the Sioux and Apaches. Jack never portrayed himself as an Indian killer, but rather as a trail-smart scout risking his life in a hostile and dangerous environment. Feelings of danger, suspense, and eventual triumph over hardship were the sensations that Captain Jack imparted to his audience. In contrast, Crawford touched the hearts of his listeners by telling the story behind the tender poem about his children, entitled "Little Ones Praying at Home," composed on a tranquil evening during the Victorio campaign.[64]

Although he frequently inserted contemporary matters into his entertainment, Crawford devoted most of his platform time to conjuring up a vanishing frontier. A key to his success with the audience was his ability to keep their emotions on a roller coaster, switching from gay to grim and blending humor with pathos. "Thar Was Jim," a poignant story symbolizing all that is good in America, might be followed by the humorous "Broncho vs. Bicycle." "Gambler's Prayer," a touching sermon preached from a deck of cards, might be followed by the sprightly "Sanctimonious Ike." The story of how he had faithfully kept the temperance pledge made to his dying mother and another story of his dog Hero, the constant companion of the child Crawford had called "Little Nugget," brought tears to the eyes of his listeners. Hardly taking time to catch his breath, Crawford then would relate a humorous anecdote, convulsing his audience in laughter. Throughout the performance, Crawford portrayed westerners as "good-hearted and true and with sincere regard for right."[65]

Nor did Crawford present a totally masculine West. On stage he recited tender poems about mothers, sweethearts, and women's influence on humanity. On one occasion, he recited a poem to his wife, telling of his bashful courting days. Crawford gave more attention to women in his plays and short stories, portraying them as strong hearted and capable—not the swooning heroines of the early twentieth-century westerns.[66]

Crawford usually closed his performance with an illustration of how Wild Bill Hickok defended himself from two outlaws, one approaching from the front and the other from the rear. Without much warning, Crawford made two rapid shots with his six-shooter, one in front, the other over his shoulder. With gasps and shrieks from the audience, Crawford left the stage to thunderous applause.[67]

Crawford's popularity stemmed, in part, from the fact that he symbolized the rags-to-riches success stories that nurtured nineteenth-century Americans. Moreover, the decade of the nineties celebrated masculine hardiness, a trait that the Poet Scout shared with his friend Bill Cody and other important image-makers of the day.[68] In addition, Crawford's performances reinforced commonly held views that the West was a land of adventure, opportunity, freedom, and individualism, where civilization ultimately triumphed over savagery. Then, too, he spoke of a West only recently passed into history. Americans were eager to learn of their heritage and sought to recapture some of the excitement of yesteryear. They looked upon the vanishing frontier with nostalgia, seeing it as a simpler time past.[69] Certainly, Captain Jack's West contrasted sharply with the newly emerging industrial East, with its growing restrictions, perplexing tensions, and unresolved conflicts. For all of these reasons, Crawford was a symbol to his audience of the heroic western experience.

Both on the stage and in his writing, Crawford strove for accuracy in depicting the West, and, in fact, the West had made of Crawford himself a realist rather than a romantic. He had firsthand knowledge of its dangers, hardships, inequities, and disappointments. Yet his performances were an inevitable mix of romance and realism. By using melodramatic action, by creating a highly charged atmosphere, by focusing upon picturesque western characters, and by celebrating the traits that historian Frederick Jackson Turner said the frontier had fostered, Crawford helped perpetuate a legendary West.[70]

By the time he left for the Klondike, Crawford had built a national reputation as an entertainer. After witnessing a Crawford performance, Kate Sherwood, who headed the Woman's Department of the *National Tribune* in Washington, D.C., avowed that Captain Jack was "without a rival on the platform," a sentiment shared by a Massachusetts journalist who wrote that Crawford "is without question the best entertainer in America."[71] Crawford was also one of the nation's important image-makers, for he helped thousands of Americans formulate their ideas about the American West, a land deeply embedded in Jack's soul:

Do I like the city, stranger? 'Tisn't likely that I would;
'Tisn't likely that a ranger from the border ever could
Git accustomed to the flurry an' the loud unearthly noise—

In Search of Fame and Fortune

Everybody in a hurry, men an' wimmin, gals an' boys,
All a rushin' like the nation 'mid the rumble an' the jar,
Jes' as if their souls' salvation hung upon their gittin' thar.
    Like it? No. I love to wander
        'Mid the vales an' mountains green,
    In the border land out yonder,
        Whar' the hand o' God is seen.[72]

9
TO THE KLONDIKE

Gold! Gold in the Klondike! The news ricocheted across the continent, spreading a virulent strain of gold fever from coast to coast. The stampede began almost immediately following the arrival of two heavily ladened treasure ships on the Pacific Coast. On July 15, 1897, grizzled prospectors carried suitcases bulging with gold down the gangplanks of the steamship *Excelsior,* with a curious crowd of San Franciscans on hand to witness the spectacle. Two days later, the steamship *Portland,* carrying nearly two tons of gold, arrived in Seattle. The two coastal towns went mad on Klondike gold. Mass resignations occurred in all trades and professions, as residents scrambled to find transportation for the gold fields. Within ten days of the *Portland's* arrival, fifteen hundred people had left Seattle for the Klondike.[1]

Gold fever soon reached epidemic proportions. On August 1, the *New York Herald's* financial page "carried advertisements for eight huge mining and exploration corporations all formed within a few days to exploit the Klondike."[2] In the mad

---

Captain Jack Crawford, Marshal of the Day, 4th of July celebration, 1899, Dawson, Yukon Territory. (Photo by E. A. Hegg, courtesy Special Collections Division, University of Washington Libraries, Neg. No. 2348.)

rush to get to the gold fields, a few people like Jack Crawford counseled caution. "No man with my experience, if he has a grain of sense left," Crawford avowed in August, "will attempt this trip at this season of the year." Canadian and U.S. officials alike warned against trying to reach the Klondike that fall. But the advice fell on deaf ears. People clogged the coastal ports, outfitting and embarking for the gold region. By September 1, nine thousand people had left Seattle, yet they had little chance of reaching the Klondike before the Yukon River froze in late October.[3]

The lucky prospectors aboard the *Excelsior* and *Portland* had extracted their gold from Bonanza and other creeks that fed the Klondike River a few miles above its confluence with the Yukon. Dawson City, located where the Klondike enters the Yukon, became the mecca for stampeders and the first capital of Canada's Yukon Territory. A popular route into the gold fields was by way of Dyea on the Alaskan Panhandle, across the mountains via Chilkoot Pass to Lakes Lindeman and Bennett, and then down the Yukon River to Dawson—a distance of about 1,600 miles from Seattle. Of an estimated 100,000 people who started for the Klondike during the stampede, only 30,000 or 40,000 reached Dawson. And only a few hundred ever struck it rich.[4]

For Captain Jack, the Klondike became the last great adventure of a long and exciting career. Typical of his era, Crawford had long aspired to great wealth; now he expected to reap a fortune in the land of the midnight sun. His practical knowledge of mining and willingness to endure hardships, he believed, would bring success where others would fail. The Klondike would also allow the fifty-one-year-old Poet Scout to relive the excitement of his earlier days on campaign, for the frozen wastes of the Yukon could be as dangerous and beguiling as any of his former foes. Unfortunately, the key ingredient for striking it rich—luck—continued to elude him, and he would leave the Klondike after a fruitless two-year search for his fortune.

But in the months preceding his departure for the gold region, Crawford revealed in published interviews an expert's appreciation for the difficulties ahead. He astutely predicted that not more than a quarter of the several thousand people who started for the gold fields would reach Dawson City. And most of these would return home disappointed. People going into the Yukon, he advised, should have "at least $1,000 cash, a year's provisions, a good constitution, a genial disposition and a great fund of patience." And he warned against fraudulent Klondike companies intent upon bilking the public of its money. "The number of innocent people," he avowed, "who will be absolutely robbed within the next twelve months is beyond calculation."[5] Ironically, within a year of reaching the Klondike, Crawford would sever connections with the company that financed his expedition, accusing it of swindling the stockholders.

Brimming with confidence at the start of his adventure, Crawford organized his own company to exploit the Yukon. In August 1897, the Captain Jack Crawford Alaska Prospecting and Mining Corporation was incorporated in New Jersey, with a capital stock of 250,000 dollars. Incorporators included, in addition to Crawford, Horatio C. King of Brooklyn, William T. Fales of Kansas City, and George B. Corsa of New York. Captain Jack served as president and general manager, and his longtime friend Horatio King was vice president. Crawford planned to lead a party of carefully selected miners to the Klondike in the spring. The company's prospectus assured stockholders that "reports from the field of operation over Captain Jack's signature will be authentic and trustworthy." But it also warned that "unless you can afford to lose, you should not invest." "There is no absolutely sure thing in mining enterprises of any kind," the prospectus declared, "but we have faith that 'Captain Jack' will succeed if any one can."[6]

Within four months of its organization, the Captain Jack Crawford company acquired a valuable placer claim on Minook

Creek (several miles downriver from Dawson) from Hank Summers, an experienced miner who had prospected with Captain Jack both in the Canadian Cariboo and in New Mexico's Black Range. After spending several years in the Yukon, Summers again teamed up with Crawford, becoming a stockholder in his company in December 1897. Summers sold the Minook claim for a nominal sum and planned to accompany Crawford to Dawson in the spring.[7]

In February 1898, Jack's company merged with the better-financed Klondike, Yukon and Copper River Company, incorporated in Montana in October of the previous year with a capital stock of twelve million dollars. Frank B. Vrooman, a former Presbyterian minister from Chicago, was president of the company, and Captain Jack became its first vice president and assistant general manager. Hank Summers served briefly as its second vice president. The company's board of directors included Senator John L. Wilson of Washington; Assistant Secretary of War G. D. Meiklejohn; a former U.S. senator from Kentucky; and a former U.S. commissioner of pensions.[8]

The company's prospectus outlined the grandiose plans of company officials. Their primary object was "to carry on extensive sub-aqueous placer operations with steam dredges." Accordingly, the company had secured twenty-year leases from the Canadian government for dredging nearly 100 miles of property on the Klondike, Yukon, Stewart, Indian, and Hootalinqua rivers. It also obtained options for hydraulic mining and applied for a townsite of 160 acres on the Hootalinqua, where its trading post would serve as a supply base for the upper Yukon district. In addition, the company acquired ten placer claims "of extraordinary value" in the heart of the gold fields, located on Bonanza, El Dorado, and Too-Much-Gold creeks, as well as Hank Summers's claims on Minook Creek. It also planned to establish the "Klondike, Yukon and Copper River Reindeer Express," employing one hundred reindeer purchased from the U.S. government to carry passengers and freight over Chilkoot Pass.[9]

Late in February, Crawford returned to New Mexico for a family reunion before departing for Seattle to organize a party of miners for the trek to the Yukon. On March 1, he signed papers authorizing Maria to act as his attorney in his absence. About a week later he boarded a train for San Francisco, where on the evening of March 16 he staged a benefit entertainment for the Maine Memorial Fund—created to honor the memory of the "martyrs" of the Battleship Maine.[10]

Crawford received wide coverage in local newspapers as he continued his journey to Seattle. A Portland journal headlined its story "Captain Jack Crawford, Poet-Scout and Goldhunter." The *Seattle Post-Intelligencer* carried a two-column article on the Poet Scout, accompanied by a drawing of Jack in his buckskins.[11] By the time he reached Seattle, the major port of embarkation for stampeders, gold-crazed men and women clogged its business district, seeking supplies, information, and passage northward. But already, many disappointed miners were returning home with their hopes shattered. The disillusioned stampeders encountered by Jack advised others to stay out of the Yukon unless they were thoroughly outfitted to withstand its rigors. He also discovered that it was "next to impossible" to get any reliable information regarding trails at Skagway and its sister city Dyea.[12]

Crawford's chief worry, however, concerned the reliability of his new partner. Before leaving for the Pacific Coast, Crawford had reached an understanding with Frank Vrooman that five hundred dollars would be awaiting him in Seattle to outfit his party. When the money failed to appear, Crawford expressed his displeasure in a strongly worded letter dated March 25. Many people had invested in the Klondike, Yukon and Copper River company, Jack claimed, because they believed in his honesty. He warned Vrooman, "Unless I am satisfied beyond the question of a doubt that you are conducting a legitimate business, I will not only re-organize the Capt. Jack Crawford Company but expose you to the world." In the act of writing this threat, Crawford received a tele-gram notifying him that the five hundred dollars had been wired that very same day; consequently, he filed the letter away—unmailed—"for future reference." [13]

Shortly thereafter, both Vrooman and the money appeared in Seattle, and Crawford's innate optimism again took hold. Com-pany plans for exploiting the Yukon apparently were proceeding magnificently. The company's first steam dredge was on its way to Seattle from the Vulcan Iron Works in Kansas City, and a steam-ship, which the company would use to transport men and supplies on Yukon rivers, was being built in Philadelphia. Crawford pur-chased about four tons of goods and machinery in Seattle, as well as his personal gear, but found that he could purchase groceries cheaper in Dyea. Among his Seattle purchases was a seven-month-old Saint Bernard (which he named Hero) and the services of an Indian boy to train it for pulling a sled. [14]

While in Seattle, Crawford learned that the company's one hundred reindeer would be delivered to him in the interior—along with several Laplanders to assist in establishing the reindeer express. The story of the Klondike reindeer is one of the strangest to emerge from the gold rush, and it is worth repeating here. It begins the winter of 1897–98, when rumors of starvation in Daw-son City began to reach Seattle. [15]

A few hundred stampeders had made it across the moun-tain passes and reached Dawson in the fall of 1897. As the town's population mushroomed, supplies ran short, people began to panic, and some predicted a famine during the coming winter. By December 1, about 900 people had fled Dawson, which probably helped to avert a major calamity. Although provisions ran low that winter, nobody starved. Nonetheless, when news of Dawson's "famine" reached the outside, Congress voted in December to appropriate 200,000 dollars to purchase a reindeer herd, to be sent to the Klondike as a source of meat. Subsequently, 539 head of reindeer were purchased in Norway, shipped to New York, transported by rail across the continent to Seattle, and then loaded on steamships bound for Haines Mission and the Dalton Trail, an alternate route into the Yukon that began near Dyea. Commanded by the U.S. Army, the Klondike Relief Expedition included forty-three Laplanders, ten Finns, and fifteen Norwegians to herd the reindeer.

To aid the starving miners, the government also shipped a large quantity of provisions to Dyea, where they awaited arrival of the reindeer. By the time Crawford reached Seattle, however, Secretary of War Russell A. Alger had decided to abandon the project, convinced that Dawsonites were not facing starvation. In mid-April, the government auctioned off these provisions, greatly benefiting Crawford and other stampeders.

After canceling the relief expedition, the army organized three parties to explore alternate routes into the Yukon, planning to use the reindeer for transportation. Once the explorers reached Circle City, 220 miles downriver from Dawson, one hundred of the animals were to be turned over to Crawford. However, without adequate forage (reindeer moss), the reindeer quickly became unfit for travel, and plans for using them as pack animals had to be canceled. It is impossible to know precisely what arrangements were made thereafter for uniting Captain Jack with the reindeer. Apparently, some were judged fit for travel in May, when at least 164 reindeer and their herders started up the Dalton Trail. The next nine months proved to be a nightmare for man and beast, as the expedition "pushed their way over mountains, glaciers, and snowfields, slowed by swamps and hummocks."[16] The reindeer finally reached Dawson City in January 1899, with the herd now numbering about 135 animals. But Crawford resigned his position with Vrooman's company about this time, and nothing more is found in the records concerning the Klondike, Yukon and Copper River Reindeer Express.

Crawford left Seattle with five men and supplies on the evening of April 11, 1898, bound for the Klondike. For eighteen dollars each, they secured passage on the steamship *Brixham,* commanded by Captain James Durie.[17] Like the majority of stampeders, they traveled up the Inside Passage from Puget Sound to Skagway and Dyea, a distance of about one thousand miles. At the beginning of this great adventure, Crawford kept a daily journal in two small notebooks; he later incorporated this material in letters sent to major U.S. newspapers, intending them for publication. As difficulties with the company mounted, however, he lost interest in the journal, and we must rely on his letters to Maria and a few newspaper clippings to flesh out the story of his Klondike experience.

Many stampeders left Seattle or San Francisco in overcrowded, unseaworthy, and overpriced vessels. Martha Munger Purdy and her brother George Munger, about two months behind Crawford in their journey to the Klondike, sailed from Seattle on the steamer *Utopia,* which Martha described as dirty and "loaded to the gunwales with passengers, animals, and freight. . . . The captain was seldom, if ever, sober." Although she had booked passage for a separate stateroom, at a cost of 120 dollars, Martha was forced to share it with a gambler and his female companion.[18]

Compared to Martha's experience, Crawford traveled north on a luxury liner. In his journal, Crawford highly praised the *Brixham*'s officers and accommodations. Captain Durie and Purser Watson were "indefatigable in making [their] passengers comfortable," and cabins and tables were as luxurious as any that Crawford had experienced on his trip to Europe. The Boston and Alaska Transportation Company, owner of the *Brixham,* was "the first to break the combine of exorbitant prices in freight and passenger rates." Crawford also praised the humanitarian spirit of the wife of the company's general manager, Mrs. D. H. Pingree, whom he met before leaving Seattle. In Mrs. Pingree's presence, Crawford remarked that he expected to stage occasional entertainments in the Klondike to help "some poor, sick and pennyless man or boy" to return home. Thereupon, Mrs. Pingree opened her card case and wrote on the back of her husband's card: "To any Capt. of the B. and A. Co. This man without money. Capt. give him work; if ill, bring him home. If well enough he will work his way. [signed] Anna Eva Fay Pingree, wife of D.H.P." Handing the card to Crawford, she said: "There now, Capt. Jack, that is the way I am going to help some worthy person you may find in distress perhaps sick." [19]

The voyage to Dyea took six days. Crawford's fellow passengers included three doctors, three lawyers, fifteen mechanics, four engineers, several surveyors, carpenters, and boat builders, along with many women ("mostly with their husbands") and a one-month-old baby boy. On the second day out, the ship encountered rough water, and many on board became seasick. But despite a brief bout of "sqeamishness," Crawford enjoyed the voyage. He found the scenery superb, writing in his journal that for a thousand miles they were "dodging in and out around mountains towering thousands of feet high[,] then snowy peaks rubbing the clouds while thousands of duck and geese are flying in all directions." On the evening of April 12, Crawford entertained "a lot of the boys" in the captain's cabin, and the next evening Durie returned the favor, telling exciting stories of his seafaring career. [20]

On leaving Seattle, Crawford had been handed a letter from Vrooman containing sealed orders to be opened at sea. Vrooman's melodramatic gesture must have amused the Poet Scout, for he later commented: "At first I thought perhaps [Vrooman] expected us to meet and annihilate the Spanish fleet." The orders placed Crawford fully in command of the expedition, requiring other "expeditioners" to obey orders and to perform their share of the work. Vrooman also instructed Crawford to "avoid Chilkoot Pass, if possible."[21]

A week prior to Jack's departure from Seattle, a horrifying avalanche on Chilkoot Pass had claimed the lives of more than sixty stampeders. Thus, when the *Brixham* landed at Skagway, on April 16, Crawford went into town to inquire of transportation companies the cost of transporting supplies across White Pass to Lake Bennett, an alternate route leading to the Yukon. The lowest price offered was thirteen cents per pound—too steep for Jack. He returned to the *Brixham* for the three-mile trip to Dyea, where it docked about 8:30 P.M. With two companions, Crawford walked into town over "one of the worst roads I have ever seen—up and down hill, through mud, slush, rocks and corduroy," returning to the ship about midnight. Later that same night, Crawford contracted with the Dyea-Klondike Transportation Company to carry about seven tons of supplies and equipment across Chilkoot Pass to Lake Bennett for nine cents a pound—thus effecting a considerable savings for his company.[22]

Crawford remained in Dyea about four days, staying at the Pacific Hotel for two dollars per night plus fifty cents for meals. Within a year, Dyea would resemble a ghost town, its gold-rush economy ruined by completion of a railroad over White Pass. While in Dyea, Crawford met Colonel Thomas M. Anderson, commanding U.S. troops in the area, and submitted a bid on the government supplies stockpiled there for the defunct Emergency Relief Expedition. On April 18, the army turned over to Crawford about three hundred dollars worth of provisions—flour, sugar, beans, rice, coffee, butter, canned milk, and so forth.[23]

On the twentieth, Crawford left Dyea for Canyon City, a tent city eight miles up the Chilkoot Trail, where stampeders reassembled their supplies before continuing their journey. Crawford dashed off a letter to Vrooman from this point, noting that he had purchased a town lot and a large tent to be used as a warehouse opposite the power house of the new tramway. The warehouse, Crawford believed, would greatly benefit later expeditioners sent out by the company. He also wrote that he expected "to get over the tram from here this P.M. or tomorrow A.M." [24]

Unlike Crawford, the majority of stampeders lacked money to hire packers or to use the aerial tramways for hauling gear over Chilkoot Pass. Consequently, they packed most of their supplies over the Chilkoot Trail on their backs or on heavily loaded sleds. Following the Dawson starvation scare, the Northwest Mounted Police strictly enforced an edict requiring each stampeder to carry into the Yukon a year's supply of food—1,150 pounds. [25] Stampeders also would have to pack tents, cooking utensils, bedding, and other equipment needed for survival. This meant they had to relay their supplies over the trail, carrying a load forward a few miles, caching it in a tent city like Canyon City, and then going back for another load. Gold seekers might spend three months or more in getting their supplies across Chilkoot Pass to the lakes beyond, where they could be loaded on boats and floated downriver for the remainder of the trip.

The tramway that Jack mentioned was built by the Chilkoot Railroad and Transportation Company and linked Canyon City with Crater Lake on the other side of Chilkoot Pass. The Dyea-Klondike Transportation Company's tram linked The Scales (seven or eight miles beyond Canyon City) with the summit. Both were meant to carry supplies, not passengers. In fact, when a member of Crawford's party heard that Jack intended to ride a tramway bucket to the summit, he advised against it. Writing from The Scales, Jack's associate warned: "Capt. I think you ought nought to try to come over on that wire as the buckets are dropping off here every once in a while. It dont [sic] work wright [sic]." [26]

Crawford and his men spent about five days in overseeing the relaying of their supplies from Canyon City to The Scales, a flat ledge at the base of the final ascent of Chilkoot Pass. On April 25,

Crawford left Canyon City on horseback and arrived at The Scales at 11:00 A.M., in the midst of "a fearful storm," the worst since the "big slide." His horse had twice broken through the snow and rolled over, with Jack narrowly escaping injury. Because of the storm, the tramways stopped operating, and Crawford failed to detect a single stampeder climbing "the Golden Stairs" to the summit.[27]

On an average day, gold seekers readjusted packs at The Scales, preparing for the coming ordeal—a climb of fifteen hundred steps chiseled into the steep ice-covered slope leading to the summit. In good weather, a solid line of stampeders inched their way up the Golden Stairs—from a distance looking more like a string of ants than human beings. It took a man carrying a fifty-pound pack (the average load) about an hour to reach the summit.[28] Even without packs, stampeders found the final ascent a challenge in stormy weather.

When Jack reached The Scales, he learned that all of his freight, minus his personal baggage, was already on the summit and en route to Lake Bennett. This worried him because he had not paid Canadian customs. "So in spite of protests from the boys and packers who had returned unable to face the storm," Jack later noted, "I determined to climb the summit." He started about 2:00 P.M., carrying his bedding on his back. Footing was treacherous, for snow had filled the ice-carved steps. "After about three quarters of an hours climb, the hardest I had ever experienced, I reached the custom office on top to find it closed [because of the storm] for the first time [since] the opening."[29] A Northwest Mounted Police post also stood on the summit, marking the international boundary. Despite the raging blizzard, the Mounties invited Jack to a roast-beef dinner, after which he bedded down on the floor of the custom agent's tent.

The next day, April 26, Crawford recorded that between one thousand and fifteen hundred people were on the summit, along with thousands of dogs and some mules and horses. He and his men started for Lake Lindeman that afternoon with two sleds, each pulled by six dogs. Jack estimated that at least two thousand men and some women were on the trail between the summit and Lindeman, with "many of the women . . . dressed exactly like the men. Some drive 3 to 6 dogs, some packing and some pulling a sled with husbands or brothers." Snow along the route was "red with blood from the horses feet breaking through the crust." Crawford's party pulled into Lindeman at 7:30 P.M., having covered a distance of nine or ten miles in four and a half hours. The next morning, Jack moved on to Lake Bennett and camped near the headquarters of Major James M. Walsh, the first commissioner for the newly created Yukon Territory.[30]

In the spring of 1898, thousands of tents and shacks lined the shores of Lake Bennett, with their owners awaiting the breakup of the ice so they could set sail for the Klondike. Enterprising stampeders opened up a plethora of small businesses: canvas saloons, cafes, hotels, bakeries, bathing and barbering facilities—all found in what has been called "the greatest tent city in the world." Lake Bennett also resembled a giant shipbuilding yard, where men rushed to build the boats that would carry them to Dawson.[31]

Crawford and his men (identified in a newspaper clipping as Chief Surgeon Dr. L. Orville Wilcoxon, Joseph H. Crook, John W. Cassidy, A. Laraway, and Andrew G. Kidder) remained at Lake Bennett for approximately two months. In fact, they lingered in camp—awaiting funds from Vrooman—about a month after other stampeders had started their frantic race down the Yukon. During this delay, Crawford's party did not escape the squabbling and irritations that destroyed so many Klondike business arrangements. The physical hardships of the trail, long delays in camp, and enforced intimacy of shared tents and bedding often caused tempers to flare and partnerships to fail.[32]

The day after arriving at Bennett, Crawford wrote in his journal that "no one but Kidder seem to take hold or want to see to anything. Orders are reluctantly obeyed." On April 30, Jack complained that after the men brought in two sleds of wood, they played cards the rest of the day. Crawford was tired of "telling them what to do[;] don't seem to want to work." The next day he lectured Crook that "ten hours work is expected" and if Crook wished to write letters he must do so after working hours. Before leaving Lake Bennett for Dawson, Crawford recorded that the men had become rebellious, "some of them claiming that the Company had gone to pieces." [33]

Despite these rumblings of discontent, Captain Jack found pleasure in the beauty of his surroundings and in the mass of humanity swirling around him. Two days after his arrival at Bennett, he called upon Major Walsh and "found him to be a splendid good man, just and fearless." Walsh, who was on his way to Dawson to assume duties as commissioner, gave Jack some "valuable information" about the Hootalinqua and other sites downriver. On May 1, Crawford spent a "delightful evening" with the commissioner, leaving his tent at 11:30 on a "lovely moonlight night." He also met young Duff Pattullo, Walsh's secretary, who, years later, would become premier of British Columbia. Pattullo was also the nephew of Tom Pattullo, whose death in the Cariboo, in 1878, Jack had commemorated in verse. [34]

While at Lake Bennett, Crawford made the acquaintance of a Canadian official who was to become a legend: Samuel B. Steele, superintendent of the Northwest Mounted Police. Steele had arrived at Lake Bennett in late March 1898 and established his headquarters in a log building, where he labored from 5:00 A.M. until 10:00 P.M. in dispensing justice and information and settling disputes among stampeders. In his memoirs, Steele recorded that he had received many callers at Lake Bennett, "no two alike." But he remembered Crawford with special fondness, for the Poet Scout had entertained him with tales of Wild Bill Hickok and the Indian wars.[35]

Crawford also helped to entertain ice-bound stampeders as they tried to create a community on the banks of Lake Bennett. On the evening of May 2, the "ladies" of the camp gave the "first social entertainment of the season" at the Union church. The program included violin and cornet solos, two vocal solos, and several recitations. Captain Jack spoke for about a half-hour, delivering a brief talk on temperance and reciting "Broncho vs. Bicycle" and other poems. Major Walsh contributed sandwiches, coffee, and doughnuts to the crowd of thirty women and two hundred men. The evening closed with the singing of "America" and "God Save the Queen," followed by rousing cheers for Old Glory and the Union Jack. Crawford took part in a similar entertainment lasting three hours on the evening of May 16, and in yet another staged a week later.[36]

On May 24, the Lake Bennett community celebrated the Queen's Birthday with games, speeches, songs, and food. Captain Jack recorded that five hundred people attended the festivities, which featured, among other events, the Anderson brothers playing duets on the guitar and mandolin, a speech by Captain Jack, and a cornet rendition of "God Save the Queen" and "The Star Spangled Banner." The day's games included a girls' potato race, using lemons instead of potatoes. "Lemons had to be returned, worth 25 [cents] each." It was, Jack concluded, "a Great Day."[37]

On May 30, while hundreds of boats set sail for Dawson, Crawford helped to stage Memorial Day services in the church, decorated with wreaths, Union Jacks, and American flags. His journal entry for the day provides another glimpse of his community spirit: "Memorial Services most successful. . . . Raised $42 towards paying $50 due on church. Went around second time and raised $12 more."

Only a week after reaching Lake Bennett, Crawford returned to Dyea, with Dr. Wilcoxon, to purchase supplies and to check for mail from company headquarters. Crawford recorded details of this arduous sixty-mile round-trip in his journal, providing a good look at trail conditions during the late spring. The trail between Bennett and Lindeman was "in a fearful state," and he walked most of the distance with wet feet. He found between three hundred and four hundred people camped at the head of Lake Lindeman, with many whipsawing lumber for boats.[38]

Crawford spent the night at the lake, in the tent of a friend named Petterson, and witnessed that evening one of the many altercations that disrupted the stampeder community. The fracas started after "Dutchy," Petterson's employee, had an emaciated horse shot and killed on the ice of Lake Lindeman. Thereupon, a miner rushed up to Dutchy and threatened to have him lynched, fearing the dead horse would pollute the lake. At this point, Petterson dashed out of his tent in his underwear to defend his employee and "used language not usually heard in church." Promising to return with two hundred men to carry out his threat, the miner left—shortly to return with fifteen men armed with Winchesters. Fortunately, a Mountie stopped them "within 100 yards of where over 50 guns and pistols were all ready for them" and ordered the men back to their tents. The powder keg had been deftly diffused, although Crawford noted: "Just such idiots as this man [the miner] have caused much bloodshed."

Early the next morning, Crawford and Wilcoxon started for Chilkoot summit, meeting en route two women alone pulling over eight hundred pounds on their sled. Once on the summit, the two men took the quickest route to its base—sliding down a tobogganlike lane cut in the snow. Crawford later wrote that he "would not have missed seeing the Chilkoot summit and climbing it, and sliding down again to its base for a thousand dollars."[39]

On the trail to Canyon City, Crawford met a brother and sister traveling together, the young man carrying a guitar and the young curly-headed woman dressed in boy's clothing with a .44 Colt pistol strapped to her waist. When Crawford remarked that they surely would "get through all right," the spunky woman replied: "Oh that's no lie." Crawford and Wilcoxon stopped briefly at the Red Onion Hotel in Canyon City for a plate of ice cream, with Jack insisting that "the Red Onion dishes up as good a meal as one could get in [New York]." The two men then caught the stage for Dyea, where they arrived about 4:00 P.M. on May 5.[40]

Apparently, no mail awaited them either at Dyea or Skagway, but news arrived on the day after of Admiral Dewey's victory in the Philippines. Crawford recorded his reaction: "Put feather in hat. Went over town with copy of bulletin yelling like an Apache. Everybody wild." While in Dyea, Crawford ordered supplies at Young's Hardware Store and the Alaska Trading Company and dined with Colonel Anderson. He also wrote a long letter describing his trip from Seattle to Lake Bennett, hiring a typist to run off several copies to send to newspapers.[41]

On May 8, Crawford started his return to Lake Bennett, spending the night at the Red Onion Hotel. The next day he found the trail approaching The Scales to be in terrible condition. At one place, the pack horses "had to step straight up nearly three feet and worm their way in and out between rocks, sometimes tumbling over with their packs." A blizzard of rain and snow struck them at The Scales, where Crawford and Wilcoxon helped the packer unload their supplies for reloading on the tram. While Wilcoxon journeyed on to Lake Bennett, Crawford stayed on the summit to pay the duty. Although a storm raged through the night, Captain Jack staged an entertainment for the Mounties and custom officers.

Crawford reached Lake Bennett on the morning of May 11 and immediately set his men to work. Cassidy and Wilcoxon went prospecting for quartz, while Crawford and Kidder sunk a prospect hole. "No reason why something should not be found here,"

Crawford wrote in his journal. The men also spent time in assembling four steel boats, the parts of which they had brought from Seattle. Crawford had the boats painted white and named after Dewey's squadron in the Philippines. While awaiting funds from Vrooman, Crawford also constructed a large scow, with his men whipsawing some of the necessary lumber.[42]

Jack wrote at least two letters to his wife from Lake Bennett. In a letter misdated May 6, he enclosed a check for one hundred dollars and told her that he had lost fifteen pounds due to hard work and "some worry." Only part of his letter dated May 27 has survived. In it, he states that the company's dredge was at Seattle and would be sent up the Yukon via St. Michael. He also told Maria that on the previous day he had traveled downriver in a Peterborough canoe to where his men were getting out logs for the scow. "Several times we were jammed in between the ice and had hard work to get out," he reported.[43]

On May 29, ice began breaking up on the Yukon lakes, and within forty-eight hours more than seven thousand boats set sail for Dawson. But Crawford and his men remained behind, building their scow and awaiting money from Vrooman. On June 16 Crawford recorded: "Too buisy [sic] to keep up diary, losing interest. Disapointed [sic] very much by Mr. Vrooman." Finally, "when I had not a dollar in my pocket," he received two hundred dollars from Vrooman's agent in Seattle. On June 29, Crawford's expeditioners set sail from Lake Bennett, embarking on a journey they would not soon forget.[44]

Three miles into the voyage, "a terrific wind came up," and Crawford's fleet of six vessels fairly flew down the lake. About twelve miles below Bennett, the storm drove the forty-by-twelve-foot scow, christened the "Concord," onto the rocky shore. Crawford and Ed Donaldson, a new company employee, jumped overboard into icy, waist-deep water to secure the boat. After six hours of hard work, and wet from head to foot, the men saved the scow from being pounded to pieces against the rocks. Meanwhile, Mrs. Donaldson and her eight-year-old daughter, Alta, weathered the storm in the scow's kitchen-cabin, becoming "very seasick." Crawford slept for an hour and then stood watch at 1:00 A.M., writing of the day's events in his journal while seated on a rock beside a blazing fire of driftwood. The storm continued through the night, with ten-foot-high waves rolling onto shore and breaking into "great sheets of spray."[45]

Within twenty-four hours, five other boats had been driven into nearby rocks—"most of them more or less damaged and all lost some of their outfits." Only one boat in Crawford's fleet, however, was badly damaged in the storm. Manned by Cassidy, the only experienced boatman in Crawford's crew, the "Baltimore" had been hurled onto rocks across the lake from Crawford's location. On July 2, three more boats landed on rocks below the "Concord." Two had a woman on board, Jack noted, adding that "there is little if any danger of loss of life going ashore but the wetting is very disagreeable, especially when it is snowing half a mile above and almost at the freezing point."

At 8:30 P.M., on July 3, Crawford and his men got the scow and other boats under way again. Becalmed during the night, they passed the police station at Lake Tagish at 3:00 P.M. on the following day. With a blizzard in sight, they soon went ashore for the evening to allow stock on board the scow—three horses and a burro—to graze. Crawford recorded in his journal: "This is about the [meanest] 4th of July I have ever known except when I had the meazels [*sic*]."

The next day was even "meaner." A storm kept the fleet on shore, with the men working hard to save boats and supplies. Waves dashed over the scow, drenching everything—including bedding. At midnight, Jack broiled a piece of bacon on a stick and ate some hardtack for supper. "No sleep for me tonight," he wrote, "this is fearful. Ice, snow, rain." At 1:00 P.M. on July 6, the men set sail again, making slow progress during the next thirty-six hours. Part of the time they had to row or pole their crafts across lakes and around rocky abutments. A journal entry documents Crawford's mounting frustration with his inexperienced crew: "Have not had one nights rest since I left Bennett owing to fact that I have with me some of the most worthless men I have ever known. They want to sleep and eat all the time."

Crawford's party approached Miles Canyon, the most dangerous stretch on the trip, at about 7:00 P.M. on July 9. Because so many of the initial stampeders had lost their boats at this point, the Northwest Mounted Police soon forbade vessels from passing through the canyon and White Horse Rapids two miles below without an experienced pilot.[46] Crawford arranged with the Barnes Brothers to pilot his fleet through this stretch for sixty-five dollars. The pilots delayed their departure until 8:00 P.M. on July 11, awaiting calm weather. Stampeders found shooting the rapids to be a breathtaking experience, and Crawford was no exception. His terse journal entry on this date reads: "[Vessels] came through O.K. Running the canon and rappids [*sic*] is a wonderful experience." But Jack also recorded that his boat "got hung up on a pile of logs" and that he and the two pilots aboard had to jump into the water to disengage the craft. In camp that night, Crawford slept soundly despite the swarms of mosquitoes that tormented the gold seekers.

Onward Crawford's party sped, spending the next night at the head of Lake Laberge, immortalized in Robert Service's "Cremation of Sam McGee." Caribou meat and fresh trout now supplemented their rations. On the afternoon of July 16, they approached the head of Thirty Mile River, where Crawford paid a police sergeant twenty-five dollars "to run us down 7 miles below the rocks." The following day, after passing the mouth of the Hootalinqua without recognizing it, they returned to locate a townsite on the banks of that mighty river.

The Hootalinqua (also known as Teslin River) was a major artery of an alternate route into the Klondike, known as the Stikine River Route. Crawford's company envisioned great wealth, not only from dredging the river but also from selling supplies to two hordes of stampeders floating by the townsite, one disgorging from Lake Bennett and the other from Lake Teslin and beyond. Thus, Crawford's first serious effort to realize his dream of striking it rich in the Klondike began here on the banks of the Hootalinqua, about 365 miles from Dawson City. And even though troubles soon nearly overwhelmed the Poet Scout, he continued to espouse his own optimistic formula for success. He had shared this code with other gold seekers in a whimsical poem he recited at a farewell social held in the Lake Bennett church. The last stanza follows:

But joking all aside, good friends,
Success or failure all depends
On you. Each one must do his part,
Must work with hands and brain and heart,
For there is no such word as fail,
Except to those who will not sail
When winds are fair. So come what will,
Despite the rushing stream or hill,
Press on! and climb. Say "never die,"
And you will get there bye and bye.[47]

10
Two Years in the Gold Fields

Crawford spent two months on the Hootalinqua hastening to establish a base camp before the Yukon winter prevented access to the outside. He labored under the twin handicaps of a noncommunicative company president and a rebellious crew. His journal entry for July 19, 1898, reflects his growing frustration: "I am pretty nearly disgusted after such a trip to not find a line or a dollar here. I can only wait and keep men at work, altho they only do what they cannot avoid. They are disgruntled and want Delmonico feed."[1]

Jack put the men to work building a cabin, while he went prospecting along the riverbanks. But the men chafed under his supervision. Younger than Crawford, they would not or could not work with the same intensity that he brought to a task. Wilcoxon and Cassidy refused to carry logs for building the cabin, insisting that a horse be utilized. Impatiently, Crawford explained that the logs were light and that the horses were in such poor condition they would not survive the winter unless allowed time to recover. "Other miners build their cabins without horses and there is no excuse for you not to do the same." In an outburst of pique, he

Captain Jack's Wigwam in Dawson, Yukon Territory. (Courtesy Rio Grande Historical Collections, New Mexico State University Library.)

threatened to expel them from camp unless they carried out his instructions.[2]

While the cabin was under construction, Crawford slept in a tent, pleasantly surrounded by his books, writing table, and other mementos. Mrs. Donaldson and daughter Alta lived on the scow, which also doubled as a store. Stocked with surplus company provisions, the enterprise soon did a brisk business and would provide Jack with funds to proceed to Dawson. Later that fall, laborers completed a large log trading post and converted the scow into a bunk house and restaurant.[3]

But even before winter cabins were built, Crawford and three of the men began sluicing gravel at the mouth of the river. Two men dipped water into the sluice boxes, while Jack shoveled in gravel and another man forked out the coarse material. This process produced a residue of black sand, which Crawford would carry to Dawson to have tested for platinum.[4]

Crawford and the others also cleared land for spring planting. Donaldson, a practical farmer who was to winter on the Hootalinqua, believed that he could raise enough vegetables to supply all future expeditioners. In a letter to Maria dated August 24, Jack reported that the potatoes he had planted twelve days before as an experiment were already three inches above ground: "Radishes planted 3 weeks ago are almost ready to eat." He enclosed a few berries, "perfect orange color, good to eat," instructing her to plant some in rich black soil in the house. They would look pretty, he said, with flowers and wreaths.[5]

Crawford also wrote of personal matters. "I cannot tell you how sore and tired I am," he lamented. "The little black flies (not mosquitoes) have eaten my hands so that in my sleep I tear them. Am using salt and watter [*sic*]." He found joy in the company of little Alta, who bestowed a kiss upon Captain Jack each morning and evening. "If it had not been for the presence and influence of this little 8 yr. old girl," he avowed, "I would sometimes forget I was not among savages." Crawford expressed concern about his son Harry, who apparently was considering leaving a job with the railroad to farm the Crawford property at Fort Craig. In writing of his son, the Poet Scout could not refrain from chiding a younger man for his inability to sustain hard labor. "While railroading may be hard," he wrote to Maria, "it dont compare with the work a man must do on a ranch and Harry never cared to put in 10 hours every day at real labor."[6]

In another letter dated August 28, intended for publication, Crawford described the limited amusements at the camp: whist, seven-up, euchre, and sometimes penny ante, with beans to represent pennies. "We have in camp," he added, "two Mandolinists, one Violinist, one Accordianist, and a half dozen Mouth Harmoniconists. So we have music, and the drama occasionally." They also encountered a stream of visitors, including two young men from Albuquerque—Ortiz and Merritt—who were prospecting on the Hootalinqua. Young Lucien Pierce of Boston, another visitor, operated a small dredge at the mouth of the river. "This dredge," Crawford reported, "is the first on the upper Yukon."[7] Jack lamented that his own dredge probably would not arrive on the Hootalinqua before spring. Still, he envisioned a bustling community sprouting on the company's townsite within twelve months, capable of sustaining at least one hundred expeditioners. Later that winter, in fact, Donaldson supervised building operations, reporting to Jack, on December 2, the completion of his wife's cabin, a stable, and a large addition to the main building.[8]

Loading supplies and equipment on two boats and a raft of logs, Crawford started for Dawson on September 13, accompanied by Cassidy, Wilcoxon, Kidder, and possibly photographer George Cantwell, who had joined Crawford's party at Lake Bennett. Although river travel below Hootalinqua was fairly safe, Jack left no record of his nine-day trip down the Yukon. Traveling this same route several weeks earlier, Martha Purdy had found smooth sailing, though she later recalled: "Day after day we passed unbroken mountain ranges and wooded river banks—a sameness of scenery which became monotonous."[9]

But Crawford sped down the Yukon, aware that winter was close at hand. The first snow fell in Dawson on September 14, and cakes of ice dotted the river on the twenty-second, about the time he approached the ramshackle town. By mid-November the river would be completely frozen over, with temperatures falling to fifty degrees or more below zero.[10]

Stampeders like Purdy and Crawford found Dawson to be a raw, frontier mining town, sporting a floating population of several thousand people. Hundreds of boats lined the wharves and littered the shoreline, with tents, shanties, log cabins, saloons, and gambling and dance halls jumbled together along mud-clogged streets. Lumber was exorbitant, and good town lots sold for forty thousand dollars. Fortunately, some departing Californians let Jack have their cabin, enabling him to use his raft for firewood.[11]

Crawford arrived in Dawson without Cassidy and Wilcoxon, however, for the younger men had headed straight for the gold creeks. Captain Jack later claimed that they deserted the company. Nonetheless, he immediately set to work in building a cache to store goods and supplies, while Kidder "fixed up" the cabin, hauled firewood, and cooked. Crawford also made a tour of the company's placer claims, which, as we shall see, turned out to be worthless.

Although his dreams for achieving great wealth were about to be shattered, the Poet Scout quickly gained distinction in Dawson as an entertainer welcomed by "respectable" audiences. Numerous saloons, gambling dens, and dancing halls catered to Dawson's predominantly male population, but there were few places of entertainment where "good women" felt comfortable. Still, civic-minded stampeders like Crawford organized entertainments and social events to improve the quality of life for the entire community, thereby providing acceptable social events that the good women of Dawson could attend.

Typical of such social gatherings, although one not lacking in controversy, was a gala entertainment that the Benevolent and Protective Order of Elks staged on October 25, with the proceeds to go to charity. That afternoon, seventy-five horn-clad Elks, accompanied by the Tivoli Theatre band, kicked off festivities by parading down First Avenue, with Captain Jack serving as grand marshal. A planned serenade at the *Klondike Nugget* had to be aborted, however, when the band instruments froze up in the cold. Later that evening, the "Best People on Earth" filled the Tivoli Theatre to the rafters. "Dawson's society simply turned out en masse," the local press reported, "and a more brilliant assemblage probably cannot be seen in any theater, than merrily applauded the various turns which rapidly succeeded each other upon the stage." [12]

Captain Jack gave the opening address, closing his remarks with "Broncho vs. Bicycle." Seventeen other presentations followed, ranging from songs and recitations to a club-swinging exhibition. Cad Wilson, a well-known dance-hall entertainer, concluded the evening with a selection of songs. But her presentation outraged some members in the audience. Exactly what she did is not known, although in reporting on the incident Crawford said that she had insulted "respectable Ladies, Brother Elks, and other Gentlemen, by vulgar acting and unwomanly conduct." The *Klondike Nugget* censured Wilson in its October 29 edition, stating that Cad's

> act caused ladies to reach for their wraps and many and severe were the comments at the conclusion. They felt they had been inveigled to a charity benefit under false pretenses. . . . the ladies in front hung their heads and their escorts wished they had never brought them. . . . Words are hardly strong enough to express our condemnation of anyone who deliberately and premeditatively insults the better part of an audience. [13]

About three weeks later, Captain Jack entertained in Pioneer Hall, presenting in verse and story "graphic descriptions of Western phases of American life." The *Klondike Nugget* labeled the evening "an unqualified success." Because of its earlier condemnation of Cad Wilson's performance, the *Nugget*'s praise for Captain Jack is worth repeating, for it underscores his popularity with middle-class Americans.

> That was a remarkable audience for Dawson which attended Captain Jack's entertainment at the Pioneer hall. It was remarkable in that so large a proportion were ladies, some of them even with infants in their arms. The reason is apparent to everyone, for the Captain has been with us long enough and his reputation is such that his name was a guarantee to all that the performance would be absolutely clean and above cavil. The large patronage demonstrates that there is an opening in Dawson for a class of entertainment where gentlemen may safely take their wives and daughters.[14]

On November 15, Crawford presided as master of ceremonies at the opening of the Regina Club, a men's organization with quarters in the recently constructed Regina Hotel, owned by the North American Trading and Transportation Company. The tallest building in Dawson, the Regina Hotel featured a spacious dining room on the first floor, with the club's main rooms on the third. "They are about the only rooms in Dawson," the press remarked, "where one is surrounded with the same degree of comfort and elegance as in the most pretentious of the outside cities." A gymnasium was on the fourth floor, where club members engaged in fencing, boxing, and other athletic amusements. For the formal opening, local entertainers presented a program of songs, stories, violin solos, and a sparring match. During the performance, Crawford preserved order by using "his silver mounted revolver as a gavel." Among important guests in attendance were Commissioner William Ogilvie (Major Walsh's successor), Gold Commissioner Thomas Fawcett, and U.S. Consul James McCook.[15]

In one of the Elks' last social sessions of the year, Captain

Jack again shared the stage with Cad Wilson. Her performance garnered neither praise nor condemnation in the local press, but Crawford and a few brother Elks protested the appearance on the program "of the same character [who] had insulted the ladies who attended our last benefit entertainment." In fact, Crawford threatened to prefer charges "of conduct unbecoming a gentleman" against the Elk responsible for inviting Wilson to the stage. The tempest eventually blew over, but for weeks the episode provided the ice-bound community with an absorbing diversion.[16]

Crawford's emotional state at this point was anything but tranquil, for since arriving in Dawson he had experienced both agony and ecstacy. The agony came first and would have a more lasting effect. Sometime before the river froze over, Dr. G. F. Washburne slipped into town with orders from Frank Vrooman to investigate Crawford's management of company affairs. He apparently also arrived with credentials replacing Captain Jack as the company's chief representative in the field. Not surprisingly, Crawford took umbrage at this move and shortly thereafter tendered his resignation as the company's assistant general manager. Already suspicious of Vrooman's honesty, Crawford would soon conclude that Vrooman was swindling the stockholders.[17]

Before making a complete break with the company, however, Crawford joyfully announced that he had finally struck it rich. Shortly after arriving in Dawson, he employed Willis E. Everette, a mining engineer, to analyze the black sand scooped up on the Hootalinqua. The sand proved to be rich in platinum. Crawford printed one hundred copies of Everette's report to send to friends, newspapers, and members of the company. He shared this information with Maria in a letter dated December 2. "Well I have mighty good news for you," he announced. "I have made the most important discovery that has been made in this country. . . . Nothing discovered has caused so much excitement [in Dawson] as the discovery of Platinum in such quantities as well as gold in these gravels." In fact, during the first week in December the *Klondike Nugget* ran two feature articles on Jack's discovery.[18]

The December 2 letter and another that Crawford wrote to Maria on January 15 shed light on conditions in Dawson during the winter of 1898–99 and also on Jack's consuming drive to achieve financial success. In the December 2 letter, he told Maria that stomach problems had kept him confined to the cabin the past ten days. Sickness, in fact, was widespread. "Strong men are dying here every day," Crawford wrote, "mostly from typhoid fever." This terrible disease also claimed the life of twenty-three-year-old May Edgren shortly after she gave birth to a baby girl. Crawford "wept like a child" while delivering her eulogy at the Methodist church, where the casket was draped in his big American flag.[19]

Crawford admitted to Maria that he would have to take better care of himself. "I did abuse myself fearfully going 15 miles up creek when thermometer was 45 below zero. Walked 7 miles alone and my leg gave out from old wound. Could scarcely drag myself along." Although Jack's letters were being sent out, none were coming into Dawson. He began his letter of January 15: "Not a word yet from home or from company. No mail in 3 months. I am very much discouraged."[20]

Despite this glum pronouncement, Crawford wrote optimistically of various financial schemes. He hoped "to make big money" from a half-interest in the "Newberry Washer," a machine that George W. Newberry invented for washing gold from gravel. Crawford had two of the machines in Dawson and predicted that "every bench claim will need one." He also wrote of marketing some kind of plant or herb in one-pound packages as an antiscorbutic. Samples introduced earlier in Dawson had been enthusiastically received: "Everyone here is wild about it—[it] is a great scurvy remedy." And he wrote of "big money" to be made by shipping burros into the Klondike, expressing the hope that Harry would arrive with a herd in the spring.

Although company worries and the harsh environment placed severe strains on his sunny disposition, warmth and good-will suffuse the Christmas greeting that Crawford sent to friends. Yuletide, in fact, found Dawson enveloped in subzero temperature and near perpetual darkness. Superintendent Sam Steele recalled that for twenty-seven days, in January 1899, Dawsonites did not see the sun, and lamps had to be lit all day.[21] The final stanza of Jack's short Christmas poem follows:

> *And I feel the sunshine twinkling*
> *Through the icy atmosphere;*
> *While the Christmas bells are tinkling,*
> *Tolling—Christ again is here.*
> *Faith and hope were never stronger,*
> *Since I started up Life's hill,*
> *I can wait, and hope, yet longer,*
> *Aye, and trust the Master still.*[22]

Crawford did not wait very long, however, before denouncing Frank Vrooman as a swindler and the Klondike, Yukon and Copper River Company as a fraud. His case against the company and its president is stated most clearly in two newspaper stories appearing in April 1899. The *Yukon Sun* headlined its story "Crawford Says It's a Swindle," while a San Francisco paper shouted "Captain Jack Crawford Tells a Tale of Woe of the Yukon." In these accounts, Crawford claimed that the company's prospectus made false claims; Vrooman had exaggerated the value of the company's properties to obtain money from stockholders. The firm owned only five placer claims in the gold district, Crawford discovered, rather than ten, as stated in the prospectus. Moreover, Jack had solicited testimony from Gold Commissioner Fawcett and Mining Recorder R. B. Craig showing that the claims were of no great value.[23]

The prospectus also stated that within a short distance of the company's claims on Eldorado Creek, "Hank Summers, the noted Alaska pioneer and prospector, owns a claim, out of which he is said to have taken $800,000 in gold, and $102,000 of which he took out in thirteen days." Crawford avowed that Summers had never made this statement. Indeed, when Summers cut his ties with the company several months earlier, he demanded that Vrooman remove this statement from the prospectus.[24]

Crawford still believed the dredging properties might prove valuable, but even on this issue Vrooman had deceived the public. Vrooman had advertised that the company owned dredging privileges for twenty years, yet Crawford discovered that the rental fee for this privilege amounted to 17,500 dollars per year— an amount beyond the company's ability to pay. Furthermore, the law required that a dredge be placed on each of the dredging claims, yet the company had failed to place a single machine in the Yukon. And Crawford claimed that because he had refused to send out glowing accounts of the richness of the company's properties, Vrooman sent Washburne to replace him and "to represent the claims as valuable."[25]

Henry M. Wallace, another disillusioned stockholder, joined Crawford in denouncing Vrooman and even tried unsuccessfully to obtain a receiver for the company on grounds that it was insolvent. In papers filed in court, Wallace claimed that the company had lacked finances to transport to the Klondike several stockholders who had invested as much as fifteen hundred dollars for the privilege of prospecting for the company. When faced with litigation over violation of the men's contracts, Vrooman had accepted Wallace's proposal to raise four thousand dollars to transport these "delayed expeditioners" from Ann Arbor, Michigan, to the Klondike, in exchange for eight thousand shares in the company. Wallace claimed, however, that the company violated its agreement, forcing him to take even more expeditioners who had been stranded in Chicago, Seattle, and Dowagiac, Michigan, awaiting funds from the company. When Wallace and his party finally reached the Hootalinqua, they were nearly destitute because the company failed to pay for transporting their supplies from Dyea. Wallace subsequently returned to Chicago to confer with Vrooman; when the company president refused to aid the men on the Hootalinqua, Wallace filed suit in court.[26]

Vrooman mounted a vigorous counterattack, charging that Wallace, Crawford, and other minority stockholders had "conspired to wreck the company and get possession of its assets in dredging rights and mining claims." The fate of the Klondike, Yukon and Copper River Company is unknown, but a letter that its directors issued on October 27, 1899, partially vindicates the stand of Wallace and Crawford. After expounding on the alleged riches in the Hootalinqua dredging property, the directors asked stockholders to subscribe for an additional twenty-five thousand dollars in stock. Rental fees of six thousand dollars on the Hootalinqua had to be paid to the Canadian government within two months. Moreover, despite its earlier claims, the company owned not a single dredge. The one shipped to Seattle the previous year, the directors stated, had been sold without their consent. Thus, the directors needed an additional nineteen thousand dollars for building and transporting a dredge to the Hootalinqua.[27]

A man with lesser determination than Jack might have sulked through the long Klondike winter, bemoaning his ill fortune. With characteristic energy, however, Crawford rebounded from his split with the company and found other opportunities for accumulating funds. On February 25, 1899, he wrote Maria that he had made more than one hundred dollars the previous week by staging entertainments and that he would continue this work until spring, "when I hope to have a good little stake to come out with." After a quick trip to New Mexico to "prove-up" some mining claims, he planned to return to Dawson to look after valuable property that he did not want "to sacrifice." [28]

Exactly what property Crawford did not want to sacrifice remains a mystery. But we do know that by the time he eventually left Dawson in the summer of 1900, he had acquired some "promising" mining claims and a Dawson town lot on which he had erected the "Wigwam," a combination eating house and trading post. Crawford advertised this establishment in the following manner: "When in town stop at Capt. Jack's Wigwam. Warmest stable in Dawson. Grain and hay always on hand. Cigars and tobaccos. Good comfortable beds. Drinks of all kinds (soft). Warm and cold storage. Groceries and general merchandise. Special attention given to orders from creeks. Goods shipped promptly and satisfaction guaranteed." [29]

In an interview with the press upon leaving the Klondike, Crawford implied that he had built the Wigwam soon after breaking with the company. From the beginning, Jack stated, he intended "to make it a strictly cash affair." Thus, he placed the following sign in a conspicuous place:

> *I've trusted many friends through life,*
> *Whose bills stand unadjusted.*
> *Not only did I lose these friends,*
> *But credit, too, and busted.*
> *And so I say to friends today,*
> *Within this frozen region:*
> *"Don't ask for trust,*
> *And narie a bust,"*
> *And friends will still be legion.* [30]

Crawford hired a sign painter to attract attention to his unique establishment, which was located just above the court house. In gaudy colors, the signs listed the Klondike luxuries sold inside: "Ham and eggs, $1; coffee and pie or cake, 25 cents; coffee and sandwiches, 25 cents; figs, dates and candies; fresh cow's milk, 25 cents per glass." A special feature of the Wigwam was ice cream, the price of which was omitted from the signs.[31]

In addition to his business enterprises, Crawford staged entertainments and performed at public functions. On February 21, 1899, he presided at the Volunteer Fire Department's social, during which he recited a descriptive poem about a recent fire and the heroic actions of the Dawson fire fighters.[32] He also attended church regularly, on occasion visiting the Methodist church on a Sunday morning and the Presbyterian church in the evening.

On Sunday, March 5, he and Dr. Mary E. Mosier stood up as godfather and godmother to little baby Mae Eldorado Edgren during her christening at the Presbyterian church. That evening, Dr. Mosier hosted a dinner for widower Edgren, Reverend Dickey, Captain Jack, and other invited guests. Mosier and Baby Edgren, in fact, became minor Klondike celebrities. Soon after the christening, Mosier invited one hundred friends—including Captain Jack—to celebrate her recent admission to the ranks of Dawson's practicing physicians. She also became the baby's foster mother and cried copious tears when Mae Eldorado was sent to live with relatives in Wisconsin. Before the baby's departure, Captain Jack and others staged a benefit entertainment, with the proceeds going to the motherless infant.[33]

During the first quarter of the new year, Crawford kept up a voluminous correspondence with Maria and a host of friends, including James Barton Adams, Marie Madison, Jim Tanner, A. C. Wendell, and others. He also worked at revising *Tat; or Edna, The Veteran's Daughter,* the play he had coauthored with Jim Adams. On several occasions, Jack read the play to friends gathered at the Regina Hotel or at some other convenient location.[34]

The arrival of spring revived sagging spirits, and Klondikers began working their claims with renewed energy. Captain Jack must have felt this same sense of renewal, for he elected to remain in the Yukon another year. Superintendent Steele recalled that the summer of 1899 "was delightful," while Martha Purdy singled out June as "the loveliest month of all the year." "The trees budded into leaf," she went on to say, "and the ground and hillsides were carpeted with wild flowers."[35]

Basking in the sun's radiance, Dawsonites staged a gala Fourth of July celebration, which began one minute after midnight when a gun was fired and a horde of Americans and Canadians commenced parading through the streets. A more orderly parade got under way in midmorning, after the populace gathered on the waterfront near the Alaska Commercial Company's store to march to the police barracks. As grand marshal of the day, Captain Jack led the parade on horseback, followed by a twenty-three-piece band. After the throng arrived at the Northwest Mounted Police Square, Colonel C. O. Davis presided over a program of band selections and speeches, including "a patriotic speech and recitation by Captain Jack Crawford." The crowd responded with cheers for the Queen of England and the President of the United States. The remainder of the day was devoted to sports and games.[36]

But summer also witnessed a steady stream of Klondikers departing for the outside. Among those to leave was Superintendent Sam Steele, who had orders to report to Montreal. Dawsonites gave Steele a royal send-off, clogging the wharves and cheering as his steamer started upriver for White Horse Rapids. A few days later, Captain Jack's poem, "A Tribute to Colonel Steele," appeared in the *Klondike Nugget*.[37]

With the coming of winter, Klondikers again settled in to endure subzero temperatures and near-perpetual darkness. It was a season to try one's soul. Jeremiah Lynch, who spent three years in the Klondike, states in his reminiscences: "This is a fearful place for one to live in throughout his life, or even for a single winter. It is so cold, so cold, that energy, ambition, and even life itself, seem not worth the value of a warm fire and a comfortable apartment."[38]

Crawford would have understood Lynch's assessment, for a second winter in the Klondike found the Poet Scout close to despair. His letter to Maria dated January 25, 1900, is filled with expressions of gloom and self-pity. He assured his wife that he was "still hustling," though he had experienced "some close calls" while traveling alone with his mule in sixty-degree-below-zero weather. One close call (which he failed to report to Maria) occurred two weeks earlier, when Crawford and his mule fell through the ice into the Klondike. Had he not received aid from two passing travelers, he would have frozen to death. Jack told Maria that he had not been sleeping well. "I twist & jump around all night." "Oh how I wish I had never come in here," Jack lamented, "and the scoundrel who has played me false will account to me some day as sure as there is a God." Problems at home preyed on his mind: a land company lay claim to the Crawford property at Fort Craig, and "jumpers" reportedly had commandeered his copper camp in the San Andres. Crawford concluded his lengthy letter with this uncharacteristically gloomy passage:

> My life has been a great big bubble the worst kind of a fizzle and a total failure. I cannot expect to do anything now. I am out of date and a back number and in order to get recognized there is only one thing for me to do *and that is die.* Then you will be pleased with the beautyfull [*sic*] obituarys [*sic*] which you will read from all over the union.[39]

Jack was still feeling glum on March 4, when he turned fifty-three. "My birthday and a sad one for me," he wrote Maria, "I feel so lonely and I have a bad cold." Nonetheless, he had resumed staging entertainments. On the last day of February, he gave a two-hour performance to a crowded house on Hunker Creek. A newspaper correspondent reported the next day: "This is the fifth time I have listened to the Poet Scout on Hunker, and I find him always new and original. Capt. Jack is a gentleman, a soldier and a patriot, and is deserving of success." To Maria, Jack noted that he would start up the creeks on the fifth to give six more entertainments. But "it is hard to get people out when it is 40 below zero." [40]

Despite his winter pessimism, Captain Jack still retained his amazing ability to please a crowd. On the evening of April 1, the people of Dawson packed Pioneer Hall "to hear and enjoy the many quaint stories and sayings of the Poet Scout." "For over two hours," the *Dawson Daily News* reported, "Captain Jack held his audience and the hearty applause that greeted his every effort was the best evidence of the satisfaction he was giving." Following one recitation that captured the house, the audience showered the stage with silver coins. [41]

In following weeks, Crawford overcame his despondency and resumed his relentless pursuit of the American Dream. Early in June, he informed Maria that a wealthy young miner had agreed to finance the staging of Crawford's play in the states. Crawford planned to leave Dawson in two weeks, and "immediately when I get out," he wrote, "I will be making money." Having regained some of his old optimism, Jack predicted: "There is a big field for me and a good nest egg for our old days." "Here goes for one more effort," he confided to Maria. "Let me fail in this and I am ready for retirement." He continued to worry about his New Mexico property, but he instructed Maria to "be of as good cheer as you can." "If all [property] goes," he counseled, "we must rise up phoenix like from our ashes and make a little home somewhere. But not in New Mexico." [42]

On June 15, the *Dawson Daily News* announced Jack's departure from the Klondike, in a lengthy article headlined "Captain Jack is Going, His Play to be Put on in 'Frisco." The *Daily News* assured its readers that "nobody in the Klondike region has a wider personal acquaintance and fewer enemies than Captain Jack." "The captain hasn't got rich in keeping with his deserts in this country," the press went on to report, "but nobody may say he has not a brave heart and infinite good temper." A few days later, Dawsonites staged a benefit performance for the Poet Scout, during which they presented him with a token of their esteem: a combination badge, representing the Eagles, Grand Army of the Republic, and Elk lodges, made of Klondike gold.[43]

Crawford left Dawson on June 25 and reached St. Michael at the mouth of the Yukon on July 2. Later that evening, he boarded the steamer *Utopia* for Nome, Alaska, arriving the next afternoon. Two years earlier, gold had been discovered on the sands of Nome, sparking a stampede during the summer of 1899. Gold seekers continued to pour on to these Alaskan beaches the following summer, when Jack arrived on the scene.[44]

Crawford spent about ten days in Nome, giving a brief address at the rousing Fourth of July celebration. He had intended his stay to be even shorter, but the threat of a smallpox epidemic kept shipowners from sailing, fearing they would not be allowed to land at San Francisco or Seattle. While in Nome, Crawford met Maria's brother Billy Stokes, who shared Jack's dream of striking it rich in the gold fields. In a letter dated July 6, Jack told Maria that her brother was "very comfortably fixed for quarters," but would soon start into the interior with a partner to "see if they can find anything." Jack closed his letter by stating that his health was good and that he was sleeping in a tent on the tundra.[45]

Crawford's arrival in San Francisco on July 27 was heralded in the local press, for despite his failure to make a fortune in the Klondike, Captain Jack remained a celebrity. His stage career, in fact, would depend upon keeping his name before the public. That Crawford continued to draw large audiences in later years negates his winter assessment of being "out of date and a back number."

But Crawford's gamble in trekking to the Klondike had not paid off. Instead of gold nuggets, Crawford reaped a harvest of unpaid debts, broken promises, and personal doubts. Still, he became a respected member of the Klondike community, with his goodwill and charitable deeds making life more bearable for the ice-bound stampeders than might otherwise have been the case. And in the end, he overcame his own despair to embark yet again on a stage career. An unwelcome consequence of the Klondike gamble, however, was the strain it placed on the Crawford marriage. Even though his Klondike letters make it clear that he envisioned an old age with Maria at his side, Crawford eventually would ask for a divorce. No mortal is guaranteed perpetual happiness, yet Jack would persist in its pursuit with undiminished energy. "Here goes for one more effort" sums up a personal creed that would not admit of defeat.

When your head is bowed in sorrow
And your soul is out of tune,
When the prospects of tomorrow
Are behind a veil of gloom,
Can't you see the light beyond it—
Just a glimmer of the prize?
Keep a groping and you'll find it
Just a blessing in disguise.[46]

11

"A Genius in Buckskin"

Boston journalist Nixon Waterman labeled Captain Jack "A Genius in Buckskin" soon after his return from the Klondike. In introducing the Poet Scout to his readers, Waterman quoted a line from Shakespeare, "And one man in his time plays many parts," adding that in writing this line the bard of Avon must have had Captain Jack "in his mind's prophetic eye." After describing Crawford's checkered career, Waterman touched upon a character trait that endeared the Poet Scout to his audiences and closest friends—his unfailing optimism. "He is a perpetual sunshiner," Waterman observed, "looking on the bright side of life with so much of success that those about him find themselves doing the same thing and discovering bits of blue sky while the cynic and pessimist would do nothing but bewail the stormy weather."[1]

Crawford's great optimism, in fact, meshed perfectly with the nation's prevailing mood at the turn of the century. Progressives of that era expressed enormous faith in American potential, for the United States had just completed a victorious war and eco-

Captain Jack as he appeared on stage in his later years. (Courtesy Rio Grande Historical Collections, New Mexico State University Library.)

nomic prosperity was once again in sight. Because poverty, disease, and the misuse of political and economic power still plagued the nation, however, reformers spearheaded a broad reform campaign to create a better American society. Between the Spanish-American War and World War I, progressives worked for social justice, better education, improved working conditions, and a wide variety of other reforms.

Crawford shared with progressives a belief that people could perfect society. And he also shared their ambivalence toward great wealth, seeing it as a force for both good and evil. Above all else, however, Jack believed, like Andrew Carnegie (a man he greatly admired), that wealth carried moral responsibilities and should be used for the betterment of humankind. Crawford's special concern during this era of reform was the building of character among the nation's young men. He sought wealth, in part, to establish a boys' camp in Michigan and to launch The Boy Heroes of the World, a national organization he founded about the time that Boy Scouts of America burst upon the scene.

Unfortunately, materials to document fully the last seventeen years of Crawford's life are missing. During most of this time, however, the lecture circuit was the chief source of his income. Clearly, the Poet Scout continued to reach for the stars, laboring to keep his name before the public and to acquire the great wealth that seemed always to elude him. In his quest for success, Crawford rubbed shoulders with many of the nation's rich and famous.

In rejoining the lecture circuit, Captain Jack profited from the nation's rising enthusiasm for western subjects. Early twentieth-century magazines catered to eastern appetites for stories about cowboys, Indians, and frontier heroes, while western novels poured off the presses. Owen Wister's *The Virginian,* published in 1902, rapidly became a best-seller. And Buffalo Bill continued to thrill large audiences both in Europe and the United States with his mock Indian battles, cowboy competitions, and riding-and-shooting exhibitions.[2]

"A Genius in Buckskin"

The popularity of the Virginian, Buffalo Bill, Captain Jack, and other western heroes (real and imaginary) stemmed, in part, from the nation's headlong rush to industrialize and to reap material benefits from technological advances. This new world of giant corporations and monopolies seemed to threaten older virtues and life-styles that many Americans wanted to preserve. Many turn-of-the-century reformers, in fact, became disenchanted with eastern cities, viewing them as centers of vice and corruption. To some observers, true Americans resided in the West. Indeed, the West became an "attractive counterimage" to the industrialized East. The rhetoric of progressives like Theodore Roosevelt and conservationist Gifford Pinchot incorporated images recreating an older rural America, a western Arcadia, a land of individualism and egalitarianism. And so across the land, people looking for an alternative to an industrial and urban life-style were strongly attracted to the romanticized vision of the West offered by Wister, Cody, and Crawford.[3]

Shortly after his return from the Klondike, Captain Jack appeared in *Tat; or Edna, The Veteran's Daughter* at the Alta Theatre in San Francisco. The play had all the elements that theatergoers desired in a western melodrama: action, suspense, manly heroes, conniving villains, unmitigated love. Set in Wyoming and the Dakotas, the story has in its cast a corrupt Indian-agency clerk; a mountain girl named Tat; an educated Indian girl; her blackguard father, Lame Dog; and a young eastern girl named Edna masquerading as a boy who works to avenge the death of her father, who was killed by the corrupt clerk. In the end the hero, Jack Wallace, played by Captain Jack, saves the good people from an Indian ambush instigated by the villainous clerk, and he is in court when Edna, on trial for the attempted murder of the clerk, reveals her true identity and the reason for her murderous thoughts. She wins acquittal and Jack's hand in marriage. Woven into the story are themes of patriotism, temperance, charity, and Indian–white friendship.[4]

Chapter 11

Despite the positive reviews that *Tat* received, it must not have generated sufficient funds to warrant production in other cities. At any rate, to refill his coffers Crawford fell back on his proven ability to entertain as a lecturer. Before leaving the Bay area, he staged "The Campfire and the Trail" in San Francisco, Palo Alto, Stockton, and a few other localities, and then continued entertaining on his homeward journey.[5]

During the next two years, Captain Jack followed a demanding schedule, touring the countryside as an entertainer and laboring to develop his mines and ranches. He was in Los Angeles, in May 1901, to witness President William McKinley's arrival just months before an assassin's bullet cut short the Ohio statesman's life, making Theodore Roosevelt the nation's youngest president. Among the most memorable of Jack's entertainments, however, were those staged in Autumn 1902 in Butte, Montana, and Denver, Colorado, to raise funds for striking miners in Pennsylvania.[6]

Flushed with his success on the platform, and with the Klondike disappointments receding in memory, Captain Jack reached a crucial decision. He would go to New York City, the capital of the entertainment world, to make yet another effort to strike it rich as a lecturer.[7] Having made this decision, Crawford nearly ceased to be a resident of New Mexico; for the next decade, he was constantly on the road, making only brief visits to San Marcial and his San Andres holdings.

Upon reaching New York City in late November 1902, Crawford became a human dynamo, racing from one engagement to another, seeking contacts that would open new avenues to fame. During the first week in December, he entertained at the banquet of the Loyal Legion, at Delmonico's, and at the Snow Festival, at the Waldorf-Astoria, where he spent nearly a half-hour in conversation with Mrs. Russell Sage, wife of one of New York's great financiers. Jack confided in a letter to a friend that the good woman, soon to become the nation's foremost woman philanthropist, had invited him to visit and entertain at her home. Crawford followed these triumphs with a Sunday evening visit with the talented Ella Wheeler Wilcox, a well-known poet and journalist, who thereafter kept up a sporadic correspondence with the Poet Scout. Crawford also boasted to his friend that in a forty-eight-hour period, he had dined "by special invitation with gentlemen representing over 100 millions of wealth."[8]

Crawford's persistence reaped a whirlwind of dividends. His photograph soon graced the front page of the New York *Journalist,* and requests for personal appearances mounted. During the first half of 1903, he crisscrossed the eastern half of the U.S., entertaining in New York, West Virginia, Florida, Georgia, Kansas, and Missouri. In Jack's eyes, however, his greatest triumph during these months came in April, when he substituted for the eloquent General John B. Gordon, commander in chief of the United Confederate Veterans, at the Albany, Georgia, chautauqua, where he entertained before an audience of four thousand.[9]

In November 1903, Captain Jack embarked upon an extended lecture tour through the South, entertaining in such urban centers as Nashville, Atlanta, Birmingham, and Savannah. His praise of the Confederate war dead and his longtime devotion to cementing friendship between Union and Confederate veterans helped endear the Poet Scout to southern audiences. When the *Atlanta Journal* announced the death of General Gordon in January 1904, it published Jack's tribute to the fallen hero, entitled "Hail to the Chief." This and several other poems by Crawford, including "The Gray and the Blue Under One Flag," appeared a few weeks later in the Atlanta *Gazette,* a journal devoted to temperance.[10]

Crawford was on the road during much of 1904. The summer was particularly memorable. In June, he was the guest of Ella Wheeler Wilcox at her summer home at Short Beach, Connecticut; and on the Fourth of July, he entertained at the Lexington, Kentucky, chautauqua. The following month, he toured the grounds of the Louisiana Purchase Centennial Exposition, then under way in St. Louis. And, in fact, he interrupted his lecturing to serve briefly as director of amusements at the exposition.[11]

Later that fall, Crawford descended upon the nation's capital to entertain at the Soldiers' Home. Soon after his arrival, he received an audience with President Roosevelt in the White House. Crawford undoubtedly felt a kinship with the president, for the two men shared a deep love for the outdoors and a practical knowledge of western ranching. Captain Jack, in fact, idolized Roosevelt, calling him "the greatest man on earth today." Even though he endorsed Roosevelt in the coming election, Crawford would not be making political speeches as he had in the past, he told a reporter, because the Republican party had insufficient funds to pay him.[12]

Crawford continued lecturing through the winter and into the following spring, leaving a trail of delighted listeners in his wake. On April 3, 1905, the New Orleans *Daily Picayune* began a two-column article on the popular entertainer by stating: "Captain Jack Crawford, the poet scout, quite won the hearts of a hundred or more boys in the big auditorium of the Young Men's Christian Association yesterday afternoon." A few days later in San Antonio, Texas, he witnessed President Roosevelt's triumphal visit to the city and then attended a reception held in the president's honor.[13]

In mid-May 1905, Captain Jack was in Atlanta on another lecture tour through the South. Thereafter, he crisscrossed the country, reportedly filling fifty-seven engagements between June 12 and early September. The grueling pace continued thereafter, with Crawford sometimes traveling through the night to meet his next day's engagement.[14]

Crawford spent a joyous Christmas that year in East Aurora, New York, as the guest of Elbert Hubbard, a flamboyant writer, lecturer, and popular philosopher, who gathered about him in his Roycroft community a glittering array of the nation's great and near great. Hubbard is best remembered for publishing a monthly magazine, *The Philistine,* in which he attacked conventional social and religious mores. At his Roycroft community, named for the seventeenth-century English bookbinders Samuel and Thomas Roycroft, Hubbard also oversaw the production of quality furniture, tooled leather-bound books, rugs, baskets, stained-glass lamps, and a variety of other home-crafted items. Dressed in flannel shirt, baggy trousers, and heavy shoes, and adorned with shoulder-length hair, Hubbard presided over a semisocialistic community, where employees and invited guests shared meals, menial labor, and evening discussions and entertainments. Those who knew Fra Elbertus, as he styled himself, either worshipped or hated him; few were indifferent.[15]

Captain Jack had traveled to East Aurora to arrange for the publication of a new volume of poetry. Once there, he fell under Hubbard's spell. Hubbard's "health-and-salvation gospel," featuring "fresh air, honest toil, individualism, and positive thinking" mirrored Crawford's own philosophy. Moreover, Crawford found the camaraderie of Hubbard, his wife Alice, and the other Roycrofters irresistible. During his Christmas visit, Crawford staged five entertainments for the Roycrofters. Hubbard later praised Jack in the pages of *The Philistine,* saying, in part:

> There is only one poet in America who can read his own stuff with an equal pull on our heart strings, and that is James Whitcomb Riley. I'll go you a "Stetson" against a stogie that Harvard, Yale, Columbia, and Princeton have not a man on their roster that can hold an audience of two thousand people for two hours, and not a person leave, or want to leave. Captain Jack can do it, and moreover can adapt himself to any kind of an audience, from Chicago newsboys to a parliament of religious. The man is a marvel of manly strength, fluid intelligence, flowing wit and oratorical grace.[16]

Crawford was to remain friends of the Hubbards until they met an untimely death with the sinking of the *Lusitania* in 1915.

During the first part of 1906, families across the Midwest and in Texas flocked to the Poet Scout's performances. In March, he received a great deal of public acclaim when he appeared in Vicksburg, Mississippi, for the dedication of the Pennsylvania Monument at Vicksburg National Park. The complete text of Crawford's touching ten-stanza poem, written for the occasion, "Roll Back the Years," appeared in the Vicksburg *Daily Herald.*[17]

Seemingly without pause, Crawford continued his hectic pace. Between May 30 and September 6, Captain Jack reportedly filled forty-one paid engagements. May Crawford joined her father for part of this summer tour, handling secretarial chores. In mid-August, she accompanied Captain Jack to the Grand Army national encampment in Minneapolis, where the Poet Scout was one of the star attractions. Crawford's old friend Jim Tanner presided over the encampment as commander in chief of the national organization. But a sadness occasioned by Mrs. Tanner's death, two months earlier, muted any joy the two men might have experienced in their reunion.[18]

During the next five years, Crawford crisscrossed the country, entertaining thousands of Americans with his poetry and stories. Certain memorable performances punctuated his frenetic drive for fame. In mid-January 1907, Captain Jack entertained ninety guests of millionaire mine-owner Thomas F. Walsh, at his palatial home on Massachusetts Avenue in the nation's capital. Among those present were ten members of the U.S. Senate, twenty members of the House, Associate Justice Joseph McKenna, and Secretary of Treasury Leslie M. Shaw. At a gathering at the Walsh residence on the following evening, Crawford entertained thirty-five select guests, including Vice President Charles W. Fairbanks, Associate Justice John M. Harlan, and Mrs. Marshall Field. Later, Walsh sent a congratulatory note to Jack, assuring him that "Washington is ringing with your praises."[19]

Crawford made his second appearance among the Roycrofters at Thanksgiving in 1907. It was as joyous an occasion as his Christmas visit two years earlier. There was time for horseback riding, wood chopping, and high jinks. (Someone placed cockleburs under Jack's saddle, and then everyone watched the sixty-year-old Poet Scout give a rodeo exhibition as he rode the bucking horse to a standstill.) On Thanksgiving night, Crawford entertained a packed Emerson Hall, where "enthusiastic applause greeted every poem, song, or story." [20]

In the spring of 1908, Crawford was again on tour in the South. The following January found him lecturing on the East Coast, where he staged a performance at the U.S. Military Academy at West Point. [21] He also found time to show "cousin" Isabel Crawford the sights of Washington, D.C. A missionary to American Indians, Isabel was touring the country and giving public lectures. Her biographer claims that she saw Captain Jack perform in 1907 for the first time and liked him right away. "She considered him jolly, witty—and a gentleman. Though he was much older than Isabel, she went out of her way to befriend him." Believing that she and Jack might be distant relatives, she wrote to a genealogist in Belfast, requesting an investigation. Although the researcher found nothing to connect Captain Jack with Isabel's family, the two became close friends, calling each other *cousin.* On occasion, the two Crawfords appeared on the platform together, with Jack dressed in buckskin and Isabel in Indian costume. [22]

The capstone of Crawford's 1909 tour came on March 9, when he entertained at Dungeness, an island off the coast of north Florida owned by Lucy Coleman Carnegie, Andrew Carnegie's sister-in-law. Lucy's husband, Tom, had built a mansion on the island before he died in 1886, and she had added several cottages in later years. It was here that Andrew Carnegie found a restful retreat from New York during the winter months. In December 1908, Crawford had sent him a copy of his newest book of poetry, along with a brief statement about his work among American boys.

The outcome was an invitation to perform at Dungeness. Crawford spent a day there, entertaining an audience of Carnegie guests and employees, playing golf with Andrew and his friend Tom Miller, and dining with the Carnegies in the mansion. Captain Jack left the island with a five-hundred-dollar check from the great industrialist.[23]

Later that year, Crawford made his debut on the vaudeville stage in Pittsburgh, performed at Keith's Theatre in Philadelphia, and entertained Effie Germon and other aging thespians at the Actors' Home on Staten Island.[24] For two weeks in January 1910, he made daily appearances at the Eden Musee, a popular amusement center on Twenty-third Street in New York City. In March, Crawford was among speakers who lauded Commander Robert E. Peary at a dinner given in the explorer's honor at the Hotel Astor.[25] During the rest of that year, and continuing through 1911, Captain Jack traveled the countryside entertaining wherever he could secure dates. In the spring of 1912, he made a memorable trip to the Panama Canal Zone at the government's expense to stage a series of entertainments for construction workers and their guests. And later that fall, Crawford campaigned in New York City on behalf of Teddy Roosevelt and the Progressive party.[26]

But financial problems now weighed heavily upon the peripatetic entertainer. On January 23, 1913, his secretary, Mrs. Eugene L. Cox, the former Polly Goerke, informed Maria Crawford that Captain Jack "has had but very few dates of late." In fact, his expenses had been so heavy that he had given up his residence at the Broadway Central Hotel in New York City and was boarding with the Coxes on West 104th Street.[27]

Despite a sharp decline in entertainment dates, Crawford remained a popular figure at gatherings of Civil War veterans. On July 4, 1913, he was in Gettysburg, Pennsylvania, to commemorate the fiftieth anniversary of the Battle of Gettysburg. At this memorable meeting, attended by more than sixty thousand veterans,

Crawford helped to organize the United American Veterans, a new society comprised of Union and Confederate ex-soldiers. In September, he traveled to Chattanooga to attend the national encampment of the Grand Army of the Republic. On the Sunday preceding opening ceremonies, the *Chattanooga Daily Times* printed two of Crawford's patriotic poems. The same newspaper singled out Captain Jack as one of the most colorful figures in the massive parade that saw twelve thousand Union veterans march through the city's streets.[28]

Starting about 1914, the focus of Crawford's entertainments shifted slightly to reflect changing world conditions. In mid-April of that year, President Woodrow Wilson ordered the occupation of the Mexican port of Veracruz in an attempt to unseat the reigning dictator, Victoriano Huerta. At the same time, war clouds building in Europe threatened to blanket the entire world. And in fact, less than three months after U.S. Marines entered Veracruz, Archduke Franz Ferdinand, heir to the Austro-Hungarian throne, was assassinated, precipitating World War I.

During the spring of 1914, Crawford entertained troops aboard the U.S.S. *Texas,* bound for Mexican waters, and was scheduled to perform on the *Wyoming* the following week. But his biggest plunge into the nation's growing involvement with world events came in the following year, when he took part in filming *The Battle Cry of Peace,* a spectacular movie preaching military preparedness. Although his role was to be a small one, Crawford's expectations were high. On April 10, 1915, he wrote to his daughter Eva: "I have every reason to believe that within the next few months I will be a leading star in one of the big moving picture companies."[29]

Before the public had a chance to see Captain Jack on screen, however, the nation was rocked by the sinking of the *Lusitania,* a tragic event that heightened patriotism in the United States and bolstered the military-preparedness campaign. Patriotism had long been a feature of Crawford's platform performances; now his patriotic poems and stories would receive even more publicity. On May 16, the *Brooklyn Daily Eagle* carried a two-column article on the Poet Scout, featuring his latest composition, "My Mother Raised Her Boy to Be a Soldier." Crawford wrote this song, the press reported, to protest the singing in the public schools of "I Didn't Raise My Boy to Be a Soldier," which he considered unpatriotic.[30]

Proponents of military preparedness, such as Crawford himself, saw no imminent threat to the United States in 1915, nor did they push for immediate intervention in Europe. But they did want to expand the army and navy.[31] Their cause received an enormous boost with the showing of *The Battle Cry of Peace.*

The movie was based on Hudson Maxim's book, *Defenseless America.* Maxim argued "that America could keep out of the war only by making itself a mighty military nation." The British-born movie pioneer J. Stuart Blackton turned the book into the movie extravaganza, which featured a cast of thousands and made a star of Norma Talmadge. The film shows a defenseless America being invaded by enemy forces. Enemy battleships lob big shells into congested districts of New York City. Enemy airplanes drop bombs into the heart of the city. Panic-stricken Americans flee the approach of marching columns of enemy soldiers. Homes go up in flames, the capitol in Washington crumbles.[32]

Crawford plays only a small part in the film. He is shown at a great Fourth of July celebration, where a large crowd of veterans gather about a stars-and-stripes covered platform. With long white hair streaming to his shoulders, a buckskin-clad Captain Jack delivers the oration of the day to the cheering throng.[33]

The Battle Cry of Peace was shown for the first time before an invited audience in New York City on August 6, 1915. Four days later, it was shown to government officials and military officers gathered at the National Press Club in Washington. Many eastern audiences thereafter had the pleasure of seeing Captain Jack in person when the movie premiered in their city. To stir up patriotism, Blackton hired Crawford to deliver a five-minute speech prior to the showing of the film. By mid-November, Jack had appeared for four weeks at the Vitagraph Theatre on Broadway, two weeks at a Chicago theater, and one week in Boston. Later he introduced the movie in Philadelphia and spent two weeks doing the same in Washington, D.C. At the close of his speech, Crawford would take the American flag from a stack of guns and, raising it aloft, give a tribute to Old Glory. Shouldering the flag, he made his exit to warm applause.[34]

As fighting in Europe intensified in 1916, Jack continued speaking out for preparedness. During these same months, he scrambled to pick up a few paying engagements, but at age sixty-nine he no longer commanded the public attention of former days. Still, for at least a decade following his return from the Klondike, Crawford had repeatedly subjected audiences to his own vision of the American West. Although striving for authenticity, he used his talents to romanticize America's frontier past. Like other image makers of the day, he viewed western expansion as progress, the fulfillment of the American Dream. The West was a land of freedom, prosperity, abundance, and manly self-reliance. His optimistic and inspiring message infused audiences with national pride. But the image he and others projected was to become so imprinted on the American mind that modern-day historians have difficulty in separating myth from reality.[35] In an increasingly urban and industrial society, Crawford helped define the western experience.

Crawford imparted this same vision in his writing. Indeed, despite a demanding lecture schedule, Captain Jack scored several literary triumphs, producing during his last years three volumes of poetry, two plays, and several short stories. In 1904, William A. Bell of Sigourney, Iowa, published Crawford's *Lariattes, A Book of*

Poems and Favorite Recitations. A longtime friend of the Poet Scout, Bell operated a printing shop and mainly filled orders for the amusement world—publicity brochures, posters, programs, and so forth. He had little experience in publishing books, and after producing *Lariattes,* he vowed not to publish another. The finished product was a disappointment.[36]

Because of *Lariattes*'s technical flaws, Crawford was eager to produce another poetry book. This led him to East Aurora, where, in 1908, Hubbard's Roycroft printing shop published *The Broncho Book,* available either in limp-leather or hard-cover binding. Crawford later admitted that he gave away three copies for every one he sold. He mailed an appropriately autographed copy to President Roosevelt, who sent, in return, a brief note of appreciation. "My dear Captain Jack," the president wrote, "That beautifully bound book of the Broncho has come. I value it for its own sake and for the sake of the author."[37]

Late in 1910, Crawford's slender volume, *Whar' the Hand O' God Is Seen,* was published by the New York Lyceum Publishing Company. A second and slightly enlarged edition appeared in 1913, and both editions carried James Barton Adams's attractive foreword. Although most of the poems had already appeared in print, Jack believed the public would welcome this new collection.[38]

Within a span of two years, Crawford copyrighted two plays: *The Dregs,* in 1907, and (in collaboration with Marie Madison) *Colonel Bob: A Western Pastoral in Five Acts,* in 1908. *The Dregs* is a short dramatic monologue depicting the downfall of a drunkard, while *Colonel Bob* is a romantic drama thinly based on Crawford's Klondike experience. But we have no information on the staging of either play.[39]

Nor do we have a complete listing of Crawford's published short stories. One that attracted considerable notice, "The Last of the Indian Chiefs," appeared in the February 1905 issue of *Mun-*

sey's Magazine, a popular illustrated monthly. Congratulatory letters inundated the Poet Scout, for *Munsey's* previously published authors included such notables as Theodore Roosevelt, William Dean Howells, and Bret Harte.[40]

About the time the *Munsey* article appeared, the New York sculptor August Zeller completed a clay bust of Captain Jack, which was then cast in bronze. The finished bust was mounted on a tall pedestal, bedecked with small figures depicting Crawford's life in the West. Crawford and Zeller both were delighted with the sculpture, with Zeller writing to Jack: "It has even passed my highest expectations." Thereafter, the Poet Scout often pictured the bust in his publicity brochures.[41]

Another of Crawford's creative endeavors was his collaboration with the talented musician Albert D. Liefeld, an expert on several instruments. Liefeld gained fame as a composer and director of Liefeld's Venetian Orchestra of Pittsburgh (an all-woman orchestra). At least two songs, the words by Captain Jack and the music by Liefeld, appeared in 1907, and included "Faith," a memorial hymn in honor of Mrs. William McKinley. Five more Liefeld–Crawford songs were to follow.[42]

Crawford achieved several literary successes in 1908, in addition to *Colonel Bob.* In January, the *Philistine* published his sensitive poem, "The Womanhood of Man," and the *Banner of Gold* published his short story, " 'Madcap Nellie,' A Story of a Texas Cattle Ranch." *Farm and Fireside,* a popular farm magazine, devoted an entire page to Captain Jack in its February 10 issue; the subtitle of the article read: "An Appreciation of Captain Jack Crawford, the Poet Scout, and His Great Work for the Uplifting of Young America." [43]

Some of Crawford's literary projects never reached publication. On April 12, 1910, for example, he signed a contract with publisher Richard G. Badger of Boston to produce "Scouting in the Sunshine," a book of poems, stories, and reminiscences of life on the frontier, designed to appeal to the American boy. Crawford's Billy the Kid story was to be in the book, along with an account of his Klondike battle with grasping capitalists. Even before signing the contract, Jack had asked Tom Nicholl, a Chicago artist, to do the illustrations. For reasons that Crawford did not record, however, the book was never completed.[44]

Crawford also intended to write a book on the life of Wild Bill Hickok. While entertaining on the Pacific Coast in 1900, Crawford visited with Joseph "White Eye" Anderson, Wild Bill's sidekick, and persuaded him to write down the details of Hickok's last days. It is no longer possible to corroborate Jack's avowal of friendship with the colorful Wild Bill, assassinated in Deadwood during the Black Hills gold rush. Still, Crawford became one of Hickok's chief defenders in later life. When Calamity Jane died in 1903, for instance, Crawford wrote a long article, published in the New York *Journalist,* to set the record straight about the alleged romantic connection between Calamity and Wild Bill. In the last eighteen months of his life, the Poet Scout diligently solicited stories and reminiscences from Hickok's surviving family and comrades. But death intervened before the biography was written.[45]

On stage and in his writing, Crawford often exhibited the soft side of his nature—a certain quality that others found attractive. Jack celebrated this quality in "The Womanhood of Man," a poem that redefines the concept of masculinity. For want of a better term, he was exalting the femaleness that is found in men and women alike—the tenderness and sensitivity that allows us to show our humanity when others are most in need of it. In the last stanza, Crawford says:

> *'Tis the womanhood of manhood*
> *That is always reaching out;*
> *It has been my lone companion*
> *While on many a dangerous scout,*

"A Genius in Buckskin"

And wherever fate may place me
I shall do the best I can,
To be worthy of the manhood
Of the Womanhood of Man.[46]

Crawford, in fact, presented a new role model to the nation's youth, a manly man unafraid to express emotions and to write of his love for a male friend. Victorian boys had been taught to hide emotions, to suppress tender affections. The nation's "cowboy" president, Teddy Roosevelt, epitomized the super-masculine hero who leapt from the pages of late nineteenth- and early twentieth-century magazines. Fascinated with manliness, Roosevelt worshiped the strong man and the strenuous life. For this reason, he found much to admire in the stories of Owen Wister, who, in Roosevelt's words, wrote of "grim, stalwart men."[47]

With his emotional openness and soft male side, Crawford was helping to redefine masculinity in an age of rapid industrialization. And it was this openness, this tender masculinity, that helped to win for him a substantial following among the nation's young men. Since first mounting the rostrum, in fact, Crawford had been deeply committed to their moral development. At every opportunity he spoke to boys in schools, churches, Y.M.C.A. auditoriums, and correctional institutions, advising them, in his own inimitable style, to lead good lives and to avoid strong drink and trashy literature.

During the first decade of the new century, Crawford stepped up his activities on behalf of American boys, sharing with other progressives a deep concern for their physical and moral well-being. After listening to one of his preachments, the boys in Las Cruces, New Mexico, organized the Captain Jack Crawford Company of the Order of the American Boy.[48] A few years later, in 1906, Crawford devised plans for opening a boys' camp at Onekama, Michigan, a small settlement on Portage Lake near the Lake Michigan shoreline. Captivated by Onekama's spectacular scenery, Crawford saw it as an ideal setting to continue his efforts to make better men of boys. He outlined his plans in a form letter soliciting entertainment dates so that he could earn money to finance his dream. He would instruct the boys in "horsemanship, shooting, hunting, and all athletic pastimes." He would take them on tramps through the woods, camp out under the stars, and "put confidence in them such as they cannot get from any other source and teach them the principles of self reliance." With his poems and stories, he would entertain the boys and elevate their character.[49]

Crawford's dream of running a boys' camp never fully materialized. Sometime in 1907, he purchased property at Onekama and leased a building suitable for staging entertainments. By the following summer, "The Scout's Retreat" boasted two four-room tents, each fourteen by twenty-one feet, which he rented for twenty dollars per month. Although Crawford struggled to finance his camp, even approaching Maria about mortgaging their house (which she refused), he would eventually lose his Michigan property, unable to keep up the payments.[50]

Even more ambitious was his attempt to create a national boys' club. During the spring of 1911, Crawford entertained five hundred boys at the Rahway, New Jersey, State Reformatory. It was at this memorable meeting that Crawford's Boy Heroes of the World was conceived. Typically, when speaking to incarcerated youth, Crawford gave a heartrending talk on temperance that frequently left the boys in tears. As Captain Jack concluded this speech, the Rahway superintendent called upon the boys to be real heroes. "Liquor has put most of you here," he declared, "and I want every Boy Hero before me to raise his hand with me and swear . . . never to touch intoxicants from this day on forever."[51]

The sight of practically five hundred hands going up provided Jack with inspiration. He asked the boys to write to him, telling him that they meant to keep the pledge. In return, he would send each boy his photograph, and to the youngster writing the best letter, a copy of his new book of poems. The response was overwhelming. Within a week, Crawford received more than four hundred letters. Shortly thereafter, he announced plans to start a boys' organization, to be called Boy Heroes of the World.

As Crawford envisioned it, Boy Heroes were to be organized on both sides of the reformatory wall. His goal was to encourage American boys to lead pure and upright lives. Consequently, Boy Heroes pledged themselves against intoxicants, cigarettes, trashy literature, and vulgar speech. Boys on the outside, in addition, promised to act as brothers to reformatory youth, assisting them to make good once they had gained their freedom. Boy Heroes were to be organized into local camps, each with its own boy commander. Although extant Crawford papers fail to illuminate fully the organizational structure of the Boy Heroes, Crawford clearly envisioned some kind of an adult national advisory body, with himself as provisional chief of scouts.[52]

Crawford was to claim that within three years of the organization's birth, more than seventy-five hundred boys had joined, many of them high school and college students and members of Sunday schools. And although the number is impossible to verify, the *New York Evening Sun* reported, upon Crawford's death in 1917, that twenty-five thousand Boy Heroes were then scattered "all over the world."[53]

The most successful boys' organization at this time was the Boy Scouts of America (BSA). Tradition credits a British general, Robert Baden-Powell, for creating Boy Scouts in Great Britain in 1907, and then exporting the idea to the United States, where the BSA was officially begun in 1910. Forerunners of the BSA included Ernest Thompson Seton's Woodcraft Indians and Daniel C. Beard's Sons of Daniel Boone. Although Jack worked on a much smaller scale, his efforts among boys overlapped that of Seton, Beard, and

Baden-Powell. And while this trio concentrated their efforts primarily on middle-class boys, Crawford worked among boys cast aside by society. In the end, however, Crawford lacked both the finances and organizational ability to make the Boy Heroes a permanent fixture in American society.[54]

Crawford also lacked the finances to protect and develop his New Mexico properties, a failure that must have been among his life's greatest disappointments. In 1894, the owners of the Armendaris land grant entered suit against Crawford for ejectment from his Fort Craig ranch, which they considered to be part of the grant. That same year, an agent for the owners, then known as the Valverde Land and Irrigation Company, purchased government buildings on the abandoned Fort Craig reservation. Jack vowed to fight the company, believing his soldier's homestead claim would stand up in court. The case was scheduled to come to trial soon after he returned from the Klondike. But for reasons not apparent in surviving records, the case was settled out of court in 1902, when Crawford relinquished claim to the ranch in exchange for fifty-seven lots in San Marcial.[55]

Sometime earlier, possibly when Jack departed for the Klondike, Maria and daughter May had left the Fort Craig homestead and moved into San Marcial so that May could attend school. Still, loss of the ranch was a crushing blow; for more than twenty years the Crawfords had worked to improve the property. In negotiating a settlement with company officials, Jack wrote that he would always "regret that I could not have made a permanent home for my old age under the old cottonwoods [at Fort Craig]."[56]

About four years after losing their ranch, the Crawfords began building a new residence in San Marcial. Maria supervised its construction, for by this date Jack had rejoined the lecture circuit and was rarely home. It was to be a spacious house, consisting of two bedrooms, a big dining room, kitchen, and a large living room with a bay window. A screened sun porch separated the dining and living rooms, and a roofed porch extended across one side of the building. Elsewhere on the property, which covered half a block in the middle of town, were chicken coops, barn, and a pasture for horses.[57]

Although Crawford lost his ranch, he had more success in holding on to his mining claims, even though he failed to profit from them. Prior to his return from the Klondike, a sudden jump in copper prices caused the mining world to go "copper mad." Miners from nearby areas stampeded to the San Andres Mountains, some intent upon jumping Crawford's claims. During this troublesome time, A. J. Harrison supervised Crawford's assessment work and succeeded in protecting most of his property.[58]

Crawford hoped to capitalize on this renewed interest in copper by organizing a development company that would use his holdings as a nucleus for further expansion. To attract eastern capital, he issued on April 15, 1901, a five-page description of his mines and ranches, a detailed map of the area, and a brief report from surveyor W. W. Jones, who said that Jack's copper mines were the best in the country. Despite Crawford's optimism, however, the mines failed to attract many investors.[59]

Nonetheless, Jack would not abandon his dream. In 1909, he organized a new development company, his last major push to realize a return on the small fortune that he had sunk into these mines. On September 28, he conveyed to the Captain Jack Crawford Copper Mines Company ten mining claims and five mill sites in the San Andres Mountains. With characteristic optimism, Jack wrote to a friend the following spring: "I have everything in my own hands and expect my new Prospectus will be out in a few days and am confident I will get enough money to do considerable development work and know I can uncover a big body of ore." And indeed, the company raised several thousand dollars through the sale of stock in the months that followed.[60] But Crawford died without ever realizing a return on his investment; nor, apparently, did any of the investors or his family benefit from his mines.

Jack's precarious finances, in fact, coupled with his prolonged absences from home, severely strained the Crawford marriage. A letter he wrote in late 1903, in which he scolded Maria for her unnecessary pessimism, reflected their growing estrangement. Two years later, about the time he first visited the Roycrofters, he broached the subject of divorce. In justifying his actions, Jack would later complain that Maria had never sympathized with his stage and platform ambitions and, in fact, had ridiculed his efforts. Maria explained their marital discord by referring to Jack's long absences and to the family savings he had squandered in worthless mining schemes.[61]

But the divorce did not come about, for the Crawfords could not reach agreement. Jack offered to deed the home in San Marcial to Maria and to provide alimony payments. Maria, however, wanted, in addition to the house, a cash settlement of three thousand dollars—an amount Crawford could not or would not muster. Since neither wanted to settle the matter in court, they merely agreed to go on living much as they had in the past. Crawford acknowledged his estrangement from Maria in a letter to May, dated September 16, 1906: "You know how matters stand between your Mother and I. And it is better so there will be no more quarreling. We will be good friends."[62]

After Crawford died in 1917, his name was linked romantically with that of Polly Cox, his secretary. Much younger than Captain Jack, she had started working for him while still a single woman, about a year or two after he first asked Maria for a divorce. Years later, when applying for a widow's pension, Maria testified that she and Jack had finally separated in 1912, although he continued to write and, on occasion, to send money. At the time of his death, Jack was living with the Coxes in Woodhaven, Long Island. May Crawford, testifying on behalf of her mother's pension application, stated that when she visited her father during his final sickness, she had gained the impression that "his relations with Mrs. Cox had passed beyond the bounds of convention." The letters Mrs. Cox wrote to James B. Adams following Jack's death seem to corroborate May's statement. That Polly Cox grieved deeply for Captain Jack and loved him dearly is beyond dispute.[63]

In the last years of his life, Crawford took pride in his children's accomplishments and enjoyed hearing news of his grandchildren. He saw his family infrequently, however, and probably never returned to New Mexico after 1912. Indeed, the Crawford separation troubled his relations with his children. May and Harry rarely wrote to their father, although years later May's daughter recalled that her mother had never sat in judgment of Captain Jack. Crawford gained the strongest support from his oldest child, Eva, his "broncho girl" of old Fort Craig. Although Eva struggled to understand her parents' predicament, she kept her father informed of family matters and sent pictures of the grandchildren.[64]

But Eva Reckhart was too ill herself to be with her father during his last illness. Early in January 1917, Jack visited evangelist Billy Sunday in Boston, where he caught a severe cold that turned into pneumonia. On January 30, both the *New York Times* and the *Minneapolis Evening Tribune* carried stories that the sixty-nine-year-old Poet Scout was dying.[65]

Even as death approached, Crawford remained the perennial optimist. The *New York Times* had this to say in its report of Captain Jack's final illness:

> Captain Jack Crawford, a picturesque survivor of Indian fighting days and known as "the Poet Scout," was reported as seriously ill last night at his home in Woodhaven, L.I. Although he had Bright's disease, asthma, and pneumonia, the veteran refused to believe that he would not recover. His physicians held a consultation and agreed that he could not live more than a few hours, whereupon he dismissed them.
>
> "I'll try Christian Science," he whispered. "I am not ready to give up yet." Two healers were summoned at his request, and the Captain sent out word to reporters last night that he felt much improved.[66]

Polly Cox wired the Crawfords in New Mexico of Captain Jack's illness, and May Crawford (engaged to a young man from

New York) was dispatched as the family emissary. She stayed in New York City about a week; then left when her father seemed much improved. On February 1, Captain Jack dictated his last poem, thanking friends who had sent flowers during his illness. Among messages he received at this time (according to a New York press release) was one that Theodore Roosevelt sent, which read: "I know the Broncho will pull through."[67]

But John Wallace Crawford, the Genius in Buckskin, died at 3:00 A.M. on February 28, 1917, at his home in Woodhaven. Newspapers across the nation reported on the event, with one writer paying tribute in these words: "[Crawford] was a real scout, and a real poet—a man with a warrior's soul and the heart of a woman."[68] The *New York Evening Sun*'s account of Crawford's death called attention to his friendship with Buffalo Bill Cody, who had died in January of that same year.

> As [Crawford] lay in bed ill from a complication of diseases he got the news that Colonel Cody, with whom he had ridden in many a wild charge against the Sioux, had gone over the great divide. It depressed him.
>
> "So Bill Cody has gone!" said Captain Jack. "I guess they will be sounding taps over me pretty soon. Well, when we meet Tall Bull and that tough old codger Sitting Bull on the other side and stick up our hands, palms forward, and say, 'How, Kola!' there will be a lot to talk about."[69]

On March 2, 1917, funeral services were held at the Nostrand Avenue Methodist church, with Dr. Herbert B. Munson delivering the eulogy. A Presbyterian minister also spoke, reviewing Captain Jack's career as soldier, scout, poet, and patriot. Honoring Jack's request, the Ulysses S. Grant Post of Brooklyn conducted Grand Army services. Although none of Crawford's immediate family was present, a large delegation of veterans attended in uniform.[70]

Captain Jack was buried at the National Cemetery in Brooklyn; an American flag was interred with his remains. Today, a simple white government-issued slab marks his final resting place, with the inscription reading, "John Crawford." This simplicity is fitting, for despite his relentless drive for recognition, Jack was, at bottom, unpretentious and openhearted. With characteristic humor, the Poet Scout once said: "I am simply Jack Crawford, boy soldier, rustic poet, scout, [and] bad actor."[71]

> *Sleep, soldier, sleep! Rest thou in peace.*
> *No more thy silvery voice shall ring.*
> *Our love of country must increase*
> *While sentiments from you we sing,*
> *And as you mingle with the boys,*
> *The dear old boys, so brave, so true,*
> *With Stonewall, Lee and Grant rejoice*
> *And tell them we are coming, too.*[72]

Epilogue:
"If I But Could"

A BRONCHO PHILOSOPHER

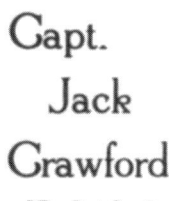

Capt. Jack Crawford

"*The Poet Scout*"

Writes:-

"I'd rather find a wayward stray,
And help him to his own,
Than entertain the angels at
A picnic round the throne."

And that is exactly what "Jack Crawford" has been doing for over thirty-five years. No living man "of equal means" has 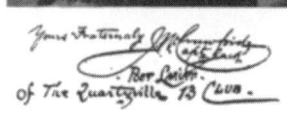 given more to help suffering humanity than has the "Poet Scout," and his thirty-five years of platform and dramatic experience makes him the peer of any man living as *an all around Unique, Clean, Versatile and Uplifting Entertainer,* and no living elocutionist can read the "Poet Scout's" poems as can the "Poet Scout" himself.

Jack Crawford spent his entire life in pursuing the American Dream. His quest took him from one part of the North American continent to another, from Ireland to the United States and then briefly back again to the British Isles. A man of remarkable talent and enormous drive, he had a personal magnetism that attracted a wide following among the elite, common folk, eastern urbanites, western settlers, and, especially, the nation's youth. De-

Publicity material for the Poet Scout. (Courtesy Rio Grande Historical Collections, New Mexico State University Library.)

spite certain foibles, he was a good man. Some who fell under his spell even called him a great man, "A Genius in Buckskin."

Crawford spent more years on the stage entertaining audiences than he did in the field scouting for the army, yet it was his reputation as a daring frontier scout that first captured the public's imagination. His accomplishments in the West were real and not imaginary, however; he actually lived the adventures he described. His companions in the Sioux campaign knew him as a brave man, a man of great physical endurance, and a boon companion around the campfire. Few accounts of the Black Hills gold rush fail to mention his exploits as miner, scout, and civic leader. Hence, South Dakota has claimed him as "The Poet Scout of the Black Hills."

In truth, South Dakota residents are more likely to recall Crawford's deeds than are residents of New Mexico, where the Poet Scout settled and raised a family. This lack of recognition among New Mexicans is ironic, for during his lifetime he labored to advance the state's political and economic development, earning the gratitude of his contemporaries. Because of his celebrity status, he gained wide coverage in the New Mexico press, with his name becoming a household word during the last two decades of the nineteenth century.

Even though South Dakota and New Mexico both claimed the Poet Scout as their own, his talents were too large to be appropriated by any one state or territory. He rightfully can be called the Poet Scout of the West, a platform virtuoso who captured the hearts of the entire nation with his poetry and stories. Modern critics find little merit in his poetry, but this was not so of readers in the middle to late nineteenth century. As one journalist phrased it at the time of Jack's death, his verses "struck a popular chord. They were unpolished but wholesome. . . . He put universal thoughts into common place words. He reached an audience that seldom read the major poets . . . but his influence was altogether good."[1]

Crawford's life was seldom dull. He sought adventure on the battleground and in the gold fields. But two compelling desires permeated his life—to write and to perform. Indeed, he came alive before an audience, whether he appeared in an outdoor amphitheater, a San Francisco theater, or on the chautauqua platform. He had a magnificent stage presence and an uncanny ability to capture his audience. Hudson Maxim, author of *Defenseless America*, explained part of Crawford's success in this manner: "He has a full, sonorous, musical, powerful voice, tone-colored to every emotion—a voice that compels the heart's sympathy and wells tears up into the eyes, or makes the eyes flash with indignation, as with fine dramatic ability he touches correspondent chords of feeling." [2]

For more than thirty years, Crawford entertained audiences with tales of the American West. In describing his impact upon listeners, one journalist claimed that it was not so much what Jack had to say as the way he said it. "It is the fire of genius in his eyes," the writer declared, "the perfectly infectious musical laugh, the kaleidoscopic face, and withal a jolly off-hand way that wins every heart and makes every one happy and at home." [3]

Although Crawford frequently drew tears from his audience, his goal was to uplift their spirits, to make people look on the bright side of life. He knew about the wrongs and evils in American society, but he believed in the "remedial properties of optimism." "Much of the misery and disaffection," he told a reporter, "comes from artificial gloom of which many people seem to have a fondness." [4]

On the platform and in his writings, Crawford conjured up for thousands of Americans vivid images of the vanishing frontier. He sought to portray the authentic West and to negate the misconceptions generated by dime novels and the Wild West shows of Buffalo Bill. But in his role as a showman, he inevitably romanticized the West, creating in the minds of his listeners a land of excitement, freedom, and opportunity, where good people always triumphed over adversity. Having established a reputation as a bold frontiersman, Crawford became a symbol of America's heroic frontier past. He was also among the nation's most influential image makers, helping to create a mythic West that continues to baffle and fascinate modern-day historians. But Crawford's own career, with its failures and disappointments, gives a more honest representation of life in the West than the images he projected on stage and in print.

The West that Crawford described was a land of spectacular beauty, which he celebrated in his writings and performances. He found spiritual renewal in the western landscape, especially at his ranches along the Rio Grande. Yet Crawford did not lament the passing of the old West. He worked for its transformation; he eagerly sought development funds that would radically change the texture of western society. Although he loved the West, he spent the last years of his life in New York City, an urban metropolis already feeling the blight of industrialized society. He lived in the East primarily to further his stage career, but he also enjoyed its bustling social life, which was unavailable to him in New Mexico.

Crawford's celebrity status exacted a price, for he was constantly on the road, filling one engagement after another. This meant prolonged absences from Maria and the family, a pattern he had established even before becoming a popular platform entertainer. There is no doubt that these absences contributed to the dissolution of the Crawford marriage. Yet Crawford's travels were dictated as much by his concern for his family's financial security as by his thirst for adventure. Like other nineteenth-century American men who left home to improve family fortunes, Crawford corresponded regularly with his wife, sent money, gave instructions for managing the ranches and finances, and appealed to neighbors to aid her whenever possible.[5]

Although always hard pressed for money, Crawford never lived in actual want. Many of his friends said that he was too generous and trusting to be a good businessman. Crawford himself recognized his lack of certain business qualities. Yet, with pride, he told a friend: "I may be wild, erratic and devoid of one iota of business sense, but I am honest."[6] Crawford, in fact, represented the best of the Gilded Age entrepreneurs. While relentlessly pursuing his golden dream, he remained a man of principle, honest and loyal to his friends. Yet he typified many Gilded Age Americans, with his willingness to endure privations to achieve personal gain. He also embraced the values of turn-of-the-century progressives, who celebrated progress, civic improvement, and moral betterment.

Friends and fans alike viewed Crawford as a kind, witty, upright, and unselfish man, one who "would not knowing[ly] misrepresent anything."[7] One newly acquired friend sent this heartfelt testament: "Ah, Captain, if there was more men like you—men who lived more for the uplifting of humanity and less for themselves what a bright world this would be. I wish instead of there being one of you that there was a thousand."[8] Many people found his tender manliness attractive; others responded to his sincerity and lack of vanity. Even the editor of the New Mexico *Daily Optic*, who chided Crawford on occasion for his relentless pursuit of fame, concluded that he was "a genuinely modest man."[9]

Crawford's most loyal friends always believed he deserved the same kind of fame that the nation bestowed upon Bill Cody. They claimed that Crawford's refusal to allow authors to glorify his deeds kept him from reaching Buffalo Bill's level of stardom. After the Poet Scout's death, William A. Bell joined forces with Eva Reckhart and other family members to publish a book about Captain Jack and his western adventures. Bell wanted it to be a "Wild West blood and thunder" story, something that would have life to it. "That is what the public wants," Bell avowed, the "kind of a book poor Jack never wanted to get out."[10] Although Bell and the Crawford family collected material for this book, it never became a reality.

James Barton Adams possessed the talent to write a biography of his friend, but Adams died of pneumonia in 1918 in Vancouver, Washington. Maria Crawford lived the last days of her life with her married daughter, May, in San Antonio, New Mexico, a few miles north of San Marcial. Maria died at San Antonio on March 11, 1925. Harry Crawford worked many years for the railroad, though in 1909 he moved his family from San Marcial to Clovis, New Mexico, where he opened a fuel yard and became the town's mayor. He died in Albuquerque in 1945. He and his wife raised five children, three of whom are still living as this book goes to press: Marion Crawford Hageman, who lives in Carlsbad, California; Fred Crawford, a resident of Silver City, New Mexico; and Harry Richards Crawford, who lives in a retirement home in Socorro, New Mexico. Harry R. Crawford's daughter, Harriett Crawford Richardson, has spent years collecting Captain Jack memorabilia, donating the core of her collection to New Mexico State University in 1985.[11]

Eva Crawford Reckhart lived most of her adult life in El Paso, Texas, where she died in 1948. Her son, Francis, died in an accident while still a young man; her daughter, Irene, married but remained childless. May Crawford married Ernest C. Brechtel soon after her father's death. Two of the Brechtels' four children are alive today, Evelyn Brechtel Lewis of Oakland, California, and Dorothy Brechtel Flumerfelt of Portland, Oregon. Their mother, May Crawford Brechtel, died in 1962 in Moab, Utah.[12]

Family and friends lamented the passing of their "fallen hero." Crawford was a product of his time, however, displaying qualities typical of nineteenth-century men of action—burning ambition, enormous physical stamina, the propensity to take risks. Yet he was also unique. His striking personality won him a legion of friends. His uplifting entertainments taught Americans about their frontier heritage, instilling in them a pride of country. He crusaded passionately for temperance, the American boy, miners, veterans, and preparedness, and against dime novels and fake western heroes. Sincere in his convictions, he worked to improve American society. He rarely ever faltered in his belief that he would succeed, though recognizing that some goals lay beyond his grasp. Still, it was his willingness to accept challenges that allowed him to reach new heights in his career. And in his lifelong quest for fame, he never lost his humanity or his passion in assisting troubled souls.

> *If I could clothe each jeweled thought*
> > *That comes to me from Nature's bowers*
> *In classic language, such as taught*
> > *Away from western woods and flowers,*
> *If I could sing the sweet refrains*
> > *That in my soul in silence cluster,*
> *From many a heart I'd strike the chains,*
> > *And give the star of hope new lustre.*[13]

NOTES

Preface

1. John W. Crawford, *Whar' the Hand O' God Is Seen and Other Poems,* 2d ed. (New York: New York Lyceum Publishing Co., 1913), p. 3.

2. Nixon Waterman, "Capt. Jack Crawford, A Genius in Buckskin," unidentified newspaper clipping, copyright 1901, located in John W. Crawford Papers, Rio Grande Historical Collections, New Mexico State University.

3. From "Our Martyred Dead," Crawford, *Whar' the Hand O' God Is Seen,* 2d ed., p. 145.

Chapter 1

1. See the biographical sketches of John W. Crawford in John W. Crawford, *The Poet Scout: A Book of Song and Story* (New York: Funk and Wagnalls, 1886), pp. x–xi; *Dictionary of American Biography,* vol. 4 (New York: Charles Scribner's Sons, 1930), pp. 522–23; *The National Cyclopaedia of American Biography,* vol. 8 (New York: James T. White and Co., 1924), pp. 175–76.

2. Cecil Woodham-Smith, *The Great Hunger, Ireland, 1845–1849* (New York: Harper and Row, 1962), pp. 39–104, 140, 158, 194, 206–16.

3. John W. Crawford, *The Poet Scout: Verses and Songs* (San Francisco: H. Keller and Co., 1879), p. xi.

4. "Life of Capt. J. Crawford," by Hugh J. Mohan, John Wallace Crawford Papers, Western History Department, Denver Public Library (hereafter cited as, Mohan, "Life of Capt. J. Crawford"); "St. Patrick's Day: A Scotch-Irish Inspiration," undated, unsigned manuscript, private collection of Harriett Richardson, Socorro, N.M. The exact date of Susie Crawford's emigration to the U.S. is not known.

5. *Schuylkill County in the Civil War,* Historical Society of Schuylkill County, vol. 7 (no. 3, 1961), pp. 35–36; John A. Crawford, Compiled Military Service Records, Civil War, Pennsylvania Volunteers, Records of the Office of the Adjutant General, Record Group 94, National Archives, Washington, D.C. (hereafter cited as Military Service Records).

6. Information supplied by Harriett Richardson from family records.

7. On conditions in the mining region, see C. K. Yearley, *Enterprise and Anthracite: Economics and Democracy in Schuylkill County, 1820–1875* (Baltimore: Johns Hopkins Press, 1961), pp. 165–73; Harold W. Aurand, *From the Molly Maguires to the United Mine Workers, The Social Ecology of an Industrial Union, 1869–1897* (Philadelphia: Temple University Press, 1971), p. 27; Rowland Berthoff, "The Social Order of the Anthracite Region, 1825–1902," *The Pennsylvania Magazine of History and Biography,* 89 (July 1965): 266.

8. Mohan, "Life of Capt. J. Crawford."

9. Ibid.

10. See Crawford, *Poet Scout* (1886), p. xi.

11. John A. Crawford, Military Service Records.

12. *Schuylkill County in the Civil War,* p. 58; John A. Crawford and John Crawford, Military Service Records. (Jack Crawford enlisted as John Crawford, without recording his middle initial.)

13. See also Crawford, *Poet Scout* (1886), p. xi.

14. John Crawford, Military Service Records.

15. Oliver Christian Bosbyshell, *The 48th in the War, Being a Narrative of the Campaigns of the 48th Regiment, Infantry, Pennsylvania Veteran Volunteers, during the War of the Rebellion* (Philadelphia: Avil Printing Co., 1895), pp. 145–46; Joseph Gould, *The Story of the Forty-Eighth, A Record of the Campaigns of the Forty-Eighth Regiment Pennsylvania Veteran Volunteer Infantry during the four eventful years of its service in the war for the preservation of the Union* (Philadelphia: Alfred M. Slocum Co., 1908), p. 161; Crawford to Wells, Oct. 25, 1894, John W. Crawford Papers, Rio Grande Historical Collections, New Mexico State University (hereafter cited as RGHC).

16. Bosbyshell, *48th in the War,* pp. 146–47; Gould, *Story of the Forty-Eighth,* pp. 173–74.

17. Bosbyshell, *48th in the War,* p. 147; J. G. Randall and David Donald, *The Civil War and Reconstruction* (Lexington, Mass.: D. C. Heath and Co., 1969), p. 418.

18. *The War of the Rebellion: A Compilation of the Official Records of the Union and Confederate Armies,* 128 vols. (Washington:

Government Printing Office, 1880–1901), series 1, vol. 36, pt. 1, pp. 18, 927–28 (hereafter cited as OR); Bosbyshell, *48th in the War,* p. 148; Gould, *Story of the Forty-Eighth,* p. 174–76.

19. William D. Matter, *If It Takes All Summer, The Battle of Spotsylvania* (Chapel Hill: University of North Carolina Press, 1988), pp. 3–4.

20. OR, series 1, vol. 36, pt. 1, pp. 19, 928; Bosbyshell, *48th in the War,* pp. 149–50; Gould, *Story of the Forty-Eighth,* pp. 176–82; Matter, *If It Takes All Summer,* pp. 248, 257.

21. Crawford to Eldridge, Jan. 23, 1896, James William Eldridge Collection, EG Box 13, Huntington Library.

22. Pottsville *Miners' Journal,* Oct. 8, 1864; Matter, *If It Takes All Summer,* p. 267.

23. Bosbyshell, *48th in the War,* p. 150; John A. Crawford, Military Service Records; Pottsville *Miners' Journal,* June 11, 1864; OR, series 1, vol. 36, pt. 1, pp. 19, 929.

24. OR, series 1, vol. 36, pt. 1, pp. 69, 229–31, 234–35, 270.

25. John W. Crawford, "My First Theatrical Experience," unpublished manuscript, Richardson collection.

26. John W. Crawford, "The Reunion," unpublished essay, John W. Crawford Papers, RGHC; John G. Scorer, "A Unique Character in American Literature, Capt. Jack Crawford, 'The Poet Scout,'" *Central Magazine,* 1 (Apr. 1895): 56–57.

27. John W. Crawford, "My First Theatrical Experience"; *Scranton Truth* (Pennsylvania), Dec. 6, 1909 (copy in John W. Crawford Papers, RGHC).

28. "Who is he?" undated, unsigned manuscript, Richardson collection; Crawford to Eldridge, Jan. 23, 1896, James William Eldridge Collection, EG Box 13, Huntington Library; John Crawford, Military Service Records.

29. Bosbyshell, *Forty-Eighth in the War,* p. 162.

30. Ibid., pp. 163–70; Randall and Donald, *Civil War and Reconstruction,* p. 424; James M. McPherson, *Battle Cry of Freedom, The Civil War Era* (New York: Oxford University Press, 1988), pp. 758–60.

31. Gould, *Story of the Forty-Eighth,* pp. 280–81, 470; Bosbyshell, *48th in the War,* p. 183.

32. John W. Crawford, "Lincoln in the Hospitals with His Boys, A Poem and a Story," unpublished manuscript, Richardson collection.

33. John W. Crawford, "Reunion."

34. Gould, *Story of the Forty-Eighth,* pp. 281–82.

35. Ibid., pp. 284–85.

36. Bosbyshell, *48th in the War,* pp. 185–86; Gould, *Story of the Forty-Eighth,* pp. 294–300; OR, series 1, vol. 46, pt. 1, pp. 612, 1056.

37. Crawford to Ed. Natl. Tribune, May 1, 1887, John W. Crawford Papers, RGHC; John W. Crawford, "Lincoln in the Hospitals with His Boys, A Poem and a Story." This essay was published in *The Iron Trail Magazine,* a Minneapolis publication, in April 1909. A copy is located in Memo Book, 1907–1908, John W. Crawford Papers, Western History Department, Denver Public Library.

38. Jim Bishop, *The Day Lincoln Was Shot* (New York: Harper and Brothers, 1955), pp. 39–43; Ida M. Tarbell, *The Life of Abraham Lincoln,* vol. 4 (New York: Lincoln History Society, 1909), pp. 21–24.

39. Crawford, *Poet Scout* (1879), p. 197; John W. Crawford, "Lincoln in the Hospitals." See also Crawford to Eldridge, Jan. 23, 1896, James William Eldridge Collection, EG Box 13, Huntington Library.

40. Crawford, *Poet Scout* (1879), pp. 197–99. See also Tacoma, Washington, *Morning Globe,* May 4, 1889. This account of Jack Crawford's military experiences erroneously states, however, that from City Point Crawford was sent to Saterlee Hospital. It contains other errors as well.

41. Crawford to Eldridge, Jan. 23, 1896, James William Eldridge Collection, EG Box 13, Huntington Library; Bosbyshell, *48th in the War,* p. 187; Gould, *Story of the Forty-Eighth,* pp. 306–7.

42. Pottsville *Miners' Journal,* July 22, 1865.

43. John A. Crawford, Military Service Records.

44. From "New Year's Day in the Black Hills—1876," Crawford, *Poet Scout* (1886), p. 82.

Chapter 2

1. Annie D. Tallent, *The Black Hills; or, The Last Hunting Ground of the Dakotahs* (St. Louis: Nixon-Jones Printing Co., 1899), pp. 140–41, 289; *Omaha Daily Bee,* Apr. 10, 15, May 3, 6, 9, 13, 1876.

2. John W. Crawford, untitled, unfinished manuscript pertaining to experiences in the Black Hills, private collection of Harriett Richardson, Socorro, N.M. (hereafter cited as Crawford, "Reminiscences of the Black Hills"); Tallent, *Black Hills,* p. 291. See description of Crawford in James E. Smith, *A Famous Battery and Its Campaigns, 1861–64. The Career of Corporal James Tanner in War and Peace. Early Days in the Black Hills with Some Account of Capt. Jack Crawford, The Poet Scout* (Washington: W. H. Lowdermilk and Co., 1892), p. 219.

3. John W. Crawford, Pension Application Files, Civil War Series,

Records of the Veterans Administration, Record Group 15, National Archives, Washington, D.C. (hereafter cited as Pension Application Files).

4. Information supplied by Harriett Richardson from family records.

5. Crawford to Wells, Oct. 25, 1894, John W. Crawford Papers, RGHC.

6. See Crawford to Wells, Oct. 25, 1894, and John W. Crawford, "Reunion."

7. John W. Crawford, Pension Application Files; Pottsville *Miners' Journal,* Nov. 23, 1867, Nov. 14, 1868, May 13, 1871; *The Dove,* Mar. 12, 1868, and undated, unidentified newspaper clipping containing the poem, "My Mother's Died," Richardson collection.

8. John W. Crawford, "Snatcher Jack," unpublished essay, John W. Crawford Papers, RGHC. Baseball was a popular sport in the Pennsylvania coal towns, and Crawford never lost his love for the game.

9. John W. Crawford, Pension Application Files; Pottsville *Miners' Journal,* Aug. 3, 10, Sept. 14, 21, 1867.

10. Aurand, *From the Molly Maguires to the United Mine Workers,* pp. 67–68; Donald L. Miller and Richard E. Sharpless, *The Kingdom of Coal, Work, Enterprise, and Ethnic Communities in the Mine Fields* (Philadelphia: University of Pennsylvania Press, 1985), p. 152; Crawford to Editor, *Scranton Truth,* Sept. 17, 1900, and Crawford to O'Brien, McCormick, and Galloway, Sept. 18, 1902, John W. Crawford Papers, RGHC; Shamokin *Herald,* undated newspaper clipping, located in John W. Crawford Papers, RGHC; Pottsville *Miners' Journal,* July 4–August 22, 1868.

11. Pottsville *Miners' Journal,* Apr. 17, 24, 1869.

12. John W. Crawford, Pension Application Files; Pottsville *Miners' Journal,* Nov. 14, 1868. Information on the Stokes family supplied by Harriett Richardson from family papers. Anna Maria Stokes was known both before and after her marriage as Maria.

13. Population Schedules of the Ninth Census of the United States, 1870, Pennsylvania, Bureau of the Census, Record Group 29, National Archives, Microfilm Publication 593, rolls 1329, 1449; dates of children's birth and date of senior Crawford's death supplied by Harriett Richardson from family records.

14. Pottsville *Miners' Journal,* Apr. 29, May 13, June 10, 17, 1871; John W. Crawford, *Poet Scout* (1879), p. xiv.

15. Pottsville *Miners' Journal,* July 8, 1871.

16. Albert Johannsen, *The House of Beadle and Adams and Its Dime and Nickel Novels,* vol. 1 (Norman: University of Oklahoma Press, 1950), pp. 3–6, 30–31; Daryl Jones, *The Dime Novel Western* (Bowling

Green, Ohio: Bowling Green State University Popular Press, 1978), p. 5; see also Henry Nash Smith, *Virgin Land, The American West as Symbol and Myth* (New York: Random House, 1950), pp. 99–125.

17. Edmund Pearson, *Dime Novels; or, Following an Old Trail in Popular Literature* (repr., Port Washington, N.Y.: Kennikat Press, 1968), p. 49; Smith, *Virgin Land,* p. 100.

18. Pearson, *Dime Novels,* p. 46; Christine Bold, *Selling the Wild West, Popular Western Fiction, 1860 to 1960* (Bloomington: Indiana University Press, 1987), p. 3.

19. Dixon Wecter, *The Hero in America, A Chronicle of Hero Worship* (repr., Ann Arbor: University of Michigan Press, 1963), p. 344.

20. *Scranton Truth,* Dec. 18, 1895, Richardson collection; Crawford to Wells, Oct. 25, 1894. (Punctuation added in second quote to benefit reader.)

21. Pottsville *Miners' Journal,* Apr. 3, 1869.

22. Johannsen, *House of Beadle and Adams,* pp. 5, 56. The best biography of William F. Cody is Don Russell's *The Lives and Legends of Buffalo Bill* (Norman: University of Oklahoma Press, 1960); see p. 501.

23. See, for example, Jones, *Dime Novel Western,* pp. 19, 22, 137, 154–55.

24. Russell, *Lives and Legends of Buffalo Bill,* pp. 192–213; Pottsville *Miners' Journal,* Dec. 12, 1873; Sandra Sagale to author, June 16, 1992.

25. Pottsville *Miners' Journal,* July 4, 1873; Robert M. Utley, *Frontier Regulars: The United States Army and the Indian, 1866–1891* (New York: Macmillan Publishing Co., 1973), pp. 242–43.

26. Utley, *Frontier Regulars,* p. 244; Robert M. Utley, *Cavalier in Buckskin, George Armstrong Custer and the Western Military Frontier* (Norman: University of Oklahoma Press, 1988), pp. 134–40; William S. Greever, *Bonanza West, The Story of the Western Mining Rushes, 1848–1900* (Norman: University of Oklahoma Press, 1963), p. 289.

27. Utley, *Frontier Regulars,* pp. 244–45; Greever, *Bonanza West,* p. 292; Watson Parker, *Gold in the Black Hills* (Norman: University of Oklahoma Press, 1966), p. 63; *Cheyenne Daily Leader,* Oct. 18, 1875. For the date the Jenney party left Fort Laramie, see *Laramie Daily Sun,* Oct. 20, 1875; Julia B. McGillycuddy, *McGillycuddy, Agent, A Biography of Dr. Valentine T. McGillycuddy* (San Jose: Stanford University Press, 1941), p. 31; Merrill J. Mattes, *Indians, Infants and Infantry, Andrew and Elizabeth Burt on the Frontier* (Denver: Old West Publishing Co., 1960), p. 200.

28. Crawford, *Poet Scout* (1879), pp. v, xiv; John W. Crawford,

Poet Scout (1886), pp. xi–xii. An often repeated and highly unlikely story is that Crawford was one of the first party of seven men to enter the Black Hills. See, for example, Scorer, "Unique Character in American Literature," 57.

29. Chloride, N.M., *Black Range,* Jan. 16, 1885; McGillycuddy, *McGillycuddy, Agent,* p. 33; Parker, *Gold in the Black Hills,* pp. 54, 64; *Omaha Daily Bee,* Sept. 18, 1875. A poem appearing in this issue of the *Daily Bee,* signed by J. W. C., clearly establishes Crawford's presence in Omaha.

30. *Omaha Daily Bee,* Oct. 7, 1875.

31. Crawford, "Reminiscences of the Black Hills"; Chloride, N.M., *Black Range,* Jan. 16, 1885; *Cheyenne Daily Leader,* Nov. 8, 1875, Jan. 12, 1876; *Laramie Daily Sun,* Nov. 5, 9, 1875; Parker, *Gold in the Black Hills,* pp. 70–71. When Jack reached Custer City in January 1876, he composed a poem, "To the Miners in Custer," which indicates that he had previously been in the area. The first stanza reads: "I'm with you once again pards,/ And you bet, I'm going to stay;/ But tell me, how you made it go,/ While I have been away." See *Sidney Telegraph,* Feb. 12, 1876.

32. Utley, *Frontier Regulars,* pp. 245–48.

33. Parker, *Gold in the Black Hills,* pp. 45–49; *Cheyenne Daily Leader,* Jan. 12, 1876.

34. *Omaha Daily Bee,* Jan. 14, Mar. 15, 1876.

35. *Omaha Daily Bee,* Jan. 6, 15, 1876; Crawford, "Reminiscences of the Black Hills"; Parker, *Gold in the Black Hills,* p. 46.

36. *Omaha Daily Bee,* Jan. 15, 24, 1876.

37. Ibid., Jan. 24, Feb. 7, 1876.

38. Ibid., Feb. 7, 1876.

39. Ibid., Feb. 7, 1876.

40. Ibid., Feb. 19, Mar. 7, 27, 1876.

41. Ibid., Apr. 10, 11, 15, May 9, 1876. Swearingen later moved to Deadwood, where he established the Gem Theater. See Parker, *Gold in the Black Hills,* p. 154.

42. *Omaha Daily Bee,* Mar. 18, June 20, 1876; Parker, *Gold in the Black Hills,* pp. 152–53.

43. *Omaha Daily Bee,* Apr. 11, May 13, 1876; Richard B. Hughes, *Pioneer Years in the Black Hills,* ed. Agnes Wright Spring (Glendale, California: Arthur H. Clark Co., 1957), p. 69.

44. *Omaha Daily Bee,* Feb. 26, 1876; Hughes, *Pioneer Years in the Black Hills,* p. 113; Crawford, *Poet Scout* (1886), p. 77.

45. *Omaha Daily Bee,* May 6, 1876.

46. Ibid., Feb. 26, 1876; Crawford, *Poet Scout* (1886), p. 136.

47. *Omaha Daily Bee,* Mar. 27, 1876; Crawford, *Poet Scout* (1886), pp. 141–42.
48. *Omaha Daily Bee,* Mar. 20, 1876.
49. Ibid., Apr. 1, 1876.
50. Ibid., Mar. 7, 1876; Parker, *Gold in the Black Hills,* pp. 71–72, 78.
51. *Omaha Daily Bee,* Apr. 15, 1876; Crawford, "Reminiscences of the Black Hills."
52. *Omaha Daily Bee,* May 6, 13, 24, 1876.
53. Ibid., Feb. 23, 1876.
54. Ibid., Mar. 20, Apr. 1, 11, 12, 1876; Crawford, "Reminiscences of the Black Hills."
55. Tallent, *Black Hills,* pp. 265–68; Crawford, "Reminiscences of the Black Hills."
56. From "The Death of Custer," Crawford, *Poet Scout* (1886), pp. 106–8.

Chapter 3

1. Utley, *Frontier Regulars,* pp. 236–48.
2. *Omaha Daily Bee,* Feb. 19, 1876.
3. Undated, unidentified newspaper clipping in John W. Crawford Papers, RGHC.
4. Utley, *Frontier Regulars,* pp. 248–51; *Omaha Daily Bee,* Apr. 12, 1876.
5. *Omaha Daily Bee,* Apr. 15, 21, 1876.
6. Ibid., Apr. 22, May 3, 1876.
7. Ibid., Apr. 22, May 6, 9, 1876.
8. Ibid., May 6, 1876; Parker, *Gold in the Black Hills,* p. 135; Agnes Wright Spring, *The Cheyenne and Black Hills Stage and Express Routes* (Glendale, Calif.: Arthur H. Clark Co., 1949), pp. 135–36. Crawford identified the servant as a Mrs. Mosby; Spring identifies her as Rachel Briggs. Spring raises the possibility that Persimmon Bill and his band of renegades committed the murders rather than Indians. Historian Paul L. Hedren also concludes "that white outlaws, possibly including Persimmon Bill," may have participated in the attack. See Paul L. Hedren, *Fort Laramie in 1876, Chronicle of a Frontier Post at War* (Lincoln: University of Nebraska Press, 1988), pp. 76–77.
9. *Omaha Daily Bee,* May 9, 1876; Crawford, "Reminiscences of the Black Hills."
10. *Omaha Daily Bee,* May 13, 1876; Crawford, "Reminiscences of the Black Hills."

11. *Omaha Daily Bee,* May 18, 1876.

12. Ibid., Mar. 18, May 24, June 20, 1876; Parker, *Gold in the Black Hills,* pp. 91–92.

13. *Omaha Daily Bee,* May 24, 1876.

14. Ibid., June 20, 1876.

15. Ibid., June 20, July 6, 1876; Edwin A. Curley, *Glittering Gold, The True Story of the Black Hills* (Chicago: Edwin A. Curley, 1876), p. 80; Hughes, *Pioneer Years in the Black Hills,* p. 91.

16. *Omaha Daily Bee,* June 21, 1876; Hughes, *Pioneer Years in the Black Hills,* p. 110.

17. *Omaha Daily Bee,* Apr. 15, June 20, 21, July 6, 1876.

18. Ibid., June 19, 20, 1876; Tallent, *Black Hills,* pp. 540–42.

19. *Omaha Daily Bee,* June 19, July 7, 1876. See also Tallent, *Black Hills,* p. 332.

20. *Omaha Daily Bee,* June 19, 1876.

21. Ibid., June 19, 23, July 6, 1876.

22. Crawford, "Reminiscences of the Black Hills."

23. Richard Slotkin, *The Fatal Environment, The Myth of the Frontier in the Age of Industrialization, 1800–1890* (New York: Atheneum, 1985), p. 5; *Omaha Daily Bee,* July 6, 1876; *Cheyenne Daily Leader,* July 4, 1876.

24. *Cheyenne Daily Leader,* July 6, 1876; *Omaha Daily Bee,* July 6, 1876.

25. *Omaha Daily Bee,* May 6, 13, 1876.

26. Utley, *Frontier Regulars,* pp. 248–53.

27. Utley, *Frontier Regulars,* pp. 253–62; Utley, *Cavalier in Buckskin,* p. 179.

28. John W. Crawford, *Poet Scout* (1886), pp. 106–8; *Omaha Daily Bee,* July 11, 1876; Russell, *Lives and Legends of Buffalo Bill,* 219–22. William F. Cody included Crawford's poem on Custer's death in his autobiography published in 1879. See William F. Cody, *The Life of Hon. William F. Cody, Known as Buffalo Bill, The Famous Hunter, Scout and Guide, An Autobiography* (repr., Lincoln: University of Nebraska Press, 1978), pp. 348–49.

29. *Cheyenne Daily Leader,* June 9, 22, 1876.

30. John W. Crawford, *Poet Scout* (1879), pp. 25–26; Crawford to Editor of the *Cincinnati Times,* Mar. 20, 1877, appearing in undated, untitled newspaper clipping, located in John W. Crawford Papers, RGHC; Report of Persons and Articles Employed and Hired during July 1876, Quartermaster of 5th Cavalry, In the Field, Records of the Office of the Quartermaster General, Record Group 92, National Archives, copy supplied courtesy of Harriett Richardson. Cody also states in his autobiog-

raphy that Sheridan gave Crawford the appointment as scout. See Cody, *Life,* p. 349.

31. *Omaha Daily Bee,* July 25, 1876.

32. Crawford, *Poet Scout* (1879), pp. 25–27; *Omaha Daily Bee,* July 31, 1876; *Cheyenne Daily Leader,* July 28, 1876; L. G. Flannery, ed., *John Hunton's Diary,* vol. 2, 1876–77 (Lingle, Wyo.: Guide-Review, 1958), pp. 130–31. John Hunton recorded in his diary that Crawford arrived at Fort Fetterman on July 29, which means he would have left Medicine Bow on the twenty-eighth. See the *Omaha Daily Bee,* Aug. 7, 1876, for Crawford's account of his ride to Fetterman.

33. Jerome A. Greene, *Slim Buttes, 1876, An Episode of the Great Sioux War* (Norman: University of Oklahoma Press, 1982), pp. 1–15.

34. Ibid., pp. 23–25; Crawford, *Poet Scout* (1879), p. 34; John G. Bourke, *On the Border with Crook* (Lincoln: University of Nebraska Press, 1971), pp. 348–50. Jack Crawford and John G. Bourke, Crook's adjutant during the Sioux Campaign, both stated that Crawford arrived in camp on August 8; Greene writes that he arrived on August 9, basing this statement on the written account of newspaper correspondent John F. Finerty, who accompanied Crook's expedition. Bourke and others state the command carried fifteen days of rations.

35. Crawford, *Poet Scout* (1879), pp. 25–36; Flannery, *John Hunton's Diary,* p. 132.

36. Crawford, *Poet Scout* (1879), pp. 25–36; Cody, *Life,* pp. 349–50.

37. *Omaha Daily Bee,* Sept. 11, 1876.

38. Utley, *Frontier Regulars,* pp. 268–69; Russell, *Lives and Legends of Buffalo Bill,* pp. 244–47; undated, untitled newspaper clipping, John W. Crawford Papers, RGHC; Charles King, *Campaigning with Crook* (Norman: University of Oklahoma Press, 1964), p. 105. See also Crawford to Editor of the *Cincinnati Times,* Mar. 20, 1877, appearing in undated, untitled newspaper clipping, located in John W. Crawford Papers, RGHC.

39. Greene, *Slim Buttes,* pp. 33–34; John F. Finerty, *War-Path and Bivouac, or The Conquest of the Sioux* (Norman: University of Oklahoma Press, 1961), pp. 175–76.

40. Greene, *Slim Buttes,* pp. 35–39.

41. Ibid., pp. 39–46; see extract from the *Las Vegas Daily Optic,* Dec. 8, 1895, in Scrapbook No. 2, John W. Crawford Papers, RGHC.

42. Greene, *Slim Buttes,* pp. 46–51.

43. *New York Herald,* Sept. 17, 1876; *Omaha Daily Bee,* Sept. 22, 1876; Milwaukee *Evening Wisconsin,* Feb. 2, 1891 (copy in

John W. Crawford Papers, RGHC). Because Jack Crawford never wrote his memoirs, he failed to gain proper credit for his role in the Battle of Slim Buttes. My reconstruction of events pertaining to this battle incorporates Crawford's written correspondence about the battle appearing in the *Omaha Bee* and the *Evening Wisconsin.* Wherever possible, I have tried to verify the accuracy of his statements with other sources. I am convinced that Crawford rarely lied about his deeds; his accounts of the battle, therefore, deserve as much recognition as those of others on the expedition who published memoirs. The best general account of the Slim Buttes engagement is Greene's *Slim Buttes.*

44. Milwaukee *Evening Wisconsin,* Feb. 2, 1891.

45. *New York Herald,* Sept. 17, 1876; *Omaha Daily Bee,* Sept. 22, 1876; Chicago *Daily Inter-Ocean,* Oct. 4, 1876; Milwaukee *Evening Wisconsin,* Feb. 2, 1891; Greene, *Slim Buttes,* p. 59.

46. Chicago *Daily Inter-Ocean,* Oct. 4, 1876; Greene, *Slim Buttes,* pp. 57–60.

47. *New York Herald,* Sept. 17, 1876; *Omaha Daily Bee,* Sept. 22, 1876; Chicago *Daily Inter-Ocean,* Oct. 4, 1876; Milwaukee *Evening Wisconsin,* Feb. 2, 1891. See also Reuben Davenport to Jack Crawford, Dec. 11, 1890, Richardson collection, in which Davenport writes that Jack was "in the very thick of the first attack."

48. *New York Herald,* Sept. 17, 1876; *Omaha Daily Bee,* Sept. 22, 1876; Greene, *Slim Buttes,* pp. 64–65.

49. *New York Herald,* Sept. 17, 1876; *Omaha Daily Bee,* Sept. 22, 1876; Andrew Burt, "Account of Slim Buttes," Andrew Burt Papers, U.S. Army Military History Institute, Carlisle Barracks, Pa. See also Greene, *Slim Buttes,* pp. 74–79, for another account of the ravine fight. Some reports claim that White was shot through the head.

50. *New York Herald,* Sept. 17, 1876; *Omaha Daily Bee,* Sept. 22, 1876; Greene, *Slim Buttes,* pp. 81–88.

51. *New York Herald,* Sept. 17, 1876; Greene, *Slim Buttes,* pp. 93–98.

52. *New York Herald,* Sept. 17, 1876; draft of Crawford's letter to General Crook, dated Sept. 4 [*sic*], 1876, Richardson collection; Greene, *Slim Buttes,* pp. 98–99, 104; Finerty, *War-Path and Bivouac,* p. 202; Oliver Knight, *Following the Indian Wars, The Story of the Newspaper Correspondents among the Indian Campaigners* (Norman: University of Oklahoma Press, 1960), p. 276.

53. Crawford to Crook, Sept. 4 [*sic*], 1876, Richardson collection; *Omaha Daily Bee,* Sept. 22, 1876; Knight, *Following the Indian Wars,* p. 276.

54. *New York Herald,* Sept. 17, 18, 1876.

55. *New York Herald,* Sept. 18, 1876; Crawford to Charles King, Feb. 27, 1891, Richardson collection.

56. *New York Herald,* Sept. 18, 1876; *Omaha Daily Bee,* Sept. 22, 1876; Knight, *Following the Indian Wars,* pp. 278–79.

57. *New York Herald,* Sept. 18, 1876; Burt, "Account of Slim Buttes"; J. G. Bennett to J. W. Crawford, Mar. 26, 1877, in scrapbook, John W. Crawford Papers, RGHC.

58. Crawford to Crook, Sept. 4 [*sic*], 1876, Richardson collection; Greene, *Slim Buttes,* p. 107.

59. Crawford to Crook, Sept. 4 [*sic*], 1876, Richardson collection; *Cheyenne Daily Leader,* Sept. 22, 1876; Report of Persons and Articles Employed in the Field, Big Horn and Yellowstone Expedition, for the months of August, September, and October 1876, Records of the Office of the Quartermaster General, RG 92, National Archives.

60. *Omaha Daily Bee,* Nov. 10, 25, 1876; Crawford to Editor of the *Cincinnati Times,* Mar. 20, 1877, John W. Crawford Papers, RGHC.

61. From "Sunshine," John W. Crawford, *Whar' the Hand O' God Is Seen,* 2d ed., pp. 34–35.

Chapter 4

1. *Omaha Daily Bee,* Jan. 16, 1877. For misrepresentations concerning Crawford's ride after Slim Buttes, see two unidentified newspaper clippings in the John W. Crawford Papers, RGHC.

2. Crawford to Editor of the *Cincinnati Times,* March 20, 1877, appearing in undated, untitled newspaper clipping, located in John W. Crawford Papers, RGHC. See also a copy of the letter that Crawford sent to Cody, dated Sept. 19, 1894, private collection of Harriett Richardson, Socorro, N.M.

3. Undated newspaper clipping [Kansas City, 1877], John W. Crawford Papers, RGHC; Chloride, N.M., *Black Range,* Jan. 16, 1885; *Albuquerque Evening Democrat,* Sept. 26, 1885; J. H. Pierce, "J. W. Crawford," *Western Magazine,* 1 (May 1877).

4. *Omaha Daily Bee,* Nov. 25, 27, Dec. 8, 1876. Later, Crawford wrote that he had joined Cody in Philadelphia on Thanksgiving Day in 1876. See John W. Crawford, "My First Theatrical Experience." Cody was in Philadelphia, starring in *Life on the Border* and *Scouts of the Plains.* See Philadelphia *Public Ledger,* Nov. 20–Dec. 2, 1876. Crawford's arrival in Philadelphia is noted in the *Philadelphia Inquirer,* Dec. 1, 1876.

5. Russell, *Lives and Legends of Buffalo Bill,* pp. 3–53, 74, 84, 160, 188, 213, 477–79; Stella A. Foote, ed. *Letters from Buffalo Bill*

(Billings, Montana: Foote Publishing Co., 1954), pp. 4, 18; John W. Crawford, *Poet Scout* (1879), pp. 75–77.

6. Russell, *Lives and Legends of Buffalo Bill*, pp. 204, 214–35; Don Russell, entry for "Buffalo Bill" Cody, in Howard R. Lamar, ed., *Reader's Encyclopedia of the American West* (New York: Thomas Y. Crowell Co., 1977), pp. 230–31. The proper interpretation of the Cheyenne warrior's name is Yellow Hair, but Cody and others identified him as Yellow Hand. Hence, in *Red Right Hand*, the warrior that Cody kills is Yellow Hand. See Paul L. Hedren, *First Scalp for Custer: The Skirmish at Warbonnet Creek, Nebraska* (Glendale, Calif.: Arthur H. Clark, 1980).

7. On Burke's importance to Cody's career, see Russell, *Lives and Legends of Buffalo Bill*, pp. 202–3. For further references to good publicity and Cody's fame, see Kent L. Steckmesser, *The Western Hero in History and Legend* (Norman: University of Oklahoma Press, 1965), p. 253; and Dixon Wecter, *Hero in America*, p. 359.

8. *Rochester Democrat and Chronicle*, Oct. 2–7, 1876; *New York Times*, Nov. 5, 1876; *Omaha Daily Bee*, Nov. 11, 1876; Russell, *Lives and Legends of Buffalo Bill*, pp. 204, 253–54. Cody implies in his autobiography that he opened the season in Rochester with a new drama, *Red Right Hand*. In fact, the Rochester paper of Oct. 3, 1876, states that Cody's new play was not then ready for production. Cody and Jack Crawford later returned to Rochester and staged the *Red Right Hand* on Feb. 6–7, 1877. See the *Rochester Democrat and Chronicle*, Feb. 6–7, 1877; Cody, *Life*, p. 360.

9. Citations for quoted material in this paragraph are, in order, Metropolitan Theatre playbill, June 20, 1877, Ephemera Collection, T. C. Behymer Collection, Huntington Library; San Francisco *Daily Alta California*, May 27, 1877; *Omaha Daily Bee*, Apr. 21, 1877; Cody, *Life*, p. 360. See also Russell, *Lives and Legends of Buffalo Bill*, p. 253.

10. *Wheeling Daily Register*, Mar. 8, 10, 1877.

11. Ernest H. Cherrington, ed., *Standard Encyclopedia of the Alcohol Problem*, vol. 4 (Westerville, Ohio: American Issue Publishing Co., 1928), pp. 1838–40.

12. *Wheeling Daily Register*, Feb. 10–Mar. 8, 1877.

13. Ibid., Mar. 9, 10, 1877; copies of two letters that Crawford sent to Cody, Sept. 19, Oct. 21, 1894, Richardson collection. Cody may not have addressed the Sunday congregation, for the local press later reported only on the address given by Captain Jack. In fact, Crawford gave two addresses, one at the Fourth Street Church and the other at the Wesley Chapel. Reporting on the second address, the *Wheeling Daily Register*, for Mar. 13, noted: "The floor of Wesley Chapel sank about one

inch Sunday, under the weight of the crowd assembled in the building to hear Capt. Jack's temperance lecture."

14. See clippings from the Kansas City *Times,* [Apr. 1877], in scrapbook of clippings, John W. Crawford Papers, RGHC; *Omaha Daily Bee,* Apr. 19, 21, 1877.

15. Russell, *Lives and Legends of Buffalo Bill,* pp. 255–56; *Omaha Daily Bee,* Apr. 24, 1877; copy of the letter that Crawford sent to Cody, Sept. 19, 1894, and undated and untitled manuscript written sometime after 1908, Richardson collection.

16. See copy of the letter that Crawford sent to Cody, September 19, 1894, and undated and untitled manuscript written sometime after 1908, Richardson collection.

17. Ibid.; San Francisco *Daily Alta California,* May 13–June 13, 1877; Russell, *Lives and Legends of Buffalo Bill,* p. 256.

18. Garff B. Wilson, *Three Hundred Years of American Drama and Theatre* (Englewood Cliffs, N.J.: Prentice-Hall, 1973), pp. 201, 221–22; Laurence M. Hauptman, "Mythologizing Westward Expansion: Schoolbooks and the Image of the American Frontier before Turner," *Western Historical Quarterly,* 8 (July 1977): 269–82.

19. San Francisco *Daily Alta California,* May 31, June 3, 1877.

20. Virginia City *Territorial Enterprise,* June 24–July 1, 1877.

21. Ibid., June 30, 1877; San Francisco *Daily Alta California,* June 30, 1877.

22. Virginia City *Territorial Enterprise,* June 30, 1877; copy of the letter that Crawford sent to Cody, Sept. 19, 1894, and undated and untitled manuscript written sometime after 1908, Richardson collection.

23. San Francisco *Daily Alta California,* June 30, 1877; R. B. Davenport to Crawford, July 8, 1877, John W. Crawford Papers, Western History Department, Denver Public Library; Virginia City *Territorial Enterprise,* July 1, Sept. 5, 1877; Russell, *Lives and Legends of Buffalo Bill,* pp. 257–58; Nellie Snyder Yost, *Buffalo Bill, His Family, Friends, Fame, Failures, and Fortunes* (Chicago: Swallow Press, 1979), pp. 97–99; copies of letters that Crawford sent to Cody, dated Sept. 19, 1894, and Oct. 21, 1894, Richardson collection. The Chloride [N.M.] *Black Range,* Jan. 16, 1885, stated, obviously from information provided by Crawford, that the net proceeds from the Cody–Crawford tour amounted to twenty-four thousand dollars, "the first money that Cody had saved throughout his five years of dramatic experience and with it he purchased his ranch on Dismal river and stocked it with cattle."

24. Virginia City *Territorial Enterprise,* July 17, 18, Aug. 1, 3,

1877; Cody to Crawford, Aug. 5, 7, 1877, William F. Cody Papers, Western History Department, Denver Public Library. (Punctuation and spelling in last quotation are Cody's.)

25. Virginia City *Territorial Enterprise,* Aug. 16, Sept. 5, 1877; undated and untitled manuscript written sometime after 1908, Richardson collection.

26. Virginia City *Territorial Enterprise,* Sept. 6, 7, 11, 15, 1877; undated and untitled manuscript written sometime after 1908, Richardson collection. For Captain Jack's activities in San Francisco, see *Daily Alta California,* Sept. 12, 13, 24, 28, Oct. 1, 11, 21, Nov. 1, 22, 1877.

27. San Francisco *Daily Alta California,* Nov. 14, 18, 19, 1877.

28. Ibid., Nov. 22, 1877; *Los Angeles Herald,* Jan. 11, 16, 1878; Arty [Jim Carlin] to Crawford, Dec. 10, 1877, John W. Crawford Papers, Western History Department, Denver Public Library; undated and untitled manuscript written sometime after 1908, Richardson collection. Visscher first met Crawford in Omaha during the Black Hills gold rush, when Visscher was city editor for the *Omaha Daily Herald.* See Lewis O. Saum, "'Astonishing the Natives,' Bringing the Wild Wild West to Los Angeles," *Montana, Magazine of Western History,* 38 (Summer 1988): 7.

29. Saum, "'Astonishing the Natives'," p. 4; *Los Angeles Herald,* Jan. 15–22, 1878; San Francisco *Daily Alta California,* Feb. 3, 1878.

30. Ronald Genini, "The Fraser–Cariboo Gold Rushes: Comparisons and Contrasts with the California Gold Rush," *Journal of the West,* 11 (July 1972): 475; Winnifred M. Futcher, ed., *The Great North Road to the Cariboo* (Victoria, B.C.: Roy Wrigley Printing and Publishing Co., 1938), pp. 15–16, 24–28; Marian T. Place, *Cariboo Gold, The Story of the British Columbia Gold Rush* (New York: Holt, Rinehart and Winston, 1970), pp. 159–70; Hubert H. Bancroft, *History of British Columbia* (San Francisco: The History Co., 1887), pp. 479, 495–99.

31. San Francisco *Daily Alta California,* July 30, Oct. 10, 1877, Jan. 1, 7, Mar. 2, 1878.

32. Seattle *Daily Pacific Tribune,* Mar. 27, 1878; Victoria *Daily British Colonist,* Apr. 7–23, 1878.

33. Victoria *Daily British Colonist,* May 8, 1878; Place, *Cariboo Gold,* pp. 147–60; Futcher, *Great North Road,* p. 16.

34. Victoria *Daily British Colonist,* Aug. 9–25, 1878.

35. Chloride, N.M., *Black Range,* Jan. 16, 1885; John W. Crawford, Pension Application Files; Crawford, *Poet Scout* (1879), pp. 56–57, 134, 184.

36. Victoria *Daily British Colonist,* May 4, 6, 1879.

37. Victoria *Daily British Colonist,* May 4, 6, 1879; San Francisco *Golden Era,* June 28, 1879; San Francisco *Daily Alta California,* July 11–14, 1879.

38. Chloride, N.M., *Black Range,* Jan. 16, 1885; San Francisco *Grand Army Sentinel,* Sept. 22, 1879, Richardson collection; Crawford, *Poet Scout* (1879).

39. *Dramatic Compositions Copyrighted in the United States, 1870 to 1916* (Washington, D.C.: Government Printing Office, 1918), pp. 275, 716. The play is reprinted in Paul T. Nolan, *Three Plays by J. W. (Capt. Jack) Crawford, An Experiment in Myth-Making* (The Hague, Netherlands: Mouton and Co., 1966), pp. 89–142. See also the San Francisco *Daily Alta California,* July 20, Aug. 10, 17–24, 1879.

40. San Francisco *Daily Alta California,* Aug. 20, 1879. In later productions of the play, the scout is named Jack Crawford rather than Jack Croff. See Nolan, *Three Plays,* p. 91.

41. San Francisco *Daily Alta California,* Sept. 21, 1879; Crawford to Commander Phil Sheridan Post, G.A.R., San Jose, Aug. 15, 1900, John W. Crawford Papers, Box 2, RGHC.

42. *Los Angeles Times,* Dec. 7, 1895; Crawford to Commander Phil Sheridan Post, Aug. 15, 1900, John W. Crawford Papers, Box 2, RGHC; *Las Vegas Daily Optic,* Aug. 19, 1885.

43. San Francisco *Daily Alta California,* Sept. 22, 23, 1879; San Francisco *Grand Army Sentinel,* Sept. 22, 1879, Richardson collection; John W. Crawford, *Poet Scout,* (1886) pp. 31–32.

44. Undated and untitled manuscript written sometime after 1908, Richardson collection; undated letter from Alfred Dampier to Crawford, John W. Crawford Papers, Box 2, RGHC. On the Williamsons, see the San Francisco *Daily Alta California,* July 1, 1877.

45. Cody to Crawford, Apr. 22, June 24, 1879, William F. Cody Papers, Western History Department, Denver Public Library.

46. Cody to Crawford, Sept. 30, 1879, ibid.; San Francisco *Daily Alta California,* Nov. 10, 30, Dec. 6, 14, 1879; Crawford, *Poet Scout* (1886), pp. 71–73.

47. Dampier to Crawford, Jan. 24, 1880, John W. Crawford Papers, Box 6, RGHC.

48. Undated and untitled manuscript written sometime after 1908, Richardson collection; see also Chloride, N.M., *Black Range,* Jan. 16, 1885; Santa Fe *Weekly New Mexican,* May 17, 24, 1880. Paul Nolan, in *John Wallace Crawford* (Boston: Twayne Publishers, 1981), states that Crawford was planning to go to Australia in 1877; and when Cody refused to grant the loan, Crawford accepted employment as a mili-

tary scout in New Mexico. Although Crawford's account of his attempt to tour in Australia is in places confusing, records suggest that Crawford was planning to go to Australia in 1879 or 1880, rather than in 1877. On one fact the records are clear: Crawford rejoined the army as a civilian scout in New Mexico during the summer of 1880 and not in 1877. See Nolan, ibid., pp. 37–38. For Crawford's presence in Denver, see *Rocky Mountain News,* Apr. 14, 1880, Santa Fe *Weekly New Mexican,* May 17, 24, 1880.

49. Santa Fe *Weekly New Mexican,* May 24, 31, 1880.

50. Ibid., June 7, 1880.

51. Ibid.

52. Ibid., May 31, 1880; Utley, *Frontier Regulars,* pp. 359–60; Dan L. Thrapp, *Victorio and the Membres Apaches* (Norman: University of Oklahoma Press, 1974), pp. 220–37.

53. Crawford's involvement in this conflict is gleaned from official military communications and also from a typescript of part of a diary that Jack kept, which covered the final three months of the campaign. He later wrote an essay based on the typescript, which apparently was never published in his lifetime. The typescript and essay remain in the hands of Harriett Richardson. Through her efforts, the essay was published in 1965. See Jack Crawford, "Pursuit of Victorio," *Socorro County Historical Society,* 1 (Feb. 1965): 1–8. The original diary has never been found.

54. Valois to Stedman, June 16, 1880, transmitting list of citizen employees at Fort Craig, Record Group 92, National Archives, copy courtesy of Harriett Richardson; typescript of Crawford's 1880 diary, Richardson collection.

55. Typescript of Crawford's 1880 diary, Richardson collection.

56. Ibid.; on the death of Billy the Kid, see William A. Keleher, *Violence in Lincoln County, 1869–1881* (Albuquerque: University of New Mexico Press, 1957), pp. 341–42. See also Robert M. Utley, *Billy the Kid: A Short and Violent Life* (Lincoln: University of Nebraska Press, 1989).

57. Typescript of Crawford's 1880 diary, Richardson collection; Crawford, "Pursuit of Victorio," pp. 2–3.

58. Typescript of Crawford's 1880 diary, Richardson collection.

59. Ibid.; Crawford, "Pursuit of Victorio," pp. 3–4; *Albuquerque Evening Democrat,* Oct. 1, 1885. Casimero Grigalba may be the same individual identified as Marigildo Grijalba, a civilian military scout, in John Spring's memoirs of early Arizona. See Spring, *John Spring's Arizona,* edited by A. M. Gustafson (Tucson: University of Arizona Press, 1966), p. 52.

60. Typescript of Crawford's 1880 diary, Richardson collection; Crawford, "Pursuit of Victorio," pp. 4–7.

61. Ibid.

62. Ibid.; Martin L. Crimmins, "Colonel Buell's Expedition into Mexico in 1880," *New Mexico Historical Review*, 10 (April 1935): 139–41.

63. Typescript of Crawford's 1880 diary, Richardson collection; Utley, *Frontier Regulars*, p. 364. Crawford apparently used Buell's letter of commendation in an advertisement for the second edition of *Poet Scout*, published in 1886. The date on this letter, however, has been misprinted (Sept. 12, 1880). The published letter is in possession of Harriett Richardson.

64. From "Little Ones Praying at Home," Crawford, *Poet Scout* (1886), pp. 28–29.

Chapter 5

1. Santa Fe *Daily New Mexican*, Nov. 30, 1880.

2. *Las Vegas Daily Optic*, Nov. 18, 1880; Crawford to Lute, Feb. 28, 1881, John W. Crawford Papers, Western History Department, Denver Public Library; *Boston Globe*, Dec. 19, 1897, clipping in Scrapbook no. 8, John W. Crawford Papers, RGHC.

3. Santa Fe *Daily New Mexican*, Feb. 6, 1881; *Boston Globe*, Dec. 19, 1897, clipping in Scrapbook no. 8, John W. Crawford Papers, RGHC. The Santa Fe press erroneously reported that Jack's party was attacked on January 30. See letter dated Feb. 6, 1881, Register of Letters Received, District of New Mexico, Records of the United States Army Continental Commands, 1821–1920, RG 393, National Archives (hereafter cited as NA), Microfilm publication M-1097, roll 7.

4. Santa Fe *Daily New Mexican*, Feb. 2, 1881; Crawford to Lute, Feb. 28, 1881, John W. Crawford Papers, Western History Department, Denver Public Library; *Boston Globe*, Dec. 19, 1897, clipping in Scrapbook no. 8, John W. Crawford Papers, RGHC. In a letter to Maria, dated Feb. 28, 1881, Jack said that he had spent over two hundred dollars of his own money and sold his gold watch and other articles "for these men who would have starved had I not done so." Private collection of Harriett Richardson, Socorro, N.M.

5. Santa Fe *Military Review*, May 1, 1881, copy in John W. Crawford Papers, RGHC; Santa Fe *Daily New Mexican*, May 17, 1881; *Record Book 1*, Socorro County Courthouse (Socorro, N.M.), p. 207; *Record Book G*, Socorro County Courthouse, p. 32.

6. Contracts are in Register of Contracts, Office of the Quartermaster General, RG 92, NA; letter of Commanding Officer, Fort Craig, June 5, [1881], Register of Letters Received, District of New Mexico, RG 393, NA, M-1097, roll 7. Crawford agreed to supply Ojo Caliente with 123,256 pounds of corn at $3.25 per 100 pounds, 151,536 pounds of hay at $35.00 per ton, and 342 cords of hard wood at $4.00 per cord.

7. Theron Marcos Trumbo, "Bronco Girl of Old Fort Craig," *New Mexico Magazine,* 25 (January 1947): 17, 49.

8. The best account of Confederate activity in New Mexico is Martin H. Hall, *Sibley's New Mexico Campaign* (Austin: University of Texas Press, 1960). See also Marion C. Grinstead, "Life and Death of a Frontier Fort: Fort Craig, New Mexico, 1854–1885," Publications in History, *Socorro County Historical Society,* 7 (1973): 18–26.

9. Lee to Chief Quartermaster, June 3, 1881, Letters Sent (hereafter cited as LS), Chief Quartermaster, District of New Mexico, RG 393, NA.

10. Grinstead, "Life and Death of a Frontier Fort," pp. 7–8.

11. Post adjutant to Crawford, Dec. 5, 1881, LS, Fort Craig, Post Records, RG 393, NA.

12. Post Adjutant to Jenkins, Oct. 23, 1882, Post Adjutant to Post Trader, Aug. 12, 1883, LS, Fort Craig, Post Records, RG 393, NA; Post Trader's Daybook (1882), courtesy of Harriett Richardson; *Record Book 15,* Socorro County Courthouse, pp. 72–73; Diagram of Fort Craig, drawn by May Crawford Brechtel, Jack Crawford's daughter, Richardson collection; *Las Vegas Daily Optic,* Oct. 3, 1882. The Valverde House was also known as the Valverde Hotel.

13. The date of May Cody Crawford's birth was supplied by Harriett Richardson. For Jack's statement, see *Albuquerque Evening Democrat,* Nov. 21, 1885. For Maria working in the store, see John W. Crawford, Pension Application Files.

14. The best account of children on frontier military posts is Patricia Y. Stallard, *Glittering Misery, Dependents of the Indian Fighting Army* (Fort Collins, Colo.: Old Army Press, 1978), pp. 75–101.

15. Fort Craig, Post Returns, RG 94, NA, M-617, roll 262; Haskell to AAAG, Nov. 17, 1881, Letters Received (hereafter cited as LR), District of New Mexico, RG 393, NA, M-1088, roll 44.

16. Fort Craig, Post Returns, RG 94, NA, M-617, roll 262; Noyes to AAAG, Jan. 11, 1882, Haskell to Post Adjutant, Jan. 10, 1882, LR, District of New Mexico, RG 393, NA, M-1088, roll 45; Trumbo, "Bronco Girl of Old Fort Craig," p. 50.

17. *Janesville Recorder* (Wisc.), Jan. 27, 1894, clipping in scrap-

book in possession of Harriett Richardson; *Las Vegas Daily Optic,* Apr. 13, 1882.

18. Santa Fe *Daily New Mexican,* Mar. 1, 1883; *Santa Fe New Mexican Review,* July 3, 1883; *Las Vegas Daily Optic,* Jan. 26, 1885. Possibly later in 1885, Eva returned to Fort Craig and would ride her pony into San Marcial to attend school. See Trumbo, "Bronco Girl of Old Fort Craig," p. 50; Jack Crawford, "The Boy Scouts," *Watson's Magazine,* 13 (Oct. 1911): 508.

19. *Las Vegas Daily Optic,* Apr. 13, Nov. 2, Dec. 11, 12, 1882.

20. *Las Vegas Daily Optic,* Apr. 13, Dec. 12, 1882.

21. Daybook, 1882, Richardson collection. Crawford had special tokens coined for his saloons. On one side was stamped "Capt. Jack Crawford's Club Room," and on the other side, "Good for 1 Drink." Copy furnished by Marion Grinstead. On Oct. 4, 1883, Crawford received orders that "the Post trader's store and Saloon (excepting the Officers club room) will be closed hereafter at Taps every evening and will also be closed on Sundays, excepting for the distribution and delivery of the mail." Dodge to Crawford, Oct. 4, 1883, LS, Fort Craig, Post Records, RG 393, NA.

22. Daybook, 1882, Richardson collection; Dyer to Crawford, Feb. 5, 1882, Dodge to Crawford, July 20, 1883, LS, Fort Craig, Post Records, RG 393, NA; Crawford to Marshall, Oct. 31, 1882, LR, Chief Quartermaster, District of New Mexico, RG 393, NA; *Las Vegas Daily Optic,* Oct. 3, 1882. For Crawford's contracts at Ojo Caliente, see n. 6. In September 1881 Crawford agreed to put in 685,588 pounds of grama hay at Fort Craig at $22.00 per ton; in June 1882, he agreed to deliver 170 tons of grama hay at $26.00 per ton; and in October 1882, he contracted for an additional 330 tons of grama hay at $22.40 per ton. See Register of Contracts, Office of the Quartermaster General, RG 92, NA.

23. Chloride *Black Range,* Jan. 16, 1885.

24. *Albuquerque Evening Democrat,* Nov. 21, 1885. See also *Las Vegas Daily Optic,* Oct. 3, Dec. 12, 1882.

25. *Albuquerque Evening Democrat,* Nov. 21, 1885.

26. Keith L. Bryant, *History of the Atchison, Topeka and Santa Fe Railway* (Lincoln: University of Nebraska Press, 1982), pp. 32–63.

27. Marc Simmons, *Albuquerque, A Narrative History* (Albuquerque: University of New Mexico Press, 1982), pp. 213, 217–18; Bruce Ashcroft, *Territorial History of Socorro, New Mexico* (El Paso: Texas Western Press, 1989), pp. 12, 22.

28. T. M. Pearce, ed., *New Mexico Place Names, A Geographical Dictionary* (Albuquerque: University of New Mexico Press, 1965),

p. 146; Population Schedules, 10th Census (1880), Socorro County, San Marcial, National Archives Microfilm Publication T-9, roll 804.

29. *Las Vegas Daily Optic,* Dec. 13, 1882. My thanks to Dennis Seglem, graduate student at New Mexico State University, who compiled information about railroad organization and construction in San Marcial for a research seminar.

30. Santa Fe *Daily New Mexican,* Oct. 20, 1882, May 16, 1883; *Santa Fe New Mexican Review,* Nov. 24, 1883; *Las Vegas Daily Optic,* Dec. 13, 1882.

31. *Socorro Bullion,* July 25, 1885; population figures obtained from Territorial Census of 1885, microcopy edition of the Territorial Archives of New Mexico, roll 42. My thanks to Dennis Seglem for information on the Depot Hotel.

32. *Socorro Bullion,* Nov. 28, 1885.

33. A variety of newspaper stories testify to the presence of the Crawford family in Chloride. For population figures, see Philip Varney, *New Mexico's Best Ghost Towns, A Practical Guide* (Albuquerque: University of New Mexico Press, 1987), p. 102.

34. Chloride *Black Range,* Jan. 16, 1885; *Record Book G,* Socorro County Courthouse, p. 626; *Record Book 11,* Socorro County Courthouse, p. 240.

35. *Las Vegas Daily Optic,* Dec. 21, 1882; see entries for Jack Crawford in *Record Books, 1, 5, J,* Socorro County Courthouse.

36. *Las Vegas Daily Optic,* Dec. 16, 21, 1882.

37. Ibid., Dec. 21, 1882. Freeman probably was referring to Edward Braun, who worked for Crawford for a time.

38. *Socorro Bullion,* Aug. 1, 1883.

39. See entries for Jack Crawford in *Record Books G, 9, 17,* Socorro County Courthouse.

40. *Santa Fe New Mexican Review,* Dec. 26, 1883.

41. *Socorro Bullion,* May 1, 1883.

42. Ibid., Dec. 1, 1884.

43. Cody to Crawford, Apr. 8, May 25, 1882, William F. Cody Papers, Western History Department, Denver Public Library.

44. Cody to Crawford, June 10, 16, 1882, ibid.

45. Yost, *Buffalo Bill,* p. 116.

46. See Yost, *Buffalo Bill,* pp. 116–30; Russell, *Lives and Legends of Buffalo Bill,* pp. 285–310.

47. Wecter, *Hero in America,* p. 357.

48. Jay Monaghan, *Great Rascal, The Life and Adventures of Ned Buntline* (New York: Crown Publishers, 1951), pp. 323, 327; *Las*

Vegas Daily Optic, Mar. 24, 1882. "The Terrible Dread" was republished in 1891 with the title *Captain Jack; or, The Seven Scouts.*

49. Monaghan, *Great Rascal,* p. 274.

50. John W. Crawford, *Poet Scout* (1886) pp. 85—86.

51. Judson to Crawford, Oct. 26, Dec. 22, 1882, Feb. 6, 1885, John W. Crawford Papers, Western History Department, Denver Public Library. On Buntline's death, see Monaghan, *Great Rascal,* pp. 286—89.

52. Nolan, *John Wallace Crawford,* pp. 18—19. Even though Nolan, at one point, states that Crawford was probably sincere in his attacks on dime novels, Nolan raises so many other doubts about Crawford's motivation that the reader is led to believe that Crawford's objections to dime novels lacked conviction. Nolan, an English professor, was interested primarily in Crawford's literary talent; as a biography, his slender volume is seriously flawed because of the many factual errors that it contains.

53. Prentiss Ingraham, *The Adventurous Life of Captain Jack, The Border Boy,* no. 96, Beadle's Half Dime Library, Feb. 21, 1883. My thanks to Cheryl Wilson, Special Collections, New Mexico State University, for providing a copy of Ingraham's Captain Jack dime novel. In later years, this story was reissued under the title *Captain Jack in Rocky Roost.*

54. Crawford, *Poet Scout* (1886), p. 15; Russell, *Lives and Legends of Buffalo Bill,* p. 387. Captain Jack appeared as a minor character, however, in some of the Buffalo Bill dime novels. See Herschel C. Logan, *Buckskin and Satin, The Life of Texas Jack and His Wife Mlle. Morlacchi* (Harrisburg, Pa.: Stackpole Company, 1954), pp. 167—69.

55. Crawford, *Poet Scout* (1886), p. 15.

56. Ibid., p. 16.

57. Daryl E. Jones, "Blood 'n Thunder: Virgins, Villains, and Violence in the Dime Novel Western," *Journal of Popular Culture,* 4 (Fall 1970): 507; Wecter, *Hero in America,* p. 345; Bold, *Selling the Wild West,* p. 6; Pearson, *Dime Novels,* pp. 92, 223. See also Lewis Atherton, *The Cattle Kings* (Lincoln: University of Nebraska Press, 1961), p. 33.

58. Schwenk to Crawford, Mar. 31, Nov. 11, 1884, John W. Crawford Papers, RGHC; *Socorro Bullion,* Dec. 1, 1884; *Las Vegas Daily Optic,* Sept. 4, 1885. Schwenk served as an officer with the Fiftieth Pennsylvania Volunteers during the Civil War, then continued in the regular army, retiring in 1876. Francis B. Heitman, *Historical Register and Dictionary of the United States Army, 1789—1903,* vol. 1 (repr.; Urbana: University of Illinois Press, 1965), p. 867.

59. See copy of preemption claim, dated Oct. 31, 1882, in possession of Harriett Richardson. Patent for the claim was filed June 5,

1890; see *Record Book 30,* Socorro County Courthouse, p. 526. That Crawford ran cattle on this land is suggested from documents recorded in *Record Book 10,* Socorro County Courthouse, pp. 218, 224–25. See also *Record Book 9,* p. 59. In a two-column article devoted to Captain Jack in the *Las Vegas Daily Optic,* Dec. 12, 1882, the following appears: "[Crawford] owns several large ranches, and he has quite a lot of horses, mules and other stock."

60. [Name unclear] to Crawford, Aug. 4, 1883, LS, Fort Craig, Post Records, RG 393, NA; *Record Book 9,* Socorro County Courthouse, p. 682.

61. Santa Fe *Daily New Mexican,* May 19, 23, 1883, Feb. 25, 1884; *Santa Fe New Mexican Review,* May 31, 1884; Crawford to Wells, Oct. 25, 1894, John W. Crawford Papers, RGHC; Thomas D. Isern, "The Controversial Career of Edward W. Wynkoop," *Colorado Magazine,* 56 (Winter–Spring 1979): 1–18.

62. Schwenk to Crawford, Mar. 31, 1884, John W. Crawford Papers, RGHC; Chloride *Black Range,* Jan. 16, Feb. 27, 1885; Santa Fe *Daily New Mexican,* May 24, 1883; *Albuquerque Evening Democrat,* Feb. 24–Mar. 16, 1885; *El Paso Daily Times,* Mar. 6, 1885; Las Cruces *Rio Grande Republican,* Mar. 7, 1885; *Santa Fe New Mexican Review,* Mar. 18, 1885; *Las Vegas Daily Optic,* Jan. 26, Mar. 20, 1885. On the career of Will L. Visscher, see Saum, "'Astonishing the Natives,'" pp. 2–13.

63. Las Cruces *Rio Grande Republican,* Mar. 7, 1885.

64. Visscher to Crawford, Feb. 12, 1885, John W. Crawford Papers, Western History Department, Denver Public Library; *Las Vegas Daily Optic,* Apr. 27, 1885; St. Louis *Missouri Republican,* May 3, 1885.

65. Don Russell, *The Wild West, or, A History of the Wild West Shows* (Fort Worth: Amon Carter Museum, 1970), pp. 8–12. Russell states that Carver began his career as a marksman in 1878. However, the San Francisco *Daily Alta California,* Dec. 2, 1877, stated that Carver had given a shooting exhibition in that city on the previous day.

66. Russell, *Wild West,* p. 117; Joseph Schwartz, "The Wild West Show: 'Everything Genuine,'" *Journal of Popular Culture,* 3 (Spring 1970).

67. See advertisement in St. Louis *Missouri Republican,* May 1, 1885. Raymond W. Thorp, Carver's biographer, states that Crawford joined Carver after Carver broke with Cody in 1883; this is in error. See Thorp, *Spirit Gun of the West, The Story of Doc W. F. Carver* (Glendale, Calif.: Arthur H. Clark Co., 1957), pp. 140–43. Don Russell, Cody's biographer, repeated this error. See Russell, *Lives and Legends of Buffalo Bill,* p. 299, and Russell, *Wild West,* pp. 17–18, 122. There is no evidence

to show that Carver and Crawford toured together in a Wild West show from 1883 to 1885, as Russell states on p. 122.

68. St. Louis *Missouri Republican,* May 3, 1885.

69. Ibid., May 4, 1885; Thorp, *Spirit Gun of the West,* p. 143.

70. St. Louis *Missouri Republican,* May 4, 1885; untitled, undated newspaper article from New Haven in scrapbook, in possession of Harriett Richardson.

71. St. Louis *Missouri Republican,* May 2—4, 1885.

72. Untitled, undated newspaper article from New Haven in scrapbook, in possession of Harriett Richardson; Russell, *Wild West,* p. 24. Thorp has a more detailed explanation of the Cody—Carver fight, in which Carver can do no wrong and Cody can do no right. See Thorp, *Spirit Gun of the West,* pp. 155—63.

73. From "The Optimistic Warbler," John W. Crawford, *Whar' the Hand O' God Is Seen,* 2d ed., p. 91.

Chapter 6

1. For Sandburg quote, see Carl Sandburg, "Washington Monument by Night," *Harvest Poems, 1910—1960* (New York: Harcourt, Brace and World, 1958), pp. 71—72; for the American Dream, see Harold C. Livesay, *Andrew Carnegie and the Rise of Big Business* (Boston: Little, Brown and Co., 1975), pp. 3—5; and John Tebbel, *From Rags to Riches, Horatio Alger, Jr. and the American Dream* (New York: Macmillan Co., 1963), pp. 3—18.

2. *Las Vegas Daily Optic,* Aug. 18—20, Sept. 4, 1885; *Socorro Bullion,* Sept. 26, Oct. 3, 1885; Jack to Maria, Aug. 6, 1885, private collection of Harriett Richardson, Socorro, N.M.

3. *Las Vegas Daily Optic,* Aug. 19, 1885.

4. *Albuquerque Evening Democrat,* Oct. 4, 1885; John W. Crawford, *Poet Scout* (1886), p. 19; John W. Crawford, "In Memoriam, The Hero's Departed" (New York: J. T. Altemus, Publisher, 1885), copy furnished by the South Dakota State Historical Society.

5. Crawford, "In Memoriam."

6. Ibid., pp. 11—12; Cody to Crawford, Aug. 11, 1885, William F. Cody Papers, Western History Department, Denver Public Library.

7. Cody to Crawford, Aug. 23, 1885, William F. Cody Papers, Western History Department, Denver Public Library.

8. Fort Craig had been deactivated in October 1884, and after that only a token force remained behind to guard public buildings. Fort Craig, Post Returns, RG 94, National Archives, M-617, roll 262. In April

1885, the Interior Department selected Mariano Armijo of Albuquerque as custodian of the Fort Craig property. The army officially turned the post over to Armijo on July 1, 1885, and all remaining soldiers left the post on July 15. Armijo later resigned as custodian. See Acting Secretary of the Interior to the Secretary of War, May 2, 1885, and Scott to A.A.A. General, July 26, 1885, LR, District of New Mexico, RG 393, NA, M-1088, rolls 56, 57.

9. John W. Crawford, Pension Application Files.

10. Tamara K. Hareven, "Family Time and Historical Time," *Daedalus,* 106 (Spring 1977): 61, 64.

11. See Robert L. Griswold, *Family and Divorce in California, 1850–1890, Victorian Illusions and Everyday Realities* (Albany: State University of New York Press, 1982), pp. 93–109.

12. For Susan McSween Barber, see Darlis A. Miller, "The Women of Lincoln County, 1860–1900," in *New Mexico Women: Intercultural Perspectives,* ed. by Joan M. Jensen and Darlis A. Miller (Albuquerque: University of New Mexico Press, 1986), pp. 188–91; for women becoming heads of households when husbands travel, see Linda Peavy and Ursula Smith, *The Gold Rush Widows of Little Falls, A Story Drawn from the Letters of Pamelia and James Fergus* (St. Paul: Minnesota Historical Society Press, 1990), and Byrd Gibbens, ed., *This Is a Strange Country, Letters of a Westering Family, 1880–1906* (Albuquerque: University of New Mexico Press, 1988).

13. Nolan, *Three Plays,* p. 70.

14. Family information provided by Harriett Richardson, Evelyn Lewis, and Marion Hageman; Jack's story is from Buffalo, N.Y., *Courier,* Nov. 12, 1891, clipping in John W. Crawford Papers, RGHC. According to a neighbor, Maria was in the habit of shooting off her gun at night whenever "she thought the buildings [at Fort Craig] were being vandalized." Nolan, *Three Plays,* p. 70.

15. *San Marcial Reporter,* Feb. 7, 28, 1891. The newspaper article incorrectly placed the Hardy Ranch in the Magdalena Mountains. A later article indicated that the ranch was in the San Mateos. See ibid., June 20, 1891.

16. *Socorro Bullion,* Oct. 3, 1885; *Albuquerque Evening Democrat,* Sept. 30, Oct. 4, 10, 1885; Santa Fe *Daily New Mexican,* Sept. 29, Oct. 7, 1885.

17. Arty to Jack, Dec. 10, 1877, John W. Crawford Papers, Western History Department, Denver Public Library.

18. Gloria Adams Lusby, "Biographical Sketch of James Barton Adams," Publications in History, *Socorro County Historical Society,* 4

(May 1968): 5; Carlin to Crawford, Sept. 18, 1885, John W. Crawford Papers, Western History Department, Denver Public Library.

19. Carlin to Crawford, Sept. 18, 1885, John W. Crawford Papers, Western History Department, Denver Public Library.

20. *Albuquerque Evening Democrat,* Sept. 26, 1885.

21. Ibid., Nov. 13, 19, 21, 1885.

22. *Las Vegas Daily Optic,* Dec. 3, 4, 1885; *Socorro Bullion,* Jan. 23, 1886; New York *Graphic,* Mar. 20, 1886, *Toledo Journal* [1886], San Francisco *Daily Examiner,* Mar. 29, 1886, Richardson collection.

23. John W. Crawford, *From Darkness into Light and Other Poems* (Chicago: R. R. McCabe and Co., 1886), Richardson collection.

24. *Albuquerque Tribune,* Jan. 10, 1963.

25. M. L. Tanner to Crawford, Dec. 22, 1888, Box 1, John W. Crawford Papers, RGHC; Marie Madison, "A True American, Capt. Jack Crawford, the Poet Scout," *Western Veteran* (n.d.), pp. 21–23, Richardson collection; untitled newspaper clipping, Aug. 15, 1906, John W. Crawford Papers, RGHC.

26. *Albuquerque Morning Democrat,* Aug. 21, 27, 1886. See also entry for James Tanner in *Dictionary of American Biography,* vol. 18 (New York: Charles Scribner's Sons, 1936), pp. 297–98.

27. Marie Madison, "True American," p. 22; Santa Fe *Daily New Mexican,* June 21, 1886.

28. Santa Fe *Daily New Mexican,* June 21, 1886; see program for "The Camp Fire and the Trail," Apr. 15, 1886, Programs Collection, Box 1, Arizona Historical Society (copy furnished by Lewis O. Saum); untitled newspaper clipping, May 26, 1886, John W. Crawford Papers, RGHC.

29. Jack Crawford to Maria Crawford, Feb. 14, 1886, Richardson collection.

30. Carlin to Mrs. Crawford, Apr. 5, 1886, and Mrs. Tanner to Mrs. Crawford, Apr. 4, 1886, Richardson collection; undated, untitled newspaper clipping announcing death of "Little Nugget," John W. Crawford Papers, RGHC.

31. Gibbens, *This Is a Strange Country,* p. 97.

32. From newspaper clipping containing Crawford's poem and letter, dated Apr. 6, 1886, Richardson collection.

33. Santa Fe *Daily New Mexican,* June 21, 1886; Chloride *Black Range,* June 18, 1886.

34. Santa Fe *Daily New Mexican,* June 21, 1886.

35. At age twelve, May was christened with the name that she chose for herself, Elizabeth Esther May Crawford. Information provided by Evelyn Lewis, May's daughter.

36. *Record Book 17,* pp. 723–25, and *Record Book 18,* pp. 82–83, Socorro County Courthouse; *Socorro Bullion,* July 3, 1886. The claims would revert to Crawford should Thomas decide not to create such a company.

37. *Socorro Bullion,* July 3, 31, Aug. 7, 1886. At times Crawford had five men working on the Copper Bottom.

38. *Albuquerque Morning Democrat,* July 28, 1886.

39. Ibid., Aug. 20, 21, 27, Sept. 2, 1886.

40. *Las Vegas Daily Optic,* Feb. 10, 24, Mar. 16, 1887; Tucson *Arizona Daily Citizen,* Mar. 22, 25, 1887; *Socorro Bullion,* Mar. 26, Apr. 9, 1887; *Albuquerque Morning Democrat,* May 11, 1887.

41. *Socorro Bullion,* Mar. 5, 1887.

42. *Las Vegas Daily Optic,* Oct. 20, Nov. 18, 22, Dec. 4, 29, 1886, Mar. 17, 24, 1887; Carlin to Crawford, [1887], John W. Crawford Papers, Western History Department, Denver Public Library. Carlin's letter was not dated when it was written ; after Crawford's death, someone wrongly penciled in the year 1883.

43. *Las Vegas Daily Optic,* Apr. 8, May 10, 12, 1887.

44. *Rome Daily Sentinel,* Dec. 8, 1887, Richardson collection; *Las Vegas Daily Optic,* June 16, 1887.

45. Jack Crawford to Maria Crawford, Aug. 13, 1887, Richardson collection.

46. *New York Star,* Aug. 23, 1887, *New York Times,* Aug. 23, 1887, and *New York Leader,* Aug. 30, 1887, John W. Crawford Papers, RGHC; *Socorro Bullion,* Sept. 17, 1887.

47. Jack Crawford to Maria Crawford, Sept. 4, 1887, Richardson collection.

48. See *Kansas City Star,* May 30, 1887, John W. Crawford Papers, RGHC; *Socorro Bullion,* Oct. 15, 1887; and several undated, untitled press clippings of Crawford starring in *On the Trail,* located in John W. Crawford Papers, RGHC.

49. Mrs. Tanner to Jack Crawford, Dec. 22, 1888, Box 1, John W. Crawford Papers, RGHC; *Albuquerque Daily Democrat,* Jan. 7, 1888.

50. See *New Castle Daily Courant,* Oct. 29, 1887, and undated clipping on Crawford starring in *On the Trail,* John W. Crawford Papers, RGHC; *San Marcial Reporter,* Feb. 4, 1888; undated newspaper clipping, interview with Crawford about October 1890, Richardson collection.

51. For examples of the children's activities, see *Socorro Bullion,* July 9, Sept. 17, 1887, Feb. 18, 1888. For Bethany College, see Santa Fe *New Mexican Review,* Sept. 4, 1884, *Las Vegas Daily Optic,* Sept. 20, Nov. 22, 1887.

52. Captain Jack's granddaughter, Evelyn Lewis, is the source for

the Hispanic couple living with the Crawfords. Socorro County tax assessment records are located in the Socorro County Courthouse; microfilmed copies of these records are available at the State Records Center in Santa Fe. Crawford advertised to rent his blacksmith shop in the *San Marcial Reporter,* May 7, 1887, Richardson collection.

53. *Las Vegas Daily Optic,* Feb. 6, June 11, 1888; *Boston Daily Advertiser,* Feb. 10, 1888, Richardson collection; statement from *Boston Evening Transcript,* May 16, 1888, appearing in publicity sheet for *Fonda; or, the Trapper's Dream,* Richardson collection; Carrigan and others to Tompkins, June 8, 1888, Box 2, John W. Crawford Papers, RGHC; Santa Fe *Daily New Mexican,* Aug. 31, 1888; *Scranton Truth,* Sept. 22, 1888, John W. Crawford Papers, RGHC.

54. Santa Fe *Daily New Mexican,* Aug. 31, 1888; Jack Crawford to Maria Crawford, Oct. 6, 1888, Richardson collection.

55. Jack Crawford to Maria Crawford, Oct. 6, 1888, Richardson collection; *Las Vegas Daily Optic,* Sept. 24, 1888; *San Marcial Reporter,* Nov. 3, 1888; Crawford to Governor Prince, May 21, 1889, Territorial Archives of New Mexico, roll 103.

56. *Santa Fe New Mexican Review,* Aug. 25–Sept. 5, 1884.

57. Mrs. Tanner to Jack Crawford, Dec. 22, 1888, Box 1, John W. Crawford Papers, RGHC; for staging of *Fonda,* see *Youngstown Daily Telegram,* Dec. 28, 1888, Richardson collection, *San Marcial Reporter,* Feb. 9, 1889, and two newspaper clippings in John W. Crawford Papers, RGHC, dated Mar. 13 and Mar. 22, 1889.

58. *Charlottesville Jeffersonian,* Mar. 13, 1889, clipping in John W. Crawford Papers, RGHC.

59. Mrs. Tanner wrote, in part: "I am glad Carlin is so good & useful. There is no reason why he should not be good to you & do all for you he can, you've served him when he was needing, as well as unworthy." Mrs. Tanner to Jack Crawford, Dec. 22, 1888, Box 1, John W. Crawford Papers, RGHC. For information on *Tat: or Edna, The Veteran's Daughter,* see Nolan, *John Wallace Crawford,* pp. 72–73, and Nolan, *Three Plays,* p. 143.

60. Undated and untitled manuscript, written sometime after 1908, Richardson collection.

61. *Santa Fe New Mexican Review,* Mar. 27, 1889.

62. John W. Crawford, Pension Application Files. Tanner's problems are set forth in Mary R. Dearing, *Veterans in Politics, The Story of the G.A.R.* (Baton Rouge: Louisiana State University Press, 1952), pp. 392–96.

63. Copies of all letters of recommendation are in the Richardson collection.

64. *San Marcial Reporter,* June 1, 1889.
65. Ibid., July 13, 20, 1889.
66. Ibid., June 22, July 6, 1889; *St. Joseph News,* July 11, 1889, copy in John W. Crawford Papers, RGHC.
67. *St. Joseph Herald,* July 1, 1889, and *St. Joseph Daily Gazette,* July 7, 1889, copies in John W. Crawford Papers, RGHC; Chloride *Black Range,* Aug. 2, 1889.
68. Chloride *Black Range,* Aug. 2, 1889; *San Marcial Reporter,* July 20, 1889.
69. Robert A. Trennert, Jr., "Selling Indian Education at World's Fairs and Expositions, 1893–1904," *American Indian Quarterly,* 11 (Summer 1987): 204. The quote is from Crawford's letter from St. Joseph, Aug. 15, 1889, which appeared in a variety of New Mexico and Arizona newspapers. See Chloride *Black Range,* Aug. 23, 1889.
70. Chloride *Black Range,* Aug. 23, 1889; undated St. Joseph newspaper clipping announcing "The Indians Coming," John W. Crawford Papers, RGHC; *Las Vegas Daily Optic,* July 23, 1889.
71. *San Marcial Reporter,* Aug. 24, 31, 1889; undated newspaper clipping, dateline Albuquerque, Aug. 19, entitled "Buried Battery Recovered," John W. Crawford Papers, RGHC; Martin Hardwick Hall, *Sibley's New Mexico Campaign* (Austin: University of Texas Press, 1960), p. 169; Conrey Bryson, *Down Went McGinty, El Paso in the Wonderful Nineties* (El Paso: Texas Western Press, 1977), pp. 52–56.
72. *San Marcial Reporter,* Aug. 24, 1889; copy of contract, dated Aug. 26, 1889, with an Indian of the San Carlos Agency, Box 4, John W. Crawford Papers, RGHC.
73. *San Marcial Reporter,* Sept. 7, 1889.
74. *St. Joseph Daily News,* Aug. 29, Sept. 4, 1889; unidentified newspaper clipping dated July 13, 1889, John W. Crawford Papers, RGHC.
75. *St. Joseph Daily News,* Sept. 4, 5, 6, 18, 1889.
76. Ibid., Sept. 9–11, 1889; untitled newspaper clipping dated July 13, 1889, John W. Crawford Papers, RGHC.
77. *St. Joseph Daily News,* Sept. 13, 1889.
78. Ibid., Sept. 9, 12, 1889.
79. Ibid., Sept. 13, 1889; *San Marcial Reporter,* Oct. 12, 1889. Captain Jack's nephew, Willie Nattress, probably accompanied Harry to St. Joseph, for the San Marcial press recorded that Willie had won "the golden spurs" award in the hurdle race held during cowboy competitions at the exposition. Harry Crawford was judged "best all around rider."
80. *St. Joseph Daily News,* Sept. 16, 1889; printed souvenir for

Crawford's performance, dated 1898, containing account of the rescue of the LaFayette carriage, John W. Crawford Papers, RGHC. For the Studebaker company sending Crawford's daughter the pony cart, see Marc Simmons, *Ranchers, Ramblers, and Renegades, True Tales of Territorial New Mexico,* (Santa Fe: Ancient City Press, 1984), p. 17. Simmons, however, inadvertently places the rescue of the carriage at the Chicago Exposition of 1893, rather than at the 1889 St. Joseph Exposition.

81. *San Marcial Reporter,* Oct. 12, 1889.

82. *St. Joseph Daily News,* Sept. 19, 1889.

83. Arrell Morgan Gibson, *The American Indian, Prehistory to the Present* (Lexington, Mass.: D. C. Heath and Co., 1980), pp. 470–71; *St. Joseph Daily News,* Sept. 14, Oct. 4, 1889; *San Marcial Reporter,* Oct. 12, 1889.

84. *San Marcial Reporter,* Oct. 12, 19, 26, Nov. 2, 1889.

85. From "Our Nugget," Crawford, *Poet Scout* (1886), p. 128.

Chapter 7

1. Datebook, 1889–90, Box 6, John W. Crawford Papers, RGHC; Miller to Crawford, Oct. 14, 1889, private collection of Harriett Richardson, Socorro, N.M.

2. On the attempt to prohibit the sale of liquor to Indians, see Francis Paul Prucha, *The Great Father, The United States Government and the American Indians* (Lincoln: University of Nebraska Press, 1984), vol. 1, pp. 98–102, 312–14, vol. 2, pp. 653–55; Prucha, *American Indian Policy in the Formative Years: The Indian Trade and Intercourse Acts, 1790–1834* (Cambridge: Harvard University Press, 1962), pp. 7–8, 23, 50, 74, 75, 63, 81, 93, 102–38, 254, 257, 267–68.

3. Garrick Baily and Roberta Glenn Baily, *A History of the Navajos, The Reservation Years* (Santa Fe: School of American Research Press, 1986), pp. 73, 77, 94.

4. This reconstruction of Crawford's investigations on or near the Navajo reservation is based on his datebook, 1889–90, John W. Crawford Papers, RGHC; Crawford's report to Attorney General Miller, Mar. 25, 1890, Richardson collection; and Crawford's expense account, located in the Annual Report of the Attorney General, House Ex. Doc. 7 (Serial 2851), 51st Cong., 2d sess., 1890, pp. 142–45.

5. *San Marcial Reporter,* Nov. 30, Dec. 7 supplement, 1889; Diary, 1889–90, John W. Crawford Papers, RGHC.

6. Diary, 1889–90, John W. Crawford Papers, RGHC; Crawford to Miller, Mar. 25, 1890, Richardson collection.

7. Diary, 1889–90, John W. Crawford Papers, RGHC; Frank McNitt, *The Indian Traders* (Norman: University of Oklahoma Press, 1962), p. 208.

8. Diary, 1889–90, John W. Crawford Papers, RGHC; Crawford to Miller, Mar. 25, 1890, Richardson collection.

9. Crawford to Miller, Mar. 25, 1890, Richardson collection.

10. Ibid. In later years, newspaper stories about Captain Jack avowed that while Crawford was employed as a special agent in New Mexico he shaved his beard and disguised himself as an Indian to capture a whiskey dealer. See, for example, the *San Marcial Reporter,* Nov. 7, 1891. Since Jack's diary notations for this period are incomplete, however, it is impossible to verify this story. In his report to Miller, Crawford clearly implies that telling Hurley he had been disguised as an Indian was a scheme to trap the whiskey dealer.

11. Crawford's expense account, Annual Report of the Attorney General, Serial 2851, p. 143; *Albuquerque Morning Democrat,* Jan. 5, 7, 1890.

12. Crawford's expense account, Annual Report of the Attorney General, Serial 2851, p. 144; Crawford to Miller, Mar. 25, 1890, Richardson collection.

13. Crawford to Miller, Mar. 25, 1890, Richardson collection; *San Marcial Reporter,* Feb. 1, 8, 1890. The *Reporter* called Jack's performance "one of the best that an audience in this city ever had the pleasure of listening to."

14. Crawford's expense account, Annual Report of the Attorney General, Serial 2851, pp. 144–45; Crawford to Miller, Mar. 25, 1890, Richardson collection; *San Marcial Reporter,* Feb. 15, 1890; *Las Vegas Daily Optic,* Feb. 7, 8, 1890.

15. See Crawford's expense account and letter to Miller, Mar. 25, 1890; also *Las Vegas Daily Optic,* Feb. 14, 1890.

16. New Haven, Conn., *Register,* Apr. 1, 1890, *Washington Post,* Apr. 14, 1890, copies in John W. Crawford Papers, RGHC.

17. Diary, 1889–90, John W. Crawford Papers, RGHC; Crawford's expense account, Annual Report of the Attorney General, Serial 2851, p. 146; Crawford to Attorney General, Jan. 12, 1891, File 320-90, LR, Department of Justice, RG 60, National Archives (hereafter cited as RG 60, NA). Crawford also staged at least three performances of "The Campfire and the Trail" while in the Forest City area.

18. Crawford's expense account, Annual Report of the Attorney General, Serial 2851, pp. 146–47; Crawford's expense account, Annual Report of the Attorney General, House Ex. Doc. 7 (Serial 2942),

52d Cong., 1st sess., 1891, pp. 130–31; Crawford to Attorney General, [Jan.] 12, 1891, File 320-90, LR, RG 60, NA; Crawford to Attorney General, Jan. 22, 1891, File 5687-90, LR, RG 60, NA.

19. Tanner to Harry W. Crawford, May 9, 1890, Box 1, John W. Crawford Papers, RGHC.

20. Diary, 1889–90, John W. Crawford Papers, RGHC; undated newspaper clipping, featuring Jack Crawford's short story entitled "On the Trail of a Lion," with copyright date of 1893, Richardson collection; *San Marcial Reporter,* May 17, 1890; Jack Crawford to Maria Crawford, Apr. 30, 1890, Carlin to Jack, Oct. 1, 1890, Crawford to Tanner, June 1, 1891, Richardson collection.

21. Crawford's expense account, Annual Report of the Attorney General, Serial 2942, p. 131; *Las Vegas Daily Optic,* May 26, 28, 1890; *San Marcial Reporter,* June 7, July 19, 1890; series of letters written by Carlin to Crawford from Dripping Spring between Aug. 1890 and June 1892, Richardson collection; *Atlanta Constitution* (Ga.), Jan. 3, 1904, copy in John W. Crawford Papers, RGHC; conversation with Gloria Adams Lusby, Apr. 7, 1990. (This Atlanta clipping carries a romanticized version of Carlin's "drying out" and appears to locate the mountains in the Colorado Rockies rather than in New Mexico.)

22. Crawford's expense account, Annual Report of the Attorney General, Serial 2942, pp. 131–32; Diary, 1889–90, John W. Crawford Papers, RGHC; Report of Agent James E. Helms, Aug. 19, 1891, and report of Rev. John E. Smith, Aug. 25, 1891, in Annual Report of the Commissioner of Indian Affairs, House Ex. Doc. 1, (Serial 2934), 52d Cong., 1st sess., 1891, pp. 293–96.

23. For Crawford's travels in the Pacific Northwest, see copies of letters, dated July–September 1890, from Commissioner of Indian Affairs and Attorney General, Richardson collection; see also Crawford's expense account, Annual Report of the Attorney General, Serial 2942, pp. 131–33. For Crawford's visit to Fairhaven, see *Seattle Journal,* Oct. 13, 1890, and clipping from Miles City, Montana, Mar. 31, 1891, John W. Crawford Papers, RGHC.

24. Crawford's expense account, Annual Report of the Attorney General, Serial 2942, pp. 131–33; T. J. Morgan to Secretary of Interior, Aug. 14, 1889, Crawford to Foster, Sept. 4, 1890, and The Dalles *Times Mountaineer,* Oct. 1, 1890, Richardson collection.

25. Lang to Morgan, Nov. 9, 1890; see also Crawford to Attorney General, Nov. 9, 1890, both in Richardson collection.

26. Report of Indian Agent Jay Lynch, Aug. 10, 1891, in Annual Report of the Commissioner of Indian Affairs, House Ex. Doc. 1 (Serial

2934), 52d Cong., 1st sess., 1891, p. 462. For Crawford's lengthy report on his Yakima investigations, see Crawford to Attorney General, Jan. 6, 1891, File 4799-85, LR, RG 60, NA.

27. John W. Crawford's account of the train wreck at Lake Labish, dated Nov. 13, 1890, Richardson collection; *San Marcial Reporter,* Nov. 22, Dec. 6, 1890.

28. *San Marcial Reporter,* Nov. 22, 1890; newspaper clipping from Spokane Falls, containing Crawford's letter dated Nov. 26, 1890, Richardson collection; Detroit, Mich., *Free Press,* Aug. 10, 1891, Richardson collection.

29. John W. Crawford, "Philip Faithful," Box 4, John W. Crawford Papers, RGHC. It is also possible that Jim Carlin collaborated with Crawford in writing this story of Philip Faithful.

30. Untitled, undated newspaper clipping, ca. 1891, containing interview with Captain Jack on ideas of Indians, John W. Crawford Papers, RGHC; untitled article on Indians, Box 4, John W. Crawford Papers, RGHC.

31. On army officers' attitudes toward reservations and Indian policy, see Sherry L. Smith, *The View from Officers' Row, Army Perceptions of Western Indians* (Tucson: University of Arizona Press, 1990), pp. 8, 92–112. For Crawford's views of allotment in severalty, see Seattle *Journal,* Oct. 13, 1890, Richardson collection; untitled article on Indians, Box 4, John W. Crawford Papers, RGHC.

32. Frederick E. Hoxie, *A Final Promise, The Campaign to Assimilate the Indians, 1880–1920* (Cambridge: Cambridge University Press, paper ed., 1989), pp. 53–65; Prucha, *Great Father,* vol. 2, pp. 701–5.

33. Diary, 1889–90, John W. Crawford Papers, RGHC; Crawford to Miller, Mar. 25, 1890, Richardson collection; untitled article on Indians and undated article entitled "A Unique Figure in New York Society, Capt. Jack Crawford," Box 4, John W. Crawford Papers, RGHC.

34. Hoxie, *Final Promise,* pp. 195-98.

35. Irma Cody's copy of *Poet Scout,* with inscription, is located in the Buffalo Bill Museum in Cody, Wyoming. For the poem that Irma recited upon Cody's return to the U.S., see Crawford to Cody, Oct. 21, 1894, Richardson collection; and undated newspaper clipping containing "A Welcome to Papa," John W. Crawford Papers, RGHC. On Cody's European tour, see Yost, *Buffalo Bill,* pp. 221–27.

36. Chloride *Black Range,* Dec. 12, 1890, Jan. 23, 1891; *San Marcial Reporter,* Jan. 10, 17, 24, 1891.

37. Crawford's expense account, Annual Report of the Attorney

General, Serial 2942, p. 134; Crawford's commission as deputy U.S. marshal, dated Jan. 29, 1891, Richardson collection.

38. Green Bay *State Gazette,* Feb. 24, 1891.

39. Ibid., Feb. 24, Mar. 4, 1891. See also Crawford to Attorney General, [n.d.], File 9471-90, LR, RG 60, NA.

40. Milwaukee *Evening Wisconsin,* Feb. 2, 1891, and Crawford to King, Mar. 2, 1891, copies in John W. Crawford Papers, RGHC; Davenport to Crawford, Dec. 11, 1890, and Crawford to King, Feb. 27, 1891, Richardson collection. See also King, *Campaigning with Crook,* pp. xvi–xix. Although historian Don Russell discussed the King–Davenport imbroglio in his Introduction to *Campaigning with Crook.* Russell did not mention this literary conflict in his biography of King, published posthumously. See Don Russell, *Campaigning with King, Charles King, Chronicler of the Old Army,* ed. Paul L. Hedren (Lincoln: University of Nebraska Press, 1991). See also Harry H. Anderson, "Some Footnotes to Charles King's 'Campaigning With Crook,' " *Historical Messenger of the Milwaukee County Historical Society,* 29 (Spring 1973). My thanks to Paul Hedren for calling my attention to this article.

41. Crawford's expense account, Serial 2942, pp. 134–36; *Yellowstone Journal* (Montana), Mar. 31, 1891, clipping in John W. Crawford Papers, RGHC; Miles City, Montana *Daily Journal,* Apr. 4, 1891, Richardson collection.

42. Crawford to Scheffer, May 20, 1891, and Tanner to Crawford, May 24, 1891, John W. Crawford Papers, RGHC; Crawford to Tanner, June 1, 1891, and Tanner to Crawford, July 8, 1891, Richardson collection. In late June 1891, Crawford mortgaged to Scheffer for one thousand dollars an assortment of farm equipment, stallions, mares, and cattle, with the money to be repaid by the fall of 1892. *Record Book 29,* Socorro County Courthouse, pp. 509–10.

43. *San Marcial Reporter,* Apr. 11, July 4, 1891; *Las Vegas Daily Optic,* July 2, 1891; "The Song of the Pulsometer," by Capt. Jack Crawford, Richardson collection.

44. Crawford's expense account, Annual Report of the Attorney General, House Ex. Doc. 7 (Serial 3097), 52d Cong., 2d sess., 1892, pp. 194–97; Washington *Post,* Nov. 29, 1891, clipping in John W. Crawford Papers, RGHC; *San Marcial Reporter,* Nov. 7, 28, 1891.

45. See Miller to Crawford, Nov. 28, 1891, Fiske to Attorney General, June 27, 1891, and Cotton to Shipley, Aug. 23, 1891, Richardson collection.

46. Crawford's expense account, Annual Report of the Attorney General, Serial 3097, p. 197; *Las Vegas Daily Optic,* Dec. 23, 28, 1891.

47. Santa Fe *Daily New Mexican,* Jan. 21–28, 1892; *Las Vegas*

Daily Optic, Jan. 27, 28, 1892; Frank Luther Mott, *A History of American Magazines, 1865–1885* (Cambridge: Harvard University Press, 1938), pp. 510–12.

48. Crawford's expense account, Serial 3097, p. 198; Santa Fe *Daily New Mexican,* Feb. 11, 1892.

49. *Albuquerque Morning Democrat,* Feb. 2, 1892; *San Marcial Reporter,* Feb. 20, Mar. 5, 19, 26, 1892; Santa Fe *Daily New Mexican,* Mar. 15, 1892; *Las Vegas Daily Optic,* Mar. 16, 1892; *El Paso Times,* Mar. 23, 25, 1892. For a more complete look at Captain Jack at the El Paso encampment and his involvement with El Paso's McGinty Club, see Bryson, *Down Went McGinty,* pp. 1–9.

50. For Crawford's involvement with the Republican Convention, see *San Marcial Reporter,* Apr. 16, 23, 1892.

51. *Las Vegas Daily Optic,* Apr. 6–8, 1892. Crawford's "War's Humorous Side" appears in the April 8 issue of the *Optic.*

52. Crawford's expense account, Serial 3097, p. 199; *Las Vegas Daily Optic,* Mar. 21, 1890, Apr. 15, May 13, 1892; *Albuquerque Morning Democrat,* Mar. 29, Apr. 16, July 29, 1890; Santa Fe *Daily New Mexican,* Mar. 29, 1892.

53. *Las Vegas Daily Optic,* May 27, 1892; clipping, undated, from *Las Vegas Daily Optic,* containing letter dated May 25, 1892, signed "Prospector" but written by Crawford, and undated manuscript on Navajo Commission, John W. Crawford Papers, RGHC; Annual Report of the Commissioner of Indian Affairs, House Ex. Doc. 1, (Serial 3088), 52d Cong., 2d sess., 1892, p. 75.

54. Undated manuscript on Navajo Commission (in Carlin's handwriting), John W. Crawford Papers, RGHC; Crawford to Carlin, undated letter describing recent experiences with Navajo Commission, Richardson collection.

55. See, for example, Jim Carlin to Jack Crawford, Aug. 14, 24, 26, Sept. 3, 1890, Apr. 2, 1891, Apr. 3, 17, 1892, Richardson collection.

56. Jim Carlin to Jack Crawford, Apr. 9, 1892, ibid.

57. Jim Carlin to Jack Crawford, Aug. 14, 19, 24, Sept. 3, 1890, Apr. 2, 1891, ibid.; *Las Vegas Daily Optic,* July 7, 1891; *San Marcial Reporter,* Nov. 14, 1891.

58. For Crawford and the McGinty Club, see Bryson, *Down Went McGinty,* pp. 1–4. "The McGinty Club" is reproduced on the frontispiece of Bryson's book. For Carlin's reference to "The McGinty Club," see Jim Carlin to Jack Crawford, Apr. 9, 17, 1892, Richardson collection.

59. *Las Vegas Daily Optic,* Aug. 13, 1892; Jim Carlin to Jack Crawford, June 4, Oct. 21, 1892, Richardson collection.

60. *San Marcial Reporter,* Aug. 13, 20, Sept. 17, 1892; Chloride

Black Range, Aug. 19, 1892; Attorney General to Crawford, Oct. 1, 14, 1892, LS, Department of Justice, RG 60, NA Microfilm Publication M-699, roll 31.

61. *Las Vegas Daily Optic,* Nov. 1, 1892; New York City *Sunday Advertiser,* Oct. 30, 1892, copy in John W. Crawford Papers, RGHC; Brownell to Kenyon, Nov. 5, 1892, Box 2, John W. Crawford Papers, RGHC. While in New York City, Captain Jack entertained about fifty guests in the home of Mrs. Frank Leslie. And the November issue of *Frank Leslie's Illustrated Monthly* carried Crawford's story, "A Battle for Love." See Tame, Iowa, *Free Press,* Nov. 24, 1892, copy in John W. Crawford Papers, RGHC; *Las Vegas Daily Optic,* Oct. 29, 1892.

62. Attorney General to Crawford, Nov. 10, 15, 1892, M-699, roll 31; draft of letter, Crawford to Foster, Nov. 28, 1892, miscellaneous notebook, John W. Crawford Papers, RGHC; *Las Vegas Daily Optic,* Dec. 21, 1892; clippings from two Wisconsin newspapers, dated Jan. 19, 21, 1893, John W. Crawford Papers, RGHC.

63. *Las Vegas Daily Optic,* Feb. 3, 1893; Albuquerque *Citizen,* Apr. 5, 1893, clipping located in L. Bradford Prince Papers, file no. 17, "Capt. Jack Crawford," New Mexico State Records Center and Archives, Santa Fe; Jack Crawford to May Crawford, Feb. 7, 1893, Richardson collection.

64. Attorney General to Crawford, Mar. 14, Apr. 18, 1893, M-699, roll 31; *Santa Fe Weekly New Mexican Review,* Apr. 20, 1893; *San Marcial Bee,* Apr. 29, June 10, 1893.

65. From "The Trail I Used To Ride," by Captain Jack Crawford, published in the *Forest City Press* (S.D.) sometime in 1890. Clipping found in one of Captain Jack's scrapbooks, Richardson collection.

Chapter 8

1. Standard works on the lyceum and chautauqua movements are Carl Bode, *The American Lyceum, Town Meeting of the Mind* (Carbondale: Southern Illinois University Press, 1968), Joseph E. Gould, *The Chautauqua Movement, An Episode in the Continuing American Revolution* (Albany: State University of New York Press, 1961), and Theodore Morrison, *Chautauqua, A Center for Education, Religion, and the Arts in America* (Chicago: University of Chicago Press, 1974).

2. The Detroit story is reprinted in the *San Marcial Bee,* June 3, 1893. For the career of Joaquin Miller, see Benjamin S. Lawson, *Joaquin Miller* (Boise, Idaho: Boise State University, 1980). For the 1893 depression, see Carl N. Degler, *The Age of the Economic Revolution, 1876–1900,* 2d ed. (Glenview, Ill.: Scott, Foresman and Co., 1977), pp. 120–24.

3. Chicago *Herald,* July 30, 1893, private collection of Harriett Richardson, Socorro, N.M.; Robert W. Rydell, *All the World's a Fair, Visions of Empire at American International Expositions, 1876–1916* (Chicago: University of Chicago Press, 1984), pp. 39–45. See also David F. Burg, *Chicago's White City of 1893* (Lexington: University of Kentucky Press, 1976).

4. Marion Dargan, "New Mexico's Fight for Statehood," *New Mexico Historical Review,* 18 (Jan. 1943).

5. *Las Vegas Daily Optic,* Sept. 22, 1893; *Santa Fe New Mexican Review,* Sept. 28, 1893. In commemoration of the exposition, a new liberty bell had been cast and was rung on special occasions. Burg, *Chicago's White City,* p. 212.

6. *Las Vegas Daily Optic,* Sept. 22, 1893.

7. Ibid.; *Santa Fe New Mexican Review,* Sept. 28, 1893; *Chicago Sunday Tribune,* Sept. 17, 1893. On the seventeenth, the *Chicago Tribune* also carried a short article on New Mexico's Day at the fair, subtitled "Gov. William C. Thornton Gives an Oration and Capt. Crawford Reads a Poem." On September 10, the *Tribune* carried a two-column article written by Crawford, entitled "Captain Jack at the Fair," in which Crawford again recorded his impressions of the exposition.

8. Ray Allen Billington, *Frederick Jackson Turner, Historian, Scholar, Teacher* (New York: Oxford University Press, 1973), pp. 124–31.

9. John W. Crawford, *Camp Fire Sparks* (Chicago: Charles H. Kerr and Company, 1893); Carlin to Crawford, Oct. 21, 1892, Richardson collection; *Las Vegas Daily Optic,* Oct. 9, 1893; Boston *Herald,* Oct. 19, 1893, Richardson collection.

10. Jack Crawford, "The Government Scout," *Outing,* 29 (Nov. 1893): 148–50; Frank Luther Mott, *A History of American Magazines, 1885–1905* (Cambridge: Harvard University Press, 1957), pp. 633–37; G. Edward White, *The Eastern Establishment and the Western Experience, The West of Frederic Remington, Theodore Roosevelt, and Owen Wister* (Austin: University of Texas Press, 1989), pp. 99–101.

11. Robert Falk, "The Search for Reality: Writers and Their Literature," in *The Gilded Age, A Reappraisal,* ed. H. Wayne Morgan (Syracuse, N.Y.: Syracuse University Press, 1963), pp. 198–210; Patrick D. Morrow, "Parody and Parable in Early Western Local Color Writing," *Journal of the West,* 19 (January 1980). Crawford's "Justice on the Frontier" appeared in the *Scranton Truth* (Pennsylvania), Jan. 29, 1898, clipping in Scrapbook no. 8, John W. Crawford Papers, RGHC.

12. The poems and themes cited in this paragraph are found in John W. Crawford, *Whar' the Hand O' God Is Seen,* 2d ed.

13. Jack Crawford, "The Professor," *Banner of Gold,* 5 (April 1894): 209–11, Richardson collection; Jack Crawford, "The Fourth at Jimtown," Chicago *Evening Lamp,* June 30, 1894, Richardson collection; Brooklyn *Eagle,* May 6, 1894, and Hastings, Michigan *Banner,* Nov. 29, 1894, clippings found in John W. Crawford Papers, RGHC. A copy of Crawford's "Oriental Bum Bum" is located in the Nicholl Collection, Washington State Historical Society, Tacoma. My thanks to Professor Lewis Saum for supplying a copy. John Higham has noted that during the 1890s, "cheerful energetic tunes [like Crawford's] spread from the midways and the outdoors amusement parks. . . . Typical of these tunes was 'Ta-ra-ra-boom-der-e,' first published in 1891." John Higham, "The Reorientation of American Culture in the 1890's," in *The Origins of Modern Consciousness,* ed. John Weiss (Detroit: Wayne State University Press, 1965), p. 30.

14. *Chicago Evening Herald,* Nov. 18, 1893, Richardson collection.

15. Ibid.

16. Crawford to Wells, Oct. 25, 1894, John W. Crawford Papers, RGHC; brochures for "The Camp Fire and the Trail" and clippings in several scrapbooks, Richardson collection.

17. *Janesville Recorder* (Wisc.), Jan. 27, 1894, Richardson collection.

18. New York *Advertiser,* July 22, 1894, Richardson collection. On Jack's Scottish forebears, see John W. Crawford, *Poet Scout* (1886), p. x.

19. *Scranton Truth* (Pennsylvania), Dec. 18, 1895, Richardson collection.

20. Ibid.; *New York Mercury,* Dec. 2, 1894, clipping in Scrapbook no. 3, John W. Crawford Papers, RGHC.

21. *New York Mercury,* Dec. 2, 1894, clipping in Scrapbook no. 3, and *London Mail,* Mar. 19, 1897, clipping in Scrapbook no. 7, John W. Crawford Papers, RGHC; *Scranton Truth* (Pa.), Dec. 18, 1895, Richardson collection.

22. *Scranton Truth* (Pa.), Dec. 18, 1895, and *Westminster Budget,* Oct. 12, 1894, Richardson collection; Spokane *Spokesman-Review,* Nov. 5, 1895, clipping in John W. Crawford Papers, RGHC.

23. *Wichita Daily Eagle,* Jan. 2, 1896, clipping in Scrapbook no. 2, and draft of Crawford letter [January 1896], Box 2, John W. Crawford Papers, RGHC; Crawford to Cody, Sept. 19, 1894, Richardson collection. On William Mathewson, see Yost, *Buffalo Bill,* pp. 374–75.

24. Crawford to Cody, Sept. 19, 1894, Richardson collection.

25. Ibid.; Crawford to Cody, Oct. 21, 1894, Richardson collection. On the question of Cody's authorship, the killing of Yellow Hand, his drinking, and association with other women, see Russell, *Lives and Legends of Buffalo Bill,* pp. 232–35, 265–84, 302–4, 360–61, 422, 432–36, 477; see also Yost, *Buffalo Bill,* pp. 84–95, 243, 314–17, 419.

26. Winchester Factory records pertaining to the Winchester that Crawford sent to Cody are located in the Buffalo Bill Museum, Cody, Wyo.

27. *New York Mercury,* Dec. 2, 1894, clipping in Scrapbook no. 3, John W. Crawford Papers, RGHC; on Mrs. Frank Leslie, see Madeleine B. Stern, *Purple Passage, The Life of Mrs. Frank Leslie* (Norman: University of Oklahoma Press, 1953), pp. 125–26.

28. *Omaha World-Herald,* May 17, 1896, copy in John W. Crawford Papers, RGHC; *New York Times,* Sept. 9–13, 1895.

29. See Jack Crawford to May Crawford, Feb. 21, 1895, Box 3, John W. Crawford Papers, RGHC; PaPa Jack Crawford to May Crawford, Mar. 16, 1895, Richardson collection; *El Paso Times,* May 5, 1895; Chloride *Black Range,* July 5, 1895; Bryson, *Down Went McGinty,* p. 18.

30. Scorer, "Unique Character in American Literature," pp. 56–60; John W. Crawford, *Lariattes, A Book of Poems and Favorite Recitations* (Sigourney, Iowa: William A. Bell, 1904), pp. 5–9.

31. *New York City Life,* May 18, 1895, clipping in Scrapbook no. 4, John W. Crawford Papers, RGHC.

32. See publicity brochure, dated Dec. 18, [1895], Richardson collection; Boston *Massachusetts Ploughman,* June 22, 1895, and New York *Press,* July 6, 1895, clippings in John W. Crawford Papers, RGHC.

33. *Bicycling World,* Aug. 30, 1895, Box 3, John W. Crawford Papers, RGHC. Bicycling was one of the great crazes of the 1890s. See Higham, "The Reorientation of American Culture in the 1890's," p. 28.

34. Crawford to Wells, Oct. 25, 1894, John W. Crawford Papers, RGHC.

35. On Marie Madison, see *Dramatic Compositions Copyrighted in the United States, 1870–1916,* and program for Madison's *The Witch,* performed in Los Angeles, June 27–29, 1892, copy courtesy of Susan Naulty, Rare Book Department, Huntington Library. See also Marie Madison, "True American." On Madison's editorial work for Crawford, see Crawford to Madison, Apr. 17, 1895, and Madison to Crawford, Oct. 20, 1895, Box 1, John W. Crawford Papers, RGHC.

36. See publicity brochure, Dec. 18, [1895], Richardson collection; several letters from Spencer to Crawford, 1895, Box 1, John W. Crawford Papers, RGHC; see Speed to Crawford, Oct. 29, 1895, Box 2,

John W. Crawford Papers, RGHC, for the first mention of Wendell traveling with Captain Jack. For more on Wendell, see *Minneapolis Journal,* Feb. 28, 1917, clipping in John W. Crawford Papers, RGHC.

37. Crawford's itinerary has been reconstructed from a multitude of newspaper clippings located in John W. Crawford Papers, RGHC and the Richardson collection. See also Crawford to Russ, Dec. 26, 1895, draft of Crawford letter, dated Dec. 26 [1895], and draft of Crawford letter to Red Bath Lyceum Bureau (n.d.), Box 2, John W. Crawford Papers, RGHC; Spencer to Crawford, Dec. 31, 1895, Box 1, John W. Crawford Papers, RGHC.

38. St. Paul *Pioneer Press,* Oct. 20, 1895, clipping in Scrapbook no. 1, *San Francisco Chronicle,* Nov. 29, 1895, clipping in Scrapbook no. 2, *Davenport Republican,* Mar. 20, 1896, clipping in Scrapbook no. 4, Spokane *Spokesman-Review,* Nov. 5, 1895, John W. Crawford Papers, RGHC. For Crawford's performance fees, see draft of letter from Crawford to Frohman, [n.d.], Richardson collection.

39. Billings *Daily Gazette,* Oct. 25, 1895, Richardson collection.

40. Spokane *Spokesman-Review,* Nov. 5, 1895, clipping in John W. Crawford Papers, RGHC.

41. Woodland *Daily Democrat,* Nov. 26, 1895, clipping in Scrapbook no. 2, John W. Crawford Papers, RGHC.

42. Four of Gay's letters to Crawford have been preserved. See Gay to Crawford, Feb. 14, 1895, Jan. 26, Feb. 29, 1896, Richardson collection; see Gay to Crawford, Apr. 7, 1896, Box 2, John W. Crawford Papers, RGHC. See also Penwell (Gay's lawyer) to Crawford, Mar. 26, 1896, Box 2, John W. Crawford Papers, RGHC. Gay's execution is described in the Lead, S.D., *Evening Call,* June 10, 1896, copy courtesy Marvene Riis, archivist, South Dakota State Historical Society. On Gay's killing of Forbes, see Estelline Bennett, *Old Deadwood Days* (repr., Lincoln: University of Nebraska Press, 1982), pp. 133–34; Parker, *Gold in the Black Hills,* pp. 171–72.

43. *El Paso Daily Herald,* Dec. 17, 1895; *Las Vegas Daily Optic,* Dec. 18–19, 1895; *Raton Range,* Dec. 19, 1895, Trinidad *Evening Chronicle,* Dec. 20, 1895, and *Denver Times,* Dec. 26, 1895, clippings in Scrapbook no. 2, John W. Crawford Papers, RGHC.

44. *Scranton Truth,* Jan. 31, Feb. 1, 1896, Richardson collection.

45. *Las Vegas Daily Optic,* Apr. 6, June 29, July 2, Nov. 10, 1896. In a letter published in the *Optic* for November 10, Crawford wrote: "I represented the New Mexico delegation as a member of the notification

committee." Crawford's name, however, does not appear on the list of official members of the notification committee as published in the *New York Times* on June 29, 1896.

46. *St. Paul Globe,* Sept. 8, 1896, Stillwater *Mirror,* Sept. 10, 1896, clippings in Scrapbook no. 4, John W. Crawford Papers, RGHC; undated printed campaign speech [1896], entitled "Captain Jack, Crawford's Speech at the Pleasant Valley Meeting," copy in John W. Crawford Papers, RGHC; *New York Clipper,* Aug. 1896, Richardson collection.

47. Margaret Leech, *In the Days of McKinley* (New York: Harper and Brothers, 1959), pp. 86–91.

48. Chloride *Black Range,* Aug. 28, 1896, Jan. 29, 1897.

49. Jack Crawford to Maria Crawford, Oct. 7, 1896, Richardson collection.

50. For the New York City meeting, see Burlington, Vermont *Sunday Sun,* Nov. 8, 1896, clipping in John W. Crawford Papers, RGHC.

51. Undated printed campaign speech [1896], entitled "Captain Jack, Crawford's Speech at the Pleasant Valley Meeting," copy in John W. Crawford Papers, RGHC.

52. John Tipple, "The Robber Baron in the Gilded Age, Entrepreneur or Iconoclast?" in *The Gilded Age, A Reappraisal,* ed. H. Wayne Morgan (Syracuse, N.Y.: Syracuse University Press, 1963), pp. 28, 36; John Tebbel, *From Rags To Riches,* p. 17.

53. *Las Vegas Daily Optic,* Nov. 10, 1896.

54. Crawford to Schwenk, Nov. 23, 1895, Box 1, *Wilkes-Barre Weekly Times,* Feb. 3, 1896, clipping in Scrapbook no. 3, Harrison to Crawford, Apr. 19, 1896, Box 2, *San Marcial Bee,* Feb. 6, 1897, clipping in Scrapbook no. 5, John W. Crawford Papers, RGHC.

55. *San Marcial Bee,* Feb. 6, 1897, clipping in Scrapbook no. 5, John W. Crawford Papers, RGHC.

56. Crawford to Pope, Feb. 12, 1897, Richardson collection.

57. Adams, Mass., *Adams Freeman,* Jan. 30, 1897, and *San Marcial Bee,* Feb. 6, 1897, clippings in Scrapbook no. 5, John W. Crawford Papers, RGHC.

58. *Boston Sunday Globe,* Jan. 31, 1897, *L.A.W. Bulletin,* Mar. 19, 1897, Scrapbook no. 5, newspaper clipping containing letter of Nixon Waterman to Captain Jack dated Mar. 26, 1897, and undated newspaper clipping, "Captain Jack Crawford, A Genius in Buckskin," by Nixon Waterman, John W. Crawford Papers, RGHC.

59. *Adams Freeman,* Aug. 7, 1897, clipping in Scrapbook no. 7, John W. Crawford Papers, RGHC.

60. *Talent,* Jan. 10, 1898, clipping in Scrapbook no. 8, John W. Crawford Papers, RGHC; Crawford to Mills, Dec. 8, 1897, Richardson collection.

61. Albany *Argus,* Nov. 16, 1897, clipping in Scrapbook no. 7, John W. Crawford Papers, RGHC; newspaper item datelined Leominster, Jan. 10, 1898, Richardson collection.

62. Woodland, Calif., *Daily Democrat,* Nov. 26, 1895, clipping in Scrapbook no. 2, John W. Crawford Papers, RGHC.

63. *Omaha Daily Bee,* Jan. 5, 1896, clipping in Scrapbook no. 3 and Adams, Mass., *Adams Freeman,* Mar. 20, 1897, clipping, both located in John W. Crawford Papers, RGHC; Chicago newspaper clipping, Nov. 18, 1893, Richardson collection. Crawford often included in his performances short but effective discourses on the evils of whiskey and dime novels.

64. See Woodland, Calif., *Daily Democrat,* Nov. 26, 1895, clipping in Scrapbook no. 2, and Worcester, Mass., *Telegram,* Feb. 4, 1898, clipping in Scrapbook no. 8, John W. Crawford Papers, RGHC; see also *Scranton Truth,* Feb. 1, 1896, John W. Crawford Papers, RGHC.

65. See descriptions of Crawford's performances in the following: Denver *Daily News,* Dec. 26, 1895; Scranton, Pa., *Truth,* Feb. 1, 1896; *Wichita Daily Eagle* (Kansas), Jan. 3, 1896; Williamsport, Pa., *Times,* Apr. 20, 1897, clippings located in John W. Crawford Papers, RGHC.

66. For swooning heroines, see Robert G. Athearn, *The Mythic West in Twentieth-Century America* (Lawrence: University Press of Kansas, 1986), pp. 170–71; for Crawford's poem to his wife, see *Brockton Times* (Mass.), Feb. 5, 1898, clipping in Scrapbook no. 8, John W. Crawford Papers, RGHC.

67. *Adams Freeman,* Mar. 20, 1897, John W. Crawford Papers, RGHC. Crawford's shooting demonstration, on one occasion, led to a bystander being wounded. See newspaper clipping dated Aug. 18, 1897, clipping in Scrapbook no. 7, John W. Crawford Papers, RGHC. On the other hand, Justice Blume of Chicago saved his life when attacked by two thugs by duplicating Crawford's gunplay. "I received my inspiration from the poet-scout, Jack Crawford," the justice later explained. See *Chicago Post,* Jan. 2, 1896, clipping in Crawford Papers, RGHC.

68. On masculine hardiness and the 1890s, see Higham, "Reorientation of American Culture in the 1890's," pp. 29–30. Theodore Roosevelt, writing in the late 1880s and 1890s after his experience as a Dakota rancher, pictured a West that was inextricably linked with mas-

culinity. See White, *Eastern Establishment and the Western Experience*, p. 91.

69. Laurence M. Hauptman, "Mythologizing Westward Expansion: Schoolbooks and the Image of the American Frontier before Turner," *Western Historical Quarterly*, 8 (July 1977): 269–72; Athearn, *Mythic West*, pp. 160–89, 249–75. For another scholar's detailed analysis of the Frontier myth, see Slotkin, *Fatal Environment*. Also helpful is Ray Allen Billington, *Land of Savagery, Land of Promise, The European Image of the American Frontier in the Nineteenth Century* (Norman: University of Oklahoma Press, 1981).

70. For a discussion of western writers and their mixing of romance and realism, see Sanford E. Marovitz, "Bridging the Continent with Romantic Western Realism," *Journal of the West*, 19 (January 1980).

71. For Kate Sherwood, see testimonial dated Mar. 15, 1897, on publicity brochure for "The Camp Fire and the Trail," copy in John W. Crawford Papers, RGHC; *Adams Freeman*, Jan. 30, 1897, clipping in Scrapbook no. 5, John W. Crawford Papers, RGHC.

72. From "Whar' the Hand O' God Is Seen," in Crawford, *Whar' the Hand O' God Is Seen*, p. 7.

Chapter 9

1. Pierre Berton, *The Klondike Fever, The Life and Death of the Last Great Gold Rush* (New York: Alfred A. Knopf, 1958), pp. 99–112.

2. Berton, *Klondike Fever*, p. 113.

3. Undated article in Jack Crawford's handwriting, private collection of Harriett Richardson, Socorro, N.M. See also Berton, *Klondike Fever*, pp. 120–23.

4. Melanie J. Mayer, *Klondike Women, True Tales of the 1897–1898 Gold Rush* (Athens: Ohio University Press, 1989), p. 23; Ethel Anderson Becker, *Klondike '98, E. A. Hegg's Gold Rush Album* (Portland: Binfords and Mort, Publishers, 1967), p. 21; Berton, *Klondike Fever*, p. 417.

5. *Scranton Truth*, Sept. 18, 1897, clipping in Scrapbook no. 7, John W. Crawford Papers, RGHC.

6. Prospectus of the Captain Jack Crawford Alaska Prospecting and Mining Corporation, Richardson collection; *Adams Freeman* (Mass.), Aug. 7, 1897, and unidentified newspaper clipping dated Aug. 7, 1897, Scrapbook no. 7, John W. Crawford Papers, RGHC.

7. Newspaper clipping dated Dec. 19, 1897 and Worcester, Mass., *Telegram,* Jan. 8, 1898, Scrapbook no. 8, John W. Crawford Papers, RGHC.

8. Prospectus of the Klondike, Yukon and Copper River Company, Richardson collection; newspaper clipping dated Jan. 12, 1899, John W. Crawford Papers, RGHC.

9. Prospectus of the Klondike, Yukon and Copper River Company, Richardson collection.

10. Handwritten letter, John W. Crawford, Mar. 1, 1898, and Crawford Expense Account with Klondike, Yukon and Copper River Company, Richardson collection; San Francisco *Examiner,* Mar. 12, 17, 1898, clippings in Scrapbook no. 8, John W. Crawford Papers, RGHC. Midway into Crawford's San Francisco performance, the commander of the local Grand Army post presented Jack with an elaborate diamond-studded G.A.R. badge, the personal gift of General R. H. Warfield, a long-time friend.

11. Undated clipping from Portland newspaper and *Seattle Post-Intelligencer,* Mar. 22, 1898, clippings in John W. Crawford Papers, RGHC.

12. Crawford to Editor, *Scranton Truth,* Mar. 29, 1898, Richardson collection.

13. Crawford to Vrooman, Mar. 25, 1898, Box 2, John W. Crawford Papers, RGHC.

14. Crawford to Taylor, Mar. 24, 1898, Box 2, and *Seattle Times,* Mar. 31, 1898, John W. Crawford Papers, RGHC; Crawford manuscript dated Mar. 22, 1898, Richardson collection. Crawford named his St. Bernard "Hero," after another dog of that name, which had been the constant companion of little May Cody Crawford. Jack credited the first dog with saving him from drowning while swimming with Fort Craig soldiers in the Rio Grande.

15. For Crawford and the reindeer, see *Seattle Post-Intelligencer,* Mar. 22, 1898; undated newspaper clipping entitled "Another Alaska Company"; and *Seattle Times,* Mar. 31, 1898, John W. Crawford Papers, RGHC. I have reconstructed the reindeer story from the following: Berton, *Klondike Fever,* pp. 171–200, Archie Satterfield, *Chilkoot Pass, The Most Famous Trail in the North* (Anchorage: Alaska Northwest Publishing Co., 1978), pp. 81–85, William R. Hunt, *North of 53, The Wild Days of the Alaska–Yukon Mining Frontier, 1870–1914* (New York: Macmillan Publishing Co., 1974), pp. 52–53, and the *Klondike Nugget,* Jan. 11, Feb. 4, 1899. An accurate history of the Klondike reindeer, however, has yet to be written.

16. Hunt, *North of 53,* p. 53; Melody Webb, *The Last Frontier, A History of the Yukon Basin of Canada and Alaska* (Albuquerque: University of New Mexico Press, 1985), pp. 145–46; Crawford manuscript dated Mar. 22, 1898, Richardson collection. For 164 reindeer starting up the Dalton Trail, see *Klondike Nugget,* Jan. 11, 1899.

17. Manuscript in Crawford's handwriting [April 1898], Richardson collection; Diary, 1898–99, John W. Crawford Papers, RGHC. Crawford recorded his Klondike experiences in two small notebooks, one I have entitled Diary, 1898–99, and the other Diary, 1898.

18. Mrs. George Black, *My Seventy Years* (London: Thomas Nelson and Sons, 1938), pp. 94–95.

19. Diary, 1898–99, John W. Crawford Papers, RGHC.

20. Ibid.

21. Copy of sealed orders that Vrooman issued to Crawford, and Crawford letter from Dyea, May 7, 1898, published in several U.S. newspapers, Richardson collection.

22. Diary, 1898–99, John W. Crawford Papers, RGHC; Crawford letter from Dyea, May 7, 1898, newspaper clipping, Richardson collection.

23. Diary, 1898–99, John W. Crawford Papers, RGHC.

24. Ibid.

25. See Samuel B. Steele, *Forty Years in Canada, Reminiscences of the Great North-West with Some Account of His Service in South Africa* (Toronto: McGraw-Hill Ryerson Limited, 1972), p. 295.

26. On tramways, see Satterfield, *Chilkoot Pass,* pp. 74–80. Advice to Crawford is contained in a note, dated Apr. 22, 1898, placed inside Diary, 1898, John W. Crawford Papers, RGHC. Packers reweighed the supplies they carried at The Scales; thus it derived its name. Berton, *Klondike Fever,* p. 249.

27. Diary, 1898–99, John W. Crawford Papers, RGHC; Crawford letter from Dyea, May 7, 1898, clipping, Richardson collection.

28. Becker, *Klondike '98,* p. 25; Berton, *Klondike Fever,* pp. 249–51.

29. Diary, 1898–99, John W. Crawford Papers, RGHC; Crawford letter from Dyea, May 7, 1898, clipping, Richardson collection.

30. Ibid.

31. Berton, *Klondike Fever,* pp. 268–71.

32. Crawford's men are identified in *Dyea Press,* Apr. 23, 1898, clipping in Richardson collection. For conflict among Klondike partners, see Frederick Palmer, *In the Klondyke, Including an Account of a Winter's Journey to Dawson* (New York: Charles Scribner's Sons, 1899),

178–79; Mayer, *Klondike Women,* pp. 104–5; Berton, *Klondike Fever,* 270–71, 284–87.

33. Diary, 1898–99, John W. Crawford Papers, RGHC. See also the undated draft of the letter that Crawford sent to the Klondike, Yukon and Copper River Company, Richardson collection.

34. Diary, 1898–99, John W. Crawford Papers, RGHC; Robin Fisher, "Over the Chilkoot with Duff Pattullo," *Beaver,* 67 (August–September 1987): 4–11. See "Under the Snow," a poem commemorating the death of Tom Pattullo, in John W. Crawford, *Poet Scout* (1886), pp. 92–93.

35. Steele, *Forty Years in Canada,* pp. 298–305.

36. Diary, 1898–99, John W. Crawford Papers, RGHC; Crawford letter from Dyea, May 7, 1898, clipping, Richardson collection.

37. Diary, 1898–99, John W. Crawford Papers, RGHC.

38. Ibid.

39. Crawford letter from Dyea, May 7, 1898, clipping, Richardson collection.

40. Ibid.; Diary, 1898–99, John W. Crawford Papers, RGHC.

41. Diary, 1898–99, John W. Crawford Papers, RGHC.

42. Ibid.

43. Jack Crawford to Maria Crawford, May 6, 27, 1898, Richardson collection.

44. Diary, 1898–99, John W. Crawford Papers, RGHC; undated draft of the letter that Crawford sent to the Klondike, Yukon and Copper River Company, Richardson collection; Berton, *Klondike Fever,* pp. 276–77.

45. Diary, 1898, John W. Crawford Papers, RGHC. Crawford's penciled notations in this journal is the basis for the following description of Jack's trip down the Yukon.

46. On pilots, see Becker, *Klondike '98,* p. 60.

47. From "Impromptu Farewell Poem," Captain Jack Crawford, printed poem dated May 27, 1898, Lake Bennett, John W. Crawford Papers, RGHC.

Chapter 10

1. Diary, 1898, John W. Crawford Papers, RGHC.

2. Diary, 1898–99, Diary, 1898, John W. Crawford Papers, RGHC; Crawford to Dutcher, Dec. 8, 1898, private collection of Harriett Richardson, Socorro, N.M.

3. Jack Crawford to Maria Crawford, Aug. 24, 1898, and undated draft of the letter that Crawford sent to the Klondike, Yukon and Copper River Company, Richardson collection; undated newspaper clipping with the title "Crawfordsville, at Mouth of This River, A Promising Village," John W. Crawford Papers, RGHC.

4. Crawford to Dutcher, Dec. 8, 1898, Richardson collection.

5. Jack Crawford to Maria Crawford, Aug. 24, 1898, and Crawford letter dated Vrooman City, Aug. 28, 1898, intended for publication in newspapers, Richardson collection.

6. Jack Crawford to Maria Crawford, Aug. 24, 1898, Richardson collection.

7. Crawford letter dated Vrooman City, Aug. 28, 1898, Richardson collection.

8. Ibid.; Donaldson to Crawford, Dec. 2, 1898, John W. Crawford Papers, Box 2, RGHC.

9. Crawford letter dated Vrooman City, Aug. 28, 1898, and undated draft of the letter that Crawford sent to the Klondike, Yukon and Copper River Company, Richardson collection; Black, *My Seventy Years,* p. 117.

10. Jeremiah Lynch, *Three Years in the Klondike* (London: Edward Arnold, 1904), pp. 51–65.

11. On Dawson, see Berton, *Klondike Fever,* pp. 288–332; and Mayer, *Klondike Women,* p. 201; on Crawford's cabin, see undated draft of the letter that Crawford sent to the Klondike, Yukon and Copper River Company, Richardson collection.

12. *Klondike Nugget,* Oct. 26, 1898.

13. For Crawford's remarks, see Crawford to Brother Elks, Jan. 14, 1899, John W. Crawford Papers, Box 2, RGHC; for the *Nugget's* editorial, see *Klondike Nugget,* Oct. 29, 1898.

14. *Klondike Nugget,* Nov. 16, 1898.

15. Dawson newspaper clipping, Nov. 18, 1898, located in John W. Crawford Papers, RGHC.

16. *Klondike Nugget,* Dec. 24, 1898; Crawford to Brother Elks (and related papers), Jan. 14, 1899, and Diary, 1898–99, John W. Crawford Papers, RGHC.

17. Undated draft of the letter that Crawford sent to the Klondike, Yukon and Copper River Company, and undated Dawson newspaper clipping, Richardson collection. See also "Notice to the Public," *Klondike Nugget,* Feb. 4, 1899.

18. Crawford to Dutcher, Dec. 8, 1898, and Jack Crawford to

Maria Crawford, Dec. 2, 1898, Richardson collection; *Klondike Nugget,*
Dec. 3, 7, 1898.

19. Jack Crawford to Maria Crawford, Dec. 2, 1898, Jan. 15,
1899, Richardson collection. The *Klondike Nugget* told its readers on
Nov. 26, 1898: "Captain Jack Crawford is reported to be laid up very sick
in his cabin."

20. On problems with the mail, see Berton, *Klondike Fever,*
pp. 327–28.

21. Steele, *Forty Years in Canada,* pp. 327–28.

22. Christmas Greeting, Dawson City, 1898, by J. W. Crawford,
hand-drawn copy in Special Collections, University of Washington;
printed copy in John W. Crawford Papers, RGHC. Captain Jack also presided over Christmas festivities at the Methodist church on Dec. 26.
Klondike Nugget, Dec. 31, 1898.

23. *Yukon Sun,* Apr. 11, 1899, and unnamed San Francisco
newspaper, Apr. 17, 1899, Richardson collection.

24. See the draft of the article that Crawford wrote for publication, entitled "Capt. Jack Crawford Speaks Out in Meeting," Richardson
collection; Summers to Crawford, Mar. 30, 1898, Box 2, John W. Crawford Papers, RGHC.

25. *Yukon Sun,* Apr. 11, 1899, unnamed San Francisco paper,
Apr. 17, 1899, Richardson collection.

26. *Chicago Tribune,* Jan. 12, 13, 1899, clippings found in
John W. Crawford Papers, RGHC; Taylor to Crawford, Dec. 8, 1898, and
Statement of Facts (involving Wallace case against Vrooman), Richardson
collection.

27. *Chicago Tribune,* Jan. 13, 1899, *Chicago Times-Herald,*
Mar. 3, 1899, and Directors to the Stockholders of the Klondike, Yukon
and Copper River Company, Oct. 27, 1899, John W. Crawford Papers,
RGHC.

28. Jack Crawford to Maria Crawford, Feb. 25, 1899, Richardson
collection.

29. *Dawson Daily News,* June 15, 1900, and undated newspaper clipping, entitled "Klondike Pictures," copies located in John W.
Crawford Papers, RGHC.

30. *Dawson Daily News,* June 15, 1900, copy in John W. Crawford Papers, RGHC.

31. Undated newspaper clipping, entitled "Klondike Pictures,"
copy in John W. Crawford Papers, RGHC.

32. See Souvenir of the Dawson City Volunteer Fire Department,
dated Feb. 21, 1899, Richardson collection.

33. Diary, 1898–99, and scrap of a diary I have labeled Diary, 1899, John W. Crawford Papers, RGHC; *Klondike Nugget,* Jan. 21, Mar. 1, 11, 25, Apr. 12, June 10, 1899.

34. Diary, 1898–99, Diary, 1899, John W. Crawford Papers, RGHC.

35. Steele, *Forty Years in Canada,* p. 334; Black, *My Seventy Years,* pp. 140, 146.

36. Black, *My Seventy Years,* p. 148; Official Program, Dawson, Y. T., July 4, 1899, Box 8, John W. Crawford Papers, RGHC; *Yukon Sun,* July 11, 1899, clipping in John W. Crawford Papers, RGHC.

37. Black, *My Seventy Years,* p. 149; Steele, *Forty Years in Canada,* pp. 334–35; *Klondike Nugget,* Sept. 30, 1899.

38. Lynch, *Three Years in the Klondike,* pp. 65–66.

39. Jack Crawford to Maria Crawford, Jan. 25, 1900, Richardson collection; *Klondike Nugget,* Jan. 10, 1900.

40. Jack Crawford to Maria Crawford, Mar. 4, 1900, Richardson collection; untitled newspaper clipping with dateline, Mar. 1, 1900, clipping located in John W. Crawford Papers, RGHC.

41. *Dawson Daily News,* Apr. 2, 1900, clipping located in John W. Crawford Papers, RGHC.

42. Jack Crawford to Maria Crawford, June 5, 1900, Richardson collection.

43. *Dawson Daily News,* June 15, 1900, and undated newspaper clipping, titled "Sold Hay and Ice Cream," clippings located in John W. Crawford Papers, RGHC.

44. Undated newspaper clipping, entitled "Captain Jack Crawford Punctures the Nome Boom," Richardson collection; *Klondike Nugget,* June 21–26, 1900. For the Nome gold rush, see Hunt, *North of 53,* pp. 95–121.

45. Jack Crawford to Maria Crawford, July 6, 1900, and San Francisco *Chronicle,* July 28, 1900, clipping, Richardson collection.

46. From "The Harvest," John W. Crawford, *Whar' the Hand O' God Is Seen,* 2d ed., p. 24.

Chapter 11

1. Waterman, "Capt. Jack Crawford."

2. George E. Mowry, *The Era of Theodore Roosevelt and the Birth of Mod-ern America, 1900–1912* (New York: Harper and Row, 1958), p. 91; White, *Eastern Establishment and the Western Experience,* p. 144; Russell, *Lives and Legends of Buffalo Bill,* pp. 418–51.

3. Mowry, *Era of Theodore Roosevelt,* p. 91; White, *Eastern Establishment and the Western Experience,* pp. 175–79.

4. Nolan, *Three Plays,* pp. 143–90. Crawford performed *Tat* in San Francisco under a new title, *On the Trail.* See San Francisco *City Argus,* undated clipping in John W. Crawford Papers, RGHC; San Francisco *Evening Post,* Sept. 9, 1900, private collection of Harriett Richardson Socorro, N.M.; *San Marcial Bee,* Apr. 19, 1902.

5. San Francisco *Bulletin,* Oct. 7, 1900, and Crawford to Mrs. Phoebe Hearst, Sept. 19, 1900, Box 2, John W. Crawford Papers, RGHC; *Stockton Mail,* Oct. 23, 1900, *Los Angeles Daily Times,* Nov. 16, 1900, *Doña Ana County Republican,* Nov. 24, 1900, *Deming Herald,* Nov. 27, 1900, Las Cruces *Rio Grande Republican,* Dec. 7, 1900, Richardson collection.

6. *San Marcial Bee,* Mar. 30, May 18, 25, Nov. 2, Dec. 7, 1901, Jan. 11, Feb. 22, Mar. 29, Apr. 5, 1902. For McKinley's visit to California, see Leech, *In the Days of McKinley,* pp. 576–79. For Butte and Denver performances, see undated Butte newspaper clipping [September 1902], titled "Two Hours With A Poet," Butte *Standard,* Sept. 26, 1902, Souvenir Program, Butte, Montana, Oct. 1, 1902, and Souvenir Program, Denver, Colo., Oct. 22, 1902, John W. Crawford Papers, RGHC.

7. *San Marcial Bee,* Dec. 20, 1902.

8. Crawford to [friend], Dec. 11, 1902, Box 2, John W. Crawford Papers, RGHC. See also *New York Herald,* Dec. 21, 1902, copy courtesy of Laurie Nawman, Captain Jack's great granddaughter, residing in Rio Rancho, N.M. The Loyal Legion was a veterans' society restricted to officers. Ella Wheeler Wilcox is noted in *Bartlett's Familiar Quotations* as the author of the lines "Laugh, and the world laughs with you; Weep, and you weep alone."

9. New York *Journalist,* Feb. 28, 1903, Richardson collection. For Crawford's performances in the first half of 1903, see the following: Crawford to Stocking, Apr. 21, 1903, Program for Young Men's Bible Class of Fifth Avenue Baptist Church, and extract from the Albany, Ga., *Daily Herald,* May 1, 1903, Richardson collection; endorsements on reverse side of Crawford to Bell, May 12, 1903, John W. Crawford Papers, Western History Department, Denver Public Library; Crawford to Wendell, June 21, 23, 1903, Box 1, John W. Crawford Papers, and endorsements on publicity brochures issued in 1903, John W. Crawford Papers, RGHC.

10. Crawford to Stocking, Apr. 21, 1903, Richardson collection; *Nashville Banner,* Nov. 7, 1903, *Atlanta Constitution,* Jan. 3, 1904, *Atlanta Journal,* Jan. 14, 1904, *Atlanta Gazette,* Feb. 1, 1904, *Montgomery*

Advertiser, Jan. 27, 1904, clippings located in John W. Crawford Papers, RGHC.

11. John W. Crawford, "To the Guests," written at the summer home of Ella Wheeler Wilcox, dated June 19, 1904, Richardson collection; Lexington *Herald,* July 5, 7, 1904; Crawford essay on St. Louis Exposition, Aug. 9, 1904, "Call for Rehearsal," Sept. 16, 1904, and undated "Amusement Notice," Box 4, John W. Crawford Papers, RGHC.

12. *Washington Times,* Oct. 31, 1904, and unidentified newspaper clipping on Crawford's visit to Washington, clippings located in John W. Crawford Papers, RGHC. See also Buffalo, N.Y. *News,* Dec. 31, 1905, Richardson collection.

13. New Orleans *Daily Picayune,* Apr. 3, 1905, clipping in John W. Crawford Papers, RGHC; *San Antonio Gazette,* Apr. 7, 1905, Richardson collection.

14. *Atlanta News,* May 16, 1905, and *Deadwood Daily Pioneer Times,* Dec. 10, 1905, Richardson collection; Davidson to Crawford, Sept. 27, 1905, Box 2, John W. Crawford Papers, RGHC; Denver newspaper clipping [September 1905], and Coit to Crawford, Oct. 26, 1905, John W. Crawford Papers, RGHC.

15. Freeman Champney, *Art and Glory, The Story of Elbert Hubbard* (New York: Crown Publishers, 1968), pp. 2–5, 58–67, 181–83.

16. Champney, *Story of Elbert Hubbard,* p. 4; Haynes to Crawford, Jan. 12, 1906, Della to Maria Crawford, Dec. 30, 1906, Buffalo, N.Y., *News,* Dec. 31, 1905, Vicksburg, Miss., newspaper clipping dated Mar. 22, 1906, and Minneapolis *Progress,* May 9, 1908, Richardson collection; Elbert Hubbard, "Editorial," *The Philistine,* 22 (Mar. 1906): 117–18.

17. Unidentified Vicksburg newspaper clipping, dated Mar. 22, 1906, Vicksburg *Daily Herald,* Mar. 25, 1906, *Vicksburg Evening Post,* Mar. 26, 1906, Richardson collection; *Vicksburg Evening Post,* Mar. 24, 31, 1906, *Vicksburg American,* Mar. 27, 1906, clippings in John W. Crawford Papers, RGHC.

18. Minneapolis *Progress,* Dec. 22, 1906; see several Minneapolis newspaper clippings, Aug. 13–20, 1906, John W. Crawford Papers, RGHC.

19. *New York Herald,* Jan. 20, 1907, and fragment of Crawford letter to one of his children, dated Jan. 21, 1907, Richardson collection; see printed news release from B.P.O.E., [Jan. 1907], copy in John W. Crawford Papers, RGHC; publicity brochure, entitled "The Picturesque 'Poet Scout,'" containing Walsh letter dated Jan. 23, 1907, L. Bradford Prince Papers, no. 17, "Captain Jack Crawford," New Mexico State Re-

cords Center and Archives, Santa Fe. Walsh had been a comrade of Craw-ford's during the Black Hills gold rush. He made his fortune from a gold mine near Ouray, Colorado. His wealth allowed him to buy the famous Hope diamond for his wife. See Joseph E. King, *A Mine to Make a Mine, Financing the Colorado Mining Industry, 1859–1902* (College Station: Texas A & M University Press, 1977), p. 71; entry for Thomas F. Walsh, vol. 15, *National Cyclopaedia of American Biography,* p. 191.

20. "Thanksgiving at the Roycrofters, East Aurora, N.Y.," article in *Progress Magazine,* undated, and Minneapolis *Progress,* May 9, 1908, Richardson collection.

21. Cook to Wilkinson, Mar. 19, 1908, and Younts to Wilkinson, Mar. 19, 1908, Box 2, John W. Crawford Papers, RGHC; *El Paso Herald,* Jan. 27, 1909.

22. Salvatore Mondello, "Isabel Crawford, Champion of the American Indians," Part 3, *Foundations,* 22 (No. 2, 1979): 100–102; Cousin Belle Crawford to Cousin Jack Crawford, Oct. 26, 1909, Richard-son collection.

23. Fred High, "$500 Worth of Poetry," *The Spectator,* [1909], Richardson collection; Joseph Frazier Wall, *Andrew Carnegie* (New York: Oxford University Press, 1970), pp. 490, 954.

24. Bell to Crawford, May 16, 1909, Richardson collection; *Scranton Truth,* Dec. 6, 1909, and *Keith's Theatre News,* [Sept. 27, 1909], Box 8, John W. Crawford Papers, RGHC; Crawford to Bell, Nov. 24, 1909, John W. Crawford Papers, Western History Department, Denver Public Library.

25. Crawford form letter, Jan. 15, 1910, Box 2, John W. Craw-ford Papers, RGHC; Crawford to May, Jan. 22, 1910, Richardson collec-tion; *New York Times,* Mar. 6, 1910.

26. John W. Crawford, "The Great Panama Canal," unpublished manuscript in Box 3, John W. Crawford Papers, RGHC; Jack Crawford to Maria Crawford, [April 1912], Richardson collection. The first boats passed through the Panama Canal in 1914. On campaigning for Roose-velt, see John W. Crawford, "A Yankee Doodle Doo," copy of lyrics in Richardson collection; see also Roosevelt letter to Crawford, dated Nov. 20, 1912, incorporated in publicity brochure, located in L. Bradford Prince Papers, no. 17, "Capt. Jack Crawford," New Mexico State Records Center and Archives.

27. Mrs. Cox to Mrs. Crawford, Jan. 23, 1913, Richardson collection.

28. *New York Times,* July 2, 1913; Gettysburg *Star and Senti-nel,* Aug. 6, 1913, copy located in L. Bradford Prince Papers, no. 17,

"Capt. Jack Crawford," New Mexico State Records Center and Archives; *Chattanooga Daily Times,* Sept. 14, 18, 1913.

29. Jack Crawford to Maria Crawford, May 5, 1914, and Jack Crawford to Eva Reckhart, Apr. 10, 1915, Richardson collection.

30. *Brooklyn Daily Eagle,* May 16, 1915, Richardson collection.

31. David M. Kennedy, *Over There, The First World War and American Society* (New York: Oxford University Press, 1980), pp. 31–33.

32. Edward Robb Ellis, *Echoes of Distant Thunder, Life in the United States, 1914–1918* (New York: Coward, McCann and Geoghegan, 1975), p. 246; *New York Times,* Aug. 7, 11, 1915.

33. *Tioga County Herald* (New York), Nov. 16, 1915, and souvenir brochure of *Battle Cry of Peace,* Richardson collection.

34. *New York Times,* Aug. 7, 11, Sept. 10, 1915; *Tioga County Herald,* Nov. 16, 1915, and souvenir brochure for *Battle Cry of Peace,* Richardson collection.

35. See Gerald D. Nash, *Creating the West, Historical Interpretations, 1890–1990* (Albuquerque: University of New Mexico Press, 1991), pp. x, 197–257.

36. Bell to Crawford, Oct. 31, 1903, John W. Crawford Papers, Western History Department, Denver Public Library; Bell to Wendell, Apr. 30, 1919, Box 1, John W. Crawford Papers, RGHC; Crawford, *Lariattes,* p. 4.

37. John W. Crawford, *The Broncho Book, Being Buck-Jumps in Verse* (East Aurora, N.Y.: The Roycrofters, 1908); undated advertisement for *Broncho Book,* and Crawford to Bell, Sept. 5, 1908 (the letter is written on a copy of Roosevelt's note to Crawford, dated Aug. 31, 1908), John W. Crawford Papers, Western History Department, Denver Public Library; see also the copy of the inscription in the volume that Crawford sent to Roosevelt, dated August 1908, Richardson collection.

38. John W. Crawford, *Whar' the Hand O' God Is Seen and Other Poems* (New York: New York Lyceum Publishing Co., 1910).

39. *Dramatic Compositions Copyrighted in the United States, 1870–1916,* pp. 374, 566. For the complete text of *Dregs,* see Paul T. Nolan, "J. W. Crawford's 'The Dregs,' A New Mexico Pioneer in the Short Drama," *New Mexico Quarterly,* 33 (Winter 1963–64); for the text of *Colonel Bob,* see Nolan, *Three Plays,* pp. 191–276.

40. Crawford's printed letter to friends (concerning Munsey story), undated, copy in John W. Crawford Papers, RGHC. On *Munsey's Magazine,* see Mott, *History of American Magazines, 1885–1905,* pp. 608–14.

41. Zeller to Crawford, Feb. 26, 1905, Richardson collection; undated publicity brochure, entitled "The Picturesque 'Poet Scout,'" L. Bradford Prince Papers, no. 17, "Captain Jack Crawford," State Records Center and Archives. This brochure states that the original bronze was the property of Thomas F. Walsh and that it was on exhibit at the Carnegie Institute in Pittsburgh.

42. Copy of "Faith," located in Tom J. Nicholl Collection, Washington State Historical Society, courtesy of Lewis Saum; copy of "Savior of my Soul," located in John W. Crawford Papers, RGHC; see also Pittsburgh newspaper clipping [1907], describing a social gathering involving Liefeld and Crawford, and article on Liefeld, undated, in *Progress Magazine,* Richardson collection. A photo of Liefeld and a list of six of the Liefeld–Crawford songs are found in a Crawford publicity brochure [1907–1908], in the Richardson collection. Information on Liefeld's Venetian Orchestra provided by a distant relative, Robert Liefeld, Professor of Physics at New Mexico State University, Las Cruces.

43. John W. Crawford, "'Madcap Nellie,' A Story of a Texas Cattle Ranch," *Banner of Gold,* January–February 1908, pp. 2–9. This issue also contained a short article on Captain Jack, reprinting his poem "The Womanhood of Man," with permission of Elbert Hubbard, who had published it in *Philistine* earlier in the month. See also Eliza Shindel Marlin, "'Whar the Hand O' God Is Seen,' An Appreciation of Captain Jack Crawford, the Poet Scout, and His Great Work for the Uplifting of Young America," *Farm and Fireside,* Feb. 10, 1908, p. 20. Both of the above publications are located in John W. Crawford Papers, RGHC.

44. Copy of book contract, Apr. 12, 1910 and notation of draft of prospectus for Jack's copper company, Richardson collection; Crawford to Mrs. H. S. [Keyser], Mar. 10, 1910, Box 2, John W. Crawford Papers, RGHC; Crawford to Nichols [*sic*], Mar. 25, 1910, Tom J. Nicholl Collection, Washington State Historical Society.

45. William B. Secrest, ed., *I Buried Hickok, The Memoirs of White Eye Anderson* (College Station, Texas: Creative Publishing Co., 1980), pp. 10, 13, 217, 225; Anderson to Crawford, Nov. 18, 1900, Richardson collection; Jack Crawford, "The Truth about Calamity Jane," unidentified newspaper clipping, which states that this essay first appeared in the New York *Journalist,* clipping in John W. Crawford Papers, RGHC; Crawford to J. B. [Adams], July 24, 1915, and Celinda Hickok Smith to Robinson, Jan. 25, 1916, A. Marie Smith File, copies furnished by South Dakota Historical Society. See also two books by Joseph G. Rosa: *They Called Him Wild Bill, The Life and Adventures of James Butler Hickok* (Norman: University of Oklahoma Press, 1974), and *The West of Wild Bill Hickok* (Norman: University of Oklahoma Press, 1982).

46. From "The Womanhood of Man," in John W. Crawford, *Whar' the Hand O' God Is Seen,* 2d ed., pp. 110–12.

47. On nineteenth-century concepts of masculinity, see two essays in Mark C. Carnes and Clyde Griffen, eds., *Meanings for Manhood, Constructions of Masculinity in Victorian America* (Chicago: University of Chicago Press, 1990): E. Anthony Rotundo, "Boy Culture: Middle-Class Boyhood in Nineteenth-Century America," pp. 15–36; and Susan Curtis, "The Son of Man and God the Father: The Social Gospel and Victorian Masculinity," pp. 67–78. On Roosevelt, see White, *Eastern Establishment and the Western Experience,* p. 197.

48. Unidentified newspaper clipping, containing letters of Joe Lowe to Capt. Crawford, dated Mar. 3, 1901, and Crawford to Joe Lowe, dated Apr. 7, 1901, located in L. Bradford Prince Papers, no. 17, "Captain Jack Crawford," New Mexico State Records Center and Archives.

49. John W. Crawford, "Sunset," and undated draft of form letter in Crawford's handwriting, outlining his plans for a boy's camp, John W. Crawford Papers, RGHC; Adams to Crawford, Dec. 17, 1906, and Burmeister to Crawford, Jan. 17, 1907, Richardson collection.

50. Daily to Crawford, July 11, 1907, Box 8, John W. Crawford Papers, RGHC; Crawford to Bell, Mar. 6, 1907, Sept. 5, 1908, John W. Crawford Papers, Western History Department, Denver Public Library; Maria Crawford to Jack Crawford, Nov. 8, 1907, and undated advertisement for O-Nek-A-Ma Mineral Springs, Richardson collection. The Boys' Modoc Club of Chicago was among those enjoying Crawford's retreat in the summer of 1908.

51. Jack Crawford to Maria Crawford, Apr. 11, 1911, and printed material about Boy Heroes on back of letter, Jack Crawford to Maria Crawford, Aug. 29, 1913, Richardson collection.

52. Hugh C. Weir, "Captain Jack Crawford, the Poet Scout," in *Youth's Temperance Banner,* June 1914, copy located in John W. Crawford Papers, Western History Department, Denver Public Library; John W. Crawford, "Are You with Me Boys," unpublished manuscript, and *Tioga County Herald* (New York), Nov. 16, 1915, Richardson collection.

53. Promotional brochure, entitled "Peace, Prayers and Poetry," and *New York Evening Sun,* [Feb. 28, 1917], Richardson collection.

54. H. Allen Anderson, *The Chief, Ernest Thompson Seton and the Changing West* (College Station: Texas A & M Press, 1986), pp. 151–65. See also Jack Crawford, "Boy Scouts," 504–9.

55. Valverde Land and Irrigation Co. vs. John W. Crawford, docket no. 2840, Fifth Judicial District Court, Socorro County, May term, 1894, State Records Center and Archives, Santa Fe; Bryan and Ascarate to Commissioner of U.S. General Land Office, May 7, 1894, Records of the

Bureau of Land Management, Abandoned Military Reservations, Record Group no. 49, National Archives, Washington, D.C.; draft of letter, Crawford to Dougherty, Dec. 15, 1900, and Jack Crawford to Maria Crawford, June 2, 1901, Richardson collection; *Deed Record Book 48,* Socorro County Courthouse (Socorro, N.M.), pp. 276, 285.

56. See Crawford to Gilbert, Feb. 15, 1902, Gilbert to Crawford, Feb. 19, 1902, Agreement between the Chicago Cattle Company and John W. Crawford, Apr. 10, 1902, Richardson collection. By the time the final agreement was negotiated, the name of the corporation that owned the Armendaris grant was the Chicago Cattle Company. According to May Crawford's daughter, Evelyn Lewis, Maria Crawford taught May at home before they moved into San Marcial.

57. Crawford to Jones, Oct. 6, 1906, Box 2, John W. Crawford Papers, RGHC; Maria Crawford to Jack Crawford, Feb. 5, 1907, Richardson collection; interview with Marion Hageman and Fred Crawford (Harry Crawford's daughter and son), Evelyn Lewis (May Crawford's daughter), and Harriett Richardson (Harry Crawford's granddaughter), Dec. 9, 1989, Socorro, N.M. Marion Hageman fondly recalled visits to her grandmother Maria Crawford's house and provided from memory a sketch of the house and adjacent property.

58. See Harrison's correspondence to the Crawfords, dated Apr. 14, 1896–Jan. 3, 1901, Richardson collection.

59. *Capt. Jack Crawford's Mines and Ranches in the San Andreas [sic] and South Oscura Mts., Socorro County, N.M.,* Apr. 15, 1901, Richardson collection.

60. *Record Book 68,* Socorro County Courthouse (Socorro, N.M.), pp. 469–76; Jack Crawford to May Crawford, Jan. 22, 1910, Mrs. Cox to Mrs. Crawford, July 3, 1917, Richardson collection; Crawford to Nichols [sic], Mar. 25, 1910, Tom J. Nicholl Collection, Washington State Historical Society, copy courtesy of Lewis Saum.

61. Crawford to Maria Crawford, Dec. 10, 1903, Maria Crawford to Jack Crawford, Nov. 8, 1907, Jack Crawford to Eva Reckhart, Apr. 10, 1915, Richardson collection; Maria Crawford affidavit, Feb. 2, 1918, John W. Crawford, Pension Application Files.

62. Maria Crawford to Jack Crawford, Nov. 8, 1907, Jack Crawford to May Crawford, Sept. 16, 1906, Richardson collection; Maria Crawford affidavit, Feb. 2, 1918, Pension Application Files.

63. Maria Crawford affidavit and May Crawford Brechtel affidavit, both dated Feb. 2, 1918, Pension Application Files; series of letters from Polly Cox to Jim Adams, dated Feb. 28, 1917–Feb. 28, 1918, Richardson collection.

64. Jack Crawford to Eva Reckhart, Apr. 10, 1915, Dec. 27, 1915, Apr. 28, 1916, and part of letter Jack wrote to Eva sometime in 1915, Richardson collection; interview with Evelyn Lewis, Apr. 13, 1989, Socorro, N.M.

65. *New York Evening Sun,* Feb. 28, 1917, Richardson collection; *Minneapolis Evening Tribune,* Jan. 30, 1917; *New York Times,* Jan. 30, 1917.

66. *New York Times,* Jan. 30, 1917.

67. John W. Crawford, Pension Application Files; untitled poem, dated Feb. 1, 1917, Box 3, John W. Crawford Papers, RGHC; *New York Evening Sun,* Feb. 28, 1917, Richardson collection.

68. Undated clipping reporting death of Captain Jack Crawford, Richardson collection.

69. See the *Evening Sun*'s "The Poet Scout," quoted in *Literary Digest,* 54 (Mar. 24, 1917): 837.

70. Bell to Wendell, Apr. 5, 1917, John W. Crawford Papers, Western History Department, Denver Public Library.

71. See entry for John W. Crawford, *Dictionary of American Biography,* vol. 4, pp. 522–23; Simmons, *Ranchers, Ramblers, and Renegades,* p. 17.

72. From John W. Crawford, "'Hail to the Chief'—Gordon!" found in undated newspaper clipping, entitled "Tribute to General Gordon," L. Bradford Prince Papers, no. 17, "Capt. Jack Crawford," New Mexico State Records Center and Archives.

Epilogue

1. Unidentified newspaper clipping, [Feb. 1917], entitled "Capt. Jack Crawford Is Dying," private collection of Harriett Richardson, Socorro, N.M.

2. Publicity brochure for *Battle Cry of Peace,* Richardson collection.

3. *Omaha Daily Bee,* Jan. 5, 1896, Scrapbook no. 3, John W. Crawford Papers, RGHC.

4. *Augusta Chronicle* (Ga.), Apr. 4, 1909, clipping in Memo Book, 1907–1908, John W. Crawford Papers, Western History Department, Denver Public Library.

5. Peavy and Smith, *Gold Rush Widows of Little Falls,* pp. x–xi.

6. See newspaper clipping, dated Dec. 8, 1895, Scrapbook no. 2, John W. Crawford Papers, RGHC.

7. Fair to "whom it may concern," Jan. 26, 1883, letter accom-

panying Crawford's application for position as special agent, Richardson collection.

8. Martin to Jack Crawford, Jan. 14, 1906, Box 2, John W. Crawford Papers, RGHC.

9. *Las Vegas Daily Optic,* May 27, 1890.

10. Bell to Wendell, Apr. 5, 1917, Eva Reckhart to Mr. and Mrs. Wendell, Apr. 27, 1919, John W. Crawford Papers, Western History Department, Denver Public Library; Bell to Wendell, Apr. 30, 1919, Box 1, John W. Crawford Papers, RGHC.

11. Lusby, "Biographical Sketch of James Barton Adams," 6. Information about the Crawford family provided by Harriett Richardson and Evelyn Lewis. See also *El Paso Times,* Mar. 13, 1925.

12. Information provided by Harriett Richardson and Evelyn Lewis. See also *El Paso Times,* July 2, 1948.

13. From "If I But Could," John W. Crawford, *Whar' the Hand O'God Is Seen,* 2d ed., p. 58.

BIBLIOGRAPHY

Manuscript Sources

Arizona Historical Society, Tucson, Arizona
 Programs Collection
Buffalo Bill Museum, Cody, Wyoming
 William F. Cody Collection
Denver Public Library, Western History Department, Denver, Colorado
 William F. Cody Papers
 John W. Crawford Papers
Henry E. Huntington Library, San Marino, California
 T. C. Behymer Collection
 James William Eldridge Collection
National Archives of the United States, Washington, D.C.
 RG 15. Records of the Veterans Administration
 Pension Application Files, Civil War Series
 RG 29. Records of the Bureau of the Census
 Population Schedules of the Ninth Census, 1870, M-593, Pennsylvania,
  rolls 1329, 1449; Population Schedules of the Tenth Census, 1880,
  T-9, New Mexico, roll 804
 RG 49. Records of the Bureau of Land Management
 Abandoned Military Reservations
 RG 60. Records of the Department of Justice
 Letters Received; Letters Sent
 RG 92. Records of the Office of the Quartermaster General
 Register of Contracts
 Report of Persons and Articles Employed and Hired during July 1876,
  Quartermaster of Fifth Cavalry, In the Field
 Report of Persons and Articles Employed in the Field, Big Horn and
  Yellowstone Expedition, for the months of August, September, and
  October 1876
 RG 94. Records of the Office of the Adjutant General
 Compiled Military Service Records, Civil War
 Fort Craig, N.M., Post Returns

Bibliography

RG 393. Records of the United States Army Continental Commands, 1821–1920
District of New Mexico
Fort Craig, N.M., Post Records
New Mexico State Records Center and Archives, Santa Fe, New Mexico
District Court Records, Socorro County
L. Bradford Prince Papers
Territorial Archives of New Mexico, microfilm edition
New Mexico State University, Rio Grande Historical Collections, Las Cruces, New Mexico
John W. Crawford Papers
Private Collection of Harriett Richardson, Socorro, New Mexico
Socorro County Courthouse, Socorro, New Mexico
Deed Books
South Dakota State Historical Society, Pierre, South Dakota
A. Marie Smith File
U.S. Army Military History Institute, Carlisle Barracks, Pennsylvania
Andrew Burt Papers
Washington State Historical Society, Tacoma, Washington
Tom J. Nicholl Collection

Government Publications

Dramatic Compositions Copyrighted in the United States, 1870 to 1916. Washington, D.C.: Government Printing Office, 1918.
United States Congress. House of Representatives.
1890. 51st Cong., 2d sess., House Ex. Doc. 7, Serial 2851, Annual Report of the Attorney General.
1891. 52d Cong., 1st sess., House Ex. Doc. 1, Serial 2934, Annual Report of the Commissioner of Indian Affairs.
52d Cong., 1st sess., House Ex. Doc. 7, Serial 2942, Annual Report of the Attorney General.
1892. 52d Cong., 2d sess., House Ex. Doc. 1, Serial 3088, Annual Report of the Commissioner of Indian Affairs.
52d Cong., 2d sess., House Ex. Doc. 7, Serial 3097, Annual Report of the Attorney General.
The War of the Rebellion: A Compilation of the Official Records of the Union and Confederate Armies. 128 vols. Washington, D.C.: Government Printing Office, 1880–1901.

Newspapers

Albuquerque Evening (and *Morning*) *Democrat*
Arizona Daily Citizen (Tucson)

Black Range (Chloride, New Mexico)
Chattanooga Daily Times (Tennessee)
Cheyenne Daily Leader (Wyoming)
Chicago Tribune
Daily Alta California (San Francisco)
Daily British Colonist (Victoria, British Columbia)
Daily Inter-Ocean (Chicago)
Daily New Mexican (and *Weekly New Mexican,* Santa Fe)
Daily Pacific Tribune (Seattle, Washington)
El Paso Daily Herald
El Paso Daily Times
Evening Call (Lead, South Dakota)
Golden Era (San Francisco)
Herald (Lexington, Kentucky)
Klondike Nugget (Dawson, Yukon Territory)
Laramie Daily Sun (Wyoming)
Las Vegas Daily Optic (New Mexico)
Los Angeles Herald
Los Angeles Times
Miners' Journal (Pottsville, Pennsylvania)
Minneapolis Evening Tribune
Missouri Republican (St. Louis)
Morning Globe (Tacoma, Washington)
New York Herald
New York Times
Omaha Daily Bee (Nebraska)
Philadelphia Inquirer
Public Ledger (Philadelphia)
Rio Grande Republican (Las Cruces, New Mexico)
Rochester Democrat and Chronicle (New York)
Rocky Mountain News (Denver, Colorado)
St. Joseph Daily News (Missouri)
San Marcial Bee (New Mexico)
San Marcial Reporter (New Mexico)
Santa Fe New Mexican Review
Socorro Bullion (New Mexico)
Socorro Chieftain (New Mexico)
State Gazette (Green Bay, Wisconsin)
Sydney Telegraph (Nebraska)
Territorial Enterprise (Virginia City, Nevada)
Washington Post (Washington, D.C.)
Wheeling Daily Register (West Virginia)

Bibliography

Oral and Written Communications

Crawford, Fred. Dec. 9, 1989.

Hageman, Marion. Dec. 9, 1989.

Lewis, Evelyn. Apr. 13, Dec. 9, 1989, May 30, 1991.

Lusby, Gloria Adams. Apr. 7, 1990.

Richardson, Harriett. Apr. 29, 1988; Apr. 13, Dec. 9, 1989; Jan. 27, 1990; May 20, 1991.

Sagala, Sandra. June 16, 1992.

Books

Anderson, H. Allen. *The Chief, Ernest Thompson Seton and the Changing West.* College Station: Texas A & M University Press, 1986.

Ashcroft, Bruce. *The Territorial History of Socorro, New Mexico.* El Paso: Texas Western Press, 1989.

Athearn, Robert G. *The Mythic West in Twentieth-Century America.* Lawrence: University Press of Kansas, 1986.

Atherton, Lewis. *The Cattle Kings.* Lincoln: University of Nebraska Press, 1961.

Aurand, Harold W. *From the Molly Maguires to the United Mine Workers, The Social Ecology of an Industrial Union, 1869–1897.* Philadelphia: Temple University Press, 1971.

Baily, Garrick, and Roberta Glenn Baily. *A History of the Navajos, The Reservation Years.* Santa Fe: School of American Research Press, 1986.

Bancroft, Hubert H. *History of British Columbia.* San Francisco: The History Co., 1887.

Becker, Ethel Anderson. *Klondike '98, E. A. Hegg's Gold Rush Album.* Portland: Binfords and Mort, Publishers, 1967.

Bennett, Estelline. *Old Deadwood Days.* Reprint. Lincoln: University of Nebraska Press, 1982.

Berton, Pierre. *The Klondike Fever, The Life and Death of the Last Great Gold Rush.* New York: Alfred A. Knopf, 1958.

Billington, Ray Allen. *Frederick Jackson Turner, Historian, Scholar, Teacher.* New York: Oxford University Press, 1973.

———. *Land of Savagery, Land of Promise, The European Image of the American Frontier in the Nineteenth Century.* Norman: University of Oklahoma Press, 1981.

Bishop, Jim. *The Day Lincoln Was Shot.* New York: Harper and Brothers, 1955.

Black, Mrs. George. *My Seventy Years.* London: Thomas Nelson and Sons, 1938.

Bode, Carl. *The American Lyceum, Town Meeting of the Mind.* Carbondale: Southern Illinois University Press, 1968.

Bold, Christine. *Selling the Wild West, Popular Western Fiction, 1860 to 1960.* Bloomington: Indiana University Press, 1987.

Bosbyshell, Oliver Christian. *The 48th in The War, Being a Narrative of the Cam-*

paigns of the 48th Regiment, Infantry, Pennsylvania Veteran Volunteers, During the War of the Rebellion. Philadelphia: Avil Printing Co., 1895.

Bourke, John G. *On the Border with Crook.* Lincoln: University of Nebraska Press, 1971.

Bryant, Keith L. *History of the Atchison, Topeka and Santa Fe Railway.* Lincoln: University of Nebraska Press, 1982.

Bryson, Conrey. *Down Went McGinty, El Paso in the Wonderful Nineties.* El Paso: Texas Western Press, 1977.

Buel, J. W. *Heroes of the Plains, Lives and Wonderful Adventures of Wild Bill, Buffalo Bill, Kit Carson, Capt. Payne, Capt. Jack, Texas Jack, California Joe.* St. Louis: Historical Publishing Co., 1881.

Buffalo Bill and the Wild West. New York: Brooklyn Museum, 1981.

Burg, David F. *Chicago's White City of 1893.* Lexington: University of Kentucky Press, 1976.

Casey, Robert J. *The Black Hills and Their Incredible Characters.* New York: Bobbs-Merrill Co., 1949.

Cattermole, E. G. *Famous Frontiersmen, Pioneers and Scouts; The Vanguards of American Civilization.* Chicago: Donohue, Henneberry and Co., 1890.

Cawelti, John. *The Six-Gun Mystique.* 2d ed. Bowling Green, Ohio: Bowling Green State University Popular Press, 1984.

Champney, Freeman. *Art and Glory, The Story of Elbert Hubbard.* New York: Crown Publishers, 1968.

Cherrington, Ernest H., ed. *Standard Encyclopedia of the Alcohol Problem.* 6 vols. Westerville, Ohio: American Issue Publishing Co., 1925–30.

Cody, William F. *The Life of Hon. William F. Cody, Known as Buffalo Bill, The Famous Hunter, Scout and Guide, An Autobiography.* Reprint. Lincoln: University of Nebraska Press, 1978.

Crawford, John W. *The Broncho Book, Being Buck-Jumps in Verse.* East Aurora, N.Y.: The Roycrofters, 1908.

———. *Camp Fire Sparks.* Chicago: Charles H. Kerr and Company, 1893.

———. *From Darkness into Light and Other Poems.* Chicago: R. R. McCabe and Co., 1886.

———. *Lariattes, A Book of Poems and Favorite Recitations.* Sigourney, Iowa: William A. Bell, 1904.

———. *The Poet Scout: A Book of Song and Story.* New York: Funk and Wagnalls, 1886.

———. *The Poet Scout: Verses and Songs.* San Francisco: H. Keller and Co., 1879.

———. *Whar' the Hand O' God Is Seen and Other Poems.* New York: New York Lyceum Publishing Co., 1910.

———. *Whar' the Hand O' God Is Seen and Other Poems.* 2d ed. New York: New York Lyceum Publishing Co., 1913.

Curley, Edwin A. *Glittering Gold, The True Story of the Black Hills.* Chicago: Edwin A. Curley, 1876.

Dearing, Mary R. *Veterans in Politics, The Story of the G.A.R.* Baton Rouge: Louisiana State University Press, 1952.

Bibliography

Degler, Carl N. *The Age of the Economic Revolution, 1876–1900.* 2d ed. Glenview, Ill.: Scott, Foresman and Co., 1977.

Dippie, Brian W. *Custer's Last Stand, The Anatomy of an American Myth.* Missoula: University of Montana, 1976.

Ellis, Edward Robb. *Echoes of Distant Thunder, Life in the United States, 1914–1918.* New York: Coward, McCann and Geoghegan, 1975.

Finerty, John F. *War-Path and Bivouac, or The Conquest of the Sioux.* Norman: University of Oklahoma Press, 1961.

Flannery, L. G., ed. *John Hunton's Diary.* Vol. 2, 1876–77. Lingle, Wyo.: Guide-Review, 1958.

Foote, Stella A., ed. *Letters From Buffalo Bill.* Billings, Mont.: Foote Publishing Co., 1954.

Futcher, Winnifred M., ed. *The Great North Road to the Cariboo.* Victoria, B.C.: Roy Wrigley Printing and Publishing Co., 1938.

Gibbens, Byrd, ed. *This Is a Strange Country, Letters of a Westering Family, 1880–1906.* Albuquerque: University of New Mexico Press, 1988.

Gibson, Arrell Morgan. *The American Indian, Prehistory to the Present.* Lexington, Mass.: D. C. Heath and Co., 1980.

Gould, Joseph. *The Story of the Forty-Eighth, A Record of the Campaigns of the Forty-Eighth Regiment Pennsylvania Veteran Volunteer Infantry during the four eventful years of its service in the war for the preservation of the Union.* Philadelphia: Alfred M. Slocum Co., 1908.

Gould, Joseph E. *The Chautauqua Movement, An Episode in the Continuing American Revolution.* Albany: State University of New York Press, 1961.

Greene, Jerome A. *Slim Buttes, 1876, An Episode of the Great Sioux War.* Norman: University of Oklahoma Press, 1982.

Greever, William S. *The Bonanza West, The Story of the Western Mining Rushes, 1848–1900.* Norman: University of Oklahoma Press, 1963.

Griswold, Robert. *Family and Divorce in California, 1850–1890, Victorian Illusions and Everyday Realities.* Albany: State University of New York Press, 1982.

Hall, Martin H. *Sibley's New Mexico Campaign.* Austin: University of Texas Press, 1960.

Hedren, Paul L. *First Scalp for Custer: The Skirmish at Warbonnet Creek, Nebraska.* Glendale, Calif.: Arthur H. Clark, 1980.

———. *Fort Laramie in 1876, Chronicle of a Frontier Post at War.* Lincoln: University of Nebraska Press, 1988.

Heitman, Francis B. *Historical Register and Dictionary of the United States Army, 1789–1903.* 2 vols. Reprint. Urbana: University of Illinois Press, 1965.

Hoxie, Frederick E. *A Final Promise, The Campaign to Assimilate the Indians, 1880–1920.* Cambridge: Cambridge University Press, 1989.

Hughes, Richard B. *Pioneer Years in the Black Hills.* Edited by Agnes Wright Spring. Glendale, Calif.: Arthur H. Clark Co., 1957.

Hunt, William R. *North of 53, The Wild Days of the Alaska–Yukon Mining Frontier, 1870–1914.* New York: Macmillan Publishing Co., 1974.

Ingraham, Prentiss. *The Adventurous Life of Captain Jack, The Border Boy.* No. 96, Beadle's Half Dime Library, Feb. 21, 1883.

Johannsen, Albert. *The House of Beadle and Adams and Its Dime and Nickel Novels.* 2 vols. Norman: University of Oklahoma Press, 1950.

Johnson, Allen, and Dumas Malone, eds. *Dictionary of American Biography.* 20 vols. New York: Charles Scribner's Sons, 1928–1936.

Jones, Daryl. *The Dime Novel Western.* Bowling Green, Ohio: Bowling Green State University Popular Press, 1978.

Keleher, William A. *Violence in Lincoln County, 1869–1881.* Albuquerque: University of New Mexico Press, 1957.

Kennedy, David M. *Over There, The First World War and American Society.* New York: Oxford University Press, 1980.

King, Charles. *Campaigning with Crook.* Norman: University of Oklahoma Press, 1964.

King, Joseph E. *A Mine to Make a Mine, Financing the Colorado Mining Industry, 1859–1902.* College Station: Texas A & M University Press, 1977.

Knight, Oliver. *Following the Indian Wars, The Story of the Newspaper Correspondents among the Indian Campaigners.* Norman: University of Oklahoma Press, 1960.

Lamar, Howard R., ed. *The Reader's Encyclopedia of the American West.* New York: Thomas Y. Crowell Co., 1977.

Lawson, Benjamin S. *Joaquin Miller.* Boise, Idaho: Boise State University, 1980.

Leech, Margaret. *In the Days of McKinley.* New York: Harper and Brothers, 1959.

Livesay, Harold C. *Andrew Carnegie and the Rise of Big Business.* Boston: Little, Brown and Co., 1975.

Logan, Herschel C. *Buckskin and Satin, The Life of Texas Jack and His Wife Mlle. Morlacchi.* Harrisburg, Pa.: Stackpole Co., 1954.

Lynch, Jeremiah. *Three Years in the Klondike.* London: Edward Arnold, 1904.

Matter, William D. *If It Takes All Summer, The Battle of Spotsylvania.* Chapel Hill: University of North Carolina Press, 1988.

Mattes, Merrill J. *Indians, Infants and Infantry, Andrew and Elizabeth Burt on the Frontier.* Denver: Old West Publishing Co., 1960.

Mayer, Melanie J. *Klondike Women, True Tales of the 1897–1898 Gold Rush.* Athens: Ohio University Press, 1989.

McClintock, John S. *Pioneer Days in the Black Hills.* Deadwood, S.D.: John S. McClintock, 1939.

McCullough, David. *The Path between the Seas, The Creation of the Panama Canal, 1870–1914.* New York: Simon and Schuster, 1977.

McGillycuddy, Julia B. *McGillycuddy, Agent, A Biography of Dr. Valentine T. McGillycuddy.* San Jose, Calif.: Stanford University Press, 1941.

McNitt, Frank. *The Indian Traders.* Norman: University of Oklahoma Press, 1962.

McPherson, James M. *Battle Cry of Freedom, The Civil War Era.* New York: Oxford University Press, 1988.

Miller, Donald L., and Richard E. Sharpless. *The Kingdom of Coal, Work, Enter-*

prise, and Ethnic Communities in the Mine Fields. Philadelphia: University of Pennsylvania Press, 1985.

Monaghan, Jay. *The Great Rascal, The Life and Adventures of Ned Buntline.* New York: Crown Publishers, 1951.

Morrison, Theodore. *Chautauqua, A Center for Education, Religion, and the Arts in America.* Chicago: University of Chicago Press, 1974.

Mott, Frank Luther. *A History of American Magazines, 1865–1885.* Cambridge: Harvard University Press, 1938.

———. *A History of American Magazines, 1885–1905.* Cambridge: Harvard University Press, 1957.

Mowry, George E. *The Era of Theodore Roosevelt and the Birth of Modern America, 1900–1912.* New York: Harper and Row, 1958.

Nash, Gerald D. *Creating the West, Historical Interpretations, 1890–1990.* Albuquerque: University of New Mexico Press, 1991.

National Cyclopaedia of American Biography. 49 vols. New York: James T. White and Co., 1898–1966.

Nolan, Paul T. *John Wallace Crawford.* Boston: Twayne Publishers, 1981.

———. *Three Plays by J. W. (Capt. Jack) Crawford, An Experiment in Myth-Making.* The Hague, Netherlands: Mouton and Co., 1966.

Palmer, Frederick. *In the Klondyke, Including an Account of a Winter's Journey to Dawson.* New York: Charles Scribner's Sons, 1899.

Parker, Watson. *Gold in the Black Hills.* Norman: University of Oklahoma Press, 1966.

Pearce, T. M., ed. *New Mexico Place Names, A Geographical Dictionary.* Albuquerque: University of New Mexico Press, 1965.

Pearson, Edmund. *Dime Novels; or, Following an Old Trail in Popular Literature.* Reprint. Port Washington, N.Y.: Kennikat Press, 1968.

Peavy, Linda, and Ursula Smith. *The Gold Rush Widows of Little Falls, A Story Drawn from the Letters of Pamelia and James Fergus.* St. Paul: Minnesota Historical Society Press, 1990.

Place, Marian T. *Cariboo Gold, The Story of the British Columbia Gold Rush.* New York: Holt, Rinehart and Winston, 1970.

Prucha, Francis Paul. *American Indian Policy in the Formative Years, The Indian Trade and Intercourse Acts, 1790–1834.* Cambridge: Harvard University Press, 1962.

———. *The Great Father, The United States Government and the American Indians.* 2 vols. Lincoln: University of Nebraska Press, 1984.

Randall, J. G., and David Donald. *The Civil War and Reconstruction.* Lexington, Mass.: D. C. Heath and Co., 1969.

Rosa, Joseph G. *They Called Him Wild Bill, The Life and Adventures of James Butler Hickok.* Norman: University of Oklahoma Press, 1974.

———. *The West of Wild Bill Hickok.* Norman: University of Oklahoma Press, 1982.

Russell, Don. *Campaigning with King, Charles King, Chronicler of the Old Army.* Edited by Paul L. Hedren. Lincoln: University of Nebraska Press, 1991.

————. *The Lives and Legends of Buffalo Bill.* Norman: University of Oklahoma Press, 1960.

————. *The Wild West, or, A History of the Wild West Shows.* Fort Worth, Tex.: Amon Carter Museum, 1970.

Rydell, Robert W. *All the World's a Fair, Visions of Empire at American International Expositions, 1876–1916.* Chicago: University of Chicago Press, 1984.

Sandburg, Carl. *Harvest Poems, 1910–1960.* New York: Harcourt, Brace and World, 1958.

Satterfield, Archie. *Chilkoot Pass, The Most Famous Trail in the North.* Anchorage: Alaska Northwest Publishing Co., 1978.

Schuylkill County in the Civil War. Historical Society of Schuylkill County, 7 (No. 3, 1961).

Secrest, William B., ed. *I Buried Hickok, The Memoirs of White Eye Anderson.* College Station, Tex.: Creative Publishing Co., 1980.

Simmons, Marc. *Albuquerque, A Narrative History.* Albuquerque: University of New Mexico Press, 1982.

————. *Ranchers, Ramblers, and Renegades, True Tales of Territorial New Mexico.* Santa Fe: Ancient City Press, 1984.

Slotkin, Richard. *The Fatal Environment, The Myth of the Frontier in the Age of Industrialization, 1800–1890.* New York: Atheneum, 1985.

Smith, Henry Nash. *Virgin Land, The American West as Symbol and Myth.* New York: Random House, 1950.

Smith, James E. *A Famous Battery and Its Campaigns, 1861–1864. The Career of Corporal James Tanner in War and Peace. Early Days in the Black Hills with Some Account of Capt. Jack Crawford, The Poet Scout.* Washington: W. H. Lowdermilk and Co., 1892.

Smith, Sherry L. *The View from Officers' Row, Army Perceptions of Western Indians.* Tucson: University of Arizona Press, 1990.

Spring, Agnes Wright. *The Cheyenne and Black Hills Stage and Express Routes.* Glendale, Calif.: Arthur H. Clark Co., 1949.

Spring, John. *John Spring's Arizona.* Edited by A. M. Gustafson. Tucson: University of Arizona Press, 1966.

Stallard, Patricia Y. *Glittering Misery, Dependents of the Indian Fighting Army.* Fort Collins, Colo.: Old Army Press, 1978.

Steckmesser, Kent L. *The Western Hero in History and Legend.* Norman: University of Oklahoma Press, 1965.

Steele, Samuel B. *Forty Years in Canada, Reminiscences of the Great North-West with Some Account of His Service in South Africa.* Toronto: McGraw-Hill Ryerson Limited, 1972.

Stern, Madeleine B. *Purple Passage, The Life of Mrs. Frank Leslie.* Norman: University of Oklahoma Press, 1953.

Tallent, Annie D. *The Black Hills; or, The Last Hunting Ground of the Dakotahs.* St. Louis: Nixon-Jones Printing Co., 1899.

Bibliography

Tarbell, Ida. *The Life of Abraham Lincoln.* 4 vols. New York: Lincoln History Society, 1909.

Tebbel, John. *From Rags to Riches, Horatio Alger, Jr., and the American Dream.* New York: Macmillan Company, 1963.

Thorp, Raymond W. *Spirit Gun of the West, The Story of Doc W. F. Carver.* Glendale, Calif.: Arthur H. Clark Co., 1957.

Thrapp, Dan L. *Victorio and the Membres Apaches.* Norman: University of Oklahoma Press, 1974.

Timmons, W. H. *El Paso, A Borderlands History.* El Paso: Texas Western Press, 1990.

Utley, Robert M. *Billy the Kid: A Short and Violent Life.* Lincoln: University of Nebraska Press, 1989.

———. *Cavalier in Buckskin, George Armstrong Custer and the Western Military Frontier.* Norman: University of Oklahoma Press, 1988.

———. *Frontier Regulars: The United States Army and the Indian, 1866–1891.* New York: Macmillan Publishing Co., 1973.

Varney, Philip. *New Mexico's Best Ghost Towns, A Practical Guide.* Albuquerque: University of New Mexico Press, 1987.

Wall, Joseph Frazier. *Andrew Carnegie.* New York: Oxford University Press, 1970.

Webb, Melody. *The Last Frontier, A History of the Yukon Basin of Canada and Alaska.* Albuquerque: University of New Mexico Press, 1985.

Wecter, Dixon. *The Hero in America, A Chronicle of Hero Worship.* Reprint. Ann Arbor: University of Michigan Press, 1963.

White, G. Edward. *The Eastern Establishment and the Western Experience, The West of Frederic Remington, Theodore Roosevelt, and Owen Wister.* Austin: University of Texas Press, 1989.

Wilson, Garff B. *Three Hundred Years of American Drama and Theatre.* Englewood Cliffs, N.J.: Prentice-Hall, Inc., 1973.

Woodham-Smith, Cecil. *The Great Hunger, Ireland, 1845–1849.* New York: Harper and Row, 1962.

Yearley, C. K. *Enterprise and Anthracite: Economics and Democracy in Schuylkill County, 1820–1875.* Baltimore: Johns Hopkins Press, 1961.

Yost, Nellie Snyder. *Buffalo Bill, His Family, Friends, Fame, Failures, and Fortunes.* Chicago: Swallow Press, 1979.

Articles

Anderson, Harry H. "Some Footnotes to Charles King's 'Campaigning with Crook.'" *Historical Messenger of the Milwaukee County Historical Society,* 29 (Spring 1973): 2–25.

Berthoff, Rowland. "The Social Order of the Anthracite Region, 1825–1902." *The Pennsylvania Magazine of History and Biography,* 89 (July 1965): 261–91.

Crawford, Jack [John W.]. "The Boy Scouts." *Watson's Magazine,* 13 (October 1911): 504–9.

———. "The Government Scout." *Outing,* 29 (November 1893): 148–50.

———. "In Memoriam, The Hero's Departed." New York: J.T. Altemus, Publisher, 1885.

———. "Pursuit of Victorio." Publications in History, *Socorro County Historical Society*, 1 (February 1965): 1–8.

Crimmins, Martin L. "Colonel Buell's Expedition into Mexico in 1880." *New Mexico Historical Review*, 10 (April 1935): 133–42.

Curtis, Susan. "The Son of Man and God the Father: The Social Gospel and Victorian Masculinity." In *Meanings for Manhood, Constructions of Masculinity in Victorian America*, edited by Mark C. Carnes and Clyde Griffen, pp. 67–78. Chicago: University of Chicago Press, 1990. .

Dargan, Marion. "New Mexico's Fight for Statehood." *New Mexico Historical Review*, 18 (January 1943): 74–79.

Falk, Robert. "The Search for Reality: Writers and Their Literature." In *The Gilded Age, A Reappraisal*, edited by H. Wayne Morgan, 196–220. Syracuse, N.Y.: Syracuse University Press, 1963.

Fisher, Robin. "Over the Chilkoot with Duff Pattullo." *The Beaver*, 67 (August–September 1987): 4–11.

Genini, Ronald. "The Fraser–Cariboo Gold Rushes: Comparisons and Contrasts with the California Gold Rush." *Journal of the West*, 11 (July 1972): 470–87.

Greenleaf, J. Cameron. "Captain Jack Crawford: The Poet Scout." *Arizoniana*, 2 (Summer 1961): 18–21.

Grinstead, Marion C. "Life and Death of a Frontier Fort: Fort Craig, New Mexico, 1854–1885." Publications in History, *Socorro County Historical Society*, 7 (1973): 1–56.

Hareven, Tamara. "Family Time and Historical Time." *Daedalus*, 106 (Spring 1977): 57–70.

Hauptman, Laurence M. "Mythologizing Westward Expansion: Schoolbooks and the Image of the American Frontier before Turner." *Western Historical Quarterly*, 8 (July 1977): 269–82.

Higham, John. "The Reorientation of American Culture in the 1890's." In *The Origins of Modern Consciousness*, edited by John Weiss. Detroit: Wayne State University Press, 1965.

Hubbard, Elbert. "Editorial." *The Philistine*, 22 (March 1906): 117–20.

Isern, Thomas D. "The Controversial Career of Edward W. Wynkoop." *Colorado Magazine*, 56 (Winter–Spring 1979): 1–18.

Jones, Daryl E. "Blood 'n Thunder: Virgins, Villains, and Violence in the Dime Novel Western." *Journal of Popular Culture*, 4 (Fall 1970): 507–17.

Lusby, Gloria Adams. "Biographical Sketch of James Barton Adams." Publications in History, *Socorro County Historical Society*, 4 (May 1968): 4–9.

Marovitz, Sanford E. "Bridging the Continent with Romantic Western Realism." *Journal of the West*, 19 (January 1980): 17–28.

Miller, Darlis A. "The Women of Lincoln County, 1860–1900." In *New Mexico Women: Intercultural Perspectives*, edited by Joan M. Jensen and Darlis A. Miller, 169–200. Albuquerque: University of New Mexico Press, 1986.

Bibliography

Mondello, Salvatore. "Isabel Crawford, Champion of the American Indians." Part 3, *Foundations,* 22 (No. 2, 1979): 99–115.

Morrow, Patrick D. "Parody and Parable in Early Western Local Color Writing." *Journal of the West,* 19 (January 1980): 9–16.

Nolan, Paul T. "J. W. Crawford's 'The Dregs,' A New Mexico Pioneer in the Short Drama." *New Mexico Quarterly,* 33 (Winter 1963–64): 388–403.

Pierce, J. H. "J. W. Crawford." *The Western Magazine,* 1 (May 1877): 97–99.

"The Poet Scout." *Literary Digest,* 54 (March 24, 1917): 837.

Rotundo, E. Anthony. "Boy Culture: Middle-Class Boyhood in Nineteenth-Century America." In *Meanings for Manhood, Constructions of Masculinity in Victorian America,* edited by Mark C. Carnes and Clyde Griffen, pp. 15–36. Chicago: University of Chicago Press, 1990.

Saum, Lewis O. "'Astonishing the Natives,' Bringing the Wild Wild West to Los Angeles." *Montana, The Magazine of Western History,* 38 (Summer 1988): 2–13.

Schwartz, Joseph. "The Wild West Show: 'Everything Genuine.'" *Journal of Popular Culture,* 3 (Spring 1970): 656–66.

Scorer, John G. "A Unique Character in American Literature, Capt. Jack Crawford, 'The Poet Scout.'" *Central Magazine,* 1 (Apr. 1895): 56–60.

Tipple, John. "The Robber Baron in the Gilded Age, Entrepreneur or Iconoclast?" In *The Gilded Age, A Reappraisal,* edited by H. Wayne Morgan, 14–37. Syracuse, N.Y.: Syracuse University Press, 1963.

Trennert, Robert A., Jr. "Selling Indian Education at World's Fairs and Expositions, 1893–1904." *American Indian Quarterly,* 11 (Summer 1987): 203–20.

Trumbo, Theron Marcos. "Bronco Girl of Old Fort Craig." *New Mexico Magazine,* 25 (January 1947): 17, 49–52.

INDEX

Index

Index

Index

Index